D1789410

Documentary, World History, and National Power in the PRC

Documentaries have recently become a favourite format for Chinese state-directed media to present an officially sanctioned view of history. Indeed, this is not confined to Chinese national history. In stark contrast to the earlier self-centred preoccupation with Chinese history, there has been an upsurge in interest in foreign history, with a view to illuminating China's role not only in world history, but also on the global stage today, and in the future.

This book examines three recent Chinese documentary television series which present the officially sanctioned view of the rise of the modern West, the reasons for the end of the Soviet Union, and the legitimisation of the present-day Chinese government via a specific reading of modern Chinese history to argue for a 'Chinese rise' in the future. With a focus on these documentaries, Gotelind Müller discusses how history is presented on screen, and explores the function of visual history for memory culture and wider society. Further, this book reveals how the presentation of Chinese and foreign history in a global framework impacts on the officially transmitted views on Self and Other, and thus provides a keen insight into how the Chinese themselves regard their 'global rise'.

Documentary, World History, and National Power in the PRC will be welcomed by students and scholars working across a number of fields, including Chinese studies, East Asian studies, media studies, television studies, history and memory studies.

Gotelind Müller is Professor of Chinese Studies at the University of Heidelberg, Germany.

Chinese Worlds

Chinese Worlds publishes high-quality scholarship, research monographs, and source collections on Chinese history and society. 'Worlds' signals the diversity of China, the cycles of unity and division through which China's modern history has passed, and recent research trends toward regional studies and local issues. It also signals that Chineseness is not contained within borders – ethnic migrant communities overseas are also 'Chinese worlds'.

The series editors are Gregor Benton, Flemming Christiansen, Delia Davin, Terence Gomez and Hong Liu.

Documentary, World History, and National Power in the PRC

Global rise in Chinese eyes

Gotelind Müller

Routledge
Taylor & Francis Group

LONDON AND NEW YORK

First published 2013
by Routledge
2 Park Square, Milton Park, Abingdon, Oxon OX14 4RN

and by Routledge
711 Third Avenue, New York, NY 10017

Routledge is an imprint of the Taylor & Francis Group, an informa business

Publication of this volume was generously funded by the Deutsche Forschungsgemeinschaft (German Research Foundation) within the Cluster of Excellence 270/1 'Asia and Europe in a Global Context' at Universität Heidelberg.

British Library Cataloguing in Publication Data
A catalogue record for this book is available from the British Library

Library of Congress Cataloging in Publication Data
Müller, Gotelind.
Documentary, world history, and national power in the PRC : global rise in Chinese eyes / Gotelind Müller.
    pages cm — (Chinese worlds ; 32)
    Includes bibliographical references and index.
    1. Documentary television programs—China—History and criticism.
    2. Historical television programs—China—History and criticism.
    3. Television and history—China.   4. History on television.   I. Title.
    PN1992.8.D6M86 2013
    070.1'95—dc23
                                                                2013016633

ISBN: 978–0–415–81169–9 (hbk)
ISBN: 978–0–203–06992–9 (ebk)

Typeset in Times New Roman
by RefineCatch Ltd, Bungay, Suffolk

Printed and bound in Great Britain by
TJ International Ltd, Padstow, Cornwall

Per Salva

Contents

Acknowledgements

This book would not have been possible without the help of several institutions and people which I am more than happy to acknowledge: the Heinz Götze Foundation kindly supported earlier phases of this project, and the Cluster of Excellence 'Asia and Europe in a Global Context' at Heidelberg University has provided crucial funding for a sabbatical semester in 2010 to be able to concentrate on drafting most of this manuscript without the demanding schedule of teaching. I am deeply indebted also to the students participating in related courses I taught in Heidelberg from 2007 to 2009, bearing with (over)loads of Chinese-language materials and documentaries discussed in this book which back then were just out on the market. So, thanks to Kristina Bodrozic-Brnic, Florian Frehmeyer, Guido Gottheil, Anastasios Kalfas, Benjamin Kemmler, Darja Krieger, Florian Richter, Stefanie Schmidt, Miriam Schumacher, Miriam Seeger and Agathe Zikeli for the at times lively debates, their questions and contributions to the seminars.

Very special thanks go to the library staff of the Institute of Chinese Studies, Heidelberg, namely Hanno Lecher and, above all, Anne Labitzky who throughout the years was as supportive as a librarian can be, alerting me to some new publications, patiently handling so many last minute orders and going out of her way to make things accessible from wherever in the world. No scholar can do without such great support.

In the later stages of this book, I am very much indebted to Gregor Benton for taking an immediate interest in the book project for the Routledge series 'Chinese Worlds', and Stephanie Rogers from Routledge was not only very helpful with organising the peer review process and all that comes with it but patiently dealt with all the petty questions that arose here and there. Her never failing good humour and knowledgeable advice I appreciated very much. Hannah Mack from Routledge joined in, always swiftly helping with many practical issues along the way. Thanks go also to the two anonymous reviewers and their suggestions. I have tried my best to take up their comments. Daniela Schaaf has been the one to carefully guide the book through all pitfalls of formatting while expecting her baby; she also prepared the index with great care, which then was kindly taken over and finalised by Mariana Münning. Joshua Pawaar from RefineCatch competently watched over the production itself, and Belinda Cunnison put great efforts into the copy edit.

Finally, thanks go to my family, my sons wondering what I was doing all the time, and especially to my husband, whose viewpoints from a very different perspective made me rethink many issues I had considered obvious before. I gratefully dedicate this book to him.

Gotelind Müller
Heidelberg, April 2013

1 Introduction

'Global rise' has become a buzzword in the early twenty-first century and many people immediately think of China in this context: both outside China, and also within. In fact, Chinese and foreigners alike assume China is already in the midst of a 'global rise' and the only question is how to deal with it. Western attitudes waver between pragmatic approaches of accommodation and at times cautious encouragement at one end of the spectrum, and fears of a 'China threat' on the other. Asian neighbours are concerned about the regional implications and hope, above all, that China's 'rise' will be a peaceful one, which will not lead to imbalances and regional instability. But how do the Chinese themselves see their assumed 'global rise'? Not surprisingly, the topic is central to the political aspirations of the state which tries to define, manage, and push China's 'global rise' in a way that does not antagonise others (and does not endanger party rule, of course), but it is also dear to the public, pleasing national pride but also inviting reflection on how others managed to 'rise' historically (and why China did not do so earlier – or why it lost out in historical competition in spite of one-time greatness). The topic therefore comes up in various guises and formats, and one of the formats that provide a window on Chinese visions of 'global rise' is the historical documentary.

Documentaries have recently become a favourite format in Chinese media and come with an aura of objectivity and study. By taking up the issue of 'global rise' in a historical perspective, they step back from a narrow 'presentist' policy focus to provide a larger context and allow for more general discussion of the 'historical laws' behind such a 'rise', its opportunities and dangers, and therewith can legitimate also present-day political options. From the perspective of the state, TV (television) history is a useful tool for presenting and disseminating officially sanctioned views of history to the public. The media and academia, on their part, reflect the timeliness of the topic by their activities, be they directly connected to the state (as explicitly elicited or financed as 'academic key projects', etc.) or not, because they perceive also the public's growing interest – and the possibility of meeting with market success in generating societal influence.

Even though history was already a favourite topic on Chinese TV, with the 'global rise' theme the conventionally self-centred preoccupation with Chinese history in the PRC (People's Republic of China) has given way to new developments: an unprecedented upsurge of interest in foreign/world history is a notable phenomenon, and even discussion of Chinese history is now carried out with a view to China's being part of world history. The driving forces behind the design of early twenty-first century historical presentations are cultural, economic and political asymmetries and their workings in the past and prospective future. In its 'utilitarian' aspect, the Chinese conception of 'using the past to serve the present' is, however, firmly linked to tradition.[1] And it is this 'application' vision of '*historia magistra vitae*' (Koselleck 1967) that underpins and frames this continuing interest in historical topics, including the 'rise to global power' of other nations in former times, making for an approach to history that focuses on positive (or negative) examples ('exemplary history') to attain the goal of national 'rise' or 'revival'.

Issues and contexts

The notions of national Self and foreign Other in China are in themselves historical and subject to shifts over time. To follow up on these shifts and address the present-day (political) relevance of these notions, this book proposes to look into the genre of historical documentaries by focusing on three very recent documentary series presenting the Chinese officially accepted view of the rise of the modern West (and Japan), of the reasons for the end of the Soviet Union, and of the legitimisation of the present-day Chinese government via a specific reading of modern Chinese history that argues for a Chinese 'rise' in the future on the global 'stage'.

   The aim in discussing these documentaries is to analyse the framing of visions of (selected) foreign and Chinese history – understood from the viewpoint of nation states precisely because they are designed to serve the national interest – which are embraced or at least acknowledged by the Chinese state.[2] In each case the discussion will clarify how far the historical presentation is a direct or indirect political endeavour by looking into the production processes and actors involved; the ends attached to this enterprise; and its impact on shifting popular views of national Self and foreign Other in a medially transmitted global context, though paying attention also to reception processes and cues that might go astray of the roads that the state or the producers envisaged. In other words, it looks into filmic methods of historical representation and their reflections of contemporary society, culture and politics on the basis of an analysis of production, content and reception.[3] This is done in a way that also pays heed to current memory studies' calls for taking into consideration mediation and dynamic processes of interaction, rather than the 'produced' static 'views' as the results (i.e. process, not finished product) (cf. Erll and Rigney 2012). Beyond 'classical' reception studies, there is a pluri-medial network in which these history productions are embedded horizontally, and they are to be seen as part of signifying processes that include the 'before' and the 'besides', not only the 'after' vertically (cf. Erll and Wodianka 2008). Therefore we will look also into 'prefigured' (Ricoeur) historical views, as well as into side productions to integrate the 'before' and the 'besides' in the discussion of the documentaries chosen.

As for history on screen in general, some research has been done predominantly on Western countries,[4] thus providing this study with comparative aspects in terms of methodology, specific problems with production contexts, receptions with various audiences, and implications of the workings of this particular medium. Hopefully, this study will be able to broaden the presently Euro-centred discussion on history in film and television, which automatically presupposes a 'Western' television production environment, by presenting the Chinese case within a very different political setting, discussing how far, nevertheless, the public is involved in it as well via its reaction to the whole process, in order to prevent a simplistic 'liberal' vs. 'authoritarian' dichotomy (cf. Müller 2011a).

The Chinese media in general are a very vibrant field of research (see below) and also draw a lot of attention from Western journalists, but most discussions focus on the structural systemic side, on censorship for example (cf., e.g. Brady 2008). Here, very often the focus is on print media or – more recently – the Internet. With visual media, Chinese film has been the format that received most scholarly attention, due to several internationally successful productions, and more recently also with a view to 'alternative' or 'underground' film culture (cf. Pickowicz and Zhang (eds) 2006; Berry *et al.* 2010). Less work, however, and only starting relatively recently, has been done on television, and the work that has been done tends to discuss soap operas and the like rather than historical series (see below). The specific role of documentaries as a format in China has barely started yet to be considered in any depth (see Chu, Yingchi 2007).[5] Notably, presentations of foreign history in the media, being a fairly new development,[6] have not yet received much attention in this context, in spite of the fact that people admit they mostly take their 'knowledge' on other countries from TV.[7] This book tries to fill that gap, connecting the specific framing of foreign and Chinese history to investigations into the shifting perceptions of national Self and foreign Other as a reaction to globally shifting asymmetries on the economic, political, and cultural level, centring around the key question of global rise and its conditions. This also enlarges the scholarship in this regard, which up to now has mainly addressed the question of China's 'rise' in terms of policy and security concerns.[8]

My personal starting point for this endeavour is the issue of the formation of historical consciousness, which is guided first of all by history education in school (cf. Müller 2008 and Müller (ed.) 2011c).[9] On the other hand, historical conscious-ness is clearly also framed today by popular media, including television, film and Internet (see Müller 2006–, 2007a and 2007b). The Chinese government, the publishing and the media industry (and in part the academic world) all realise the potential of various media, and thus construct a net of interdependent interests, actors and so on, which criss-cross a simple dividing line between 'public' and 'private' in the realm of the media, presenting a layered web of socio-political complexities as the basis on which different historical visions are negotiated (cf. Müller 2011a). The Chinese state with its power of defining the boundaries of action evidently sets up the limits, but also actively takes up the potential of the new media to promote its own desired reading of history (which is not necessarily taken up by the audience as originally intended, however).[10]

More concretely, the book's focus on the three chosen recent documentary series serves to analyse the ways in which the Chinese officially favoured view of history is transmitted via the media so as to guide perceptions of foreign and Chinese history towards legitimisation of PRC policies. Besides the aspects of governance involved via the media system itself and the use of documentaries also in the formation of cadres (the top-down intention), cultural flows are marked in introducing Chinese spectators to foreign history with a hitherto unknown intensity as well as in the subsequent reframing of China's own history, putting her consciously in a global context (top-down by the producers; bottom-up in terms of the use Chinese spectators make of it; Lull 1991: 211–12). And the relations between different media outlets and consumer groups add the 'horizontal' dimension.

The sources to be used are mainly the three chosen recent documentary series of influence in a political – and partly in a market – sense:

1   *Daguo jueqi* (The Rise of the Great Powers), i.e. Portugal, Spain, the Netherlands, the UK (United Kingdom), France, Japan, Germany, Russia/Soviet Union, the US (United States) and their rise since the fifteenth century.
2   *Fuxing zhi lu* (The Road to Revival), basically explaining modern Chinese history as a rise from the ashes thanks to CCP (Chinese Communist Party) guidance with the prospect of China gaining international 'Great Power status' herself in the twenty-first century.
3   *Ju an si wei* (Alert to Danger while Dwelling in Safety) on the history of the Soviet Union (SU) and the Soviet Communist Party which was obligatory (!) for cadres to watch in order to 'correctly understand' why the SU failed and what they might learn from it to prevent China's meeting a similar fate.

The three series are interconnected:

1   on a general level via the subject (foreign and domestic history and their implications for China's future: the first and third on foreign, the second on Chinese history in a global perspective, each reflecting on China's future in a different way: the first as a model to mostly emulate, the second as China's 'historically proven' potential, the third as a warning on what to avoid);
2   on a practical level via the producers (the first and second);
3   on the level of the time that they came out (the first and third appeared almost simultaneously in late 2006, the second was a direct sequel to the first, being aired in late 2007), thus providing also a temporal focus on 2006–7.

The first two productions were accompanied by and promoted via a host of 'side' productions in print, special exhibitions, and so on, and have been discussed intensively also in blogs set up on purpose by CCTV (China Central Television) (as well as in independent internet forums) and in the general media. The third one was explicitly designed for cadres; however, it now has come more into the open and is flanked by several books on Soviet history which appeared over the last 20 years, most recently in connection with the twentieth anniversary of Soviet demise in 2011.

This book will carefully document and screen the three documentaries (in Chapters 2, 3, and 4) to find out how China's history and the history of other countries is reframed, what ends this will serve, how these documentaries as a very special genre are designed and why at all this kind of genre became popular. Is there anything specific that makes documentaries especially useful for propagating a desired historical view? Naturally, the question of claimed authenticity is of particular interest (cf. the ongoing theoretical discussions in scholarship on Western documentaries, addressed in Chapter 5). Further research questions are: Why are the particular countries' histories chosen? How does this form of presentation relate to other ways of 'memory culture'? How far are shifts discernible to earlier notions of the historical Self or the foreign Other?

Beyond this 'Sinological' aspect, however, the visions and presentations of foreign and Chinese history respectively from a particular point of interest (the more-or-less official Chinese one) and directed consciously to a particular audience (the Chinese viewer) create cultural flows of which the outcome remains to be ascertained. How do these intended flows work in practice? Do they stick to the asymmetrical assignments that the producers' side envisaged? Or do they generate unintended shifts? Which actors are involved or consciously involve themselves in these processes?

Furthermore, the involvement of foreign and Chinese 'experts' in the documentaries is a notable new feature, introducing the audience to a variety of voices and faces, aiming at a new 'international' scholarly image with Chinese participating naturally and on an equal footing with Westerners, Japanese or Russians. (However, a second glance may reveal various fissures by deliberate cuts, or 'translations' not necessarily fully in accord with the original statements, and a marketing 'differentiation' between Chinese and foreign interviewees.) In sum, the new global image is not only present in content but in presentation as well, requiring a look at the specific workings of the making of these documentaries and – as far as possible – at the reception and reactions these documentaries have provoked with various audiences.

Consequently, in the remainder of this chapter I will first sketch out the setting, addressing the motivations that drove the production of these documentaries and the lessons one hopes to retrieve from a consideration of 'world history' as the accumulation of others' experience. Then the context of the media system in the PRC, coupled with the 'history market' in today's China – since historical documentaries are just one aspect of the latter – will be discussed. In Chapters 2, 3, and 4 the three documentary series will be investigated in detail, considering their production context, the historical interpretations they provide, and – as far as possible – their impact and reception with various audiences. Finally, Chapter 5 will consider the examples in a comparative and broader view to look into similarities and divergences between the role of historical documentaries in China and the West. The central question of the whole undertaking to produce these Chinese historical documentaries is taken up as to their implications for the officially desired transmitted views on the national Self and the foreign Other by presenting Chinese and (selected) world history in a global framework on Chinese screens and for a Chinese audience.

'Global rise', national power, and 'world history': motivations and lessons

Paul Kennedy, author of *The Rise and Fall of the Great Powers* (1987), who was an inspiration for the historical reading especially of the documentary series *Daguo jueqi*, summarised the main lesson of the historical 'Great Powers' in the following way:

> The history of rise and later fall of the leading countries in the Great Power system since the advance of western Europe in the sixteenth century . . . shows a very significant correlation *over the longer term* between productive and revenue-raising capacities on the one hand and military strength on the other. [Emphasis in original]
>
> (Kennedy 1987: xvi)

With a view to linking history and present-day developments, Kennedy further argues that:

> economic shifts heralded the rise of new Great Powers which would one day have a decisive impact upon the military/territorial order. This is why the move in the global productive balances toward the 'Pacific rim' which has taken place over the past few decades cannot be of interest merely to economists alone.
>
> (Kennedy 1987: xxii)

Kennedy, who maintains that the history of rise and fall goes on all the time and change, therefore, is normal and unavoidable, is taken up in China as scientifically arguing for the possibility of 'new-comers' to rise. However, in the above quotations he argues not only for the primary importance of economics in a nation's possible rise but also for its military and territorial impact later on. From the Chinese perspective, as we will see when looking into the documentaries, the argument for the primacy of economics is undisputed, but the second aspect, understandably, is toned down so as not to provoke ill feeling and suspicion with neighbours and competitors on the global scene. In fact, even the terminology used in the documentaries had to be adjusted for diplomatic considerations, as a too unabashedly-pushed Chinese 'rise' could feed into images of a 'China threat' that could arouse opposition and therefore would be detrimental to the aim of extending China's national power. In fact, military or territorial ambitions, were continually denied in favour of 'peaceful development' as the new 'politically correct' term (see Chapter 2), or even of 'revival' (see Chapter 3), implying that one only 'comes back' to the stage where one has originally been.

(Here, there is an interesting parallel to present-day Russia where there are similar claims of 'rising again'.[11]) Our documentaries were produced precisely during the internal Chinese disputes about terminology and provide an interesting window into this negotiation process to position China in the globalised world without antagonising 'established' powers (or immediate neighbours).

Furthermore, another concept held and holds considerable appeal in China for furthering national power globally: 'soft power', made popular mainly by the writings of Joseph Nye, who – like Kennedy – was an interviewee in the Chinese documentary *Daguo jueqi* discussed in Chapter 2 and also in *Fuxing zhi lu* discussed in Chapter 3.[12] The Chinese government has picked up this strategy, and it uses historical documentaries as part of a move to diversify its means of 'soft power'. At times, even less 'aggressive' terms are used without the word 'power' and more in line with advertising (cf. 'nation branding'), implying an attempt to attract rather than to manipulate or even coerce.[13] By this, the issue of 'hard power' is relegated to the background, at least for the benefit of observers from abroad, even if internal discussions might go in a more self-assertive direction. (We will look into the various Chinese modes of reception for the particular documentaries, as far as possible.)

Kennedy suggested the 'rise' of the 'western world' since 1500 was set against the earlier but then declining powers Ming China, the Ottoman Empire and Mogul India, with Japan and Russia still waiting in the wings. Therefore, one may argue, China's present-day 'rise' is rather a 'comeback'. To help with this 'comeback', the 'lessons' provided by 'world history' are going to serve. 'World history' is part of mandatory school education in China and therefore on principle familiar to every Chinese citizen. However, 'world history' as taught in the PRC still very much follows ex-Soviet style in design. Even though in certain historiographical evaluations the present-day Chinese ones differ from Soviet one-time 'orthodoxy' and in spite of some 'modernisation' efforts since the 1990s, the basic outlook is still similar, including the continuing very Eurocentric approach.[14] On non-European parts of the world only limited information is included, usually as a relic of the Mao-time 'anti-colonial' legacy, i.e. with anti-colonial 'liberation movements' around the globe. Here (alongside some 'ancient civilisations' such as the Babylonians, Egyptians, or Mayas), Africa, Latin America and western or southern Asia figure, though briefly. In sum, the countries presented in the historical documentaries discussed in this book are largely those that a 'normal' Chinese viewer would expect to be discussed in 'world history',[15] at least since 1500: Great Britain, France, Germany, and the US mainly, adding Japan and Russia in some respects. However, in some ways the documentaries go beyond the 'usual' scope, for example when addressing the Iberian countries, the Netherlands, or the Soviet Union after Stalin, which are rarely mentioned in Chinese standard world history education. In this sense, they 'add' to existing knowledge, but they do not challenge the fundamental assumptions of what 'counts' as the historically relevant 'world'. Furthermore, as the presentation of 'world history' here is clearly connected to the aim of 'learning lessons' from it to further national power, only examples of success (or spectacular failure) are addressed. This motivation has to be considered when evaluating the historical documentaries in the following chapters.

That China is at first not integrated in the 'world history' presentation offered in the documentary series *Daguo jueqi* is striking, but explicable considering school history as well: 'world history' and 'Chinese history' were clearly separated throughout the twentieth century, reinforced in PRC times by the similar Soviet case from where early PRC 'world history' textbooks were translated. Therefore, even though Western references like Kennedy clearly did have China on their minds – be it Ming China, be it present-day China – the Chinese producers of the documentary *Daguo jueqi* did not integrate the recent Chinese 'rise' into their narrative but rather had China 'added' with a separate documentary: *Fuxing zhi lu*. By this they evaded the tricky problem of integrating China into 'the world' without going against the equally politically normative motto of 'Chinese characteristics', precisely arguing for China's being peculiar. What is to be learned from history is therefore only what a country needs in order to 'rise' (as shown by the first documentary, *Daguo jueqi*), what potential one can build upon (as shown by the second documentary, *Fuxing zhi lu*) and what one should avoid (as shown by the third documentary series, *Ju an si wei*).

Television, the history market, and documentary in present-day China

TV and the media in the PRC

Chinese television, being part of the whole media system of the PRC, is closely – even if no more exclusively – monitored by the state.[16] Although the huge leading enterprise, China Central Television (CCTV),[17] is not straightforwardly a state enterprise any more in the sense that in spite of being 'owned' by the state it financially depends overwhelmingly on non-state funding, namely advertising,[18] it is nevertheless the dominating agent for providing state-desired 'information' to households (mouthpiece function),[19] reaching a larger audience than even the newspapers.[20] Especially in rural areas and with non-elite audiences TV is *the* means for people to get information (Miao 2011: 96). The fact that it is easily accessible and affordable and does not presuppose either much literacy (as newspapers do) or technical skills (as the Internet does) makes for TV's outstanding relevance and sensitivity for societal impact (Zhang, Xiaoling 2011: 110). Local TV stations, mostly organised along the lines of different levels of government administration (provincial, municipal, county) (Miao 2011: 92), largely depend on CCTV as a 'mother' institution (Brady 2008: 108), though some have succeeded in profiling themselves (for example Hunan Satellite TV),[21] and become competitors in the sense that they can now be received nationally, if not internationally. More recently, in 2010 the official Xinhua 新华 News Agency also started to build up its own TV network, broadcasting around the globe via satellite (Hong 2011: 390). However, Xinhua is focused on news stories and does not provide the ample programming offered by CCTV.

Besides these 'official' TV stations, there are some privately run satellite TV channels, including Murdoch's STAR TV/Phoenix – for a long time the only foreign channel permitted to broadcast in China (Brady 2008: 160); programmes, however, have to comply with limits set by the Chinese state in terms of content. (This has provoked various scandals, for example when STAR TV took off BBC programmes that were 'too critical': White, James D. 2005: 197–206). This state supervision is carried out by SARFT (State Administration of Radio, Film and Television).[22] Basically, 'examination' of programmes is done in two categories: the first one *ex ante*, the second *ex post*, which keeps a record of public 'reactions' so as to decide whether some series might have to be stopped.[23] However, due to the state's successfully enlisting additional outlets of de facto control, be it various competing media, or the courts, the necessity for the state to intervene directly 'from above' has waned, as self-censorship or 'horizontal control' often lead to the desired outcome.[24] Foreign productions are also shown on Chinese TV, though on a very limited scale since the government wants to encourage Chinese homegrown production, and thus restricts foreign programmes.[25] Prime-time TV especially is officially required to put on only Chinese productions (Berry 2008: 76). In special cases topics are promoted outright by the state through targeted funding and sustained by a highly malleable award system (Zhao, Yuezhi 2008: 214). And for reasons of controlling outcome, serialised programmes are not usually all finished before airing, so that changes can be made, if necessary or required, during production. In this way productions run less risk of being taken off (which would imply an enormous financial loss as production is now mainly privately funded). On the other side of concern, the market,[26] for a long time audience research was inadequate (Lull 1991: 34). But recently technical means have improved and audience research has become professionalised.[27] Thus it is now easier to guess at what the market demand might be, which is crucial for advertising investment. Several TV formats and additional media outlets even try to engage viewers into participating, thereby also eliciting feedback.

TV, in recent years often referred to as *the* leading medium in China, has come to this position only slowly. Through the early years of the PRC, TV sets were rare and mostly found in work or public settings, and the first Chinese TV broadcasting started only in 1958 with very modest development until 1978. Thus it was only in the 1980s that TV sets also became more common in normal households (Lull 1991: 21). In the 1990s, TV started to overtake other media in penetration density, and as of the early 2000s almost every Chinese household all over the country possessed a TV.[28] In tandem with ongoing semi-privatisation, in the sense that even state enterprises, including CCTV, had to raise funds themselves which was done mainly by advertising, the channels also multiplied. Whereas the second channel of CCTV was available only from 1986 onwards, soon channel numbers grew exponentially. In 2005 there were already nearly 400 TV channels available in China, of which CCTV provided 16, soon adding 11 subscription channels and 28 online channels (Hong *et al.* 2008: 46–7). The number has continued to grow. Thus using TV additionally to 'market' politics is an attractive option with a high dissemination probability.[29]

TV is, of course, not the only decisive medium in the PRC. Newspaper and radio are long-term rivals. Whereas the radio, for a long time the dominant medium in everyday life throughout the country, lost some of its hold (due also to the fact that it uses Mandarin, which is not easily understood everywhere, whereas TV can work with subtitles),[30] newspapers and magazines are still very influential, mainly in urban areas.[31] The official newspapers have always been *the* mouthpiece of the government. For decades, people looked to the *Renmin ribao* 人民日报 ('People's Daily') to detect political developments. And the Xinhua News Agency still monopolises what news stories were and are distributed.[32] Due to the spread of the Internet,[33] it might well be that TV will lose its present status as leading medium, even though many Internet users also watch TV programmes on their computer screens or mobile phones (or read online newspapers). In fact, the Chinese government reacted to the rise of the new media and now actively promotes the merger of TV with them by founding CNTV (China Network Television) in 2009. Either way, the media market has become much more complex, as recent research in this brimming field has abundantly shown,[34] and one of the interesting developments is that semi-privatisation does not lead automatically to 'better' information (as the market – and democracy – optimists would have it) since the necessity to cater to populist feelings for the purpose of making money pressures media at times in directions that might not be in line with the official one, but which are nevertheless biased – a problem certainly not unique to China but at least novel to her.[35] And the state also actively takes up various media for its own purposes, having become 'smarter' in marketing politics.[36] In fact, whereas Jiang Zemin still clung to the principle of 'guidance of public opinion', the new buzzword in Hu Jintao's era became 'public opinion channelling', indicating a shift to more indirect means (Qian and Bandurski 2011: 56). At least to some degree, the commercialisation of the media has actually contributed to regime stability, not least because commercialised media tend to avoid clashing with the official line in practice and thus may, ironically, be more effective in disseminating the latter, due to their higher credibility with the audience vis-à-vis openly recognisable 'mouthpiece' outlets.[37] In sum, recent research suggests that even if pluralisation in the field of media undeniably offers more possibilities of accessing and disseminating 'alternative' information, these are circumscribed by market considerations and political indirect/'horizontal' (or – if necessary – direct/'vertical') supervision; and they are set in competition with an updated way of directly or indirectly selling the official line.

The 'history market'

The Chinese history market, in turn, has become more complex as well: whereas the main tool to provide citizens with history views remains school education,[38] there are now more channels open to diversify the historical image. Textbooks have to stick to quite detailed guidelines (since 2000, the even stricter 'curriculum' has been replaced by 'guidelines'), but are available now produced by several publishing houses and they differ slightly, making for a qualified diversification even in this highly controlled genre.[39] But beyond textbooks, history is present in 'lieux de mémoire' (in the words of Pierre Nora), such as museums and memorial sites,[40] in books, old photographs, films, and TV.

The pluralisation of history set in during the 1980s in the context of the 'opening up' policy and the decisive 'Resolution on certain questions in the history of our party since the founding of the PRC' in 1981, which for several historical aspects provided a more secure basis for historiography, for example by also making it possible now to speak about the Chinese recent past within prescribed limits (and by this finally taking school history beyond 1949). Furthermore, the fad for old photographs (*lao zhaopian* 老照片) and local history, including urban history to 'preserve' or 'develop' distinctive building patterns (*hutong* 胡同 in Beijing, *shikumen* 石库门 or *lilong* 里弄 in Shanghai, and so on) bespeak a desire on behalf of the populace to be 'taken in' with 'their' views on history which are at times widely at variance with the official one.

The state, on the other hand, did not only grant more space to the 'public' to express private or local variants, but joined actively in the 'market' itself, either directly by providing its specific products or indirectly by accepting chosen commercial proposals. These activities cover a broad range of fields, be they historical theme parks (Ap 2003), 'red tourism' (Rioux 2007), 'patriotic education' in its various expressions, including the impressively stepped-up construction of museums and memorials throughout the country since the 1990s,[41] or whatever else. In a quest for 'nation branding', the state tries to promote a certain image of China to its own people and to foreigners as well.[42] And here, history plays a crucial role in defining 'Chineseness' and 'mobilis[ing] the population by promoting shared identity through shared history' (Berry and Farquhar 2006: 20). In fact, the scope of the massive 'patriotic education' campaign since the 1990s (to check on and redirect domestic discontent, which had exploded in 1989)[43] is to cover and bind together all these activities, using various media and performance types, from ceremonies through travel to films. Targets of the campaign are primarily youth, but 'education' is not exclusive to them, as the general public must be addressed as well. All levels of bureaucracy and institutions are forced to draw up concrete plans to disseminate 'patriotic spirit', the TV being ordered to reserve prime time for broadcasts suited to the topic (the so-called *zhuxuanlü* 主旋律 or 'main melody' productions), and even local TV stations are called to prevent any broadcast or commercial 'damaging national dignity'.[44] By this, history and national dignity are two key elements in the public representation of Chinese identity in the context of 'state-led nationalism' (Tilly). This is all the more the case as China's 'history of humiliation' through foreign encroachment, emphasised since the 1990s to step up patriotism, is now to be contrasted with a new self-esteem in the twenty-first century, engineered from the side of the state by cultural governance and consumed by the broad public.[45]

That televised history images are of great practical relevance has also become clear in Chinese studies on audience reaction. According to an investigation using questionnaires, roughly at the time our three Chinese documentaries were done, 71.5 per cent of the people who were asked admitted they took much of their historical 'knowledge' from historical TV plays, although they were aware they might not be all correct. In case of doubt they would rely on historians' explanations. The best-liked topics were historical personalities (with emperors Qin Shihuangdi 秦始皇帝, Tang Taizong 唐太宗, Kangxi 康熙 and Genghis Khan heading the list, and integrating only one 'cultural' figure: Confucius), showing the level of interest in personalised and 'hero-ised' history (which, however, is not unique to China).[46] On the other hand, nearly half of the people questioned answered that they disliked history textbooks in school and found them wanting, even if they did not consider them 'false' but rather 'boring'. Thus, the study concluded, the state would do well to bring history education in school closer to what the audience appreciated with history TV: liveliness (*Lishi jiaoyu ruhe kaolü gongzhong kouwei*; 7 December 2006). The production of historical TV documentaries is therefore in line with these expectations.

History on Chinese TV: the role of the documentary

The high popularity of TV history is a fairly recent development. Whereas historical *films* have been part of the propaganda since the beginning of the PRC and also at times recommended teaching material (given, as already stated, that private TV sets were rare, but cinemas were available, and also given the Soviet example of preference for newspapers and cinema to reach the 'masses'),[47] TV started somewhat later to come up with historical issues (Zhu *et al.* (eds) 2008: 5). The earliest cases were biographies of outstanding people ('biopics'), which were still very close in their format to the film genre. (As the recent questionnaire referred to above suggests, biography is still popular with the audience.) The usual term for this 'story-telling' format was *gushipian* 故事片. Then new genres such as trilogies, and so on, were developed exploiting the specific advantages of the TV medium, namely serialisation. Some non-biographical historical *documentaries* had already become popular by the 1980s,[48] starting mainly with the huge historical–geographical co-productions with the Japanese on the Silk Road, the Yangzi, the Yellow River or the Chinese Wall, all running over several instalments, which had an enormous impact not only on cultural self-esteem, but also technically with the advanced Japanese production skills (Hong 2007: 31; Hong *et al.* 2008: 41).[49] Such 'topic-centred' productions are usually termed *zhuantipian* 专题片 ('topical pieces'). Capitalising on this wave, the serialised Chinese documentary *Heshang* 河殇 (River Elegy, 1988), which took up the historical–geographical format, though with a highly politicised intent precisely to take issue with 'traditional' (and in fact contemporary) Chinese culture, enjoyed enormous success and created a stir in public opinion. Whereas the Japanese co-produced series (and their Chinese follow-ups) had presented the 'beautiful' side of Chinese geographical diversity and awe-inspiring age-old civilization, *Heshang* attacked the latter polemically, arguing that its stagnation had made China lose out in worldwide competition. Reforms – the insinuation goes – were mandatory. Although at first backed from above, *Heshang* soon ran into trouble for political reasons: its 'contested' historical readings, representing the political faction that was ousted following the Tian'anmen Square Massacre in 1989, provoked discontent in many. It is said to have been backed, for example, by then prime minister Zhao Ziyang who was forced into house arrest after the massacre. Therefore, it was banned in 1989.[50] Notably, *Heshang* had already used interviews – a new documentary mode, as opposed to the traditional 'didactic' 'voice of God' narrator-led one – to prop up the intended 'ideological' message. (This, however, backfired in a way when the series was criticised in the wake of the crack-down on the protest movement of 1989, as there were easily identifiable 'responsible people' besides the official makers of the series – those visible on screen.)[51]

After the cataclysmic events of 1989, which led to a temporary evasion of political issues, the popularity of (basically non-political) TV *soap operas* grew,[52] inspired by foreign (US, Japanese, Latin American and then Korean) models,[53] going at times into dozens of episodes. The historical *drama* followed suit and became one of the favourite TV genres during the 1990s.[54] TV dramas continue to be one of the best received genres and also at the time of our three documentaries discussed in this book they made for more than half of the advertising income of TV (Xu Sheng; 29 December 2006). Thus, in terms of history on TV, there are films, costume dramas, comical renderings (*xiju* 喜剧), 'serious' historical dramas (*zhengju* 正剧), and documentaries, which again may be roughly subdivided into narrator-led and interview-added ones. (Since I am concerned here with historical documentaries, I leave out other forms of documentaries, such as the 'independent' documentary as an art form as studied by Berry (cf. Berry 2010),[55] or other forms dealing with aspects of present-day life, for example in the context of investigative journalism, or the ethnographic documentary.) Interview-added programmes are the more modern ones in style and have been chosen here in two examples, whereas our third example is rather traditional with the single, dominating, unseen narrator.

The *documentary*, though all but new as a genre in China, as Chu and others have stressed,[56] became popular fairly late in the context of history on TV, being a form of 'infotainment'. Since 'serious' historical dramas (*lishi zhengju* 历史正剧), which depended on re-enactment to recast the past,[57] had run into problems with the huge 2003 series *Zou xiang gonghe* 走向共和 (Towards the Republic) for its disputed view on Chinese history in the years 1890–1917,[58] the documentary format obviously provided new possibilities for discussing history. The historical documentary (*lishi jilupian* 历史纪录片, literally: 'historical recording piece') oscillated between a strongly educationalist function (demonstrating history 'as it was', typically in the 'expository' – Nichols – or the 'dogmatic mode' – to use Chu's term)[59] and a more modern discursive pattern, integrating interviews as authoritative 'readings' or interpretations by experts of what had been seen. This, arguably, made the interpretations less vulnerable to attack (and shifted responsibility for contents or viewpoints partly to those interviewed), since CCTV tended to become very careful after the 'painful lesson' of the historical drama *Zou xiang gonghe*, which had caused a huge loss of money when the order came to take it off the screen.[60] And it went well with the growing popularity of the documentary style (*jishizhuyi* 纪实主义, literally: 'recording reality') in general on TV,[61] as the wave of transmissions like *Dongfang shikong* 东方时空 (Oriental Horizon, setting up in 1993), *Jiaodian fangtan* 焦点访谈 (Focus, setting up in 1994) and other types of present-related 'investigative' journalism broadcasts demonstrates.[62] In fact, as Chu – concentrating on 'societal documentaries' in her work – has stated, 'there are not many better ways of trying to come to grips with the social changes in China today than having a careful look at the television documentaries' (Chu, Yingchi 2007: 2). This, I would argue, holds true also for historical documentaries, though certainly in a less immediate way than in the case of 'societal' documentaries.

According to Berry, *jishizhuyi* can be seen as contrasting with the official form of 'realism' ('socialist realism', *xianshizhuyi* 现实主义; Berry 2008 and 2010). However, documentaries are still also produced on official order (or in line with official/political preferences, including those discussed in this book), which means that the state 'appropriates' the popular documentary format as well. In our three cases, *Daguo jueqi* is called a *jilupian* 纪录片 (literally: 'recording piece') – the most current, general term for a historical documentary; *Fuxing zhi lu* a *zhenglun-pian* 政论片 (literally: 'piece discussing politics') – marking it as of political intent; *Ju an si wei* a *cankaopian* 参考片 ('reference piece') – assigning an educational function to it for 'study'. In this, we can see the whole range of functions connected to the 'official' documentary: to document, to transmit political views, and to educate. Therefore, I would argue, the documentary format as such is used here as an 'update' rather than as an 'oppositional mode' to 'socialist realism', and this format is used from 'above' as well as from 'below'. In sum, government backing, high interest in society and consequently high viewing rates together made for the historical documentaries' particular success in China since the 1990s (Liu Xiliang (ed.) 2007: 336).[63]

Looking further into the development and subtypes of the documentary genre in China, Liu Xiliang 刘习良, a Chinese scholar trying to systemise documentaries in China in the 1980s, has proposed to distinguish according to topics between scenic (*fengguang* 风光), socio-economic reform (*shehui jingji gaige* 社会经济改革), biographic (*renwu* 人物), revolutionary tradition (*hongyang geming chuantong* 弘扬革命传统) and scientific–explorative (*kexue kaocha he tanxian* 科学考察和探险) documentaries; according to style, Liu differentiates essayistic (*sanwen fengge* 散文风格) and political (*zhenglunxing* 政论性) documentaries (Liu Xiliang (ed.) 2007: 214–15). Here, evidently, the category 'historical documentary', which would cut across this systematisation, is not used for the 1980s, though one might argue that at least the biographic and the revolutionary tradition types are usually 'historical' in practice. For the 1990s, however, Liu names as 'outstanding' the historical document-based (*lishi wenxian lei* 历史文献类), the ethnographic (*renleixue* 人类学) and the independent (*duli zhipianren zhizuo* 独立制片人制作; Liu Xiliang (ed.) 2007: 339), although the 'independent' ones that include some politically sensitive productions are not detailed, given Liu's focus on 'official', 'unproblematic' productions. This indicates that 'historical documentary' as a distinct genre in China is relatively new, dating from around the 1990s.

The documentary format as such is close to a news style,[64] suggesting an unmitigated window on the events shown, in contrast to (historical) dramas, which are clearly staged. Therefore, this apparent verisimilitude is also an asset for propagating desired beliefs: that all is going well with propaganda aims. (For more on this, see Chapter 5.) What is 'documented' seems true. Thus, for example, Shanghai Documentary Channel came up with the idea to rename itself *zhenshi* 真实 ('true'; Berry 2008: 85). However, documentaries, above all when on historical topics with no immediate contemporary or investigative appeal, also need to entertain to keep audiences engaged with the screen. Of the three cases discussed in this book, this is clearly in the background of *Daguo jueqi*, which markets visual experience to conform to touristic curiosity. The series did sell and had to sell well to make a profit from this costly production, with several film crews shooting on location overseas, whereas *Fuxing zhi lu* could reuse easily available footage on Chinese history, and *Ju an si wei* was virtually pieced together from film archives. Therefore, the latter two, especially the last one, were low-cost productions and did not need to consider public reaction to such a degree, whereas the first one had to meet the costs and bring in profit. All three, however, grew out of political will – as will be shown in the following chapters: *Daguo jueqi* was set off by a political study session of the Politburo on what could be learned from the rise of the Great Powers in history (see Chapter 2), *Fuxing zhi lu* was to 'add' China under CCP rule to the list of the Great Powers as the Great Power-to-be (see Chapter 3), going in tandem with the Seventeenth Party Congress of 2007 and illustrating a motto dominating the following years, and *Ju an si wei* was a cadre-educational piece grown out of a study programme set up at CASS (Chinese Academy of Social Sciences) about what lessons should be drawn from the Soviet Union's fatal demise to prevent China (or rather the CCP) from ending up in disaster as well (see Chapter 4). *Daguo jueqi* and *Fuxing zhi lu* were both marketed in various ways with side publications, but only *Daguo jueqi*, being focused on foreign history, proved a market success, creating a hype, whereas *Fuxing zhi lu* was less original (its side-productions being of more long-term influence than the TV series), and given its overly 'political' tone praising the achievements of the CCP, had to be pushed on the market. It could only partly capitalise on nationalist feelings in the populace. *Ju an si wei*, designed for internal use of the party to 'educate' cadres, did not bother at all about the 'popularity' of its reception.

In sum, the three documentaries chosen here also represent three different cases of historical views that were officially sanctioned/promoted for Chinese audiences. In each case, the state's political intent and the audience interacted differently. With *Daguo jueqi*, the move to make this study session topic into a TV series came up (at least officially) from the TV's side: a 'safe' topic, since sanctioned by this political background, but appealing to the public, given the 'exotic' subject of foreign history and growing outbound Chinese tourism. Furthermore, it also catered to 'educational' prestige and went down well with a Chinese society that was more and more globalised, being now also integrated in world matters in the World Trade Organisation (WTO) and other international organisations. This all promised high profit with low political risk (paying heed to the warning of the ill-fated historical drama *Zou xiang gonghe*).

With *Fuxing zhi lu*, the producers pointed out, they expected to follow up on *Daguo jueqi*'s success, arguably also responding to Chinese complaints about leaving China out of the picture of the 'Great Powers'. However, the fact that this *zhenglunpian* ('political piece') only reproduced in content what everybody had learned in school or had heard from the news, including several speeches of Chinese leaders, besides being assembled in a fairly short time, predictably encountered much less enthusiasm with the audience than its predecessor. By bringing out some side productions and by adding an exhibition, all in the context of a party congress, the impression is that the state was in fact the one to push for that documentary in a barely concealed propaganda attempt. Thus, it did not matter whether the documentary or the side productions did sell very well by themselves, and whether the exhibition was mainly visited by groups shuttled there for 'education'. The topic remained, as we shall see, central to the political agenda, and was re-adapted in various guises, including a huge celebratory epic – being only the third of its kind since the founding of the PRC – and was reworked finally into the 'standard' view of Chinese history in the official national permanent exhibition on modern Chinese history. In this way, *Fuxing zhi lu* clearly remained of long-term influence.

With *Ju an si wei*, finally, the state's role is paramount, since this documentary was explicitly designed for cadre education by a study group set up at CASS and was obligatory watching for cadres. Here, questions of visual appeal were totally secondary, since there was no need to attract viewers in order to pull advertising revenue via commercials as in 'normal' TV programming. Therefore, this documentary is fairly unmitigated by any further constraints in its propaganda effort. Given the fact that the Soviet Union also was discussed in *Daguo jueqi*, the views on her fate can be seen in a rather 'unfiltered' form in *Ju an si wei*, as compared to the 'market' version in *Daguo jueqi*.

What can be drawn from these three cases is a layered relationship between (official) TV and the state, demonstrating that this relationship is not uniform.[65] It moves from the most market-oriented (*Daguo jueqi*) to the most party-oriented (*Ju an si wei*) framing of historical Others and the national Self. By this, it provides insights into the workings of TV as part of the Chinese media in the specific political context of the PRC and how the state interacts and uses the media with peculiar formats to get across its favoured historical views.

Notes

1 Cf. Unger (ed.) (1993). The classical phrasing is 'using the past as a mirror'.
2 I fully agree with those scholars who stress that 'world history' in China functions as a 'stage' for the Chinese performance only with the precondition to focus on nation states as given units (see for example Spakowski 2009). This is hardly surprising, given the fact that there is no political interest in 'merging' China into the world or into some regional entity.
3 For more on this, see Chapter 5.
4 A key scholar setting off this trend in the West was Rosenstone. The empirical data are explicitly or implicitly taken predominantly from the US, the UK, France, and

Germany. There is also some notable work on the Soviet Union. For more details, see Chapter 5.

5 For more references on media studies concerning China, see below. Beyond the Chinese case, more general literature will be addressed in Chapter 5. Here I limit myself to some brief hints.

6 Insofar as foreign countries were presented in the media earlier, this was done either in the context of 'Third World solidarity' in 'Maoist' times or with tourist and lifestyle interest since the 1980s (cf. Chu, Yingchi 2007: 79). Both, however, were concerned mainly with the present, not history.

7 For example, a poll in 2008 revealed that 92 per cent took their information on Japan from TV, including the news but also TV dramas, documentaries and movies (see Reilly 2012: 184).

8 To name a few examples: Guo (ed.) (2006); Glaser and Medeiros (2007); Friedberg (2011); Nathan and Scobell (2012). A very recent contribution in this field which acknowledges the importance of domestic perceptions in 'rising' countries in a comparative view is Nau and Ollapally (eds) (2012).

9 See also, e.g. Vickers and Jones (eds) (2005), Lall and Vickers (eds) (2009).

10 For the first, see Brady (2008), for the second de Certeau (1984). Stockmann (2013) has justly argued that it might be misleading to simply assume that the mere 'consumption' of a media product (which is usually and more easily 'counted') necessarily translates into its being 'accepted' by the recipient. As her media credibility studies demonstrate, Chinese consumers tend to differentiate between different media outlets, which they 'consume' for various reasons.

11 See Merridale (2003: 21), who notes the popularity of 'Russia will rise again' slogans.

12 Nye has made the concept popular since the early 1990s. He has written mostly on American soft power, but also addressed China. See for example Nye (1990) and Nye (2004). Nye's concept has become very popular in China since 1993, when it was introduced in China (Lai 2012: 11), although it has been criticised by Chinese academics based in the West as contradictory, not befitting the Chinese case and neglecting the dynamics of relative perception of what is seen by whom, when and where as 'hard' or 'soft' (see especially Zheng and Zhang 2012).

13 For recent scholarship on Chinese 'soft power' and 'nation branding', see for example Kurlantzick (2007), Ding (2008), Li, Mingjiang (ed.) (2009), Lai and Lu (eds) (2012), Barr (2012), Ramo (2007), Wang, Jing (2008).

14 For the impact of Soviet historiography on Chinese world history and its inherent Euro-centrism, see for example Martin (1990) and Martin (1998). Regulations on world history education through the twentieth century can be found in Kecheng jiaocai yanjiusuo (2001). For the newer regulations, see Zhonghua renmin gongheguo jiaoyubu (2001a, 2001b, 2003). The image of Europe emerging in Chinese history textbooks, in turn, has been looked into in Müller (2011b).

15 On the development of world history in China, see the studies of Wang, Q. Edward (2003, 2010), Spakowski (2009), Sachsenmaier (2007a), Hsiung (2004), Croizier (1990), and Littrup (1989).

16 For the state's use of TV as a propaganda tool, and how that use shifted from micro- to mainly macro-surveillance, see Brady (2008: 17 and 140–2). Liebman (2011) adds the perspective on emerging 'competing' supervision of media in general, notably by the courts.

17 CCTV's predecessor Beijing TV was renamed as such in 1978. For a very recent Western book-length treatment of CCTV, basing itself mainly on interviews with key agents, see Zhu, Ying (2012).

18 For some figures, see Hong *et al.* (2008: 44–5). See also Wang, Jing (2008: Chapter 7), for a view on CCTV and TV in general from an advertisement and branding perspective.

19 The 'mouthpiece' metaphor was used already by Marx in relation to the press, and in China it was adopted even before the Communists took power. It then became part and

parcel of Communist understanding of the function of media in society. (Cf. Zhao, Yuezhi 2011: 210).

20 For overviews on the development of Chinese TV, see Liu Xiliang (ed.) (2007), and Guo Zhenzhi (1997). A recent short assessment of scholarship on Chinese TV and its trends with regards to works in Chinese and English is given by Zhu, Ying (2008: 13–18). To this one might add the German language works on Chinese TV by Kramer (2004 and 2006) and Zhang, Wei (2012). See also Curtin (2007), covering film and TV in Greater China, and Chan (2010), Cooper-Chen with Liang (2010) and the overview article of Miao (2011) on Chinese TV and the most recent developments.

21 Hunan Satellite TV landed its major own hit with the singing competition 'Super Girl', a show modelled on the US show *American Idol* (itself copied from a British one), in 2004. It tries to profile itself in the field of popular entertainment. (Zhu, Ying 2012: Chapter 9).

22 SARFT is the bureaucratically downgraded version of the earlier State Ministry of Radio, Film and Television following a 1998 reshuffle of administrative structures. A merger has just been announced (March 2013) between SARFT and the supervising body for publications.

23 For the two types of 'examination' and some examples, see Miao (2011: 98–100) and Zhao, Yuezhi (2008: 213).

24 Especially the work of Liebman on courts (2011); and of Stockmann (above all: Stockmann and Gallagher 2011 on media and most recently Stockmann 2013) points to 'system-stabilising' aspects of horizontal control.

25 See the volume by Kops and Ollig (2007), which looks in various ways at international exchanges of programmes, including also the practical experiences of German TV programme makers in trying to sell programmes to China.

26 Zhao, Yuezhi (1998) has referred to the position of the media as 'between the party line and the bottom line'. See also Zhao's 'follow-up' book (2008).

27 Audience research is now mainly done by CSM, a joint venture between CCTV's China Viewership Survey Center and French TN SOFRES, and American ratings company Nielsen Media Research (see Zhang, Tongdao 2008: 175).

28 Cf. Chinese Television Rating Yearbook 2005, cited in Zhang, Tongdao (2008: 172).

29 For a discussion of the shifts, and ways to positively 'advertise' politics, see Stockmann (2011a) and Stockmann and Gallagher (2011).

30 For the development of radio, see Chen and Liu (2010) who, however, do not refer to the language issue. They argue that radio was sidelined by TV in the 1990s and has only recently started a comeback with deregulation and more commuting people listening while driving.

31 For a general assessment, comparing also the various levels of commercialisation of print media, see Qian and Bandurski (2011). Stockmann (2013: 66), referring to several surveys, concludes that more than 80 per cent of the urban population read newspapers.

32 On the development of Xinhua, see Hong, Junhao (2011).

33 There is a quickly growing literature on the Internet in China (see for example Tai 2006; Zhou, Yongming 2006; Zheng, Yongnian 2008; Yang, Guobin 2009; Lei 2011; Mou *et al.* 2011). As Tai (2006: xiii) points out, the first decisive cases of internet influence on 'public opinion' in China were in 2003. In general, Tai and Yang are very 'optimistic' about the Internet's role in China, Zheng and Lei are cautiously optimistic, whereas Zhou is more reserved, and Brady (2008) who focuses on the state's control mechanisms, even more so. Mou *et al.* share this pessimism. The latter is in line with some of more general Internet literature (see for example Goldsmith and Wu 2006; Chapter 6 deals specifically with China).

34 For some recent work on media in China (where further information on earlier studies in this thriving field is also readily available), see for example Susan L. Shirk's edited volume (2011c) and the recent special journal issues on media in China in *Political*

Communication (Tang and Iyengar 2011) and *China Quarterly* (e.g. Stockmann 2011a), both in 2011, as well as the March (2012) issue of the *Chinese Journal of Communication* (Curtin 2012). Scotton and Hachten (eds) (2010) also covered the various Chinese media types recently in one volume. For a view on how the interplay of state and the media furthers the cultural transformation of and the political communication in China, see Yu, Haiqing (2009) and Zhang, Xiaoling (2011). Brady (ed.) (2012) offers some case studies on new themes and methods of control in terms of 'thought management'.

35 This point has been substantiated by evidential research done by Stockmann (2011b), for example, for the case of newspapers.

36 Cf. Reilly (2012: 5 and Chapter 6) who convincingly argues that the propaganda state is all but dead. For a case study on *Huanqiu shibao* 环球时报 ('Global Times'), a newspaper to market PRC (foreign) policies and the 'Chinese rise' to Chinese elite readers, see Lee (2010) and Shirk (2011b: 227–30).

37 This point has been stressed, for example by Stockmann (2013) who has studied the case of newspapers.

38 On this, see for example Vickers and Jones (eds) (2005); Lall and Vickers (eds) (2009); Müller (ed.) (2011c).

39 For more information on available Chinese history textbooks and the guidelines for designing them, see the chapters of Li Fan, Su Zhiliang and Müller in Müller (ed.) (2011c).

40 See Denton (2005 and 2007), Hevia (2007) and Mitter's (2000) works on this kind of memory culture in China.

41 The early phase of this trend was been studied back in the 1990s by Barmé (1999). For 'patriotic education campaigning' see for example Zhao, Suisheng (1998), Callahan (2006 and 2010) and Wang, Zheng (2008).

42 On China's 'nation branding', see for example Barr (2012). See also the UK think tank report by Ramo (2007), which was received in Western political circles, although it is – academically speaking – problematic due to several factual misunderstandings and free-wheeling linguistic 'fantasies'. A more advertisement-inspired approach is Wang, Jing (2008).

43 See Callahan (2006: 186), who argues 'patriotic education' was not primarily to 're-educate' unruly youths but rather to channel discontent away from home, playing upon an 'us against them' theme.

44 The central text for the 'patriotic education campaign' of 1994 has been translated into English. See: 'Action plan for patriotic education' (2006: 14–15).

45 Cf. Callahan (2006 and 2010), who stresses the interdependence of producing and consuming nationalism in China. See also Wang, Zheng (2008) on the 'marketing' of 'humiliation history' since the 1990s.

46 That this is a feature not unique to China can be seen, for example, in Russia where during *glasnost* as well as after the crumble of the Soviet Union, biographies of individuals were bestsellers, either because they had 'disappeared' from history in Soviet times, or because the public looked for a 'fresh' approach to key Soviet figures, disclosing 'unknown' information. Cf. Merridale (2003: 23) who links this trend back to Stalinist heroised historiography (even though I would argue this is only part of the whole story, as personalised history is popular also in the West).

47 For a collection of Chinese history curricula in the twentieth century, see Kecheng jiaocai yanjiusuo (2001). In some cases films are suggested as additional teaching material. How Chinese cinema is still tightly interwoven with the national is discussed by Berry and Farquhar (2006): Chapter 2 addresses the role of time and history more specifically.

48 For a systematic categorisation of documentaries in the 1980s, see Liu Xiliang (ed.) (2007: 214–15). For a more general assessment of Chinese documentaries, based on media theory, from a Western academic perspective, see Chu, Yingchi (2007).

49 For a short summary on co-produced TV series with the Japanese (mostly with the national broadcaster NHK, but also with the Tokyo Broadcasting System, TBS), see Fang Fang (2003: 311–26), and Liu Xiliang (ed.) (2007: 211–12). By the way, the noted documentary *Heshang* (see below) also made use of footage filmed in the context of the *Yellow River* series done with NHK. (Notably, the two producers of the *Heshang* documentary, Wang Song 王宋 and Guo Baoxiang 郭宝祥, and the director of *Heshang*, Xia Jun 夏骏, had been involved in the *Yellow River* co-production and might have been the ones responsible for this take-over).

50 There have been many works on *Heshang*, including Chen, Xiaomei (1992), Neder (1996), and an English guide by one of the main authors: Su, Xiaokang *et al.* (1991). For background to the series' production, see Chen and Jin (1997), Jin having been directly involved in it. See also Wang, Jing (1996) on general contexts, and Barmé (1999). Some people involved in the banned series were able to reintegrate after a hiatus, such as the director of *Heshang*, Xia Jun, who was eventually taken on by CCTV again. Cf. Zhu, Ying (2012: 120).

51 For example, some interviewees of *Heshang* ended up in prison for their alleged involvement in the 1989 movement, and others went into exile (see Su, Xiaokang *et al.* 1991: 179, note 62; 216, note 47; 218, note 54).

52 For the top ten television genres in China, where TV drama ranks directly after the weather forecast and the news, see Zhang, Tongdao (2008: 172). For the emerging pop culture since 1989, including TV soaps, see Zha (1995).

53 Latin American telenovelas were very successful also in China (see Keane 2008: 147). Japanese TV dramas are popular since *Oshin* おしん, aired in 1986 (Lull 1991: 175–9), and recently the 'Korean wave' has also had its grip on China (see Chua and Iwabuchi (eds) 2008). Chan (2010) stresses that regional East Asian influences on TV are an even stronger influence than 'global' ones, arguing for a more pronounced regional perspective.

54 See Bai, Ruoyun (2007a) and the introduction of Zhu *et al.* (eds) (2008: 7). For the particular fad for late Qing dramas, see Li and Wang (2008) and Niedenführ (2008).

55 See also the sections on *duli zhipian* 独立制片 in Fang Fang (2003: 346–401).

56 On the documentary genre in China, see the works of Fang Fang (2003), He Suliu (2005), Liu Xiliang (ed.) (2007) and the only Western language book-length study by Chu, Yingchi (2007) who concentrates on 'societal' documentaries.

57 On re-enactment, see Agnew (2007) and the whole special issue of *Rethinking History*, vol. 11, no. 3.

58 For this series, see Müller (2007b).

59 Cf. Nichols (2001), who has proposed an influential categorisation for documentary modes as poetic, expository, observational, participatory, reflexive and performative (see also Chapter 5). Chu, Yingchi (2007: 26) adds to Nichols' categories the 'dogmatic mode' as typical for China in the Maoist period, above all, but also relevant, albeit in reduced form, since then. Chu's term also integrates the context of production, etc. For a discussion of terms, see Chapter 5.

60 This expression 'painful lesson' is used by Bai, Ruoyun (2007b: 95).

61 Thus, in the early 1990s, starting with the creation of the Scientific Committee for Documentaries, a whole range of new 'documentary societies' sprang up. And Shanghai TV started a separate documentary programme (see Liu Xiliang (ed.) 2007: 332). This was the basis for setting up its own documentary channel (see Berry 2008). And in 2011, CCTV followed suit and started one of its own as well.

62 One of the models for this type was CBS' *60 Minutes*, very popular in the US. However, Zhang, Xiaoling and others suggest that *Focus* was more 'conformist' and state-related than usually assumed, being designed to pick up certain 'scandals' at certain times (and leave out others; see Zhang, Xiaoling 2011: 171–83).

63 Liu argues that with the 1993 historical documentary on Mao Zedong a new style was established for documentaries that clearly assess historical importance from a

present-day point of view, which is one including comment, rather than suggesting they show history 'as it was'. After this 'new' documentary, many more followed, basically either on outstanding people or on historical events (mostly revolutionary ones).

64 In fact, the early PRC organisational terminology reflected the close relationship between news and documentary in the Central News Documentary Film Studio (*Zhongyang xinwen jilu dianying zhipian chang* 中央新闻纪录电影制片厂), which was integrated into CCTV in 1993, by shifting official documentary production mainly to TV (cf. Chu, Yingchi 2007: 28 and 30).

65 Keane and Berry in particular have repeatedly stressed the complex relationship between the media and the state.

2 Foreign models for the public

The TV documentary *Daguo jueqi* (The Rise of the Great Powers)

In late 2006 a new TV documentary series made it into the headlines and created a public stir in China: it was the first time foreign history was extensively discussed in this format, dominating Chinese prime time TV. The series was greatly acclaimed, introduced various new features also in terms of visual presentation, and immediately attracted a huge audience, soon setting off a veritable 'foreign history boom'. Obviously, the documentary, focusing on the 'rise' of the so-called 'Great Powers' in early modern to modern times, hit a nerve, and its topic was perceived as timely. However, the documentary was not simply some smart TV maker's brainchild but had some more specific background to it that is worth considering when evaluating the interplay of entertainment, 'public education' and politics.

From 'study session' to TV: the 'Great Powers' hype

When Hu Jintao 胡锦涛 came into power in late 2002, being appointed general secretary of the Chinese Communist Party (CCP) and finally in March 2003 also president of the People's Republic of China (PRC), the CCP leadership started a new format of policy consulting: the so-called 'collective study sessions of the Politburo of the CCP' (*zhonggong zhongyang zhengzhiju jiti xuexi* 中共中央政治局集体学习). These sessions focus on various rather broad subjects, often with comparative views to how other countries deal with them, ranging from law through environmental problems, economics, agriculture, the military, societal, or health issues to purely ideological ones.[1] They are held by scholars from prestigious universities, the Chinese Academy of Social Sciences (CASS) or other think tanks, arguably to update the leadership with information for helping them to make up their minds on policies concerning the respective issues in China (or to reflect upon steps already taken).[2] These study sessions, staffed by experts, also convey to the public the impression that leading circles were handling policies 'scientifically' and 'collectively' and that they were willing to 'learn' though this seems to be more symbolic than real (Lu, Yiyi 2007).[3] The general framework of each study session is decided upon beforehand, leaving it to the experts to fill in the details.

Study Session Number Nine took place on 24 November 2003, and was dedicated to an 'investigation into the development of major countries (*zhuyao guojia*

主要国家) in the world since the fifteenth century', held by two historians special-ising in world history: Qian Chengdan 钱乘旦 and Qi Shirong 齐世荣.[4] This was the first session on a purely 'historical' topic. From an interview with Qian Chengdan, at that time professor of history at Nanjing University (now at Beijing University and member of the CASS),[5] a clearer picture emerges as to how the session was organised: there were 90 minutes of talk and some 20 minutes for questions. The countries addressed were Portugal, Spain, the Netherlands, the UK, France, Germany, Japan, Russia/the Soviet Union, and the US. This suggests these countries were 'dictated' (*Duihua Qian Chengdan*; 4 December 2003).[6] At the end, President and General Secretary Hu Jintao concluded the session by pointing out the importance of studying historical examples around the world in order to refine governance in today's China.

For Qian Chengdan himself, the main point, more concretely, was to reflect upon those aspects to learn from other countries' experience, since China, as a latecomer in modernisation with many negative experiences in the past, needed to look to positive examples. That certain countries could become leading powers, even though they might be fairly small in size, was due to their 'grasping the historical current', thus leading to the question: how did they manage to interpret their times so well? Since they were able to do this, they were also able to invent new structures and create innovative systems. As a precondition, according to Qian, they needed unity, a strong government, a stable society, and mercantile success. And from this historical example China could learn to build her own future (*Duihua Qian Chengdan*; 4 December 2003). This also meant that modern-isation and historical supremacy were the yardsticks, and this, in turn, made for a heavily Eurocentric vision of foreign history, as proposed by the lecture.[7]

The draft for this lecture had been sketched out by the two lecturing professors, Qian Chengdan and Qi Shirong, the latter from Capital Normal University, Beijing, together with Professor Zhang Hongyi 张宏毅 from Beijing Normal University. The selection of countries, however, had obviously been done before-hand but reflect, according to Qian, the outstanding role these countries played during at least some period since the fifteenth century (*Duihua Qian Chengdan*; 4 December 2003). The whole preparation for such study session lectures is moni-tored by the General Office of the Party's Central Committee (*Zhonggong zhongyang bangongting* 中共中央办公厅) and the Central Committee's Policy Research Office (*Zhongyang zhengce yanjiushi* 中央政策研究室), who have to approve also the lecture draft before the session takes place (Ma Shiling; 3 January 2007). As the preface to the print version of the later documentary reveals, this study session was repeated at various party and governmental department levels (Zhao Huayong 2007), which bespeaks the great importance the leadership attached to this topic and their obvious interest in having this 'lesson' circulated more broadly.

These inner-party activities thus were expanded beyond the purely political realm into a broader sphere by getting the mass media involved. The decisive step came with the project to make the topic into a TV documentary series by the state-owned China Central Television (CCTV), something never done before with any other study session topic! CCTV's head at the time, Zhao Huayong 赵华勇, referred to the stir this particular topic made with the public, which at the time of recent change in leadership was especially alert to political signals: people wondered why such a historical topic was taken up at that time by their leaders. For the programme makers, this seemed a good opportunity to capitalise on that interest, but CCTV being a state-owned entity was also very probably made to ponder this decision as a way of publicising state policies, since circulation of these 'lessons' – as seen above – was considered important. Zhao, though, officially deflected any assumption of having received any political order – such an 'order' would hamper marketing efforts – and argued in terms of audience appeal and nationalism: the documentary series, according to him, intended to address the dream of being a great power that was in the heart of every Chinese, and to reflect the rising status of present-day China which 'cannot be ignored any longer by any country in the world'. But as those great powers in history also wrought calamities for others (including China), China, in its 'peaceful rise'[8] should also learn from those countries' negative example to evade that problem (Zhao Huayong 2007). This, obviously, fit well with the current baseline of the Hu Jintao government's foreign policies of appeasing China's worried Asian neighbours and being careful not to provoke any further talk of a 'China threat' by referring to China's historical victimisation by the West (or Japan).[9]

Notably, Study Session Number Nine only had spoken about 'development', but the TV documentary picked up the motto of (peaceful) 'rise' (*heping jueqi* 和平崛起), originally coined by Zheng Bijian 郑必坚, an influential political advisor already active under Deng Xiaoping (1904–97; and ill-fated reformer of the 1980s, Hu Yaobang 胡耀邦, 1915–89!), and now a close collaborator of Hu Jintao.[10] Zheng had promoted this term after a visit to the US in late 2002 (in implicit reaction to Western views on China's 'rise' since the 1990s, recently taken up by US political scientist John Mearsheimer in his book of 2001: *The Tragedy of Great Power Politics*, focusing on rivalry and China's assumed 'unpeaceful' rise).[11] In fact, according to Zheng, it was he who suggested after his return to China 'that this topic be the subject of research' (Zheng, Bijian 2005: 57).[12] This would imply that the entire study of other countries' development and thus Study Session Number Nine were at least partly spurred by the US visit of the delegation led by Zheng Bijian (and the topic would also be assigned via publicly sponsored projects to several academic institutions thereafter).[13] 'Peaceful *rise*' as a topic was, in fact, addressed by the following Study Session of the Politburo, Number Ten, on security issues, in February 2004. This was done after the term had been publicly taken up by premier Wen Jiabao 温家宝 during a visit to the US (which again demonstrates that the concept was primarily seen in the context of Sino–US relations, as the US was the potentially endangered status quo power that would be replaced by China) and then by President Hu Jintao at Mao's (1893–1976) one-hundred and tenth birthday, both in December 2003. But then, in the course of 2004, 'rise' was dropped again in favour of 'development' (*fazhan* 发展) – which was also ideologically 'sanctioned' by Deng Xiaoping's concept of 'peace and development'.[14]

Glaser and Medeiros enumerate several reasons for this shift: 'peaceful' might be interpreted as renouncing a military option as a solution to the Taiwan problem; (Zheng Bijian expressly denied this); it might be simply impossible to rise 'peacefully', since others will try to prevent it; the term *jueqi* with its implied abruptness will appal neighbours; it goes against Deng Xiaoping's motto to 'bide our time and hide our capabilities'; it could be detrimental to military modernisation; it might let popular nationalism spin out of control; it is merely a slogan and no substitute for 'real' politics (Glaser and Medeiros 2007: 302–6). As Zheng Bijian later explained, the term 'peaceful' was to be used against the US assumption of a 'China threat', and 'development' against the second US scenario of a 'China collapse' (Zheng, Bijian 2005: 56). As Glaser and Medeiros observe, even though the term (peaceful) 'rise' was dropped from official vocabulary (mainly for diplomatic reasons) during the year 2004, the concept was tacitly sustained nevertheless. (Zheng Bijian, for example, now officially in retirement but with important unofficial functions, continued to use it openly and explained it was 'the same' as 'peaceful development', just a term better suited to other 'contexts', and that a 'great rejuvenation/revival'[15] 'coupled with rapid development qualify as a "rise" '; Zheng, Bijian 2005: 54–7.) Thus, 'his' theory of 'peaceful rise', Hu Jintao's official 'peaceful development' and the popular 'great revival' of China were identified as all the same. As Zheng Bijian argued again in 2005 (with the Americans as the primary intended audience), China's 'rise' was not to follow 'bad' examples like European-style colonialism or the Soviet Brezhnev-style arms race and expansionism. Neither would it follow the German or Japanese examples of the World Wars (Zheng, Bijian 2005: 6).[16]

Thus, one may conclude, the views expressed by Zheng Bijian were basically behind the intention for Study Session Number Nine to study other countries' experiences of 'rise',[17] and its later spin-offs, including the TV documentary. In fact, that CCTV kept using the term 'rise' through 2006/7 in spite of official disuse since 2004 might be seen as a concrete example of further support for this concept. It could well be that this also had to do with intended audiences, as the documentary was directed at a Chinese audience, and 'rise' (*jueqi* 崛起)[18] was predictably a better selling point on the Chinese TV market than the rather unexciting (and long-term) notion of 'development'. Furthermore, the TV documentary openly acknowledged its indebtedness to Western historian Paul Kennedy's famous 1987 book, translated also into Chinese (*The* Rise *and Fall of the Great Powers*) (emphasis added), even though the Chinese translation of 1989 had been titled *Daguo de xingshuai* 大国的兴衰, notably *not* using *jueqi* for 'rise' back then, but the more 'conventional' dynastic–cyclical term *xingshuai* 兴衰 (literally: 'blossoming and withering'). Kennedy would also be one of the 'foreign experts' interviewed for the documentary. However, the 'fall' part of the 'rise and fall' paradigm was barely addressed in the documentary and left out of the documentary's title altogether which concentrated on the 'rise' element, and included the binomial *jueqi*, which has become current only in recent years,[19] instead of *xingshuai*. This bespeaks the primary interest in those aspects of the 'Great Powers' that were worthy of emulating in order to get up the ladder, in short, their applicability for China. Similarly, the more mundane description of the study session's subject-matter, as 'major countries' (*zhuyao guojia* 主要国家), was also replaced by the Kennedy-style reverential term 'Great Power' (*daguo* 大国) – which was officially sanctioned by Jiang Zemin's use of it at the Sixteenth Party Congress of 2002 in any case. As the market success of the series proves, CCTV had calculated well in framing the title the way it did.[20]

After the decision to render the study session topic into a TV series, the documentary was planned in more detail and divided into 12 instalments on the nine countries, combining Portugal and Spain in the first, but giving special attention to the UK, Russia/the Soviet Union and the US in assigning two instalments to each of them, and a final instalment to 'draw conclusions'. As this was, according to CCTV, the first time they sent out film crews to the respective countries (roughly simultaneously in late summer and autumn 2005) to film original sites and interview local experts during a stay of about one to two months,[21] the process of making of this documentary series would be marketed as well, offering glimpses into the film crews' adventures abroad to curious Chinese readers who might not have yet the economic means to travel abroad themselves. Thus, the details of the itineraries, written by the respective directors in charge,[22] were published in the accompanying book series to the documentary (see below). The historical narrative, as Ren Xuean 任学安 (the general director of the project) reveals, had been mainly prepared by history professors of Beijing University,[23] and then turned into the documentary's script by CCTV's Chen Jin 陈晋 (and Ren Xuean) under declared supervision of a host of advisors (on the production process, see below). The chief responsible scientific advisor of the whole TV series, however, was Qian Chengdan, who had lectured at the Politburo's study session. The filming then was arranged with the help of the respective embassies,[24] and the series could be broadcast finally in late 2006, accompanied by an eight-volume book series.[25] Its success is bespoken by the fact that the TV documentary series was not only repeated three times (Lou Hejun 2007),[26] but also by summer 2007, more than 400,000 authorized DVDs had been already sold and innumerable copies of several pirated versions were circulating (Wang, Q. Edward 2010: 274).[27] Of the book series, the first 10,000 sets were sold out in only 13 days and were reprinted 12 times in 11 months (Zhao Buhui 2008).[28]

The TV documentary series was first broadcast on prime time in the evening at 9.30 pm on CCTV's channel two, the finance and economics channel, 13 to 24 November, and because of high demand already started a second airing on the same channel on 27 November. Besides the broadcasting, several books came out, some planned to accompany the documentary, others capitalising on its success. The publisher Zhongguo minzhu fazhi chubanshe 中国民主法制出版社 (China Democracy and Legal System Press) in Beijing, which is run by the National People's Congress and thus a highly 'official' publisher, put out the already-named eight-volume book series bearing the official CCTV logo: Daguo jueqi *xilie congshu* 大国崛起系列丛书 (2006). This set was divided according to the individual countries (except for Portugal and Spain, which made up only a single volume). Later this larger eight-volume set was flanked by a three-volume set by the same publisher (see Daguo jueqi: *12 ji daxing dianzi jilupian* 2007). Basically, comparing both sets, the contents of the three-volume set and the eight-volume set are the same, covering the spoken commentary of each instalment, some background information on the particular countries' history, and the itinerary of the film crew. The eight-volume set had only a looser layout, more and larger pictures, and the text of some interviews. Since the eight-volume set came out in tandem with the airing of the documentary (late in 2006, followed by various further printings within weeks), the three-volume set (appearing in spring 2007) seemed to be a condensed 'second selling' of the same thing in a more handy format to respond to excessive demand. The script authors and supervisors of the country volumes are identified by the general director, Ren Xuean, in his afterword to the three-volume set, which allows the reader to follow the production process and interplay between various actors more closely.[29] Whereas the original narrative prepared by history professors of Beijing University obviously was divided country by country (but for the Iberian ones), some script authors of the country volumes' narratives in the book series now wrote simultaneously on several countries, the (still country-specific) supervisors being academic historians – but mostly different ones from those that provided the first narrative.[30] This demonstrates the desire to involve as many people (or as much expertise) as possible; it may, however, also explain some problems in narrative coherence (see below on the historical portrayals).

CCTV's Chen Jin 陈晋 then took over, being the responsible author of the final TV script, basing himself on the drafts of CCTV's Zhou Yan 周艳, Zhang Xiaoyu 章晓宇, Sun Min 孙岷 and Cui Wenhua 崔文华. This shows that there was a process of narrowing down authorship, with only Sun Min and Zhang Xiaoyu being involved in both the preparation of the TV script and the writing of some country volumes in the book series. There was clearly a process of shifting the TV script more and more from historians to CCTV people, Zhou Yan being the responsible film director of the TV series, Zhang Xiaoyu being one of the directing group,[31] himself having filmed in Russia. Thus, Zhou Yan and Zhang Xiaoyu embody the influence of the 'TV filmic concerns' on the script. Chen Jin then gave the TV script the final touch, with Ren Xuean taking on the responsibility as head of project. These shifts and the plurality of authors and supervisors – apart from further people taking active part in the production and 'censoring' process – should be kept in mind when assessing the homogeneity or heterogeneity of the message in the TV documentary below.

However, the TV documentary has to be seen in a larger publishing context rather than just the accompanying book series. Following the study session of 2003, other publishers had come out with similar book projects even before the airing of the TV documentary. This makes also for some interesting comparisons (and partly indirect relations to the historians connected to the TV documentary):[32] in 2004 Chen Xiaolü 陈晓律, Qian Chengdan's colleague at Nanjing University who would be also interviewed for the documentary on the UK, edited the book *15 shiji yilai shijie zhuyao fada guojia fazhan licheng* 15 世纪以来世界主要发达国家发展历程 (The course of development of major advanced countries in the world since the fifteenth century), which included two more countries, Italy and Canada, in its chapter-wise discussion of 'major countries' (still keeping the book title close to the study session's wording; see Wang, Q. Edward 2010: 275).[33] In this case, the tamer (and unquestionably positive) title 'development of major advanced countries' was used, in line with historiographical scholarship at Nanjing University, which had a focus on 'Modernisation Studies'.

However, the publisher Sanqin chubanshe 三秦出版社, located in Xi'an, which came out with its own book series in 2005 on basically the same countries as the later TV documentary (and nearly the same division as the eight-volume book series referred to above, notably, however, *minus* Russia/the Soviet Union), opted for a much stronger title: *Qiangguo xingshuai shi congshu* 强国兴衰史丛书 (The history of the rise and fall of the powers series). The term *qiangguo* clearly implied a more aggressive vision of the 'Powers' (and one may note that this book series also included the 'fall' in its 'traditional' *xingshuai* title). Significantly, this book series was edited by Qi Shirong (Qi 2005b), one of the two lecturers at the Politburo, who had edited also a single volume (Qi 2005a) the same year with the publisher Guangdong renmin chubanshe: *15 shiji yilai shijie jiu qiang de lishi yanbian* 15 世纪以来世界九强的历史演变 (The historical evolution of the nine world powers since the fifteenth century), again using *qiang*, with its aggressive ring, in the title. This suggests that the similar framing of 'power' in the title, chosen by these two publishing places far away from each other, could be due to their common editor and reflect his historical interpretation. Ironically, the *Qiangguo xingshuai shi congshu*, though edited by Qi, nonetheless claimed on the blurb to be 'based on Professor Qian Chengdan's lecture to the Politburo's Ninth Collective Study Session', marking the younger Qian as the key figure among the two lecturers there. In spite of the overlap as to the countries chosen, the arrangement of the *Qiangguo* series of volumes was different from the later eight-volume series accompanying the airing of *Daguo jueqi*. Although there was no explanation as to the ordering of the volumes, it seems the order rather went along today's perceived importance (which would fit with the much more aggressive and less positive term *qiangguo*, ranking the countries according to strength, vis-à-vis the TV documentary's more reverential term *daguo*) than in the chronological (neutral) sequence followed in the documentary. That is to say, the *Qiangguo* series started with the US, followed by Germany, the UK, Japan, France, Spain, and Portugal (the originally planned final volume on the Netherlands did not appear).[34] Interestingly, the volume on Portugal and Spain – for which there are not many experts around in China – provided a personal overlap between Qi's *Qiangguo* series and the later eight-volume book series accompanying the TV documentary, since world historian Wang Jiafeng 王加丰 authored the first and acted as advisor to the second (though not a specialist in Iberian history). Considering these publications under Qi Shirong's guidance and their title options in contrast to the TV documentary with its accompanying publications, being under Qian Chengdan's influence, this might suggest the older Qi preferred to stick to the 'conventional' historiographical image of the aggressive powers (which had harmed China in the past), whereas the younger Qian stressed modernisation as the key positive lesson to retrieve from the 'great' nations in history. Thus, the TV documentary's positive reading would set itself against the more traditional negative reading of the 'powers', which was deeply engrained in PRC historiography and school education.[35] (It might be noted that the official 'People's net' (*Renminwang* 人民网) has run a forum called 'strong power forum' (*qiangguo luntan* 强国论坛) ever since the 1999 Belgrade NATO bombings hit the Chinese Embassy, and has received some backing from leading politicians, including Hu Jintao. This, in turn, suggests that the leadership tries to acknowledge both sides of the 'Great Powers' issue: both modernisation *and* aggression – and maybe therefore also chose the two lecturers for the study session as representing two somewhat different historical lines of interpretation.)

But before the documentary was aired in late 2006, the topic obviously did not sell as it did afterwards with full CCTV backing. Thus, immediately after the airing, other publishers came out with related works to capitalise on the 'Great Powers' hype, among them the semi-official People's Press (Renmin chubanshe 人民出版社) in December 2006 with a book of the same title as the documentary: *Daguo jueqi*, edited by Tang Jin 唐晋, and the same countries covered in single chapters,[36] however without any author/advisor overlap with Qi's *Qiangguo* – or the eight-volume book series.[37] Interestingly, in this book, too, the role of Russia differs in that it is heavily centred on pre-Soviet Russia, whereas the documentary allotted one instalment to each period 'evenly'. This is an interesting hint as to the rather contested historical evaluation of the Soviet Union, since Qi's *Qiangguo* series of 2005 (Qi 2005b) had – as stated earlier– not included Russia/the Soviet Union at all. (This might be also understood as 'Russia/the Soviet Union' not being considered part of the 'aggressive' (*qiang*) powers – a term usually referring to Western countries and their aggression toward China only.) Tang Jin's book of 2006 now focused in the respective chapter rather on pre-Soviet Russia. Thus, only the CCTV productions took up the Soviet Union on an equal footing with other countries and periods, but notably chose to keep the same historical advisor on Russia and the Soviet Union throughout the production in this uniquely 'sensitive' case: Beijing University professor Xu Tianxin 徐天新, who had been educated in the Soviet Union in the 1950s.[38] Tang Jin's book was soon also published in Taiwan, adding, however, the interesting note that the rise of the PRC should, in turn, be a warning to 'little island Taiwan' (Tang Jin (ed.) 2007).[39]

Another book from the People's Press, now titled with a reference to the classical image of 'history as a mirror': *Qiangguo* (!) *zhi jian* 强国之鉴 (The mirror of the powers) and openly connected to the documentary, came out in April 2007, providing in-depth reflections of the experts in the documentary, i.e. partly the professors of Beijing University who had drafted the single countries' narratives in the beginning, partly advisors or authors of the single-country volumes in the accompanying eight-volume book series. In this way, a competing publisher tried to ride on the wave by eliciting contributions of its own from people involved in the popular documentary. This book became a bestseller even in Korea (*Renmin chubanshe xiang Hanguo shuchu 7zhong banquan*; 5 September 2007). And the same publisher came out in September 2007 with two further sister volumes to

Tang Jin's book, thus making this into a three-volume enterprise: one on 'The Road To Revival' of 'Great Powers', and the other on their 'downfall example', stressing that some countries may also reappear as great powers on the world scene (like China, which is now finally integrated here, including also other nations not discussed earlier, such as India and Brazil), whereas others never reappear (such as the bygone empires of ancient to modern times).[40] Interestingly, both sister volumes address Russia/the Soviet Union, but in a telling way: Russia is shown as an example of a country 'revived', presenting Peter the Great (1672–1725) to Lenin (1870–1924) quickly, then jumping immediately to Gorbachev and Yeltsin, thus *leaving out* the main story of the Soviet Union (!), and finally ending with Putin as embodying the Russian 'revival'. The 'downfall' volume, rather, addresses the Soviet Union as an example of an empire as bygone as the Romans![41] The use of 'road to revival' in the title of the first of these two sister volumes already marks the transition from 'rise' to 'revival' (which will be the topic of the following documentary addressed in this book – see Chapter 3), arguing that instead of China's 'rise' one should rather refer to its 'reappearance', or its 'revival' (Zhang Xiaojing (ed.) 2007: 2). And the second title integrates again – like the *Qiangguo zhi jian* volume of the same publisher – the old metaphor of history as a mirror for learning how to avoid a similar downfall.

In short, the People's Press, though not being the 'official' publisher of the CCTV production, could also live off the TV documentary quite comfortably, and continued to come out with related books.[42] Together with a host of further titles on the topic of the 'Great Powers' and China's potential to become one herself, some more historically, some more economically, some more strategically oriented, these publications were symptoms of the 'great powers hype' that set in late in 2006. The feverish activity on the book market and the contest between the historical interpretation of negative, aggressive powers and positive models of success made palpable the tension, anxieties and excitement this topic generated. And it reflects the vested interest of different sides to have their historical interpretations (with their respective political implications) circulated.

Portrayal of the 'successful' countries in 'world history'

The fact that his documentary was able to create such hype leads to the question as to how the different countries' historical experience is presented and what this implies. Therefore we will turn now to a close reading of the documentary itself, integrating also some observations on the accompanying book series and the directors' itineraries on their personal and filming experiences in the individual countries so as to approach the documentary more holistically.

Portugal and Spain: The Time of the Sea (Haiyang shidai 海洋时代)

The documentary sets in with the instalment on Portugal and Spain (the countries least familiar with a Chinese audience). Dominated visually by the sea and using the introductory images of waves to symbolising the 'rise', the key message of the whole documentary is already provided and is repeated in the introduction to all the following instalments: history is like the sea: vast, changing, with innumerable waves going up and down. The underlying music is purposefully epic. The commentary suggests the basic idea of opening up new horizons to the viewer – and introduces the key notion of competition: who would 'rise' in world history depended on who was able to use resources (the sea) first.

Even though the first instalment is set on the Iberian Peninsula, in the introduction one Chinese name is already mentioned: Zheng He 郑和 (1371–1433), the famous Chinese seafarer, suggesting that in the background there is the topic of China's rise looming. And it was indeed China's misfortune that after Zheng He, China left the sea to the Europeans, thus enabling them to 'rise'. How else could such small countries like Portugal and Spain have ever risen? But even in the case of Zheng He, it is argued, China was 'different': she did not take to the sea to open up trade opportunities, but just to 'propagate the virtue and authority of the Chinese Emperor' – a rather idealistic juxtaposition with the Europeans' motives, which are supposed to have been dominated by rivalry.

With Portugal and Spain, the surprising point is seen in the fact that they did not represent the 'centre' of their times, neither in an economic nor in a cultural sense. Thus, their 'rise' is explained by the fact that they had endured oppression themselves by the Romans, Germanic tribes, and Moors, and now went on to suppress others – something not to be emulated of course today. Portugal rose first, because she had been the first 'nation state' recognised by the Pope in 1143 and was under the unifying rule of a monarch, but she was short of natural resources. Thus, Prince Henry (the Navigator; 1394–1460) decided to take to the sea. This was spurred by the rediscovery of Ptolemy's geographical 'knowledge'. It was also a countermeasure to Arabian domination of continental trade routes, especially for spices. Thus Prince Henry set up a seafarers' academy, and had it 'ameliorate the Chinese compass' and build fast sailing ships. In other words, under Henry, the Portuguese state developed a strategy of conquering the sea. Compared with Zheng He's gigantic fleet, the Portuguese one was small, but they took more risks, driven by 'desire for wealth and strong religious faith'. And they were helped by the fact that all other potential rivals were still not ready, being absorbed in internal strife or other distractions. Thus, a dedicated leader like Henry (expressed also in the mentioned fact that he never married – a theme recurring also later in the documentary in other cases, as we will see) could allocate state funds to lay the foundations of the 'rise' of his nation – inviting the reading that this is what the Chinese state should do today as well. After Prince Henry, the Portuguese King John II (1455–95) then sent Diaz, who guaranteed the Portuguese domination of the spices trade following his discovery of Cape Horn.

However, Spain was soon ready to compete since Queen Isabella (1451–1504) managed to get the upper hand in the Reconquista together with her husband Ferdinand II (1452–1516), finally taking back all territory occupied by the Moors and triumphantly marching into the Alhambra. Whereas the Portuguese were fixed on their African route and did not believe the way towards the West would be worth exploring, thus not picking up the Genoese Columbus' (1451?–1506) suggestions to finance him to undertake such an enterprise, the latter tried his luck with Spain and found a ready ear with Isabella. The fact that a queen like Isabella would talk business with a simple foreign merchant, Columbus, even offering him a significant share of the wealth of the expected colonies, is particularly stressed: here rulers do not only grant an 'audience' – as was usual in China – but take private people seriously and elicit their service by offering them fair profit. Supported by Isabella, Columbus started the risky journey and finally arrived at the Bahamas. Pope Alexander VI then decided to divide the hemispheres between the Portuguese and the Spaniards, thus starting the long history of Europeans dividing the globe between them, culminating in the late nineteenth century – a clear hint to the Chinese audience where the beginnings of imperialism (and the 'splitting of the melon'-tactic encountered by China herself in the nineteenth century) lay. However, the 'victims' are mentioned only in passing (the Indians are briefly addressed, using – by the way – the US team's film clips; and the slave trade is not mentioned at all (!) –appearing only in the accompanying book series). Thus, exploitation is presented more in material economic terms (American silver, and so on). And with da Gama (1460/69?–1524) sailing to Asia, finally the Europeans took those parts of the world that Zheng He had already visited (but had not actually 'taken'). When asked by the Indians what he wanted, da Gama simply replied: Christians and spices. Thus, the driving forces of European expansion are again reiterated: economy and mission, and both are familiar to the Chinese audience as the 'unholy alliance' of imperialism. But heroic deeds at times have also their personal price, as demonstrated by the example of Magellan (1480–1521) who sailed around the whole world first, but was killed far away from home. This has a familiar ring as well with a Chinese audience: without people making sacrifices for their nation, no 'rise' will be achieved.

In any case, both Iberian countries managed to hold half of the world at their 'high' times, though the 'Portuguese style' is rather characterised as trade-oriented, and the 'Spanish style' as more of direct exploitation. But as with Don Quixote – one of the few Spanish literary works well-known in China – and his creator, Cervantes (1547?–1616), they tragically ended in failure and poverty. Neither country could hold on to its status, and both lost everything in the course of time. This, the commentary argues, was due to both countries investing their wealth only in religion (cf. the many cathedrals shown) and in wars, instead of developing production in their own countries, even blocking foreign merchants' enterprises for fear of the aristocrats losing control – arguably another implicit comment on present-day (Chinese) politics in favour of foreign investment, and a warning not to follow such short-sighted self-complacency. The Iberians, though, only lived off the colonies and thus could not adapt to the changing times. And this unavoidably determined their historical 'defeat' – the conclusion goes.[43]

The interviewees in this instalment are all Portuguese or Spaniards. In the accompanying eight-volume book series' corresponding volume, there is some additional information given on the key figures such as Henry and Isabella, but also on Charles V (1500–58), the House of Habsburg, Luther (1483–1546), the Spanish most well-known conquistadors, and Philip II of Spain (1527–98) who do not appear in the documentary's instalment. The 'aftermath' of both countries' 'way down' is, however, tellingly concluded by the return of the Portuguese colony Macao to China in 1999, thus providing a bridge for the Chinese viewer to connect straightforwardly to modern China's 'way up' (Daguo jueqi: *12 ji daxing dianzi jilupian* 2007, vol. 1: 80). As the itinerary written by the director reveals, the film crew encountered some difficulties due to the sometimes sloppy organisation of their visits, but at times also when interviewees did not confirm their historical reading – which they had, or wanted to cling to, nevertheless! Thus, there are certain gaps between the interviews conducted and the message conveyed in the documentary. Religious topics especially proved to be rather 'difficult' to grasp, seemingly appearing fairly alien to the crew-members. Thus, the background information added by the accompanying book series suggests that interviewees rather functioned as 'legitimisers' (cf. Chapter 5) in the documentary, whereas the content and historical interpretations were already set before filming.

Visually, the presentation in this and in the following instalments integrates present-day scenes, monuments, bird's-eye views, interviews, and occasional feature film scenes, but also documents, maps, and historical paintings (sometimes identified), often animated or reworked with CGI (computer-generated imagery) techniques, to entertain but also to illustrate certain readings that the commentary provides. The didactic aspect is most visible in the written white-on-black introductory commentary section which 'authoritatively' provides the key focus of the documentary as such: the nine countries, their mutual competition, their rise and fall, and the impact they had on the globe and what remains of it. Throughout the documentary, the commentator in 'voice-of-god' style leads the viewer through the instalment, providing a narrative bridge between the often abrupt cuts in imagery, which rather function as visual cues, for example by evoking familiar images the average viewer might expect in a particular country, here with the Iberian countries: bull fighting, Flamenco or others, or conforming to the 'tourist gaze' in showing sight-seeing spots, local costumes, dishes, and so on. The same holds true for the following instalments. Quick visual references also occasionally serve to connect historical issues with the present. Thus, visual appeal for the viewer and 'correct' interpretation provided to the listener at the same time make for a successful blend of entertainment and historical 'learning' experience.

For the audio element, the narrated parts are accompanied by epic or dramatic music (with some key motifs reappearing time and again throughout the documentary as a distinctive marker), whereas contemporary scenes may come with local folk music or street noise in a lighter mode before switching back to 'heavier' historical interpretation parts. Interviews are conducted in original voices with Chinese subtitles, the interviewee being identified as to his/her expertise at the beginning. Interviews and the commentary are interspersed with music, and sometimes the music is toned down to serve as background to the ever-present commentator. This means that speech dominates, again demonstrating the strong 'didactic' flavour the documentary comes with. This is also underlined by the structuring of the instalments in sections, always connected by rhetorical questions that are raised and then answered in the following section. This pattern is very familiar to the Chinese audience in film and TV, as well as in history textbooks in school.

The Netherlands: Small Country, Great Enterprise (Xiaoguo daye 小国大业)

The second instalment introduces the Netherlands as a very small country, just 2.5 times the size of Beijing, and 'only inhabited since the twelfth century'. With one-third of the territory below sea level (stressed by black-and-white film footage on flooding), how – the commentary asks – could such a place ever have become the economic centre of the world in the seventeenth century, counting only 1.5 million inhabitants at the time, later gaining the title by the unquestioned authority of Karl Marx (1818–83) of being the 'first maritime power'? Obviously, this was due to history's being 'as unpredictable as the sea'. And everything, the commentator argues, began with the main occupation of the Dutch: fishing for herring.

Here again, the motif of competition that spurred progress is introduced: since others were also living off fishing, for example the Scots, the Dutch fought several wars over fishing rights. However, it was not wars but the invention of a new technique that finally gave the Dutch an edge over their rivals: gutting, invented by the fisherman Willem Beukelszoon (late thirteenth century–1347?). By this new method one removed the fish's inner organs by one quick cut, and then salted them. These '*matjes*' herring could be conserved for more than one year and consumed (as is visually highlighted) uncooked almost in their entirety – probably a tantalising viewing experience for a Chinese audience accustomed to cooked and sliced fish, and traditionally associating such eating practices with 'barbarism'. However, this conservation method meant the Dutch could sell their herring all through the year to meet ever growing demand not only at home, but also in neighbouring countries, in time expanding their markets, stretching from Northeast Europe over England to Africa.

This role was facilitated by the Netherlands' geographical location: Rotterdam became the first great port for maritime trade, being also close to the mouths of important continental rivers like the Rhine and the Meuse, assisted by cross-connections that Dutch engineers built: the canals. Thus, where the Portuguese and Spaniards had based their rise mainly on the use of force, the Dutch distinguished themselves by trade (and innovations). This fitted their condition since they 'lacked' a centralised governmental power and large work force – the latter aspect being underlined visually by showing the present-day highly automated Rotterdam harbour. (In fact, one of the things the responsible director of the film crew noted in her itinerary was the enormous harbour of Rotterdam and the tiny work force active there, most of the work being done by machines, contrasting with the bustling Chinese harbours full of people working.) By skilfully integrating themselves as middlemen in trade, the Dutch even profited from Portugal and Spain's efforts overseas; offering, for example, to distribute spices carried by the Portuguese from afar to various nearby locations in Europe as a kind of sea courier. To this tactic, it was only England that in time rose as a competitor enjoying even 'more favourable' geographical conditions, disposing of more territory and people and thus becoming a challenge to the Dutch. But again, the clever Dutch found a way to compete successfully for the time being by their innovativeness: whereas the English ships were massive, carrying armour for security, the Dutch took the risk of sailing without, thus having much more room for goods to be transported on lighter, less expensively built ships. To innovation and cost-efficiency is added the particular dedication of the Dutch to trade. This is underlined by the story of a trader who would rather have his men starve then let them consume the goods destined for some client, when they were blocked by pack ice in the polar region. Thus, the Dutch could secure a reputation as trustworthy in Europe, where they were able to dominate the short-distance trade even in the sixteenth century, turning their cities into centres of trade.

However, the commentary argues, the Dutch were different from the rest of Europe in that they did not see any advantage in being governed. Thus, the cities that had originally been under the rule of the aristocracy wanted economic freedom for themselves. To achieve this, they did not stage a revolution but simply used their money to buy their freedom from the aristocracy! And roughly half of the Netherlands' population lived in these self-governing cities. Only with the rise of autocracy in the whole of Europe did the independent Dutch cities come under pressure, not being strong enough to defend their autonomy. Thus the 'idyllic' times of self-government ended in the face of outside forces 'stronger' because of a unified government under autocratic rule (a reminder to the Chinese audience that 'hard power' and unity are needed as well, notwithstanding their sympathy with the Dutch 'soft power' example). In this way a period of domination began, first by the Spaniards who did not respect Dutch economic freedom (the religious issue of the Reformation is not addressed here, demonstrating again the tendency to 'circumnavigate' religious issues in the documentary) but tried to exploit them in the traditional imperialist manner. Whereas the Dutch could bear or live under many kinds of oppression – the commentary suggests – the attack on their economic freedom provoked them finally to do what they had never done: to fight (illustrated and dramatised by short war scenes taken from feature films). In the end this led to independence from Spain,[44] but now combined with the problem of who should reign instead. The idea of seeking the protection of Elizabeth I of England (1533–1603) proved problematic, since she started to exploit the rich Dutch as well – who obviously are to be moved only by their purses. Then – typically – they tried with a republic, being the first of its kind in the modern world and on top of this being a trader-dominated one, having only stadtholders (above all from the House of Orange) as leading figures. But this structure was only very loose (notably compared by an interviewee to the EU of today!) and thus historically stood no chance against the strong autocracies around it.

Being faced with stern Spanish opposition and blockade, the Dutch were economically endangered and only at that point decided to concentrate on overseas trade now themselves, founding the Dutch East Indian Company as a joint stock company. This was a new commercial model since besides the government normal people also acted as shareholders, thus providing the company with money and leading to the founding in Amsterdam of the first stock exchange in the world. The company thus being financed officially and privately, it functioned in overseas regions in partly governmental ways, for example being entitled to wage wars if necessary, or to make contracts on its own. With this company, the Dutch snatched the profits of overseas trade away from the Iberians. Their farsightedness is characterised also by the fact that they rather invested the early profits and only afterwards provided the shareholders with their dividends. This commercial model worked well because via the shareholding everybody could take part in the profit or sell his share when needed. They could also either deposit their profits or take up loans from the first bank in the world created in this context here as well. Even foreigners were allowed to use the stock exchange and the bank. As the commentary underlines for a Chinese audience that one could assume to be awestruck: even Spanish enemies could have their wars against the Dutch financed by Dutch loans! In sum, whatever the case, business came first.

Basically, the Dutch tried to remain neutral in Europe's contemporary various conflicts but concentrated on creating a modern economic trade system. They thus were able to dominate half of the world trade in the seventeenth century, having taken Cape of Good Hope in Africa from the Portuguese to advance to South East Asia where they set up important trade posts in Indonesia, from where they could also get hold of East Asian trade routes (taking Taiwan on the way), up to New Zealand named after one of her provinces; and in the Americas they occupied Brazil and founded New Amsterdam (today's New York) at the time. The parts of the world the Dutch managed to occupy and colonise (at least for some time) are visually highlighted to show this 'small' country's huge impact on the world at its best times – and to remind the audience of the Dutch colonial presence also in East Asia. But their way of behaviour distinguished them also from other Europeans, as the example of the Dutch mission to the Qing court demonstrates: whereas other Europeans had declined to bow before the Chinese Emperor in the ritual way (*kotow*), the pragmatic Dutch quickly agreed, thus securing in 1656 an advantage in trade. This, the comment stresses, shows well the Dutch preference for profit above 'honour'.

At home, the Dutch proved different as well in that they did not invest their money in palaces or cathedrals like other Europeans, but in the city halls or private homes, as many decorations and paintings shown are to demonstrate. The latter also reflect wealthy bourgeois family life seemingly common at the time. (The prominent use of Dutch paintings and museums in general is a notable feature of this instalment.) The Netherlands only started to lose out to the rising competitor Britain when precisely one of her own leading figures, stadtholder William III of Orange (1650–1702), moved there to become king of England, Scotland and Ireland. In sum, the presentation suggests the unique Dutch merchants' way as the exception in the rule of needing a strong state to rise as a 'nation' – and as a remarkable case of economy far above politics.[45]

The film crew director's itinerary, in turn, suggests the surprise of the Chinese camera team about much in present-day Dutch life: the calmness of the cities (which also characterises much of this instalment's presentation in mood), the few and very casual people, difficulties with the weather and food, the many flowers cultivated instead of grain production, and so on, which seemed very different from Chinese realities. The interviewees, as in the first instalment with similarly 'less well-known' countries in China, were all local (but for one British expert) and included a politician; but interviews were conducted in this – and only this – instalment in English throughout rather than in the native tongue. Whereas the narrative in the documentary stresses rather the economic and peaceful aspects and largely omits religious or armed conflicts, the accompanying book series' respective volume is more explicit about these. Furthermore, there is already in the book series a short reference to Peter the Great, who appears prominently in the instalment of the documentary on Russia (though not in this instalment). Furthermore, in this instalment there are already many visual references to Great Britain, the great competitor and 'successor' on the world scene, therewith linking it to the following instalment.

The United Kingdom: Towards Modernity (Zou xiang xiandai 走向现代) and First Appearance of Industry (Gongye xiansheng 工业先生)

Two instalments are dedicated to the development of Britain, the third and the fourth, basically taking the beginning of industrialisation in the eighteenth century as the dividing line. Britain, being an 'isolated small island' at the Western tip of Europe, would, as the commentary suggests in a familiar manner (though some-what in discrepancy with the preceding one where Britain was characterised as 'geographically superior' to the Netherlands) at first glance not seem the likeliest place for a nation to become the leading one in the whole world in the eighteenth and nineteenth centuries, creating an empire where 'the sun never sets', stretching over all continents and governing more than three billion people. What then made this island so influential?

The storyline in this case starts with a belligerent image of competition: the Spanish Armada setting sail to attack England, thus linking it to the first instalment. Here, at last, the religious factor present in the Spanish–English conflict is mentioned by an interviewee as crucial besides the Chinese commentary's stress on economic competition, thus presenting the historical rivalry as one both of Spanish protection of Catholicism vs. English religious independence from the Pope, and as one of power rivalry between established Spain and upstart England. From the British side, the crucial role of Elizabeth I is highlighted (whose portrait is animated in a playful way as an entertainment device). As with Prince Henry of Portugal, her total dedication to her country is exemplified by her not marrying all through her life. Citing an English author's metaphor, Elizabeth is characterised as a hen breeding her egg that is the English nation. Following the rationale that, as the Portuguese and Spaniards demonstrated, one only needed to be the first to grasp new territory and wealth, she set out to compete with them in the 'new game' that was played above all at sea. Thus, the geographic location of Britain, being an island, could be used as an asset. Elizabeth's cleverness in relying on pirates with whom, when necessary or running into problems, she could always negate 'official' relations, makes her appear as a smart sovereign with a strong will to further her nation's interest at whatever cost. Thus, she bestowed ranks on the pirate Francis Drake (1540–96), who was not only the first to undertake and survive the complete trip around the world himself, but time and again provoked the Spaniards and snatched a huge profit for her (and all those who had financed him). When Philip of Spain finally declared war, England had only a fairly tiny fleet made up of merchant and pirate ships, but they were quicker and disposed of better cannons. And they knew their own region much better. Thus, the huge but inflexible Armada was defeated in a war that the first Chinese historian appearing in the documentary declares as having been 'decisive for Europe'. Victory, however, an interviewed British expert stresses, was only possible due to the English monarchy, since it bundled English emergent nationalism into one strong force to combat all continental rivals. Unity, in short, makes strong.

On the island itself there also occurred great changes: London grew into the first metropolis in Europe, not only claiming to be a political capital with its impressive official architecture, but also a cultural one with its lively art scene, exemplified by Shakespearian theatre. (Curiously Shakespeare, 1564–1616, is introduced in the commentary as having been praised by Marx as a great genius – as if such a figure needed 'ideological' approval.) And the latter, cultural role of London was not to be dominated by the former, political one, as can be gleaned from the fact stressed by the Chinese interviewee that even though Shakespeare's plays did not only talk about human nature in general but also were often very outspokenly critical of rulers, Elizabeth enjoyed the performances and had no idea of censuring criticism. (This, arguably, is a more than implicit reminder of the different Chinese situation.) She did not need to behave in an authoritarian way, it is insinuated, since she knew very well that she depended on the people (as she had depended on the pirates). And this (liberal) style of rule had a long tradition, even going back to William I (1028–87) and the decentralised feudal system, regulated not yet by 'law' but by convention. (Here again Chinese interviewees are presented quite extensively, explaining the difference of the use of the term 'feudalism' in China and in Europe/Britain to make sure the audience grasped the 'true' character of English feudalism as non-autocratic rule – probably also a counter-measure to not running the risk of being accused of unduly 'praising feudalism', a term heavily negative in connotation in Chinese understanding.) When King John (1166–1216) in the thirteenth century lost his continental territories and wanted to press his subjects for money to continue his wars, the aristocracy rebelled in 1215 and pressured him into signing a more formal agreement: the Magna Carta, which not only guaranteed aristocratic privileges vis-à-vis the king and regulated juridical procedures to prevent easy expropriation, but declared that rights were not bestowed by and thus dependent on the king but had rather to be respected by him, not himself having the right to expropriate or detain anyone at will. (The Chinese interviewee stressing this may again be understood as implicitly commenting on the Chinese situation.) Thus, the king of England was early on bound by law and even more restricted in his power when a parliament was created. Thus, although Elizabeth I was a strong ruler, she could never just do as she pleased but consulted the parliament, tried to act cost-efficiently and did not wage war easily. Not marrying, she freed herself also of any possible restraint that might come with alliances, marking this decision as a conscious political one to further her country's interest.

Contrasting with the highly idealised Elizabeth I in the documentary, Charles I (1600–49) appears as a negative example of a ruler too sure of himself and without consideration for others, infallibly ending in disaster. As a Chinese interviewee underlines, he had Dutch painter Rubens (1577–1640) portray him and his country as being particularly blessed by 'God's will', waged costly wars in disregard of the parliament's opposition, trying to impose taxes on his own to finance his endeavours and even ordering the snubbed parliament to dissolve. This blunt disregard of established norms, as the documentary's main supervisor and specialist of British history, Qian Chengdan, argues, necessarily led to the English Revolution of 1642, bringing about the English Republic under Cromwell (1599–1658) and ending for Charles I on the scaffold in front of the Banqueting House where he had had Rubens exalt him in painting. And this execution (which is visually repeated several times, again with animated historical paintings) under the charge of having behaved as an 'enemy of the people' shocked all of old Europe's monarchs, making them aware of the precarious legitimacy of rule. (This, again, can be seen as an implicit remark on people's consent being the precondition for legitimate rule also in China.) If formerly the conflict had been between the aristocracy and the king, it now had changed into one between the whole nation and the king.

However, since neither the republican system, which had ended up in Cromwell's dictatorship, nor the reinstated royal house under Charles' son James II (1633–1701) proved satisfactory, the second 'glorious' revolution decided to choose a middle way: to remain with the monarchical system on principle but substitute the deficient king with someone else willing to respect the people's rights. (At this point, for the first time the main intellectual point of reference for the whole documentary on the 'rise of the great powers', Yale history professor Paul Kennedy, is introduced as an interviewee.) Thus, the British invited William of Orange from the Netherlands (1650–1702) who was connected to the English royal house via his wife, the daughter of James II, to come to England to substitute his father-in-law, who had no alternative but to flee. But now, William and his wife were no longer considered as monarchs 'by God's will', but constitutional monarchs 'elected' by the parliament and bound by law. This 'Glorious Revolution' of 1688 was named that way because, it is (somewhat hazardously) argued that this time no blood was shed.[46] Just by 'reform' – a key word in present-day China – and not by 'revolution', societal progress was realised. And, as Chinese-born expert Zheng Yongnian, teaching in Nottingham, adds, only because of this inner strength that Britain developed by social consensus could she rise as a nation. In fact, after having beaten the Spanish Armada 100 years earlier and now having taken that decisive step in internal organisation, Great Britain could start her impressive economic career. Quickly, she could fight the main continental power France and snatch the intermediary trading position from the Dutch. Due to her open society, the people profited economically together with the whole nation. In this, Great Britain was different from the other great countries of the time, which were either living under autocracy (as France), were still in the making (as Russia) or not unified at all (as Italy or Germany). In East Asia – the comment adds – Japan was still stuck in ('negative') feudalism at the time, and in China the Qing had only just started their dynasty. Thus Britain moved unchallenged to the pole position to remain ahead for the next two centuries.

Linking the narrative back to China, which at the time of the height of auto-cratic rule under Kangxi (1654–1722) is set against the British starting their economic success story, initiating what later has been termed the 'Industrial Revolution', the fourth instalment introduces Great Britain from the eighteenth century onward. With overseas expansion and colonisation, the demand for goods rose, scientific knowledge and the processes of the market came into focus and in this way Britain developed her liberal economic system. Key to the whole process of the Industrial Revolution was innovation, and the latter, exemplified by James Watt (1736–1819), was driven by a positive evaluation of profit as such by Protestantism. Another factor was the economic advantage of market access that the British had achieved overseas. This could be secured by strategically elimi-nating all rivals in wars, which, a British expert argues, were fought since the 'Glorious Revolution' in consensus between the king and the people, because they were fought now in the whole nation's interest.[47]

Market demand as a driving force realised itself at first in the textile sector, above all pushing the development of weaving manufactures. In the beginning, mechanic looms could be moved only by water or wind, thus restricting the possible locations of such looms. But then James Watt invented the steam engine. This innovation grew out of a personal crisis Watt underwent, having lost his wife, his business partner suffering personal ruin, leaving him with a large family to feed and thus being in desperate need of money. (This is illustrated, for example with his personal letters giving a more intimate note to this 'hero'.) Even though a friend suggested emigration to him, Great Britain still provided the best conditions for someone technically able, as was Watt. His many technical inventions did not provide him with much profit at first. But the system of patent protection on them guaranteed that he would profit from them in the long run – demonstrating that inventions also need an adequate legal context. (This, again, has a special salience for the audience in a Chinese context, stressing the need to respect intellectual property. And the conjunction with emigration suggests that a country needs to entice able people to stay to prevent a brain drain.) Thus Britain soon realised that one could earn much more by innovation than by wars, instigating many techni-cally versed people to try at innovations themselves. Another consequence was the rise of a new class: the entrepreneurs, since technical innovations had to be trans-ferred to industrial use. Thus, it needed a Matthew Boulton (1728–1809) to apply Watt's rather complicated steam machine to widespread mechanic use in factories to get the Industrial Revolution really going.

Technical innovations, however, were also closely connected to science. Without an Isaac Newton (1643–1727), the Industrial Revolution would not have been possible either, since he stimulated human thought by finding evidence for natural laws and raising the possibility for people to 'look behind God's creation' (visually opposing natural phenomena with the 'superstitious' belief in religion, showing a *Christian service*). Newton's contribution was honoured politically by the fact that he received a state burial in Westminster Abbey, thus showing the great respect a 'mere' scientist could gain in Great Britain – again an indirect comment on the different Chinese situation. Even though Newton was not an infallible personality, as a British interviewee – referring to his bickering with other scientists of his time – suggests, the fact that a scientist could receive such honours in his country impressed even other Europeans like Voltaire (1694–1778). And after Newton had discovered and systemised natural forces mathematically, Watt then was able to use them creatively, leading to the Industrial Revolution. Thus, mankind was no longer governed by natural forces but could master them. (Marx is again cited here by a Chinese expert as a reassuring reference for acknowledging the enormous success of the Industrial Revolution – and leading over to the following short discussion of labour relations.)

New ways of production led to new social developments: where there were entrepreneurs, there were now also industrial workers. Due to rationalisation of working processes, labour was divided and thus workers repeated the same part of labour all day long. (Notably, this potentially 'critical' side of the Industrial Revolution is only briefly addressed here to move on quickly to the 'positive' stimulating side of economic competition.) But it was not only the work process that changed: lifestyles were changed as well, as was societal thinking. To illustrate this, the documentary focuses on Adam Smith's (1723–90) *The Wealth of Nations* as a symbol of intellectual change that argued for individual profit as the driving force of human behaviour. However, the 'invisible hand' present on the economic market guaranteed that in the end the individual profit would emerge as of benefit to all. (A Chinese viewer may associate here the argument forwarded by Deng Xiaoping, that if some get rich first, that means that the others will follow suit.) By this 'invisible hand', free competition would translate into a general growth in the level of wealth. And this 'invisible hand' was simply self-regulation by the market through supply and demand. This basic optimist idea argued that instead of trying to monopolise markets it would be better to let also others become rich, thus being able to sell even more to them, and raising one's own profit again. In short, where Watt created the technical basis for the Industrial Revolution, Smith articulated its economic rules. And this was translated into politics, since British parliamentarians as well as nobles were impressed by the economist's arguments.

This political option proved successful for Great Britain, being able to beat all competitors not only by her military, but above all economically. Thus Napoleon, for example (1769–1821) – who loved to belittle The United Kingdom – not only had his army defeated by the British at Waterloo, but his soldiers all wore uniforms made of British textiles. (This, of course, brings present-day dominance of Chinese textiles on world markets to mind.) However, viewers are reminded, for all the positive rhetoric connected to 'free trade', that the UK was the one to profit from that system because of her advanced products, her easy access to markets (often – as with China – 'opened' by force) and her leading market position making it in fact difficult for competitors to gain a foothold. (This argument of 'unequal' opportunities will come up also later in the documentary as a typical critique of upstarts against established competitors.) And British economic success depended on raw materials provided by all the colonies – an argument again familiar to the audience from Chinese history textbooks.

But the fact that it was an empire led also to significant changes inside the UK. Urbanisation grew, and production was redirected to new areas, namely steel production to build railways and transport, in turn needing a lot of coal for producing steel. With the new ways of production, also conceptions of space and time changed: time was measured strictly and in seconds, and new means of transport meant also another relation to spatial distances. As the comment stresses, in 1851 the UK already had rail tracks six times as long as the distance from Beijing to Guangzhou. (This evokes with the audience the issue of railways as one of the crucial contested issues in Chinese modernisation. For a long time, they were built and operated mainly by foreigners.) The UK could therefore proudly exhibit her leading position via the newly created 'world expositions', which showcased the newest inventions – and try to cater for new clients. This was actively supported by the crown, as Queen Victoria (1819–1901) who celebrated it as 'unending glory', demonstrated by inaugurating the first world exposition in London in the Crystal Palace. Unlike Elizabeth I, Victoria was a 'mother' not only to the nation, but cared for her own nine children, leaving day-to-day business to the parliament. But she guaranteed the 'invisible hand' by not interfering, leading to the UK's pivotal role under her rule. (In this way, principal support 'from above' but without 'interference' is suggested to the Chinese viewer as a very positive model to follow.) However, whereas at home things went fairly well, in the colonies opposition started to form in the nineteenth century. And the profit drawn from the colonies also decreased over time. Thus, the British opted for investing more and more in their own country in the late nineteenth and twentieth centuries. In the meantime, via the so-called 'Second Industrial Revolution', Germany and the US had caught up, and the British system of free competition led to disastrous consequences in the new century. (There are no details given, but one may assume the world wars are among those things referred to here.) When the British finally realised that their empire was at its end, a new power had already surpassed her: the US.

The end of the UK's presentation in the documentary is quite surprising in that there is almost nothing on the twentieth century, no details on the 'problems' of the British model, leaving the viewer basically with the most successful period of the eighteenth and early nineteenth century and only signalling that in the 'second half of the nineteenth century', i.e. the time when British imperialism started to be felt in China, the UK was already on an 'inward' move and thus on its 'way down' – in spite of its colonial history continuing for many decades ahead. In short, even though two instalments have been assigned to the UK, the picture drawn appears to be somehow unfinished, which is remarkable considering that Qian Chengdan, the main advisor for the documentary, is an expert in British history. Whether there were any specific motives remains speculative.[48]

Notably, the experts presented in these two instalments are a mix of Westerners (including Paul Kennedy) and several Chinese (including Qian Chengdan). However, in the accompanying book series there are only the faces and interviews of the Westerners (including the Chinese teaching abroad) presented, probably to suggest more 'authenticity' or 'internationalism'. Whereas Qian Chengdan and the other Chinese experts were most probably interviewed in Beijing, it is not clear where Zheng Yongnian was interviewed, since he teaches in Nottingham but is not mentioned in the director's itinerary as an interviewee during the crew's stay in Great Britain. Since the same holds true for some other interviewees, although this itinerary is particularly detailed on problems with interviews, it could well be that some interviews were conducted afterwards in China to supplement missing points.

The director's itinerary in this case is very informative and much more detailed than the former ones, providing interesting insights into the production process. It becomes obvious that the crew had a fixed job of whom to interview and what to film and thus not much room for spontaneous changes on the spot. Nevertheless, there were some unforeseen moments influencing the outcome like missing film permissions, bad light conditions and spontaneously filmed 'life scenes'. But the general picture emerges that in Beijing the whole outlay was fixed, including what to ask in the interviews (and more or less what the expected answers were to be!), and that the film crew was well aware what kind of pictures they were expected to provide (for example, leading to the cameraman refusing to certain spontaneous filming requested by the director on the assumption that it might not be used later, describing established documentary specialist Kang Jianning 康健宁 as the deciding figure back home for the final visual arrangement). And there was at least some interchange on the phone between the film crews in different countries, for example asking for certain shots that one could take over if conditions were not ideal in one's own case. It seems also that the generally responsible executive director of the whole project, Miss Zhou Yan 周艳, toured between some crews to see whether everything worked. As with the other crews, the one in Great Britain consisted only of the director and cameramen, i.e. without a fixed person with language skills attached to the crew. The guiding, arrangements and interviews were done locally, usually by Chinese living in the respective country who were recruited in advance. By providing all these details, this itinerary gives the most concrete insights into how the filming of the documentary was done in practice.

France: Times of Passion (Jiqing suiyue 激情岁月)

The documentary then moves on to Britain's long-time rival: France, which has been established as a great power by Louis XIV (1638–1715), symbolised visually by his palace at Versailles, swept the European continent under Napoleon and as a colonial power was only second to Britain in the world. However, it is also portrayed as the country of the enlightenment and of social experiments, that is, the country of ideals and passion.

Given this general image of France, the presentation starts dramatically with what most Chinese might first associate with French history: the French Revolution. The camera zooms in on the diary of Louis XVI (1754–93) for the entry on 14 July 1789, which stated: 'Nothing happened.'[49] In face of the foremost symbolic fight about the Bastille as representing autocratic rule (illustrated by animated French paintings of the Bastille), which at the time imprisoned only seven people but for whose liberation the attacking citizens lost 98 men, the king did not realise its meaning, asking his minister whether there was another rebellion underway. The latter, however, responded: 'No, your majesty, it's a revolution'. Thus, the mental gap between the ancient regime and the grass roots level of social movements is forcefully introduced, setting the frame for turning back to Louis XIV as the one who built up the autocratic system later attacked in the revolution.

To link the narrative back to China, Louis XIV is paralleled with the Kangxi Emperor (1654–1722) as representing the heyday of their respective countries under autocratic rule. Given his overpowering personality, however, Louis XIV could take important decisions all by himself, also famously coined in his phrase 'L'état, c'est moi', well known in China, which is explained by a French historian (and China specialist) as covering also the meaning of the monarch being the embodiment of the state's spirit, and the usefulness of this concept for effectively waging wars. (Notably, this instalment also presents French interviewees with expertise on China – albeit not openly acknowledged – whereas earlier instalments usually interviewed foreign experts with no special connection to China.) However, the country's finances were depleted by wars. Furthermore, in France it was only the third estate that shouldered the taxes. (Here, the famous caricature with the representative of the third estate carrying the other two on his back is shown, familiar to the Chinese audience from history textbooks in school.) The autocratic system, however, functioned only as long as the autocrat was a capable ruler. This became clear years later when at the times of the Qianlong 乾隆 Emperor (1711–99) in China, who enjoyed a fairly peaceful reign, in France it was Louis XVI's time: he was a calm, withdrawn person pursuing his hobbies (not unlike the art-loving Qianlong Emperor); but in his case, the country was not so calm. Although natural disasters drove up bread prices Louis XVI did not act to reduce taxes but rather increased them by levying taxes also on the two other estates for financing costly wars, thus antagonising the whole population. When he had even the National Assembly that he was forced to convene come to nothing, and ordered it to be dissolved by his troops, he lost the last chance for a peaceful solution. Revolution was imminent, aiming now at a completely new social system. This ideal was laid down in the famous 'Declaration of the Rights of Man and of the Citizen', proclaiming freedom, equality and the right to private property, negating privileges. Thus, human rights and law were to be the new basis of the social system. And this French heritage, born in the context of the autocratic state of France of the eighteenth century, later was to be integrated in the charter of the United Nations. (As with previous instalments, the original documents are shown here.)

Another feature prominent in autocratic France as formed by Louis XIV was encouragement of the arts – reminding the viewer of the instalment on pre-industrial Britain and Queen Elizabeth's support for theatre. Paris as a city was newly created as a model by Louis XIV, who founded royal academies for theatre, music, architecture, and science. Louis XIV himself liked to dance ballet. And by this cultural leadership in Europe the prestige of the French language achieved a great boost. (This may be seen as positive encouragement in the documentary for 'soft power' policies and official support for the arts – besides science, as another important intellectual endeavour.) Apart from the autocratic court's engagement in arts, in the bourgeois urban sphere a culture of the salon developed, organised by wealthy women in their homes, and the café played a similar role in the culture of urban citizens.

This newly developed culture was also the setting for new ideas coming up. Thus, a Voltaire could find an audience for his critical viewpoints toward religion and his homage for human genius. As he argued, not Caesar (100–44 BC), nor Alexander the Great (356–23 BC), nor Genghis Khan (1162?–1227), nor Cromwell, but someone like Newton (introduced in the instalment on the UK, making for a visual and narrative link between the two) should be revered, because he investigated the nature of the world whereas all others only tried to govern it. With this new focus on human ability, science and rationality, the old fetters of theology and the state were shattered, underscored by a dictum of Marx (whom it seems necessary to cite time and again) that man is defined by being conscious of himself as a human being. Thus, Voltaire left to mankind the important legacy of the freedom of the human spirit – dramatically underscored in the documentary by showing Voltaire's enshrined 'passionate' heart, carrying the inscription: 'My heart is here, but my spirit is everywhere'.

Voltaire's contribution to criticising the old regime was complemented by Rousseau (1712–78), who imagined a new one. By providing a new basis for society, grounding the latter in a 'social contract' model, Rousseau did away with power and wealth and integrated all citizens into a new society. Therewith he laid the positive foundation for the French Revolution. Consequently, on his tomb there is a hand with a torch, symbolising that after his (and Voltaire's) death the light was to be taken up by the French people. And that torch burned down the *Ancien Régime*, leading to the First Republic. The importance of this development is marked by counting the time anew, starting from the republic's foundation and the execution of Louis XVI, who represented the old forces. However, this affront to autocratic rule led to the intervention of other European autocrats in France. This tense situation expressed itself in a mounting terror, symbolised by the guillotine. 'Traitors' were discovered everywhere (probably reminding some older Chinese viewers of the times of the Cultural Revolution). And this mania made people forget their own definition of freedom from only a few years earlier in the 'Declaration of the Rights of Man'. (It is notable that the terror aspect of the

French Revolution is stressed here, since the French Revolution has been presented more and more positively in Chinese history schoolbooks during the last decades.[50]) Thus, radicalised revolutionary practice turned against its own ideals, paving the way for a new monarchic system, now however based on elections, with Napoleon.

Napoleon thus was a very different kind of monarch: he embodied hope in a powerful state, led by a strongman, and finally leading also to the subjugation of 'old' Europe. Even though he was an emperor, he nevertheless symbolised the triumph of the French Revolution over the old regimes everywhere by his new civil code exported to all countries conquered. (It is remarkable that, according to the itinerary of the directors, the Chinese crew was very puzzled at the beginning by the fact that the French chose to return to monarchy after their 'great revolution', but the interviewees explained that fact with the 'newness' of Napoleonic-style monarchy, being a sequel to the revolution rather than its negation.) The importance that Napoleon attached to this civil code as an embodiment of the ideals of the revolution is particularly stressed. In this way, though he is comparable in some ways to the earlier apogee of France, Louis XIV, he nevertheless also represents the ideals of the French Revolution, by his victories over 'old' regimes also smashing ('negative') 'feudalism'. However, since his actions in occupying many European countries contradicted the ideal of 'freedom', thus making for the conquered peoples' aversion to this 'armed missionary' (an expression the Chinese viewer will link to similar experiences in Chinese history in the nineteenth century), he was bound to fail, thus ironically reaping the fruits of the ideas he himself had sewn by his crusade for revolutionary ideas. For all his vanity and thirst for the glory of his nation, exemplified in the Arc de Triomphe, he left behind a hollow glory, marking the problems of one-man rule and creating a state of chaos shown by the many changing forms of rule the French state went through in the years that followed. (This, again, is remarkable in the documentary since the general image of Napoleon in Chinese history textbooks in the last decades has been a very positive one.[51] But the emphasis on the problems of one-man rule could be read also as an implicit comment on Maoist times.)

The French nation's unstable situation also led to her fairly slow down industrial development, making her lag behind her competitors. Thus, it was only under de Gaulle (1890–1970), the last (and most positively presented) of the three great men in French history whom the instalment profiles (after Louis XIV and Napoleon), that the French nation rose again – notably introduced by a commemorative mass in Notre Dame for the war dead on the day of liberation from the Nazis, where the bishop explicitly points out de Gaulle's merits. (Archival footage shows de Gaulle walking through the Arc de Triomphe in 1944, finally rendering that monument of Napoleon worthy of its name.) It is ex-President Giscard d'Estaing, the most prominent of the interviewees whose special attention to China and interest in being interviewed is stressed by the directors' itinerary, who details de Gaulle's contribution to leading France back to the group of the great powers, for example by securing for his country a seat on the Security Council of the UN (sitting there together with China). Under him, France came back to glory, but now based also on economic strength, being a precondition for remaining a great power, as the only Chinese expert appearing in this instalment adds. And de Gaulle looked to keeping France independent, for example by setting up her own nuclear programmes. This – again – parallels China.

De Gaulle is also credited for having 'accepted' Algerian independence and for rolling back on colonialism, furthermore ending the long-lasting animosity with neighbouring Germany. And – very importantly – he is acclaimed for being the first Western statesman to recognise the PRC! By keeping a distance from the US he established a neutral France, acting also as an in-between in international conflicts. This line of neutralism is taken up in another French politician's statement to the effect that de Gaulle respected all forms of political systems, since they have to 'suit' the people, and also that in any case every democratic country has its own kind of democracy.[52] – This statement, obviously, goes well with the (official) Chinese argumentation line of 'national characteristics'.

In short, de Gaulle's Fifth Republic guaranteed France an important role in the world again, however now respecting other countries (in marked difference from Napoleon), and in fact only now realising the ideals of the French Revolution and fulfilling the aims of the enlightenment. This, then, marks France as a great power.

This glorious side of French history is honoured by the Pantheon as the place where greatness receives respect (and it is not connected to the church, as in the British case with Westminster Abbey). And – the commentary stresses – greatness here is broadly defined, with only a tiny proportion of the revered figures being politicians (11 out of 72) and including also thinkers, artists, scientists and so on. In 2002, for example, Jacques Chirac decided to have the famous writer Alexandre Dumas (1802–70) reburied here to be honoured as one of France's great men, provoking a national debate. In his speech Chirac argued that the ideals of the French Revolution were enhanced in his writings, legitimating his reburial in the Pantheon. Thus, the Chinese commentary adds, only a country that is able to honour the greatness of human spirit in its many forms as France does may become a '*grande nation*' – probably intending an indirect comment on the Chinese less courting treatment of intellectuals as well.[53]

The itinerary of the film directors of this instalment (and the following one on Germany) is not very informative but suggests that this film crew first concentrated on the interviews (all conducted in French) and did not move around much, remaining basically in Paris and only travelling to Strasbourg to take some shots in connection with the topic of the European Union (EU) and the Maginot Defence Line – which, however, were not finally included in the instalment (but some were used in the instalment on Germany and others in the very last instalment of the documentary instead).

Comparing the instalment to the accompanying book series with its volume on France, one gets the impression that the basic account of French history had been somewhat ampler than the resulting focus on Louis XIV, the Enlightenment, the revolution, Napoleon, and de Gaulle, starting back in the fourteenth century. However, it is notable that the colonial high times of France are largely ignored by jumping from Napoleon to de Gaulle. Such break in the narrative and blank spots do occur time and again, as we noted above already, especially with the UK, making the observer wonder what the reasons might be. Besides the multiple authorship and potentially conflicting historical interpretations already named earlier, one plausible explanation for the breaks could be the narrative focus on (positive) 'greatness', thus leaving out more 'negative' phases or aspects. However, it has obviously led to a fairly imbalanced picture of the respective countries.

Germany: Spring and Autumn of an Empire (Diguo chunqiu 帝国春秋)

Following up on France, the next instalment focuses on Germany, laying out as a key theme in the modernisation of this 'country of classical music and philosophy' the particular drive to set in motion the 'Second Industrial Revolution', underpinned by special attention to higher education and innovation. However, the flip side of the medal is Germany's huge potential for destruction as exemplified in her being the driving force behind two World Wars. (All these topics are accompanied by short visual cues, for example with clips of archival footage of the first half of the twentieth century, to reactivate the viewer's assumed knowledge about this country.) Thus, Germany, a country faced with a tortuous and prolonged way towards unification, is presented on a keynote of a tragicomedy, driven by the quest for unity and strength.

The presentation starts with some glimpses of the area around the Brandenburg Gate on 3 October 2005, noting how surprisingly unspectacularly the Germans deal with their national holiday – in contrast to China. (In the itinerary of the film directors – the same two as in France, though the much more reflective tone in the itinerary of Germany suggests that the directors divided the work between themselves – a somewhat different impression is transmitted than what is conveyed in the instalment: here the nonchalance is rather appreciated and compared on a human level to ordinary Chinese people's behaviour on 'national holidays'.) Focusing on the Brandenburg Gate, the storyline sets in with Napoleon's having conquered Berlin and taken away Germany's 'goddess of peace' (the quadriga with a goddess), thus making also for a visual link with the preceding instalment on France. Geographical factors are introduced, as in every instalment, to argue for Germany's 'natural' position as a battlefield for all sides, being situated in the middle of Europe, sometimes also offering herself to others to fight wars in their stead. With the Peace of Westphalia (1648) already mentioned in the earlier instalment on the Netherlands (showing the same famous painting of the signing of the treaty), Germany's fragmentation was legalised, making for a Germany that existed only as the notion of the Holy Roman Empire but without any centralised power. Given that political fragmentation, it was small wonder that Napoleon (linking with the previous instalment again) subdued it with ease. Even the biggest of the small states, Prussia and Austria, could not oppose him, and none of them identified themselves with 'Germany' anyway. Thus, as Schiller (1759–1805) asked: where is Germany? The poets looked for her in the people, musicians tried to raise sentiments for her and philosophers dreamed of a strong state. Only in the late nineteenth century could unity and freedom finally be realised against the wishes of all other European states, which feared a unified Germany. And only then the 'goddess of peace' returned to Berlin. Thus, it was ironically Napoleon, with his attacks, who had furthered the later move of the many German states to aim at unification, providing with the ideas of the French Revolution (another link back to the previous instalment) of freedom and equality an ideological precondition for German unity.

Besides the political aspect, the instalment stresses the importance of economic unity, profiling the economist 'patriot' Friedrich List (1789–1846) who was responsible for furthering a peaceful unification between the many German states via a tariff union. (The itinerary gives a lot of further information on List, his life and concrete attempts to further German unity, marking him as a perceived key figure – which is notable, given the fact that List is usually not treated very prominently in Germany.) List realised that economic division prevented the Germans from modernising and catching up with other European competitors, given the thousands of different currencies in use alone. Due to his (a private person's) efforts, finally there was just one tariff zone from Berlin to Switzerland, since the Prussians had finally accepted his ideas. The Austrians, on the other hand, saw his activities as dangerous and threatening. Thus, List had no easy life, treated by some as a *persona non grata* and a potential revolutionary, and beset by many personal problems he ended his life in suicide. (The itinerary stresses that whereas suicide is fairly 'common' with artists or writers, List was the only *economist* ending his life this way!) But Prussian acceptance of List's ideas led also to Prussia's becoming the leader in the tariff union, paving the way for German unity under Prussian guidance – as the Chinese former minister to Germany underlines. (Here, for the first time, a Chinese diplomat is presented as an expert. This also makes for his marked use of 'orthodox' Marxist vocabulary.) From Prussian territory major projects in modernisation evolved, for example, the creation of a whole network of railway tracks and large-scale industrial production in the mid-nineteenth century. (The itinerary provides here a link to China, referring to a Chinese Manchu prince having visited Germany's iron and steel works in Völklingen. Furthermore, the outstanding Chinese official Li Hongzhang 李鸿章 (1823–1901) had been interested in German railways, already seeing in 'later-developing' Germany an important point of reference for China.)

When the revolution erupted in 1848 the 'capitalist' revolutionaries – the Chinese former minister argues – aimed at a new system in the format of the US to enhance political unity as a further step to the economic unity that was already under way. But due to the forceful suppression of the self-proclaimed parliament in Frankfurt and restoration of the old regimes, the chance for a peaceful democratic unification was lost at that time. (Again, the itinerary reveals that at least one of the directors pondered in more depth on the missed democratic chances in Germany.) Thus, it was only due to war (against France) and Prussian leadership, now supported by the decisive figure of Bismarck (1815–98), that unity was finally achieved. Bismarck, honoured also by his sovereign who was crowned

German Kaiser in Versailles, having German painter Anton von Werner (1843–1915) paint a special version of this event highlighting Bismark,[54] thus became the true 'hero' of German unity, impressing with his personality even countries as far away as China. As the commentary adds, Chinese leading official at the time, Li Hongzhang (often named 'the Chinese Bismarck') was eager to meet him, as were Japanese leaders at the time. (Here, again, the itinerary elaborates on Li Hongzhang's fondness of Germany, using also German advisors, and the great impression Bismarck made in the East.) But unity Bismarck-style meant 'blood and steel', i.e. unity by arms, rather than by a parliament (as the 1848ers had envisaged). Bismarck, however, had little alternative, given the fact that all other European powers were interested in keeping Germany fragmented. Thus he strategically knocked one after the other off the chessboard, paving the way for final unity. This he could achieve only by good tactics and his famous 'realpolitik', continuously changing alliances. (However, there are also some critical evaluations in the itinerary by the director(s) of his 'blood and steel' approach not reflected in the instalment itself. In fact, it was precisely the fairly uncritical Bismarck image the Chinese film crew was fixed upon notwithstanding other 'expertise', downplaying his problematic role in blocking Germany's way to democracy, that upset the German interviewees, as a later German interview with one of them, noted historian Heinrich August Winkler, reveals; Winkler 2006.)

But for 'blood and steel', there were however also other important reasons helping Germany to rise, one of which was education, as a Chinese expert stresses, citing General von Moltke (1800–91): Prussian victory was decided early in elementary school! Showing an old Prussian elementary school, the commentary adds that Prussian children learned even in 1820 about the great world beyond (including the Chinese Great Wall). The curriculum covered subjects like geography, sciences, arithmetic, German, calligraphy, religion, and sports. And school was gratis. In effect, those who did not send their children were fined. Thus, Prussia furthered education and military training for all her subjects well before she achieved German unity. And when in political reality there was not yet a German unified state, the Prussian king tried to prepare for it by educational means, donating a palace to the newly created Humboldt University, setting the model for science to be supported by the state but not interfered with by it – an important reminder also for the Chinese viewer of the importance of freedom to scientific study. By this promise of subsidy without interference he could attract many outstanding scientists, providing Prussia/Germany with the brainpower to rise in an unprecedentedly short time. These scientists repaid their freedom with complete dedication to their cause, being the key to German success. Thus, unlike France or the UK, Germany's way of modernisation focused primarily on education, which was her most important asset, providing her with strong innovative powers. In this way, she could quickly catch up with other European powers, taking the lead in coal, steel, and chemical production. This meant, that what Bismarck had secured on the military field was now made sustainable by education. And the state was instrumental in bringing this about. However, the state also engaged in caring for the people's social needs. In this, the commentary argues,

Germany's model was superior to the English free-market system, i.e. the strong and beneficial role of the state guaranteed success and participation of the people in the latter (making it a model for late-developing countries). But this worked only because the rise of Germany was secured by the external condition of peace – another indirect hint to the comparable Chinese situation today and the importance of innovation policy on the one hand and peaceful external conditions on the other.

However, success was spiralling out of control: whereas a sober-minded Bismarck had relied on the military only to achieve the 'positive' end of unification but never waged war for the sake of conquering territory, he was finally dismissed in 1890. Kaiser Wilhelm II (1859–1941) radically changed the political course. By relying on 'landlords and capitalists' (as a Chinese expert argues) he did not further democracy and wanted to put science and industry in the service of the military, consciously embodying militarism himself. Thus, Germany changed into an aggressive state due to the Kaiser's dream of governing the peoples of the world.

In 1913 Germany had left all European competitors far behind and was second only to the US in the world. However, the great dream ended in a nightmare, and Germany again faced division after losing the world wars (merging both into a short, nearly uncommented sequence of war footage clips, including just two shots of Hitler (1889–1945). The accompanying book on Germany, however, gives some more information on him, if briefly). To reflect upon that period of aggression and its innumerable victims (on whom some footage is shown), including the Jews, Germany set upon a path of repentance, symbolised in Chancellor Brandt's (1913–92) fall to his knees in Warsaw, 1970 – an image well-known in China and often used to criticise the Japanese for never having done anything similar. Citing a German journalist of the time, the commentary argues that Brandt personally had no reason to apologise (given the fact that he had been part of anti-Nazi resistance), but he did so for the German nation. Thus, where he fell down, his nation rose again. And the commentary stresses (probably always with a view to the Japanese) that the Germans paid huge sums to the victims and still write about their guilt in their schoolbooks today, so as to prevent similar things from ever happening again. (Again, this topic of guilt and repentance is much more detailed in the itinerary, mainly connected to a description of the Jewish memorial in the middle of Berlin. Notably, however, the victims of the Nazis 'and their allies' are stressed to be manifold, comprising not only the Soviets but also many Chinese![55] Thus, the victims' list is headed by the Soviets and the Chinese! This shows Chinese 'uneasiness' about the perceived Jewish 'monopoly' of victimhood connected to the World War II, as can be often observed, for example, in connection to the 'Holocaust' and the claim that the Nanking Massacre committed by the Japanese during the war was a 'holocaust' as well.) Due to the Germans' repentance, now they are again a respected nation and back on the world stage, being a major player in Europe. And they finally 'achieved reunification' again – without detailing the division and how it ended, but this time without blood and steel. (Notably, the Berlin Wall hardly figures at all, but since the German Democratic Republic (GDR) is completely *left out* of the instalment's narrative (!), it is only in the itinerary that more comments can be found on it, clearly denoting the Wall as a means to prevent the people from 'fleeing from the East'.) Germany's economic success after World War II was again favoured by a peaceful environment and should be taken as a lesson, the commentary states, by all countries set upon rising today.[56]

As this section on Germany's economic 'wonder' is set after reunification without a clear narrative distinction, the insinuation goes that national unity favours economic success, not only glossing over the GDR and economic difficulties resulting from the reunification, but also over the fact that integration into Europe and economic success in (West) Germany happened precisely during the time of division. Thus in the instalment on Germany, the 'forced' interpretations, conforming to previously set narrative baselines, become most obvious. In fact, German experts' complaints about their being misrepresented by contextualisation go hand-in-hand with occasional strange cuts of interviews in the middle of sentences (which, however, also occasionally happens in other instalments). Interviews were all done in German.

The fact that this instalment provides an 'evaluation' of the 'worth of a historical lesson' at the end is quite telling since it is the first time the documentary tries to 'moralise' explicitly from one country's experience. (The itinerary stresses time and again that Germany's history is something that 'makes people think', calling Germany a 'textbook of the twentieth century'.) What is most striking is that the world wars are only very briefly mentioned, almost ignoring Hitler as the other (but negative) 'strongman' in German history after the hailed strongman Bismarck,[57] presenting World War II rather in terms of human 'tragedy', and that the GDR does not figure at all. Again, one might conclude, the focus of the documentary is only on the 'way up' and the 'success story'. Thus, the clear foci of interest are the economic rise, the importance of unity, state guidance and support (without interference) for education and innovation policies, and the necessary condition of a peaceful environment.[58]

Japan: A Hundred Years of Reform (Bainian weixin 百年维新)

The next instalment, focusing on Japan, takes up several of the topics already prepared for in the previous one on Germany: the developmental model of a latecomer and the ambivalence of its legacy in the twentieth century.

After a brief strip of visual cues to Japanese culture and history, including – similar to the previous instalment on Germany – also a few seconds of archival footage on the Japanese military in the early-to-mid twentieth century, the storyline sets in with Japan being confronted with the West and Commodore Perry's (1794–1858) 'Black Ships' in 1853. (Notably, contrary to the accompanying volumes to the other countries, the one on Japan provides almost no general background to Japan, only briefly presenting contacts with foreigners in Edo times, that is the seventeenth to nineteenth centuries. Earlier periods do not even figure. This suggests an exclusive interest in the country's Western-induced modernisation, seeing everything earlier as insignificant.[59]) The Japanese, however, reacted to this 'foreign threat' differently than the Chinese had done a few years earlier (their opposition bringing upon themselves the disastrous British–Chinese Opium War); that is to say, the Japanese decided to take up the opportunity and set upon modernising themselves. In this way, their small country could in time become a major player itself, finally growing into the world's second strongest economic power. But this all started with foreign aggressor Perry, who is therefore still remembered positively. (The itinerary, officially done by the two directors, but – as the text reveals – actually done just by Bao Runfeng 包润峰, stresses the author's surprise at the Japanese fondly remembering someone who actually beat them. Several times, the 'moral gap' perceived between the Chinese and the Japanese appears here, presenting the Japanese as a people only hailing the victor of the moment, i.e. always siding with the strong, in this way juxtaposing the obvious efficiency of this approach with moral ridicule.)

The Japanese reaction to Perry is presented also in the context of the Japanese being 'used' to learning from others, since they had taken over many things from China earlier, and later studied 'Dutch knowledge' during the so-called period of isolation (1633–1853). Furthermore, the Japanese realised from the Chinese negative example with the Opium Wars that it did not pay to try to resist this overpowering Western enemy – thus arguing for China being twice an indirect contributor to Japanese success. The Japanese took the situation vis-à-vis Perry in a fairly realistic manner, immediately acknowledging their technological backwardness. The Shogun's government already realised it had to take up an active strategy to further Japan's potentials, and private people did so even more, as exemplified by the fact that two youngsters risked their lives in trying to accompany Perry back to the US in face of the prohibition to leave the country that was still in force. This heroism and dedication is acknowledged by the Chinese commentary. Although these two had to remain, others soon went in great numbers to the West to learn from there. The Japanese also sent a delegation to the world exhibition in Paris in 1867 to study Western technologies, including later 'father of Japanese modern industry', Shibusawa Eiichi 渋沢栄一 (1840–1931), who decided on the spot to remain and study Western economics and industrialisation in detail, in order to apply his knowledge later at home. And the Europeans reacted positively to Japanese curiosity and openness, the Belgian king even trying to attract Japanese attention to the products his country had to sell. Using this example of a Western 'promoting king', Shibusawa felt safe enough to counter traditional Confucian depreciation of merchants at home, arguing instead for a possible and necessary combination of Confucian ethics with economic activity (the *Analects* of Confucius plus the abacus). (This rings fairly familiar with a present-day Chinese audience accustomed to a new appreciation of Confucianism as compatible with economic success.)

On the political level, the Meiji Restoration (*Meiji ishin* 明治維新), putting the Tenno at the centre of the state, provided the other important stimulus to set upon the path of reform. As with other Asian countries, at first Western penetration had meant a loss of sovereignty (the 'unequal treaties') and economic resources (outward flow of capital). To counter these problems, the Japanese revamped the political system by restoring the Tenno to power, and restructuring their economic system. They also invested a huge sum to send the Iwakura Mission (*Iwakura shisetsudan* 岩倉使節団), abroad to investigate into various foreign countries for two years (1871–3), including half (!) of the government's staff, who thus gained first-hand knowledge of different systems. (In contrast, one might add, when China sent a similar governmental mission to other countries in the context of the 'new policy' after the turn of the twentieth century, that group was split in two and both, setting off in late 1905, remained on tour only a couple of weeks.) The Japanese policies resulted in a decisive restructuring of Japan after Western models, which had impressed the Iwakura Mission profoundly during its trips. One of the most important models was Germany, with her Bismarckian 'real-politik', to aim at strength before being eaten up by others, and her way of modernisation from above, which had led to Germany's outstanding performance in the 'Second Industrial Revolution'. In this way, the German model of a late-developing country is again presented to the Chinese audience – as in the previous instalment and with unmitigated filmic citation of the latter – as a blueprint for latecomers.

The deputy leader of the Iwakura Mission, often named the 'Eastern Bismarck', Ōkubo Toshimichi 大久保利通 (1830–78), thus took up the task of building up a modern industry in Japan upon his return, being one of the most influential politi-cians. However, as his personal paraphernalia are made to testify visually, he in fact combined Western and traditional (partly Chinese-derived) aspects (for example, the camera dwells upon his Western chair as well as a Chinese tea pot). His enthusiasm for Western industrial production, however, was not shared by all. For example when he started the first silk reeling factory, it was difficult to find people ready to work there, given the frightening machines and the noise. Only by the government's interference in asking noble families to send their daughters there to set an example – which they did, again proving the Japanese elites were ready to sacrifice individually for their nation's well-being – could workers finally be recruited. And thus the first Japanese export good was produced.

In this early acceptance of Western technology, it is argued, Japan reacted very differently from China or Islamic countries, which tried at first to pose opposition. Even more striking to Chinese minds is the fact that the Japanese high officials opted for trying to attract foreign experts in all those fields where their countries excelled with huge salaries, well beyond the Meiji officials' own ones. This will-ingness to sacrifice personal benefit for the country's well-being in the future is underlined many times in the presentation. (One might, of course, think here of the Chinese recent policies of attracting foreign know-how, and of the contrast to late Qing times when there was more interest in the products than in acquiring the know-how to produce similar things later oneself.) Furthermore, the Japanese government, which provided huge sums at the beginning of industrialisation, did not try to do everything itself, but attempted rather to provide positive incentives to private individuals and companies to take over single projects, guaranteeing them a start-up and ordering Japanese-manufactured products in order to sustain them. This, for example, was how later big trusts could get started such as

Mitsubishi 三菱, which soon proved so successful that it was able to take over the transport routes to Shanghai from US and British competitors, thus marking a first success in integrating into the 'free market'. And several officials were now willing to leave the government to participate in the economic sector, publicising the new appreciation that entrepreneurship would receive in a modern Japan.[60] Thus, for example, Shibusawa Eiichi left his official position to create the first modern Japanese financial institutes and embodied the figure of the versatile industrialist, investing in different industrial branches. In this way, the Japanese are presented as smart and flexible.

Reform ideas were present in all aspects of modern Japanese life: from changing the calendar and eating beef, to Western hairstyle and wearing suits. Just as Japan had copied Chinese models earlier, now everything Western was copied. For example, if Chinese Tang-period Chang'an had been the model for Japanese capitals, now a Western-style street (Ginza 銀座) in Tokyo showcased the Meiji state's efforts at modernising the city. However, there were also drawbacks: some Japanese felt overpowered by this path of rapid modernisation. In 1878, Ōkubo, a symbol of recent fundamental changes, was assassinated by a samurai as a mark of protest. The speed of modernisation, exemplified, for example in very radical calls such as that for the abolishment of the Japanese language in favour of English, and the more-than-close connection that was created between politics and economics led to societal imbalances and left many people dissatisfied, nearly leading to upheavals, making for the fact that only the Tenno could hold the country together. (Here, again, one might take this as an implicit statement aimed at today's China on the dangers of modernising too quickly and failing to consider people's responses so as to prevent upheavals.) When the people's dissatisfaction articulated itself ever more by the 'Freedom and People's Rights Movement' (*Jiyū minken undō* 自由民権運動), Itō Hirobumi 伊藤博文 (1841–1909), who was after Ōkubo's death the most influential politician at the time, realised the country needed some sort of constitution to appease public sentiment. He devised the latter, integrating, however, some traditional and Confucian elements with the modern structures of a parliament, all based on the fundamental idea of the centrality of the Tenno. Thus, the Tenno became the embodiment of Japaneseness, being sacrosanct and also the only one entitled to declare wars – a problematic heritage, as later times were to testify. Thus, although the parliament seemed to guarantee a system where numerous parties were represented, in reality there was militarism under the guidance of the Tenno (showing footage with the 'war Tenno' Hirohito, 1901–89). (This point is very pronounced, given the fact that to the Chinese the instrumental role and responsibility of the Tenno – often negated on formal grounds by the Japanese – is decisive. It also marks the constitution as a sort of halfway measure, guaranteeing that the parliament would not become too powerful.)

After the promulgation of the constitution, the Japanese economy boomed in an unprecedented way – suggesting to the Chinese audience the importance of a sound legal environment for economic success. However, as the constitution was in fact a mixture of Western and Japanese elements, other areas of life remained hybrid as well. In short, the Japanese did not negate everything Japanese but kept it together with or parallel with Western-derived models. (In their itinerary, the directors also accentuate time and again this parallel of Western and traditional elements to be seen also in Japanese daily life.) However, as the head of the Chinese Association for Japanese History, Tang Zhongnan 汤重南, adds with reference to a well-liked simile, looking at it closely, Japanese culture itself is like an onion, made up of several layers all permeated with foreign influences – therewith implying the absence of an onion's 'pure' heart. And as the constitution was not a line-by-line copy of a Western one, was economics not developed in a classical 'liberal' context either, but – as with Germany – in one administered from above. In fact, as in the case of Germany, besides industrial achievements such as the speedy building of railways, education was also treasured highly in Japan, providing for a high rate of school enrolment in the whole populace.

Japan soon also copied the aggressive behaviour of the West: not long after she herself had been forced to open up, she did the same with Korea. As Fukuzawa Yukichi 福沢諭吉 (1835–1901), Japan's famous reformist intellectual had argued: one needed to look to the West for what civilisation meant. And this is what is contained in the slogan of the Meiji period: 'Enrich the state and strengthen the military' (*fukoku kyōhei* 富国強兵). Thus, in tandem with the economic development, a strong military was built up, which also now enabled the Japanese themselves to expand aggressively now – again showing, as with Germany, a decisive shift around 1890 when the 'positive' building-up of the state had basically been achieved and militarism started fatally to gain the upper hand. Therefore, beginning with the Sino–Japanese War of 1894, Japan went down the road of aggression, on the way also taking Taiwan and Korea for herself and financing her further aggression also by the reparations China had to pay after her defeat in 1895. This led to all the disasters of the twentieth century, which are only enumerated – as had been done also with Germany – basically by blending in the year or event and some footage of the military or of bombings with dramatic music (the First Sino–Japanese War (1894/5), the Russo–Japanese War (1904/5), World War I (1914–18), the Manchurian Invasion (1931), the start of the Second Sino–Japanese War (1937) – notably without reference to the Nanking Massacre (1937/8)! – Pearl Harbor (1941)), and the final atomic bombing in August 1945. (It is striking that the instalment is fairly brief on the aggression, notably on the Second Sino–Japanese War, even though the directors' itinerary always returns to the topic of Japanese guilt. The atomic bombing, however, has obviously deeply impressed the crew when visiting Nagasaki. Therefore this topic, which at times is downplayed in China due to the fear that the Japanese could use it to get out of the role of the perpetrator and into the one of a victim, is notable.) In sum, as with Germany, the main lesson to be drawn from this part of Japanese experience is that aggression hurts not only others, but also oneself. Therefore, at the end of the war, Japan had lost most of what she had built up since the Meiji reforms and now faced hunger (the sight of starving Japanese – a rare sight in Chinese presentations of Japan – inviting pity).

After the war, US occupation helped the Japanese to get back on the track of modernisation with financial aid, and by this the country would live through a spectacular economic rise. This was due to the fact that although there was much material destruction through the war, the skills of the well-trained people were still there. The new constitution, redefining the Tenno as only a symbol of the state and prescribing the aim of peace, denying the right to wage war, marked the background to Japan's economic rise, and the huge business corporations were its chief agents, pushing Japan even in the late 1960s to third place in the world behind the US and the Soviet Union, just 100 years after the Meiji Restoration. Whereas it had once been the Westerners bringing the first railway to Japan, the Japanese now had not only soon built their own ones but even set world-wide standards for modern railway technology with their high-speed Shinkansen trains.

Interestingly, this instalment ends with an excuse for having to 'leave out much', probably due to the rather unexpectedly quick tour through Japanese aggressions, summing up the main lesson of the Japanese experience as the importance of providing wealth to one's people and guaranteeing peace to others – reminiscent of present-day Hu Jintao's political statements.[61]

The directors' itinerary, as noted above several times, gives a somewhat different impression from the instalment itself, suggesting they did not have too much of a say in the instalment's narrative. They continually come back to the 'mixed feelings' that Chinese harbour towards the Japanese, always trying to connect Japanese successes with some Chinese elements: in contrast, as victims or otherwise. What is also striking is that only this itinerary mentions the fact that the respective country's government actively engaged in hospitality to the film crew, insinuating that the Japanese took pains to influence positively the presentation of Japan in the Chinese documentary, which they obviously took seriously: the film crew was invited to an official dinner by the Japanese Foreign Ministry and several interviews were arranged over a governmental bureau in their rooms. (In fact, the directors leaked that they tried to hide this from the viewing public by always filming towards another angle of the same room.) Interviewees in this instalment cover also a substantial number of Chinese experts, but – as in the accompanying volumes to other countries – those appearing in the book with photos are only the local ones.

Russia/Soviet Union: Searching for a Way to Become Strong (Xundao tuqiang 寻道图强) and a Timely New Way (Fengyun xintu 风云新途)

After two examples of latecomer countries, the documentary now turns to a third one which, however, took a very peculiar development: Russia. The first instalment on Russia sets in – as usual – with a geographical assessment: today's Russian Federation is the country with the most territory on the whole globe, showing diverse Russian landscapes and the cities of Moscow and St Petersburg, accompanied by soulful music of Russian composers. But Russia is claimed to be 'special' also in other regards: on the one hand her ruler once went around everywhere to learn how one makes one's country strong and modern (which reminds the viewer of the equally eager Japanese of the previous instalment), on the other hand she did become a huge empire by basing herself on autocratic rule and the military in a very traditional way. Setting the keynote of dramatic presentation, the commentary argues that although the country went through many crises, it grew stronger by them, but even after gaining strength it still faced setbacks before long.

The narrative on pre-Soviet Russia sets out with a famous instant of public discontent: the Streltsy Uprising and Peter the Great's attending the execution of over 1,000 of their activists in 1698 (illustrated by feature film scenes). This dramatises the reason for the rebellion: the protest against Peter's travelling to Western Europe a year before. Linking back to the second instalment on the Netherlands, Zaandam, the place where Peter had studied ship building incognito, is introduced (reusing some shots of that instalment) and it is stressed that Peter lived with common craftsmen and impressed them with his quick mastering of their craft. He thus appears somewhat ambivalent as a figure between humbly studying modernisation abroad and using authoritarian if not cruel methods at home to apply it. As a Russian expert argues, he set out to learn many different things in Western Europe, including also cultural–artistic aspects, and had contacts with Newton (1642–1727) already introduced earlier in the documentary series. However, at home his travels were extremely unpopular. A Chinese expert adds that this was due to Russian self-esteem. Claiming to be the true inheritors of the East Roman Empire because of the marriage of the Archduke of Moscow to the Princess of the Byzantine Empire in 1472, the Russians always believed they had a special mission to save the world, and not the other way round. Thus, the institution of the tsar as derived from Caesar (100–44 BC) with the Byzantine crown is briefly introduced, and Moscow's claim to function as a 'third Rome', also bridging Europe and Asia. And this belief in being 'elected' also drove the Russians to expand their territory in all directions. But, as Peter realised, in spite of its vastness, the country suffered from being backward, only producing agrarian goods, but leaving the whole area of trade to foreigners. (Key shots of earlier instalments are used as cues here to remind viewers of the competitors of the time.) Therefore, Peter chose to dispense with this sense of superiority to learn from those powers that were dominant at his time (as China should arguably do now).

Since the Russian population could not follow his ideas (a hint at the necessity of getting the population on board when starting new policies and remaining in touch with it – as had been exemplified by the murder of Ōkubo in the preceding instalment on Japan), rumours were spread that in fact he had been killed in Western Europe and replaced by a double. This, in turn, sparked the Streltsy Uprising in support of a 'real' new tsar and getting rid of all the undesired foreign influences (probably reminding the Chinese audience somewhat of the Boxer Rebellion 1898–1901). And thus Peter hurried back from Venice to Russia and took his cruel revenge, after which he dictated a whole series of reform measures that would forcefully Westernise the population in its daily habits, for example changing the calendar to the Western mode and the script to the Latin alphabet as well as prohibiting the wearing of long beards and ordering the wearing of suits (again reminding the Chinese audience of similar far-reaching measures in Chinese modern history – from the cutting of queues to Cultural Revolution 'dress codes').

On the other hand he tried himself at military contests with the neighbouring Swedish so as to gain access to the Baltic Sea for the purpose of finally getting Russia into the great power game in which the maritime component was so important; but he lost out in spite of his bigger army. Thereafter, the army was completely restructured and Peter also built up a new navy. He forcefully modernised his country, sent people abroad to study and made sure, with whip in hand, that the new education system set up would also be implemented at the local level. When he took the Swedish on again in 1709, he would win, and gain for his country a new status in Europe. This move to the West was also expressed in Peter's shifting the capital to St Petersburg, creating a new European city that also attracted many foreigners.

However, Peter's iron will to rewrite Russian identity from scratch ended in tragedy, even compelling him to brutally murder his own son, when the latter disagreed with him. Since he was hard to himself he behaved the same way towards everybody else, even antagonising the Russian upper echelons whom he would not grant any more freedom. His nonchalance toward brutality even scandalised Western diplomats at his court. When he died, he therefore left a mixed legacy: on the one hand, he had opened the window towards the West, had modernised his country and gained an unprecedented status for Russia, but as all late-developing countries, the commentary warns, modernisation has to take into account local traditions (as the Japanese in the former instalment arguably had done quite successfully), and must organically evolve to avoid antagonising the populace. In fact, after Peter's death there was at first a backlash, for example Moscow replaced St Petersburg as the capital city again.

Only with the German-born Catherine the Great (1729–96), who had been educated by a French teacher and who came to Russia when she married the young Tsar Peter III (1728–62) (who was also educated in Germany), Peter the Great's legacy was taken up again. Catherine was accepted by the populace because she did everything to first 'Russify' herself, including changing her religious affiliation to Russian Orthodoxy, whereas her husband, with whom relations were strained, remained aloof from the people. (It is notable that with Catherine the usual Western associations with her unconventional sexual life are not mentioned in the instalment, though affairs are referred to in the accompanying book series. She rather appears here as somewhat similar to Queen Elizabeth I, as a ruler completely and exclusively dedicated to her nation.) However, Catherine, who succeeded her (murdered) husband on the throne, was familiar with the Enlightenment Movement and even exchanged letters with Voltaire. (Here, corresponding shots of the instalment on France reappear.) Like Peter the Great, she put a focus on education, now also including women, and sponsored publications (including satirical ones, reminding the viewer of Queen Elizabeth's 'openness' to criticism) and educational enterprises. In fact, the very place where the October

Revolution would start in later times was a women's college set up by Catherine, who argued that mothers were the primary teachers of the coming generation – an argument very familiar to a Chinese audience from Chinese modern history.[62]

Catherine also wanted to introduce Western European legal norms to Russia, but in this she collided with the interests of the landlords who did not want to abolish serfdom, for the labour supply was short and the fields to be cultivated were large. Without serfdom, the landlords feared that labourers would flee and leave the fields uncultivated. When Catherine realised she would lose the throne if she pressed any further with legal reforms, she rather stepped back. And when the French Revolution erupted, she was shocked by this outgrowth of the once-admired Enlightenment, which reinforced her 'conservative turn' to retain serfdom and rely on the nobles. Thus, unlike Peter the Great, she would not push through with reforms, thereby acknowledging also the necessity of the ruler to be accepted at least by the upper classes. But like Peter, she would reign autocratically within and try to expand Russian territory without. (The vast and expanding Russian territory is given more emphasis than the physical growth of any other great power discussed in the documentary, being dynamically represented on a map with growing areas of colour.) Russia was thus a dominating power in her time, and even after Catherine's death Napoleon would finally meet defeat in Russia, which would then preside in 1814 in the 'Holy Alliance's' victory celebration in Paris and emerge as an important power broker in Europe.

However, the failure to tackle the serfdom issue left Russia far behind in the economic contest with other European states, which were set on the way to indus-trialisation and modernisation. The commentary stresses that Catherine's mode of building up greatness simply by force was no sustainable solution. Thus, Russia's high time ended with the Crimean War (1853–6), which is explained by a Chinese expert as a contest of systems: and here the capitalist system emerged as superior. Where Russian ships were still made of wood, the English and French already had ships made of steel with overwhelming firing power. As Tolstoy (1828–1910), an author who is well-known in China and who participated in the war, is cited in evidence, Russia stood no chance in the war. In spite of some reforms undertaken in the wake of defeat such as the abolishment of serfdom, Tolstoy himself repre-sented the ambivalence of Russian modernisation Western-style: on the one hand he had been to the West to learn its ways, but on the other he realised also the dark sides of capitalism, i.e. the social problems and the nascent labour movement. Thus, Russians were divided over the course to take between those who advocated an orientation towards Western norms, and those who argued for an 'own' way for the Slavs. (Such discussions are, of course, easy to associate for Chinese viewers with similar discussions in China.) Many thinkers in Russia now started to ponder how modernisation could be achieved without losing their country's own identity, thus getting beyond the mere stage of copying or rejecting a foreign model and looking for own designs. In this context a great variety of opinions and political positions came up: from arguments for a constitutional monarchy to radical critiques of the system, from the Narodniki over assassination attacks on the tsar to socialism, culminating in the 'bourgeois' revolution of 1905. Tolstoy however, who serves as a kind of guide through all this period of Russian history, was also critical of that revolution, seeing the basic problem in the continuing existence of private property and arguing for communal property. (In this way, the critical potential of the nascent socialist movement is introduced to prepare for the instalment on the Soviet Union.) In fact, the Duma was dissolved, Tolstoy died alienated and the catastrophic World War I erupted. In sum, it needed a new force to change Russia.

This instalment on pre-revolutionary Russia concludes with the assessment that Russian intellectuals suffered from too much idealism, but even though Russia's fate was tragic, it made also for an especially strong people. In fact, the Russians were not all wrong about their sense of being somehow special with a mission to the world, and they would demonstrate this in 1917 with the October Revolution – an event obviously crucial also for today's Communist China.

The October Revolution is introduced with pathos by the 'first shots of the canon', thus dating the 'birth' of the first proletarian government in world history to 9.40 pm on 7 November 1917. And in just 20 years, this totally new government would create an industrialised power out of a backward agrarian Russia. With the October Revolution, Russia could for the first time since Peter the Great claim to be top, but this time not only militarily but also politically. The new state would make heavy sacrifices during World War II for world peace, but its main contribution to the history of the twentieth century, the commentary argues, was its completely unprecedented social experiment.

The storyline sets out with the dramatic moment of Lenin's death in 1924. As a Russian expert explains, Russians were not 'accustomed' to individualism and thus were inclined towards socialist communal ideas. Furthermore, they longed for heroes to group around, and given this leadership they would become a strong force. Thus, the commentary concludes, Russian history was always deeply influenced by great leaders, be it Peter the Great (whose legacy, in fact, had been somewhat ambivalent as presented in the previous instalment), Catherine the Great or Lenin, but the latter's significance was even extended to the whole of mankind! – to whom he opened up a new door. In fact, he went even beyond Marx, who is acknowledged to have been sceptical about Russia's socialist potential, hoping for the revolution to break out in developed Western European countries first. Lenin, however, argued that there were enough people to get a revolution started in Russia, considering that the aristocrats and landlords in power for centuries were also a minority. However, interestingly, the comment by famous US sociologist Wallerstein, who figures prominently in the later US instalments, counterbalances any 'mastermind' interpretation, emphasising that the revolution simply 'occurred' due to the crisis in the state, and that Lenin just happened to take advantage of the situation, implying that he had only taken over existing Soviets and 'bolshevised' them. That this piece of interview was retained is quite remarkable.

To highlight the problem the new state faced, the commentary explains that while the Soviet Union did away with exploitation and provided work for all, foreign countries were hostile, and the civil war took years. Natural disasters added to the problems of the young state, which at first sought to continue inflexibly centralising grain production and distribution, creating unrest among the peasants. Even the marines who had been central to the October Revolution opposed the government on this issue. In short, hunger was to sap revolutionary energy, and thus Lenin realised he had to stimulate economic growth first. (By this, in fact, Lenin's New Economic Policy (NEP), which would remind Chinese viewers of Deng Xiaoping's 'liberalisation' strategy in economics since the late 1970s, is ideologically 'excused' as a necessary device under the given circumstances.) In short, it was the foreign blockade, military pressure due to the civil war, shortage of grain, and ensuing political unrest that led to the NEP to solidify Soviet power. Lenin argued that, in fact, it was an experiment on how a society might evolve from capitalism to socialism, based on social realities (which goes well with Deng Xiaoping's stance in China after the Cultural Revolution). (As elsewhere in the documentary, intermingled shots of present-day department stores suggest that these topics are not only of historical relevance.) And, the documentary's chief Chinese expert on Russia, Xu Tianxin, assures the viewer that these 'capitalist' market devices were actually used only to further socialism. A Russian expert sustains this view that in fact it was not exactly 'the same' as capitalism. The original idea of doing away with money and simply exchanging industrial for agrarian goods had not worked, and thus financial institutions were reinstituted. Furthermore, the Soviet Union was isolated internationally, not the least because of the US, which feared communism, and thus had no possibility to borrow money or import know-how. Instead, she had to rely on herself.

But there were also other Americans, as is demonstrated by Armand Hammer (1898–1990), an American communist and merchant who went to visit Lenin and helped to establish economic ties between the Soviet Union and the US. Thus, after Lenin had secured Soviet power in the civil war, he welcomed foreign 'capitalist' investment (as China does, especially since 1978) and, aided by Hammer, in spite of the diplomatic freeze between the two countries, economic exchange intensified (suggesting that sub-governmental ties may prove important in the long run). However, the Soviet Union did not import only foreign products but concentrated upon importing know-how and capital. In fact, one of the most important symbols of Soviet industrialisation, the GAZ truck, was originally built by American Henry Ford (1863–1947). Hammer was instrumental in getting Ford to enter the Soviet 'market' by arguing that it would be economically nonsensical to lose such a big market just because of disliking Soviet ideology – again a clear reference to present-day China and the arguments for the attraction of a huge market that should not be interfered with because of 'ideological' aspects. In fact, Ford was satisfied with the profit he made by the joint-venture to build the trucks. And the introduction of market elements in socialism, Xu Tianxin underlines, was in fact a 'ground-breaking' development in Marxism. Lenin himself argued that in any case his NEP would 'soon' lead to real socialism. But his 'realistic' way was unfortunately not to be followed in the long run.

After Lenin died, Stalin (1878–1953) took on power (there is no mention in the documentary of the complicated process involved here), and he forced industrialisation in a 'harder' way, epitomised by his chosen name 'Stalin' from steel (juxtaposed with the more 'flexible' Lenin, who took his name from a river). He set out to centralise everything again, as American historian and inspiration of the whole documentary, Paul Kennedy, explains. And as Chinese expert Zuo Fengrong 左凤荣 adds critically,[63] it was the peasants who had to pay for the massive industrialisation under Stalin (which is another very pertinent topic for today's Chinese audience, who are well aware of the growing social imbalance especially vis-à-vis the rural population). With the (ideological) argument that the NEP (which had been advantageous for the peasants) had in fact only been a temporary device, Stalin wanted to press ahead with industrialisation in a way that reminded Chinese viewers of one-time Great Leap Forward arguments. (This somewhat critical take on early Stalin is largely relativised in the following, suggesting there was no unanimity in evaluation from the producers' side, which is also reflected in the notably mixed interviewees in this instalment, presenting not only local Russians and Chinese but also Americans, and in terms of viewpoints ranging from the head of the present Russian Communist Party to American proponents of world system theories and Nobel laureates in economics.) Stalin's view is explained (and excused) by the strong discrepancy between the recovering Western nations after World War I, including the US which was in its 'golden twenties', and the still very backward and isolated Soviet Union. In view of Western blockade and hostility, without heavy industry the country would have also been unable to defend itself and produce weapons – as the commentary states with explicit reference to the 'similar' Chinese case. In fact, Stalin is cited as a warning that the Soviet Union might become as powerless as China at his time! (This is accompanied visually by shots of the Forbidden City – which at that time had been deserted.) Thus, Stalin had no real choice but to go for quick industrialisation – which, by way of the parallel, would have befitted China at the time as well.

Thus, in 1929 the first five-year plan was set up. With this institution, the commentary stresses, a completely new era was started in economic history: never before had there been such detailed planning of economic development. At roughly the same time, in contrast, the US was facing the crash of stock markets, demonstrating the high risks of capitalism. In fact, American economist Joseph Stiglitz is cited with a comment on the very unequal distribution of wealth, which again characterises the early twenty-first-century US, suggesting capitalism's need of governmental check then, as today. (In fact, Stiglitz is noted for being fairly positive about the so-called 'Beijing consensus', increasingly discussed in the 2000s, which challenged the 'Washington consensus' of economic development that went necessarily in tandem with traditional Western-style liberalisation policies.)[64] The crash was economically far more devastating than the whole of World War I, the argument goes, demonstrating the crisis of a free-market system. The Chinese commentary further adds that at the time even people in America – the classic emigration destination – considered the Soviet system as a viable alternative leading to 100,000 emigration requests for the Soviet Union! (This view is visually underlined by clips of footage of hungry children in the US vis-à-vis big working machines in the Soviet Union.)

Economically, Stalin first integrated the Soviet Union into world trade by exchanging grain for foreign products and technologies. But then Soviet people had to learn how to use these imported technologies. While the stock exchange in New York crashed, the Soviets were setting up the first big truck factory in Stalingrad with the help of Americans and also Germans. At that time, the Soviets invited lots of foreign experts (as China has also been doing since 1978). Nevertheless, the Soviets were ahead of the West in the 1930s in their industrial successes and in the enthusiasm of their people, the commentary argues. As evidence, a *Pravda* article of 1935 on model mine-worker Stakhanov (1906–77) is referred to, who – in typical Great-Leap-Forward fashion – is said to have produced outstanding quantities of coal, 13 times the average output, which he later outdid again! (That this kind of blunt propaganda is repeated here at face value might be surprising even to modern Chinese cadres and can be taken as a further sign of interpretative tension behind the framing of this instalment.) In any case, Stakhanov was made into a symbol of Stalinist 'economic miracles', which reached their height under the second five-year plan to make the transition to an industrial state come true. At the end, that is to say in 1937, the Soviet Union was in fact number two in the world economy, the commentary points out, citing also present-day leader of the Communist Party in Russia, Zyuganov, who hails the economic successes in the 1930s. Thus, the balance on the whole was very positive, and thanks to the Soviet planned economy in an extremely short time the Soviet Union might catch up with the West, which had needed a very long time to achieve the same development.[65] In fact, it is stressed, the word 'planning' was even becoming fashionable in the West, including US President Franklin D. Roosevelt (1882–1945) who introduced de facto planning elements in his New Deal policy. And even author of mysteries, Agatha Christie (1890–1976), referred to five-year plans, demonstrating how widespread that Soviet notion had become.

However, all these successes were also accompanied by problems, Xu Tianxin underlines, namely for the peasants who had not profited from industrialisation (again reminding the Chinese audience of similar discrepancies in development at home). In fact, even industrialisation was very one-sided, since Stalin favoured only heavy industry whereas for progress in everyday life products of light industry would have been more pertinent. In spite of the upbeat presentation of Stalin's successes in industrialisation, the admitted fact that in terms of grain or meat production until Stalin's death the level of tsarist times was not even reached, is in fact devastating. However, the commentary tries to mitigate the point by referring to World War II, which it claimed was more decisive in these failures than problems in the planned economy as such. After China had started to resist fascism in 1937, the Soviet Union as well was finally drawn into the war, but managed to resist the attacking Nazis even though she first lost most of her industrialised Western territory. (Interestingly, in this context of general 'fascist' aggression, China and her struggle against the Japanese – a period that the instalment on Japan tended to go through very quickly, as noted before – is brought up again.) And this Soviet resistance, as a Stalin biographer stresses, was only possible because of the five-year plans, which had also set up industrial plants in other areas that now could be used to produce tanks or weapons. Due to the war, far-away Siberia especially was quickly industrialised, and thus the production of air planes so crucial in the war could double the German output in 1942. Thus, it was basically due to the economy that the Nazis were beaten! (This would explain also why the 'political' side of Stalinism receives hardly any treatment.) At Stalingrad, the former truck factory had been redesigned to produce tanks which would then be used against the Germans in battle. And the Soviet victory against the 'fascists', though at a high human cost, the commentary emphatically adds, is important enough to entitle the Soviet Union to be a 'great power'. (In fact, the commentary underlines the special salience of the Soviet contribution in defeating the Germans, while saying next to nothing about the other allies' role in it. It is also stressed that the Germans, in turn, lost most soldiers in their battles against the Soviets, thus profiling the Soviet Union as the 'key' factor – in line with conventional PRC historiography of World War II.)

After the war, the Soviet Union emerged as the second superpower besides the US and challenged the latter on all fields, including the space programme (today so dear to the Chinese leadership), even being the first to send off a satellite and an astronaut. And even Western authors like Romain Rolland (1866–1944), who had been invited by Gorky (1868–1936) to visit the Soviet Union in 1935, were so impressed by Stalinist Russia that they wanted all the critical aspects of what they had seen to be withheld from the public even after the war, for fear that this might taint the image of the basically positive development the Soviet Union represented.[66] When Rolland's 'Moscow diary' finally became public in the 1980s, long after the author's death, the Soviet Union however still had not resolved those critical aspects noted by him in the 1930s, including the rather miserable daily life, personality cult and bureaucratism. No wonder the Soviet Union would collapse in 1991, the commentary adds, implying that the chance to 'optimise' socialism was only taken up in China, with its independent path.

Thus, the Soviet Union teaches the lesson of a spectacular experiment in history which, as the Chinese commentary sums up, should be carefully measured and put in a long-term perspective. In fact, the instalment hopefully concludes, present-day Russia could well be on the road to a national revival, showing the assembled heads of state, including Hu Jintao, attending the 2005 pompous sixtieth-anniversary parade of allied victory over the Nazis in Moscow amid red flags.

All in all, this presentation of the Soviet Union, being one of the trickiest parts of the whole documentary, is notable in its argumentative twists. It adopts a basically 'conservative' note, with many Chinese experts included plus mainly communist-affiliated Russians, though with some interesting – if sometimes contradicting – American (and some critical Chinese) comments, basically presenting the Stalinist economic 'successes' and being silent about all political dark sides, namely, avoiding the topic of the purges.[67] In sum, the Soviet Union instalment ends up as the most economy-focused one of all instalments in this documentary. Furthermore, the 'sensitive' part of Soviet history after Stalin and the Sino–Soviet split is – as with the GDR in the instalment on Germany – simply omitted.[68]

The itinerary in the case of Russia is similarly evasive, being the shortest of all and mostly reflecting 'orthodox' sentiments of the film crew close to the narrative of the instalments.[69] As might be remembered, film director Zhang Xiaoyu was a key figure in the production of the documentary. He filmed in Russia and took part in writing the TV script for France and Germany as well as authoring the volumes on Russia and the US in the eight-volume book series. The lack of coherence in historical interpretation is therefore especially striking, suggesting there were more 'voices' to be accommodated in the course of production. The crew was sensible to Russian 'achievements', namely the cultural conservation of the city of St Petersburg as a showcase of ancient European architecture (in marked contrast to what is happening in skyscraper-dotted Beijing, for example). However the itinerary pronouncedly starts with present-day Russian inefficiency and ends with an expression of estranged feelings towards Russian self-aggrandisement, her fixation on territorial expansion, and her 'unpredictable' character, not failing to mention the need for a lot of security. The crew, however, also refers to its disappointment in realising that the famous Red Square is just one-fifth of Tian'anmen Square and that Chinese visitors always tend to look for signs of the deceased Soviet Union, whereas obviously hardly any Russians go to museums on Lenin any longer. In short, a feeling of estrangement towards this one-time 'socialist brother' clearly comes across and might have added to this somewhat imbalanced picture emerging especially from the instalment on the Soviet Union.

The US: New Country, New Dream (Xin guo xin meng 新国新梦) and Critical Situations and New Policies (Wei ju xin zheng 危局新政)

The last country to be presented in this documentary is the US, a country with a 'brief history' (a point always likely to be raised in China to contrast it with the latter's 'long history') and a 'European basis', but an all unique way. European migrants, coming over in waves, settled down on originally Indian territory, and out of the 13 British colonies the US was finally established. This country, the commentary underlines, has been the one able to remain economically number one in the world for over 100 years (thus side-lining the political aspects of US leadership) – and therefore is to be looked at with particular attention.

The storyline starts with Williamsburg in Virginia where the local government was located in the eighteenth century. A colonial parliament was in charge of all affairs, virtually self-governing the colony in glaring contrast to other countries' colonies around the globe. British rule was rather 'loose', but the specificity in the American case is connected to the Puritans and the Mayflower. When the Puritans split from the Anglican Church and looked for a place of refuge, they embarked on the Mayflower to sail to America. On ship, the Pilgrim Fathers made their own compact to the avail of self-governance, laws and so on. (A copy of the compact is shown.) Thus, in fact, they were compiling a free contract without any interference by any authority, thus setting the stage for a new type of state, as a Harvard historian explains. When they arrived at Plymouth, Massachusetts, in 1620, this model was finally applied.

Besides the Puritans, many other migrants with various religious and ethnic backgrounds arrived, including also black slaves, who all settled between the

Appalachian Mountains and the Atlantic to finally form the 13 British colonies. Due to their life conditions, the settlers were virtually forced to self-govern, as Chinese expert on US history, Zi Zhongjun 资中筠, stresses. (She is the only expert from China also figuring in the accompanying book series as an interviewee, whereas all other experts from China 'disappear' in the print version.) In contrast to the situation in Latin America, the Harvard history professor adds, the British opted for controlling trade, letting the colonies decide on political issues, including the levying of taxes. The situation however changed when the British were in need of more money to sustain their growing empire and the wars to be fought in this context. Thus they changed their policy without consultation so as to claim a greater share in taxes, which in turn provoked resistance with the settlers who saw their habitual rights infringed, as Wang Xi, a Chinese teaching in the US, argues. When the British tried to suppress their opposition by force, the War of Independence erupted in 1775. (This scene is illustrated by an American re-enactment.) And in 1776 independence was declared – though the battles went on – and the US established. In conclusion, the famous words of the Declaration of Independence (that all men are created equal; that they are endowed by their creator with certain unalienable rights; that among these are life, liberty and the pursuit of happiness) are cited. (A copy of the declaration is shown in tandem.)

Linking back to earlier instalments, the Chinese viewers are reminded that at the time this new country was established, Britain set upon industrialisation, France steered toward revolution, Germany was all divided, Russia lived through the tsar's reforms, and China was at the peak of her glory under the Qing. American economy had heretofore been totally integrated in the British trade system, the north setting up manufactures, the middle regions being dominated by agriculture, and the south by plantations. Independence therefore was economically challenging. But even more so was the lack of a government. De facto the States were just a loose federation; there was no president, no common foreign policy, common currency, or Supreme Court. General George Washington (1732–99) therefore stressed the need for greater integration to prevent infighting between the 13 ex-colonies. Thus, the constitutional conference convened in 1787 in Philadelphia to build up some sort of central government to stand up against the European powers. The delegates were mostly university-educated people and Washington was only presiding since he did not want to become a new king after final independence from the English one, believing that the constitutional form had to respect the special circumstances of the US, leaving all states with a high level of autonomy. He was chosen as the first president, and the constitution fixed the various responsibilities of the state governments and the central government, and the legal framework for economic development. The central government would look over the common market, establish a common currency, a unified tax system, and a national bank, and other European financial institutions were emulated as well. Although Britain tried to prevent the lost American colonies from getting on the train of industrialisation as well (and from growing into a competitor – again a topic not only of historical relevance to the Chinese viewer), some British migrants clandestinely brought new technologies to the US. With their quickly growing population, the US started to industrialise, late but very effectively. But the weakness of the central government also entailed problems.

This became salient when the differing positions of the singular states, namely with regard to the race question and slavery, became more pronounced. The South, being dependent on 'white gold', that is, cotton from the plantations mostly worked on by slaves, would hold on to racial segregation and slavery, whereas the North, mainly living off industrial production and trade, had developed a more 'liberal' attitude, also because an unrestrained capitalist system with a free-floating labour force was more profitable in economic terms. (It is interesting to note that this economic argument is clearly seen as more salient than any 'moral' one in the context of slavery and racism.) However, the North feared a split if the South were antagonised by emphasis on the abolition of slavery. In fact, when declared enemy of slavery, Lincoln (1809–65), was voted for president, the South wanted to leave the Union, thus leading to civil war. Lincoln, arguing that the South had broken the unity of the nation (a point that was most important to the political argumentation of the commentary),[70] violated the constitution and undemocratically acted against the majority vote, was ready to fight. Thus, whereas Washington founded the US, Lincoln saved it, and guaranteed the morally (as economically) stronger North victory, and the slaves freedom. And this, the commentary argues, laid the foundation for the US' power in the twentieth century.

The Civil War thus constituted a decisive moment in US history, but the presentation stresses, too, that it was also Lincoln who was instrumental in Western expansion by promising land there against money. Even though it is acknowledged that the Western expansion connected to the gold rush was already underway, Lincoln's Homestead Act of 1862 is seen as an important push from the government's side. And this experience of living as settlers in a 'new' territory taught the people their independent, self-reliant spirit and all that comes with the image of adventure, the realisation of one's dreams, and the 'American way of life'. And it rendered all other territory 'safe'. When the West was all conquered and large areas developed as a huge granary at the end of the nineteenth century, the US could concentrate on its impressive economic rise. (The shots and underlying music render the Western expansion rather elevating, peaceful and harmonious which is remarkable with such a 'problematic' topic in 'conventional' Chinese historiography, which tends to stress its 'aggressiveness'.)

This rise, however, was not only due to the resources acquired, but – as for the British case – also to innovation, as the narrative underlines with Thomas Edison (1847–1931) who started a new era in history with electricity. After Watt's steam engine, Edison now laid the foundation for the 'Second Industrial Revolution'. Edison's invention not only changed daily life but also created wealth, therewith indirectly helping the US government to secure much more tax. Being very creative, Edison added many more inventions to the electric gulp, and others joined in, making the late nineteenth century a high time in innovations. In other words, it was also technological innovations that made the US the leading power in the twentieth century.

As a Chinese expert teaching in the US points out, it was no accident that the US became technologically the leading power, since it encouraged innovation and application of innovations in business enterprises. Even though the idea of guaranteeing patents to innovators was British, only the Americans wrote it into their constitution. Thus, for technological development, the legal context is crucial. The importance of acknowledging intellectual property is also stressed by the fact that if George Washington already personally signed patents, Jefferson (1743–1826) even had been on the board of the patent office before becoming the president of America. In this way, the topic of protection of intellectual property, already addressed in the instalment on the UK, is taken up here again, demonstrating the topic's salience in Chinese view.

Brains, the narrative further argues, are an endless resource and are the key to economic success of the US, aided by the growing strength of the central government. In this way, the US could outdo the Europeans, and in 1894 was already the leading country in terms of production. Its main competitors now were Germany in Europe and the rising Japan in Asia. The US had also enlarged its territory via wars and purchase and thus consisted in 45 states at the end of the nineteenth century. By this she was ready to embark on 'her' century – the topic of the second US-instalment.

The year 1900 opened a new century; however, as the Chinese commentary points out, not very gloriously, since the year marked the eight allied powers' 'aggression' in Beijing, i.e. the Boxer War (accompanied by terrifying music, but typically not naming the Boxer Rebellion as the reason for the Western 'attack').[71] (In this way, China is integrated into the narrative of the American rise as a victim suffering from it, which even amounts to an 'epoch divide', but arguably there is a suggestion that roles will be reversed in the twenty-first century.) At the same time, though, there was also a world expo in Paris, which was illuminated by Edison's electric gulps and showcased the Powers' advanced status (contrasted with shots of agrarian Chinese tea-cultivating women). Thus, the Western powers are set against China in a twofold way: negatively in the military–political field, but positively in the economic–innovative one. The twentieth century would therefore be the century of rivalry and competition between the 'old' and the 'new' countries. And the US had started to outdo everybody else, but they lived also through periods of great crisis before becoming the world's number one.

This time the storyline sets in with a famous place in the US, representing the 'core personalities' of US history: the Mount Rushmore National Memorial with its rock carvings of the Presidents Washington, Jefferson, Lincoln and Theodore Roosevelt (1858–1919). Roosevelt as president in the beginning of the twentieth century already started a new policy, since he realised that the brimming economy and the growing monopolies of great trusts needed more governmental surveillance. One of the targets of his policies was oil magnate John D. Rockefeller, Sr (1839–1937), whose personal background is briefly introduced as a symbol of the 'American dream': stemming from a poor agrarian family, he became an apprentice first, and then set up his own small business until oil was discovered in Pennsylvania. Immediately realising the latter's economic potential, he founded an oil company: Standard Oil. Being ahead of all competitors, he was thus able to largely monopolise the trade in oil and set the prices, even being able to strike deals with the transporting agencies because of his huge market share. (The capitalist hustle and bustle is visually supported by quick-running film sequences.)

Traditionally, the US government did not interfere in economics, but the rise of many economic 'kings' in various branches who would increasingly dictate prices, monopolise transport and make for a huge gap in income, accumulating 60 per cent of wealth in the hands of just 2 per cent of the population, posed a challenge to this policy. And thus Theodore Roosevelt was moved to start a tighter control of economic activities. Furthermore, industrialisation also brought with it many social problems: pollution, labour incidents, child labour and so on, on which the instalment also visually dwells (accompanied by terrifying music). The point is further underlined by Zi Zhongjun as Chinese expert on US history. The monopolies were, as the commentary argues, a natural outgrowth of free competition. But this was detrimental to the interests of the labourers and society at large. They mercilessly crushed smaller businesses and led to widespread impoverishment. Even though anti-trust-legislation had been enforced, it did not stop the trend. Thus, the middle classes looked for some solution. In this context, the so-called Progressive Movement was born, which went well into the 1920s.

This movement, the commentary points out, was aided by investigative journalism, exemplified by a woman, Ida Tarbell (1857–1944), whose father's small enterprise went bankrupt because of the overpowering Rockefeller trust. She took up the pen to denounce the monopolist's methods, though encountering many hardships for doing so. Her work and similar endeavours received wide popularity and Theodore Roosevelt came under pressure from society to act. The state instituted a supervising anti-trust agency and in 1911 (when Roosevelt was already president no more) Rockefeller's Standard Oil Trust was finally broken up into smaller units. Basically, the value that was to be defended was the equality of opportunities, which had been jeopardised by the monopolists. Roosevelt had also hoped to bring employers and employees together at one table, and released a host of labour laws. Insinuating a causal relationship, the commentary argues that the US economy soon brimmed, especially during World War I, taking the war parties' orders for steel, ammunition and so on. At this point, the US had become the main creditor country in the world, having accumulated 40 per cent of world capital. However, after the war, which saw the US on the side of the victors, then-President Wilson (1856–1924) was unable to deal with the post-war situation internationally and thus the US started to turn again more towards themselves. (Notably, China is not mentioned here as one might expect with the Versailles Peace Treaty 1919, thus having Wilson emerge rather positively as a person of good will, but who was unable to convince the other Powers of his position. This contrasts with the usual Chinese image of Wilson as having 'betrayed' his own ideals in striking a deal with the Japanese at Versailles and letting them keep the Chinese Shandong Peninsula.)

The twentieth century was, however, also a time of great innovations: besides the first airplane, the opening of the Panama Canal, the spread of cinemas, and the development of the automobile industry marked America's new era. Henry Ford developed a totally new way of production: assembly-line production was started in 1913, leading to huge factories. The automobile changed daily life and contributed to what the world then understood as the 'American way of life'. Film and radio accompanied this new, mobile society in the 1920s, with normal people owning cars. (This emphasis on Ford is, of course, a direct link back to the instalment on the Soviet Union, which, as we have seen, relied heavily on Ford's trucks for its industrialisation.) When in 1928 President Hoover (1874–1964) was elected, he hailed the free economy, promising 'chickens and cars' for everybody.

But then came 1929 and Black Friday. Recession and bankruptcy reigned. Unemployment went up to 25 per cent and hunger became widespread. It should be noted that this emphasis on unemployment and hunger seems to have been lifted from the instalment on the Soviet Union, since the accompanying book on the US does not provide this visual material and is very brief on Black Friday. In fact, criticism is largely absent from the book version, and the itinerary of the film directors responsible for the US – nominally two, though one gains the impression that the itinerary was written by just one – is very positive towards the country throughout.[72] Black Friday was a challenge to the whole system of free economy, leading to many desperate acts like suicides which expressed the deep anxiety in American society in the early 1930s without help by the non-interfering government. Thus, President Franklin D. Roosevelt decided to change this, addressing the populace regularly over the radio to convince them of his option. At the time, only the Soviet Union had been untouched by the financial crisis (cf. the instalment on the Soviet Union). She was following her planned economy with the first five-year plan. And thus Theodore Roosevelt's earlier 'interference' approach was taken up again by his distant relative Franklin D. Roosevelt. Economists like Keynes (1883–1946) approved this line. Keynes (who is well-known also in China) even had written to the president to this avail. Whereas President Hoover had acted to the contrary, reducing the state's societal engagement, his successor Franklin D. Roosevelt responded positively to Keynes' ideas and initiated the New Deal in 1933, which is considered an epochal event by the documentary (and is in fact reflected in the instalment's title). Besides restructuring the banking system, he offered assistance to impoverished people, regulated prices on agrarian goods and invested money to revive the economy. As American noted economist and Nobel laureate Stiglitz notes: 'unconventional times needed unconventional solutions.' Thus the state had roads built and actively stimulated the economy. Building dams helped not only stop flooding but could also be used to generate hydro energy. Furthermore, the programmes by the state created employment opportunities. Social insurances were another revolutionary decision taken by the US president. And the labourers were guaranteed a minimum wage. The rationale behind these policies was that without basic economic security, no freedom could be realised. Thus, for the first time the right to a minimum standard of existence as a 'freedom from want' became part of the American credo. With this, Franklin D. Roosevelt proved an extraordinary president. In fact, as a Chinese teaching in the US adds, he saved the free market system by his New Deal, combining the invisible with the visible hand – and this is what China, per implication, should do as well.

As the US economy was recovering, however, World War II broke out. The US at first tried to stay out as it did during World War I, but finally was drawn into it. Contrary to the suggestion made in the instalment on the Soviet Union, here the documentary highlights the decisive role of the US entering the war in the allied struggle against the 'fascists', though the sequence on World War II is even shorter than in other instalments, and the audio part rendered it as no 'threat' to this country but rather as its great 'chance' to move into pole position in the world! When Franklin D. Roosevelt died in 1945, he had served the longest presidency, and his successor, Truman (1884–1972), could claim that the US was now number one in the world.

In fact, due to the wars, Germany and Japan were completely changed and would rise again only much later, whereas France and the UK lost out more and more. The US and the Soviet Union thus remained as the only superpowers, with the US being number one in industrial production, with the US dollar established as the lead currency in the world. Furthermore, the US also was present in all parts of the world militarily. Without any further specification, the commentary ends by stating that as an outcome of the turning point of World War II, since then the US has been able to manipulate the world order according to its will, leaving it to the viewer to speculate over the rising challenge of China to that position in the twenty-first century.

This presentation of the US again ends more or less with World War II, as did the instalment on the Soviet Union, notably not going into Asian issues such as the Korean (1950–3) or the Vietnam wars (1955–75) and not pointing out how the US in the end remained the sole superpower, due to the dissolution of the Soviet Union. Obviously, the narrative focuses only on the phases of establishing supremacy.[73]

The accompanying book differs slightly from the others. It is the only one featuring also a mainland Chinese scholar, Zi Zhongjun (former head of the America Institute of the CASS), whereas none of the others put on those mainland scholars interviewed and shown in some instalments, thus presenting a more 'foreign' appearance in the book version. Furthermore, this book is much more dominated by interviews than the others. It might be noted that interviewees include also some Chinese teaching in the US (parallel to the volume on the UK) but no coloured person. And – as already stated – the book version was positive throughout towards the US, its history and also on the personal experiences during filming there.

Reflecting the Great Way (Da dao xing si 大道行思)

The final instalment tries to sum up the varying experiences presented in the documentary series, which are sketched out by the short 'definitions' of the opening strip to every instalment with 'crucial dates' and a visual marker for every country: great discoveries (Portugal and Spain, fifteenth to sixteenth centuries; sailing ships), the power of capital (the Netherlands, seventeenth century; a view of Amsterdam), the 'Glorious Revolution' and industrialisation (UK, 1688 – by the date stressing the 'political' event of the 'Glorious Revolution' which is seen as a historical watershed in conventional PRC historiography; railways and the world exhibition's Crystal Palace),[74] the 'great revolution' (France, 1789; a painting of the revolution), unity (Germany, 1871; the Brandenburg Gate), the Iwakura Mission to the West (Japan, 1871; sailing ships), tsarist reform as a way to power (Russia, no date, but glossing over the Soviet Union period altogether!; a view of the Kremlin), the birth of the US to become the world's number one (the US, no date, an animated Statue of Liberty).[75] These short-hand definitions with the accompanying shots are highly telling: they present a mix of economic and political markers, on the one hand integrating conventional PRC historiography, and on the other tacitly leaving out the 'problem' (and in the end 'unsuccessful' example) of the Soviet Union, and ending on the upbeat note of how to become number one in the world. This suggests a narrative strategy from economic expansion (physical discovery and the commercial exploitation) over innovation in technical and political regards, conditioned on national unity, towards achieving supreme power status. (How far will the image of the Statue of Liberty raising the torch will be associated by Chinese viewers with the symbol of liberty that relates to events on Tian'anmen Square in 1989, and the 'Chinese Statue of Liberty', remains speculative.)

Significantly, the final instalment starts with the last phase of World War II and Soviet 'liberation' of Poland, underscoring the importance attached to the war and the Soviet (communist) contribution to ending it (in the European war theatre), thus bringing the Soviet Union (positively) into the narrative in accord with conventional PRC historiography. When people desperately longed for peace, the Yalta Conference of 1945 mapped out the post-war scenario. However, just one year later, one of the participants, Churchill (1874–1965), spoke of the 'Iron Curtain' as a new dividing line. Looking back in 2005 (which was also the year of filming of the documentary series), in marked contrast to the exclusive group's secret conference at Yalta, Russia celebrated the sixtieth anniversary of World War II's end among many heads of state and veterans of the war in a great show of publicity. The visual presentation of then President Putin honouring the many Soviet soldiers who had died, however, leaves the viewer with the impression that credit was above all due to the Soviets for ending World War II – and no reference reminds the Chinese viewer of what happened in the Pacific war theatre and who ended the war there. The commentator emphatically explains the intended message of the given pictures – that without remembering the past there will be no solid basis for future action. (The importance attached to the commentary is sustained by repeating various quick shots of previous instalments on present-day life that do not divert the viewer from listening.)

Remembering the trajectories of the 'great powers' since 1492, when the world 'truly' became one, serves this purpose. Whereas at that time a 'great power' was defined by trade and canons leading to an individual country's wealth, today's 'great powers' are no longer acting on their own but in a global context.

Qian Chengdan, chief advisor to the whole documentary, is duly the first to be cited with an evaluation, arguing that from the experience of Portugal and Spain one should realise the importance of national unity as a precondition for strength. And Paul Kennedy, whose book on the 'great powers' had stimulated the documentary's subject-matter, adds that only countries that satisfy all conditions at the right time may become strong, declining to just pick out one factor only (which he was probably asked to do by the interviewer before). Thus, Qian and Kennedy as the two most important references for the whole documentary, fix the base-line for the discussion on what should be learned from it. The oceans were essential at that early time and may be called the cradle of the great powers. This was realised by Prince Henry of Portugal who started to pursue discovery as a state policy. Isabella of Spain followed suit, accepting Columbus' desire for profit, and even sold her crown jewellery to finance him. Thus, both Iberian countries combined national unity and dominance at sea, which gave them an edge over all other countries at their time. Other interviewees (many presented here for the first time)[76] add that economic power and stable political environment were necessary as well. As former British Foreign Secretary Geoffrey Howe stresses, trust between the government and the people is essential, and other commentators add attraction, capability, military strength and internal cohesion. In other words: no outer strength is possible without an inner one.

The commentary argues that whatever factors international scholars might stress as particularly important, all are agreed that intellectual culture is essential in any rise, thus demonstrating the documentary's confidence in intellectuals' role in society. For example, Churchill's statement that he would rather lose India than Shakespeare is referred to as proof. Without a Newton, no industrialisation would have taken place, and without an Adam Smith no new economic system could have developed. In France, the Pantheon includes only a minority of politicians, and it was rather by her intellectuals that France influenced the world. In short, only those who produce new thought will rise, which underscores the central importance of education. For example, by her creativity and invention of new economic devices such as banks and stock markets, the small Netherlands could rise. The British invented a new trading system with their idea of free trade, which was successful until the 1920s when Black Friday challenged this idea, leading to the New Deal, now combining the visible with the invisible hand. All in all, it is argued, one might say that only the Netherlands, the UK, and the US were truly global countries since they were economically innovative, implying that the others only were modelling themselves after them! (How the Soviet Union with her certainly very 'innovative' system figures here, is open to question, but her being skipped here is fitting with her omission from the short-hand definitions, as mentioned above.)

Furthermore, it was Britain, as Qian Chengdan stresses, that invented a parliament and political parties which proved to be a system profitable to the economy! And his colleague at Beijing University, international relations scholar Wang Jisi 王缉思, who appears for the first time as an interviewee, adds that also in the US the combination of a constitution with a juridical system furthered the development of productive forces, thus making for a strong argument for China to 'develop' also politically and legally!

Still, it is pointed out that every country went her own way (and thus China should do so as well). Where the Netherlands, the UK and the US are examples for innovation, Russia, Germany and Japan are to be looked at for their way of how to behave as latecomers (strangely not the US, which was a latecomer, too, but is grouped here with the 'innovators'). They realised they needed a strong state to push forward the economy (which explains why also the Soviet Union could also be counted in this group, though the term 'Russia' keeps it unspecific). This entailed a top-down approach different from the UK or the US (or historically the Netherlands). Thus, these latecomers needed a strong state (arguably like China today).

As history presumably showed, only those countries that took the right decision at the right moment in consideration of their own situation could rise. In other words: history selected. However, a historical review is not only for simple interest, but those great powers in history are still major players and are to be reckoned with even today, whereas most countries in the world still grapple with the problems of modernisation. The Japanese example is important here in showing that it is in fact possible also for non-Western countries to modernise. This way up is arguably long and, as the commentary underlines, needs 'both' economic *and* political modernisation. In the end, to rise just means to modernise. However, what happens when some country (for example, China) has finally arrived at the top?

To think about this, one has to consider also the rear side of the coin. Thus, after having elaborated on the 'mystery' of how to become a great power, the next section addresses the problematic sides of the great powers in history: referring to the Treaty of Tortesillas (1494), the danger of power is demonstrated in its living at other people's expense. In history, the colonised have had to pay the price for the wealth of the colonisers. In short, the great powers of yesterday created more problems than they solved, thus bringing the narrative in line with conventional PRC historiography critical of the historical 'powers' and their impact on the rest of the world. Naturally, every great power tends to argue for the status quo and the upstarts tend to argue against it. As the example of Germany shows (which is dealt with at some length): if one pushes through as an upstart by military means, one is bound to fail. No one in history who has gone for hegemony, whether the Spaniards, Napoleon, or Hitler, has been successful, and the times of colonisation are over. Germany in particular plays an important role as a warning: as far as she influenced the world by her thinkers, she was great, but when she tried to do so by force, she ended in catastrophe. Chancellor Brandt's kneeling down in Warsaw precisely demonstrated this and marked a new turn back to reflexivity in that particular country on what 'greatness' means. Whatever the case, no country will remain at the top forever, the commentary explains, and change is normal when looking at history. As the example of the UK, in turn, demonstrates, one might lose much of what one had (the British Empire) but still remain a global player (a kind of comfort to Western nations with a view to China's rise?).

However, anybody bound to rise needs also self-confidence, as the third section on the 'way to great power' emphasises. For example, founder of Sony, Morita Akio 盛田昭夫 (1921–99), preferred to refuse an attractive US offer to assemble radios for them rather than give up his own trade mark – which means, for China, that she should not be content with being the 'work bench' of others but develop her own trademarks. And it was because of people like Morita that Japan's economy rose in the way it did after World War II. Thus, Japan is also an important model: when she tried to rise by military means, she failed, but now Japanese companies are extremely successful on markets around the globe with their own products, backed up by their government. Furthermore, Japan realised the importance of education precisely for conquering markets by know-how. Therefore, a central competition going on is the global one for brain power. And the importance of brain power holds true for all competitors. As Joseph Nye, Harvard professor, one-time US Vice-Secretary of Defense, author of *Bound to Lead: The Changing Nature of American Power* and proponent of the 'soft power' concept stresses, the US economy in fact went through a crisis in the 1980s and was regarded by many as doomed, but she nevertheless retained her leading role in information technology. Thus, as President Truman had already stated in 1945: those who have the know-how will be ahead of all others.

The US is not only the country that developed the first computer but the one that initiated the 'Third Industrial Revolution', boasting of the most important higher education facilities to back her superpower status. Today's world is, however, more and more interconnected, and no one may any longer act simply on his own. As the Asian financial crisis showed, all suffer in such processes, and thus regional or supra-regional cooperation is necessary, as Malaysia's former premier Mahathir, for example, underlines. Such cooperation will also help ease the negative consequences of globalisation for weaker countries. An example of new ways of cooperation is the European Union, which is built up around the nucleus of one-time arch-enemies: France and Germany (whose military conflicts are illustrated with several shots of the Maginot Line, then adding Adenauer (1876–1967) and de Gaulle's rapprochement, leading finally to European integration). This EU model, it is suggested, might be relevant also to other world regions and is, in fact, declared by influential US political scientist Brzezinski in an interview as the most likely organising structure for the future world.

In sum, as the final section on 'thinking about great power' points out, everybody looking at history and considering the future strategically should realise that war is no longer a means of remaining at or achieving the top position. Rather peace and development – the slogans of Hu Jintao's administration – are necessary requirements. (Visually, competition is illustrated here by reference to sports.) However, every country has her own system, and even democracy is not identical between Western states, as reinforced by the repetition of a French politician's statement from the instalment on France. Therefore, the most essential thing is to give one's own people a perspective and to acknowledge the importance of culture. In this way, the commentary summarises, the history of mankind has progressed from moving on four legs to walking on two, then to running fast in the last 500 years and in the last 100 years to flying. In short, it is no longer feasible for a great power to use the old ways today, but it rather must care about common topics such the climate or poverty, furthering its own interests not with force but with persuasion. If a country with a strong cultural tradition (arguably thinking of China) is going to rise, this should be of obvious benefit for all. And such a present-day great power must combine material and intellectual strength, 'soft' and 'hard' power. In that way, it will be attractive and dispose of real strength. Although the portrait of an ideal 'great power' is still open to contestation, the above hopes are described as reflecting present-day realities – and show a rhetorical vicinity to the Confucian-tinged Chinese state discourse of the Hu Jintao administration, though skilfully blended with Western statements, mostly from politicians.[77]

In the end, the commentary emphatically states, whereas 500 years ago the sea opened up a new dimension of space for human action, today it is the cosmos that is explored and the known world seems small again. Though nobody knows what lies beyond there, peace or competition, and how the great powers are going to develop in the future, mankind after all aims at a peaceful enjoyable common future, thus ending on the positive note of 'peaceful rise'.

Assessments and implications

The documentary *Daguo jueqi* was broadcast, as we saw when discussing its production, on prime time TV: first on CCTV 2, the finance and economics channel, sold on DVD, accompanied by several book series and soon followed by a host of mimicking productions. Given its 'new' visual appeal, combined with its 'exotic' content, it is no wonder that the reception was widespread and mostly positive. Interestingly, however, not many commentators were aware (or articulated any awareness) that the documentary aired in late 2006 had a political background as a study session topic of top cadres in late 2003. Considering the production context we have looked into above, it is very unlikely that the documentary provided information that went against the grain of politically willed directions.[78] But, as we have seen with historical interpretations, at times there are deviations from conventional school history textbooks.[79] Given the context of production, these might thus be interpreted as suggestions for a direction into which the more sensitive genre of textbooks (which are slower to produce, go through many other structural channels and are more authoritative than a TV series) should evolve. This would imply it was also designed as a kind of trial window for a future course in history politics.

Most of the Chinese comments on the documentary, whether officially in newspaper articles or unofficially voiced on blogs,[80] preferred to focus not so much on the political as on the visual aspect. The few Western media comments, however, predictably hooked up precisely with the political argument. One of the first to react was Joseph Kahn of the *New York Times*. In two closely related articles on 8 and 9 December 2006, he argued the series was Hu Jintao's effort to promote the political motto (at first cherished and then eclipsed in 2004) of 'peaceful rise', which had had to be toned down (but continued in substance nevertheless), for diplomatic and other reasons, to 'peaceful development' (cf. above). Using academics such as historian Qian Chengdan, the documentary according to Kahn, was designed to trumpet to the world the 'shy giant's shedding its false modesty' (Kahn; 8 and 9 December 2006).[81] Kahn especially picks up the presentation of the US with Lincoln and its stress on 'national unity', linking it to the Taiwan question, i.e. the issue of Chinese reunification, and on Franklin D. Roosevelt and the state's role in managing the market economy, linking it to Chinese present-day economic policies of the early twenty-first century. In fact, both points have been raised by an influential Chinese political advisor to Hu Jintao, Zheng Bijian, whom we have discussed above as the 'driving force' behind the 'peaceful rise' concept in his speeches.[82] Even though Kahn admits that state officials tend to deny a political background to the series, in his mind the documentary fits all too neatly with the recent government's moves on the international scene towards greater involvement for China. Another Western commentator, Robert Hartmann, writing for *Asia Times*, shares this impression (Hartmann; 16 March 2007). A somewhat later Western reaction is Olivier Zajec's comment in *Le Monde diplomatique* in September 2008, linking *Daguo jueqi* to China's naval ambitions (Zajec; September 2008). According to him, China's navy plans from 2000 onward go well with the documentary's thrust towards a more proactive attitude vis-à-vis the sea. Interestingly, though Zajec does not mention the link, his argument on the 'blue' strategy for deep sea development of the navy evokes the hotly discussed 1980s TV series *Heshang* (River Elegy) and its advocacy of 'blue' culture vs a 'yellow' land-oriented one (see above, Chapter 1). Zajec draws a direct line from the documentary to Chinese territorial claims in the seas and the aim to render crucial oil routes safer. That this might cause diplomatic tensions with Asian neighbours is a concern well present to the Chinese admirals, he argues (Zajec; September 2008). Looking at Chinese reactions we will note that although Kahn's and Hartmann's interpretations have some Chinese equivalents, Zajec's more 'aggressive' reading is taken up more cautiously, at least in public. For example, a book series edited by Qian Chengdan called *Easy Read: a Book Series on Foreign History* (*Qingsong yuedu: waiguoshi congshu* 轻松阅读。外国史丛书) comprises a recent volume on the 'Way of a Great Power: Navy vessels and maritime power', which includes China herself, in spite of its focus on 'foreign history', and argues precisely for a 'blue culture' in the sense of naval expansion (Zhang Wei 2011)![83]

Contrary to the Western media's suspicion of political overtones to the documentary *Daguo jueqi*, the people responsible for it, however, took pains to stress their personal agency and that they did not want to be misunderstood as mere agents of politics.[84] Their basic argument was that in fact they aimed at doing something 'new' and 'fresh', providing information in a digestible way to the audience and 'investigating' the 'deeper meanings' of historical experience. Thus, they stressed that the documentary's approach was different from conventional ones. To underline their 'independent' reading of history, they put particular emphasis on the collaboration of international interviewees to guarantee scientific objectivity – which corroborates our conclusion that these interviewees are mainly deployed here as a legitimation device.[85]

Positive reviewers added that China's 'history of shame' and the 'bad deeds' of the Powers had been taught in school sufficiently anyway, but a 'complete picture' of the great powers beyond aggression remained obscure in this conventional, 'morally tinged' teaching (Lou Hejun 2007). In other words, the documentary served to redress this knowledge imbalance. Critical Chinese comments on the policy issue, however, asked why the series was so preoccupied with the reasons because of which Western powers became great, instead of asking why China did *not*. As argued by Kong Hanbing 孔寒冰, a professor of International Relations at Beijing University and thus a colleague of Wang Jisi as one of the key supporters of the documentary, the series should have pushed for leaving behind the 'pessimistic' historical view and stimulated China to believe in her strength as a top ranking power, as she had been before the 'disaster' in modern history (Kong Hanbing; 8 December 2006). This quest would be satisfied by the makers of the series later, when taking up the sequel documentary *Fuxing zhi lu* (see Chapter 3).

Other critics, however, were rather troubled by the whole topic of 'great power': were there not more pressing issues? And what about the character of such a 'rise' to power? Would it not be more important to get ahead with democratisation in the face of concrete daily problems such as the forced destruction of old houses in China and relocation of their inhabitants, than to talk about great power status, asked a professor from Canton.[86] And well-known critical journalist Chang Ping 长平 (from the South as well) added why the series did not stick to a democratic reading of the rise of these nations, insinuating that the documentary was politically too cowardly, and missed the potential of the topic (Chang Ping; 8 December 2006).[87] Dang Guoying 党国英, a scholar of rural development from CASS, took the criticism one step further, drawing a comparison with *Heshang* (River Elegy), the famous but 'unlucky' political documentary of the late 1980s: whereas *Heshang* had been very pointed in its (polemic) message, *Daguo jueqi* was too 'simple', evading a more thorough discussion and presentation of what the 'key' might be for a rise. He took also issue with the selection of 'experts' interviewed. Basically, Dang argued, the documentary favoured 'autocratic' systems and neglected the role of technology, notably in military affairs. Wavering between looking for a universal key to rise and a 'national characteristics' approach, the central message, to his mind, became obscure (Dang Guoying; 27 November 2006). In short, where *Heshang* provoked, *Daguo jueqi* remained tame and toothless in political debate.

Another critic even condemned the documentary as a mere propaganda piece for 'good governance' in its suggestions that the 'rise' depended simply on the leaders' capacities (Wang Xiaoling 2007). And Chang Ping asked further why the series focused on 'nations' at all. Had it not been individuals and the assertion of the importance of the individual that had made many Western countries great? Taking the US as an example, he argued it was clearly not governments that were instrumental in that country's rise (Chang Ping; 28 December 2006). Thus, the focus on leaders and the nation was denounced as ignoring the historical contribution of (individual) 'people'.

Zi Zhongjun, a senior woman researcher on American history of CASS who had been also interviewed for the documentary pointed out that even though the documentary provided many interesting historical examples, one should not have left out a crucial country like Italy and, in fact, one should have taken Europe as a whole rather than splitting the narrative up between single nations (Zi Zhongjun 2007: 43). This means, the narrative focus on 'nations' seemed doubtful even to Chinese scholars involved in the documentary as interviewees. Furthermore, in Zi's opinion, the instalments on the Netherlands and the UK (interestingly not the ones on the US, for which she was interviewed) were the best, the one on the Soviet Union, however, she considered often 'erroneous' (Zi Zhongjun 2007: 46), for example in drawing parallels between the Soviet planned economy and the New Deal in the US, or in glossing over Stalin's liquidation policy. And as for the evaluation of 'rise' and 'fall', she argues, one should have first decided in which perspective one wanted to address the issue. A country 'fallen' in the perspective of a colonising power may well still be 'top' in other respects (Zi Zhongjun 2007: 47). This renders standards more relative and shows that scholars who were involved in the documentary by some capacity held widely differing opinions, not necessarily being all in favour of the final rendering of the documentary. It also shows that the documentary had to negotiate between different historical interpretations which translated into inconsistencies in narrative between different instalments as we have seen above, or in deliberate cuts in the interviews.

Against mounting criticism, the makers of the documentary countered with the overwhelmingly positive reception they received from the general public impressed by the visual appeal, and stressed they could very well have simply bought foreign productions on foreign history on to the market. The fact they decided to do their own series was precisely to show the rise of foreign countries with 'Chinese eyes'. Responding to criticism raised, they defended their use of CGI and similar 'distorting' features as filmmakers of historical documentaries do everywhere: with the lack of footage or the need to embellish and entertain. In terms of content, it seems most criticism was received as to the portrayal of France, and to the lack of homogeneity of the series. This we found as well when looking into the historical portrayals above. The makers of the documentary also admitted it (Xiao Sanlang; 9 December 2006).[88] On the other hand, some critics especially highlighted the 'fresh', unconventional treatment of the UK and the US with the stress on Elizabeth I's political 'generosity' towards Shakespeare's critical comments in his plays, with the focus on the Magna Carta, limiting the ruler's power, or – for the US – the fairly positive comments about the Western expansion: a topic that is usually described in Chinese world history textbooks as 'negative' with a focus on the Indians suffering from it. The documentary, instead, focused on the pioneering spirit of the settlers.

From the documentary makers' side, Guo Zhenxi and Qian Chengdan defended their approach, on the grounds that the negative side is already familiar with the Chinese audience and they simply wanted to provide a 'new' perspective to add to this prior knowledge, which was acquired in school, in terms of 'life-long learning' (Ren Xuean; 30 November 2006). Thus, the difference in presentation was toned down so as not to challenge acquired (textbook) knowledge, but rather to 'supplement' it. In another interview, Qian argued that one should distinguish in evaluation between a plain history TV mode that only narrates, and one that tries to ponder questions, as does this documentary. This implies that he considered the documentary as basically driven by historical interpretation (which means one does not need to give the 'complete' picture but may selectively stress key issues). He therefore concludes it should not be unduly compared to textbooks, though the documentary aims at sticking to historical reality and objectivity. This double-bind between 'objectivity' and 'message' made his defence of the documentary very delicate. To him, the main criteria to choose the nations presented were: economic development, a complete systemic structure, an attractive culture, and global influence. These four could be made the basis of historical interpretation. (As we have seen above, however, it seems that the countries chosen were 'dictated' during the preparation of the political study session and that here Qian was only trying to 'rationalise' it.) And in terms of genre, he argued, one should understand this documentary as a 'historical document' piece (*lishi wenxian pian* 历史文献片) rather than as a 'documenting/recording' one (*jilupian* 纪录片), since it presented many primary sources. (This suggested to the audience a very 'scientific', scholarly approach.) That this was appreciated by the audience proved, according to Qian, that the masses did not want to be fed only with mediocre entertainment, but yearned for something more substantial. Thus, he clearly positioned this documentary against all sorts of 'histotainment' in forms of historical comedy dramas (*xishuo lishi dianshiju* 戏说历史电视剧) and the like (Qian Chengdan; 7 December 2006). And he clearly wanted to emphasise the 'factual' basis of the documentary to take the heat out of the discussion.

People involved in the documentary in some way or other came out in favour of the series as well. A journalist who took part in the last phase to translate the US interviews detailed how intensively interviews were worked upon, but then unfortunately had to be cut severely due to time constraints (*Duihua* Daguo jueqi *Guo Zhenxi;* 1 December 2006). Thus the cuts which, as we saw, occasionally distorted the interviewees' views should be seen only as technical expediency, though interviewees did not share this impression necessarily, if they even knew about it.[89] Chinese diplomats involved with interviews in the documentary voiced their basic support of the documentary as well, highlighting certain features they had experienced personally when stationed in the particular country which sustained the documentary's reading. And Qian Chengdan argued that, being a world historian and having lived abroad, he could draw a quality comparison with foreign productions and concluded that this Chinese endeavour could stand the competition (Qian Chengdan; 29 December 2006). Wang Jisi, another main figure behind the series and head of the Institute of International Relations of Beijing University, even argued that the special feature of having foreign experts appear as interviewees in itself made the quality of the series rank much higher than a documentary with 'only Chinese interviewees' would have been. (Wang, by the way, also talked on the 'peaceful rise' concept 2006 at a conference at Beijing University precisely with the topic of 'The rise of China'; see Glaser and Medeiros

2007: 292. This suggests that Beijing University, from where the first narrative draft for *Daguo jueqi* had emerged, was fairly positive about the 'rise' concept as such; see Wang Jisi; 29 December 2006.)

From the scholarly side, the documentary received much positive evaluation, including, obviously, people who had been interviewed for it. Thus, in a way, they gave a public explanation as to why they had signed up with the project: for example Niu Dayong 牛大勇, a well-known historian from Beijing University, argued that the documentary finally made people aware that China is now part of the world, and that it is a must to understand the reasons for its rise and decline, considering especially also those cases much less known in China of countries once great but now less noted, like Portugal and Spain. Only in this way would China be able to rise and remain strong (*Zhuanjia yanzhong de* Daguo jueqi; 5 December 2006).[90] (Niu, for example, also states in another interview that the series meant for him a chance to get 'out of the lecture hall'. Thus, it could also positively serve academics as a public outlet for scholarship.) Yu Pei 于沛, at the time head of the Research Institute of World History at CASS, summarised the main lessons he thought were provided by the documentary in discussing necessary conditions for a rise: a stable development, a solid economic basis, opening up, reform and innovation, grasping the right historical opportunity (*Zhuanjia yanzhong de* Daguo jueqi; 5 December 2006). This was more or less what Qian Chengdan had argued for as well. And the head of the Chinese–Japanese History Association, Tang Zhongnan 汤重南, who had also taken part in writing 'in-depth' reflections on the documentary,[91] added a link to the Chinese historical drama series *Zou xiang gonghe* (Towards the Republic) of 2003 to stress the importance of discussing the question of how China should develop (and 'rise') without provoking a clash of civilisations, Huntington-style (*Zhuanjia yanzhong de* Daguo jueqi; 5 December 2006).[92] This link to *Zou xiang gonghe* is remarkable since Tang obviously did not see the difference in genre (documentary vs historical drama) as important, but just as two ways of addressing policy issues. And they all saw the documentary, albeit discussing 'foreign' countries, clearly as a blueprint consideration for China.

Notably, intellectuals and academics also joined in the discussion on various blogs. For example, specialists in South Asian Affairs commented on the use the series could be put to, convincing important neighbour (and rival) India about China's not being aggressive about her own rise by studying earnestly the 'Powers'' historical experience. Rather, as Guo Zhenxi from the producers' side also had stated, the aim attached to this documentary was to learn about how to rise 'harmoniously', that is to say with the model of the EU as a regional cooperative model for the future, rather than repeating the errors of the past (*Duihua Daguo jueqi Guo Zhenxi;* 1 December 2006). Thus, the whole world region could profit from China's rise, the insinuation goes.

In terms of media coverage, the makers of the series were very proud that it elicited not only domestic response, including that of the Chinese government and official media, but also reaction in Singapore and Korea.[93] As it seems, books connected to the series sold particularly well in Korea (Renmin chubanshe *xiang*

Hanguo shuchu 7zhong banquan; 5 September 2007).[94] The Russian Embassy in Beijing was said to have actually prepared for a press conference to discuss the image of Russia in the series, and domestically the first round of broadcasting was said to have attracted a four million viewing rate on average (*Duihua* Daguo jueqi *Guo Zhenxi*; 1 December 2006), and the accompanying book series of eight volumes took 80 per cent of the whole TV book market (Lu and Li; 3 January 2007). The 'official' 'People's Daily' (*Renmin ribao* 人民日报) reported on the documentary and clearly stated that it considered it to be 'politically flavoured' (*you xianming zhenglun secai de dianshi jilupian* 有鲜明政论色彩的电视纪录片) (thus negating a 'purely' academic or entertaining character), expressing very positive evaluations and calling the series a welcome 'serious' production. With a view to critical arguments questioning whether the series was suitable for the 'masses', 'People's Daily' defended the documentary arguing that 'masses' were 'relative' and not simply 'the majority'. Thus, even if viewing rates were not higher (though they were very high for a documentary!), such objections were beside the point. That the series provoked the lively response it received, showed, according to 'People's Daily', that the 'masses' were not only asking for superficial entertainment (Yin Hong; 1 December 2006). And the newspaper cited a host of well-known figures from politics, media and academics coming out for the series, thus providing a de facto official 'sanctioning' of the documentary that was visible to all (Xu Xin; 1 December 2006).

However, some critics warned that the series should be considered in the broader context of international reactions. Did not the *New York Times* or the *Times* write repeatedly about China now taking the place of the former Soviet Union as the antipode to the US? Considering that the US set its foreign policy with values as much as with 'harder' means, China should do something similar to add 'values' to her global ambitions and promote them. But the slogan of 'harmony', the critique goes, is too fuzzy to serve, and the suggestion that China wants only to do business calmly without any 'value factor' is not helpful either (*Pinglun: Daguo jueqi, heqi shengcai?*; 11 December 2006). Thus, China would have to develop an attractive 'value system' of her own to convince others of her standing.

On the other hand, a commentator from Canton suggests, a 'great' country in this context explicitly meant 'internationally of influence' (Yang Yumou; April 2007: 47). This is why all instalments stressed it was not geography or population size that mattered to a country's being chosen (and thus leading to China's not playing a part). To him, however, six points are crucial for a 'rise': the nation's [political] system, its inner cohesiveness, educational standards, a healthy economy, respect for human rights, and a favourable international context – thus adding 'human rights' as an important point to those suggested officially by the makers of the documentary (Yang Yumou: April 2007: 47). This, however, still means that state policy is all-decisive.

The ingredients of a possible 'rise' were, however, discussed even before the TV documentary was aired, since the topic was on the official agenda since the study session of 2003. Noted Canton-based critical historian Yuan Weishi 袁伟时 argued already in 2004 that the central issue for him for a country's 'rise' was freedom.[95] Comparing on his own the 'three empires on a rise in the seventeenth century', the Chinese (Qing) Empire, the UK, and Russia, he argued that tsarist Russia and the Qing were the ones to 'perish' in the early twentieth century due to both regimes' lack of freedom, whereas the UK survived (Yuan Weishi 2004). In sum, though talking about 'earlier times', he suggested that Russia and China went the wrong way, whereas 'freedom' guaranteed by the state is a true marker and precondition of a successful 'rise', then as today. In this, he had already sketched out the later 'liberal' critique of the documentary *Daguo jueqi* which, however, excluded China from direct historical comparison.

Soon criticism was also voiced as to the series being too 'elitist' and academic, neglecting the 'normal people'. In spite of the *Daguo jueqi* hype, one critic argued neither viewing rates nor technical features were very impressive, and formats like TV lecture star Yi Zhongtian's 易中天 lectures or the popular *Baijia jiangtan* 百家讲坛 (Lecture Room), presenting various experts on topics of Chinese history and culture, were more to the point. *Daguo jueqi*, on the other hand, was not purely 'educating' like those other formats, but somehow 'ideological' (Zhang Jingwei; 8 December 2006)[96] – articulating uneasiness about the documentary's 'message', but not taking into consideration that *Daguo jueqi* was addressing something less familiar to the audience: foreign history, rather than Chinese history or culture as do the two other formats.

In general, *Daguo jueqi* was considered further proof of the mounting interest in documentaries as a format at a time when specialised documentary channels (as available today also in China) were not yet common.[97] In this context *Daguo jueqi* was often named in the same breath as influential cultural–geographical documentary series, such as *Huashuo Changjiang* 话说长江 (The Yangzi River) of 20 years earlier, but now moving to the aspect of history that had been taken up more recently by successful documentary series such as *Gugong* 故宫 (Imperial Palace), *Xinhai geming* 辛亥革命 (Revolution of 1911) and others. Thus, 2006 was declared a year of 'documentary fever'. And *Daguo jueqi* was especially welcome, as it was not only entertaining but 'serious' education as well, providing an 'interpretation' as well as documentation only (Daguo jueqi *zai xi gaochao*; 5 December 2006).[98] In fact, it was stated that the success of *Daguo jueqi* sparked another huge enterprise, a subsequent documentary on 55 world civilisations in 260 instalments, mainly focusing on the 12 most important 'world civilisations'. This series, however, coming out in 2008, was designed as more purely educational–scientific, being assigned to CCTV Channel 10 on scientific education, and received much less public response (Daguo jueqi *jueqi yingping*; 29 November 2006). A later production on 'world history', covering the 'world' in a much broader sense than *Daguo jueqi* with its chosen nine countries, could not follow up on *Daguo jueqi*'s success either.[99] Thus, it seems, *Daguo jueqi*'s 'success recipe' lay in the perspective of combining the history of chosen foreign (successful) countries, the tourist gaze and the key issue of how to 'rise' to connect it implicitly to China's future. It therefore went beyond education and pure documentation to 'serve' the national identity.

The choosing of the particular countries reflected, however, not only political intentions, but in a wider sense was due also to tendencies in Chinese historical scholarship, as Edward Wang has shown (Wang, Q. Edward 2010 and 2003). Thus, it reflects the Soviet-tinged notion of 'world history' as basically Eurocentric (Martin 1990).[100] Given the historical focus, current competitive 'rising nations' (such as Brazil, India, or the 'tiger states') were not considered. Also, in history, economic development as the 'driving force' led to the focus on history since 1500, starting with the seafarers. This competed with other periodisations in 'world history' also prevalent during earlier times in the PRC, which saw the 'political' division of the 'revolution' in seventeenth-century England as crucial to the beginning of 'modernity', rather than the 'economic' one of the seafarers (cf. Müller 2011b: 40 and 45). Thus, turning to the economic factor and using 1500 as a dividing line is on the one hand a way back from 'political Stalinism–Maoism' to classical (economic) Marxism, and on the other it is also closer to Western interpretations, thus integrating Chinese historical reading more easily with international scholarship (world system theories, and so on – paying heed also to the fact that the leading proponent of the latter theory, Wallerstein, was a chosen interviewee).

As for the documentary's genre, officially labelled a TV historical documentary, 'mastermind' Qian Chengdan had already proposed the term 'historical document piece', highlighting the material, factual basis from which interpretations start. Western-based Chinese historian Wang Xi, however, who has been also interviewed for the series, has proposed to call it a 'literary reportage in film' as a hybrid of literary writing, historical research, and political commentary (Wang, Xi 2007: 296). This positions the documentary much closer to the – certainly more polemical – *Heshang* and reportage literature of the 1980s and distances it from what is central to the arguments of the makers of the series: its 'factuality'. Having looked into the production context of the series, the historical readings the documentary provided and the reception modes, one might conclude Wang Xi's evaluation is quite to the point.

Notes

1 For a list of study sessions up to the forty-fourth session in September 2007, see *Zhonggong zhongyang zhengzhiju jiti xuexi* (29 November 2005).
2 As an article on the specifics of these sessions suggests, some topics were dealt with before deciding on policies, others during the process, but others also after it (see Ma Shiling; 3 January 2007).
3 Lu analyses these sessions as of more symbolic value, promoting new policies, rather than genuine 'learning' enterprises.
4 Qian Chengdan has specialised in the history of Britain and written on different ways of modernisation, focusing on the 'reformist' British model. His vision of 'world history' can be gleaned, for example, from Qian Chengdan (2001). Qi Shirong is an established figure in Chinese world history studies. Obviously connected to the study session, he came out with the edited volume: Qi Shirong (ed.) (2005a), and a multi-volume series on the 'powers', published in Xi'an, in the same year (2005b) (see also below).
5 His case is notable in that the experts invited were mostly located in important institutions in Beijing, above all coming from the CASS. Cases like Qian, coming from somewhere else, are in the minority. His later 'promotion' to Beijing University and

CASS goes well with Ma Shiling's (2007) observation that some of the 'experts' will be 'rewarded' afterwards with higher positions.

6 Wang, Q. Edward (2010: 275) raised the question as to who might have decided upon the countries chosen. This seems to be clear, however, from the above, though Qian himself did not state it.

7 The discussion on Eurocentrism in Chinese (world) historiography is an old one. See Littrup (1989); Martin (1990) and (1998); Xu, Luo (2007), Sachsenmaier (2007a) and (2007b); Spakowski (2009), and so on. Besides early Western influence, Soviet historiography was crucial in 'cementing' Eurocentrism in the Chinese historiography of the PRC. For a critical stance on historical Eurocentrism studies see Dirlik (2002) and (2003).

8 This term entered Chinese mainstream discourse in 2003 but was then eclipsed after only several months by 'peaceful development' (for details on this process see Glaser and Medeiros 2007).

9 In general, in Chinese history education a 'victimisation' approach superseded the Mao-era 'victor's narrative' from the 1990s. By this means, instead of class struggle, patriotism was to be stimulated.

10 For more information on Zheng, see Glaser and Medeiros 2007: 293–7, the foreword to a first English collection of his speeches translated by the American Brookings Institution (Zheng, Bijian 2005: vii–x), and the foreword and preface of his recent English version of a book-length collection of his speeches translated in China but published in the West (Zheng, Bijian 2011). Zheng has been instrumental in drafting several important party documents since the late 1970s. It is notable that he could remain influential in spite of his association with Hu Yaobang who was ousted in 1987 as 'too reformist' and lenient towards the student protests of 1986. (His death would be the occasion that sparked the protests on Tian'anmen Square in 1989.) In terms of historical references, Zheng Bijian himself addressed the 'negative' historical examples of Germany, Japan and the fall of the Soviet Union, advocating a reassurance of Asian neighbours by coining the term 'peaceful rise' (Glaser and Medeiros 2007: 295). However, though the word 'peaceful' was uncontroversial, 'rise' could be interpreted as threatening. Thus 'peaceful development' was introduced instead.

11 Zheng does not refer here to Mearsheimer explicitly, but Chinese discussions on the concept of 'peaceful rise' do (see for example Peng Peng (ed.) 2005 or Hu Zongshan 2006). Notably, Mearsheimer appears in the *Daguo jueqi* accompanying book series in eight volumes in the volume addressing the UK (p. 248), but is not included in the chosen interviews shown in the documentary itself.

12 I refer here to the American translation of 2005, which was received in Western political circles and scholarship at the time.

13 For example, a project in Canton and one in Wuhan were designed to take up this topic and also to explain historically that a 'peaceful rise' is possible (see the final publications of these two projects: Peng Peng (ed.) 2005 and Hu Zongshan 2006).

14 See the foreword to Zheng, Bijian (2005: x); see also Peng Peng (ed.) (2005) and Hu Zongshan 2006: 1. Hu, for example, argues that 'rise' is more political, 'development' more economic and social (Hu Zongshan 2006: 7). For a more general treatment of various terms used in China's diplomatic lexicon, including 'peaceful rise' and 'peaceful development', see Scott (2012). Mierzejewski (2012: 75) holds that the Chinese government soon recognised the term 'peaceful rise' as a mistake. However, it seems it became only cautious about the intended audience and was not dismissing the term altogether (see below).

15 Here, the term 'rejuvenation', also translatable as 'revival' (see Chapter 3) links this term to the China 'rise' issue. The English translation 'rejuvenation' is provided by the Brookings Institution, which published the first English translation of Zheng's speeches and is maintained in the recent book translation (Zheng, Bijian 2011). In Chinese publications, Zheng uses *weida fuxing* 伟大复兴.

16 Similar arguments were forwarded by him already in earlier speeches (see Zheng, Bijian 2005: 72 and 80). That his position was taken up also by others is demonstrated by Lee's (2010) study of the Chinese semi-official elite newspaper *Huanqiu shibao* (*Global Times*) which peaked in its articles on the 'peaceful rise' concept in 2004 and stressed similarly in various articles the 'historical' parallels *not* to be followed, pointing out as well that the Soviet Union's big mistake was to have put all efforts into a neck-breaking competition with the US. This error China should not repeat.

17 This assumption is made by Peng Peng (ed.) (2005: 3).

18 The character *jue* 崛 has a nuance of 'abruptness' which preoccupied diplomatic circles, and some years earlier had been even prohibited by the previous Jiang Zemin government for use in official documents. See Guo Sujian (ed.) 2006 'Introduction', p. 1, note 2. Guo states the first to promote the term 'China's rise (*jueqi*)' was Yan Xuetong 阎学通 from Qinghua University in a book title of 1998, which caused internal debates and led to Jiang Zemin's government prohibiting the term for official use. Yan, however, stuck to his term and presented it also in a short English article on how Chinese perceive their rise as anything but threatening (Yan 2001). Mierzejewski (2012: 65) has identified an earlier, though less influential, first promotion of the term in 1995.

19 As a cursory check for Chinese book titles suggests, the term *jueqi* has been used only since the 1970s with any frequency, becoming more popular in the following decades, especially rocketing in the 2000s, that is, during Hu Jintao's government, peaking in 2007–9.

20 In fact, the documentary might well be one of the driving forces behind the peak of book titles including the word *jueqi* during the years 2007–9.

21 All in all, seven teams were sent to the nine countries, Portugal and Spain being covered by one crew, as was France and Germany. The markedly longest stay was the one in the US with over two months, the others being between four and six weeks in duration.

22 Portugal and Spain was done by the film crew headed by Liu Junwei 刘军卫, the Netherlands by Duan Jun 段骏, the UK by Gao Xiaomeng 高晓蒙, France and Germany by Shi Shilun 石世仑 and Gao Jun 高隽, Japan by Wan Jianying 万剑英 and Bao Runfeng 包润峰, Russia by Bi Yuekun 毕岳昆 and Zhang Xiaoyu 章晓宇, and the US by Li Chengcai 李成才 and Liu Ying 刘颖. Thus, Portugal and Spain were done by one and the same crew, as was Germany and France. All others had their 'special' team.

23 Edward Wang, who did some interviews at Beijing University, was told that Gao Yi 高毅 had prepared the part on France, and that Dong Zhenghua 董正华, an interviewee in the documentary, the one on the Netherlands (see Wang, Q. Edward 2010: 276). The other historians involved were Qin Haibo 秦海波, Gao Dai 高岱, Xu Jian 徐健, Song Chengyou 宋成有, Xu Tianxin 徐天新 and He Shunguo 何顺果 (see imprint of the 'official' CCTV three-volume book series *Daguo jueqi*). Interestingly, the later book, which provided the 'experts'' narratives (*Qiangguo zhi jian*, see below) replaced half of the Beijing University professors, i.e. it left out Qin Haibo, Dong Zhenghua, Xu Jian and Song Chengyou, and included Wang Jiafeng, Chen Yong, Li Gongzhen and Tang Zhongnan in their stead. (In *Qiangguo zhi jian* Wang Jiafeng wrote on Portugal and Spain, Chen Yong 陈勇 on the Netherlands, Gao Dai on England, Gao Yi on France, Li Gongzhen 李工真 on Germany, Tang Zhongnan 汤重南 on Japan, Xu Tianxin on Russia/the Soviet Union and He Shunguo on the US).

24 For details, see Ren Xuean's afterword in the three-volume set Daguo jueqi: *12 ji daxing dianzi jilupian* (2007), vol. 3: 1215–22.

25 As Zhao Buhui 赵卜惠, the responsible editor of this eight-volume series (see Daguo jueqi *xilie congshu* 2006), explained, the books were intended to give more information owing to the scripts of the TV series being very short and occasionally only glossing over certain periods because of time constraints (50 minutes per instalment). So for example topics that were familiar to and expected by Chinese viewers such as Napoleon, which the TV series could not address at length, could be presented in more detail

in the book version; and interviews, cut down heavily in the documentary, could be given in full (see *Daguo jueqi nongsuo 500 nian shijieshi. Tanxun 9 daguo bufa*; 4 December 2006).

26 The sometimes-cited version of Lou's article in the journal *Shehui guancha* 社会观察 (Social Outlook) is only an abridged reprint, which came out the same year.

27 See also Wang Xi (2007), an interviewee in the series.

28 Because of this success, the editors were more than willing to take up the sequel TV documentary series *Fuxing zhi lu* as well (see Chapter 3).

29 They are: Sun Min 孙岷 (Portugal and Spain, supervised by Wang Jiafeng 王加丰; the Netherlands, supervised by Chen Yong 陈勇; and Japan, supervised by Tang Zhongnan 汤重南); Chang Shiben 常仕本 (UK, supervised by Qian Chengdan); Wang Lingfeng 王凌峰 (France, together with Zhang Xiaoyu 章晓宇, supervised by Shen Jian 沈坚); and Zhang Xiaoyu (besides cooperation on France writing the part on Germany, supervised by Li Gongzhen 李工真; on Russia, supervised by Xu Tianxin 徐天新; and on the US, supervised by Li Jianming 李剑鸣). Notably, the only cross-over between authors and film crew was Zhang Xiaoyu who filmed in Russia, took part in writing the script for France and Germany as well as authoring the volumes on Russia and the US in the eight-volume book series (see *Daguo jueqi xilie congshu* 2006).

30 The expert on Russian/Soviet history, Beijing University professor Xu Tianxin, is the only 'overlap' between both groups of people.

31 Zhang Xiaoyu is named among the directing group on the imprint of the three-volume book series.

32 This list is not exhaustive. The literature on the 'rise and fall' of other nations has a longer history in China. I limit myself here to examples more closely related in time, content and/or authorship to the study session and TV series.

33 The book is available on the Internet: http://book.chaoxing.com/ebook/detail_11290964. html.

34 The volumes and authors are: US (authored by Bai Jiancai 白建才, Dai Hongxia 戴红霞 and Dai Baoping 代保平), Germany (authored by Wu Youfa 吴友法 and Xing Laishun 邢来顺), the UK (authored by Liu Cheng 刘成, Liu Jinyuan 刘金源 and Wu Qinghong 吴庆宏), Japan (authored by Sun Renzong 孙仁宗), France (authored by Lü Yimin 吕一民), and Spain and Portugal (authored by Wang Jiafeng 王加丰).

35 According to informal information given to Q. Edward Wang (2010: 279, note 12), Qi Shirong is now taking charge of 'revising' the TV series *Daguo jueqi*. This would fit with my interpretation of the different historiographical outlook between the two lecturers to the Politburo, and would suggest an intention to shift back to a reading more in line with conventional PRC historiography.

36 The authors of the country chapters are: Liu Hongwei 刘宏伟 (Portugal, Spain and the Netherlands), Zhou Yi 周毅 (the UK and France), Liu Dongzhe 刘东哲 (Germany, Japan and Russia) and Zhan Jiafeng 詹家峰 (the US).

37 For a critical evaluation of Tang Jin's edited book, see Lin Fengchun (2007). Lin deplores the fact that the book speaks too little of soft power and concentrates on the hard power side only.

38 Xu Tianxin (see above) is one of the rare continuities through the different stages of production.

39 There is a short two-page addendum (pp. 2–3) to the original book by Tang Jin.

40 See Zhang Xiaojing (ed.) 2007 and Liu Jinghua (ed.) 2007. The 'downfall' volume addresses the empires of old Persia, Rome, Byzantium, the Arabs, Mongols, Ottomans, Portugal and Spain, Great Britain and the Soviet Union.

41 Interestingly, this chapter is the only one besides the one on the Romans where the historical narrative written by the commissioned specialist is joined by a final evaluation written by the editor, bespeaking the sensitivity of the topic. (In this volume, by the way, the Iberian countries are again commissioned to Wang Jiafeng.)

42 For example in 2008 a historical discussion of Japan's 'rise' was published (though obviously written in 2006, judging from the preface), this time, however, starting as early as the sixteenth century and thus going further back than the treatment of Japan in the documentary *Daguo jueqi* (Zheng Pengnian 2008).

43 The text of the comment is reprinted in both the accompanying book series (see for example the condensed three-volume set Daguo jueqi: *12 ji daxing dianzi jilupian* 2007, vol. 1: 1–12).

44 The problem of religious issues connected to that split is omitted in the documentary, but in the accompanying book series it is at least addressed. This shows that the authors of the country volumes were aware of it but the TV rendering rather opted for evading these issues, focusing on economics instead.

45 The text of the comment is reprinted in the three-volume set *Daguo jueqi*, vol. 1: 110–22.

46 However, this can be said only in so far as James II fled without fighting. The whole process of course was all but bloodless.

47 A decisive step was the 'Seven Years' War', effectively side-lining the French and the Spaniards (1756–63).

48 The text of the comment is reprinted in the three-volume set Daguo jueqi: *12 ji daxing dianzi jilupian* (2007), vol. 1: 201–28.

49 In fact most of Louis XVI's entries were like this, since this was only his 'official' diary, marking special occasions or royal hunts. As the itinerary of the responsible directors reveals, they wanted to dramatise the presentation by this citation.

50 It might be added that some of the painted torture scenes shown are deliberately taken out of completely other contexts just to emphasise the cruelty. (I thank a student of mine versed in art history for pointing out the origin of the pictures, which show forms of torture no longer used at that time.)

51 Napoleon as a strongman was presented positively even in Guomindang times. After the founding of the People's Republic, due to Soviet influence (which took issue with Napoleon not the least because of this attack on Russia), the image turned negative. After the fall-out between China and the Soviet Union, and especially in recent years, Napoleon's image in China has become ever more positive. This can be gleaned from the development of the history curriculum over the twentieth century (Kecheng jiaocai yanjiusuo (comp.) (2001)), and newer standards for history education: Zhonghua renmin gongheguo jiaoyubu (2001a, 2001b, 2003).

52 Yves Guéna, politician and former president of the Conseil Constitutionnel, is chairman of the Fondation Charles de Gaulle.

53 The text of the comment is reprinted in the three-volume set Daguo jueqi: *12 ji daxing dianzi jilupian* (2007), vol. 2: 381–92.

54 This version of *The Proclamation of the German Empire* by Anton von Werner, done on request of the Kaiser, with Bismarck highlighted in a white uniform (which, in fact, he had not worn) as a present to the latter's birthday, is shown in the documentary.

55 See the itinerary, for example as given in the accompanying book on Germany in the series Daguo jueqi *xilie congshu* (2006), p. 176.

56 The text of the comment is reprinted in the three-volume set Daguo jueqi: *12 ji daxing dianzi jilupian* (2007), vol. 2: 535–47.

57 Q. Edward Wang, who provides very short summaries of the episodes in his article ' "Rise of the Great Powers" = rise of China?', strangely states Hitler is given 'ample attention' (Wang, Q. Edward 2010: 277). This is clearly not the case.

58 The accompanying book on Germany (see Daguo jueqi *xilie congshu* 2006) gives some more information not only on the topics raised, but also offers some 'pre-history' to the instalment's focus on the nineteenth and twentieth centuries, providing some room for the Thirty Years' War in particular (1618–48) in order to introduce the basic theme of division.

59 In a way, a form of disrespect for Japanese ancient culture is widespread in Chinese perceptions of Japan, where people see it as 'barbarous' or, at best, as a poor copy of China.

60 This very idealist presentation clearly accentuates only the 'model function' of those 'above' but neglects the de facto difficult position many samurai faced after the abolishment of their privileges.

61 The text of the comment is reprinted in the three-volume set Daguo jueqi: *12 ji daxing dianzi jilupian* (2007), vol. 2: 682–94.

62 Noted late Qing intellectual Liang Qichao 梁啟超 (1873–1929), for one, had continuously argued in this vein at the turn of the twentieth century.

63 Zuo Fengrong would be one of the most outspoken critics of the *Ju an si wei* documentary, discussing the Soviet Union in detail (see Chapter 4).

64 The term 'Beijing consensus' in analogy to 'Washington consensus' was popularised by Joshua Ramo (see Ramo 2004). Inside China, the term used is 'China model' (*zhongguo moshi* 中国模式) rather than 'Beijing consensus' (*Beijing gongshi* 北京共识), as there is arguably not yet a 'consensus' on anything clearly defined. In fact, against the 'prescriptive' (Ramo 2004: 4) mode of the 'Washington consensus', which implies that countries develop basically along the lines of (Western-style) liberalisation and should undertake certain kinds of reforms in all realms of society, the 'Beijing consensus' implies pragmatism, according to which every country follows its particular developmental path, for example without considering aspects of political reform (as does the Washington consensus).

65 Here, a well-known citation of the Soviet novel, *How the Steel was Tempered*, written by Nikolai Ostrovsky is included, to the effect that the basic achievement was nothing less than the 'liberation of mankind'. This novel is well-known in China and mentioned even in Chinese textbooks.

66 Rolland is said to have mandated his travel notes to be published only in 1984, after 50 years, at a time when he hoped that all problems he noted might have long been solved.

67 They are, however, mentioned in the accompanying book on Russia (see Daguo jueqi *xilie congshu* 2006).

68 The text of the comment is reprinted in the three volume-set Daguo jueqi: *12 ji daxing dianzi jilupian* (2007), vol. 3: 817–42.

69 The itinerary is signed by Zhang Xiaoyu together with Bi Yuekun 毕岳昆.

70 Cf. Chinese prominent political advisor Zheng Bijian's evaluation (2005: 64): Lincoln did everything for the Union, i.e. maintaining the integrity of the nation was his main purpose, rather than the abolition of slavery. Here Zheng Bijian, whom we have shown above as probably the one driving the political study session out of which the documentary grew, sees a link to the 'Taiwan question' (the hope for its eventual reunification with the Chinese mainland)!

71 The Chinese official 'sanguine' historiography on the Boxers has been challenged by academic historians, which led to an éclat in 2006 when historian Yuan Weishi's criticism of Chinese textbooks led to a censuring of the publication in which it was printed. (See below and also Chapter 3).

72 It might be also added here that descriptions of American history in Chinese world history classes changed in this regard in the 2000s: whereas the ensuing Great Depression and irresponsible 'capitalist' behaviour was focused upon earlier, now Roosevelt's 'positive' New Deal was integrated into the narrative to balance the account. This means that the documentary steered between the two approaches here (and also satisfied the assumed expectations of viewers who grew up with the 'traditional' narrative).

73 The text of the comment is reprinted in the three-volume set Daguo jueqi: *12 ji daxing dianzi jilupian* (2007), vol. 3: 969–81 and 982–94.

74 Following the Soviet model, the political event of the 'Glorious Revolution' is seen as the start of the modern era in world history textbooks in the PRC.

75 This twelfth part of the series has no accompanying volume of its own because the books are all country monographs, but it is equally divided between the eight volumes and added as a kind of appendix in each of them.

76 This suggests that only part of the interviews conducted could be included in the single instalments.

77 Politicians cited include former British Secretary of State for Foreign Affairs Geoffrey Howe and former French President Giscard d'Estaing.

78 This is also warned of by Sun, Bin in his blog reaction to the airing of the documentary, reflecting the stance of critical articles in *Nanfang zhoumou* 南方周末 (Southern Weekend) and similar 'critical' inner-Chinese publications (see the entries in Sun, Bin's blog on 28 and 29 November 2006). His blog is hosted in the US and focuses on Chinese affairs. Chinese voices critical of the documentary and its political implication appeared, for example on *Nanfang baoyewang* 南方报业网 ('nfmedia.com') and in *Nanfang xinwen* 南方新闻 (Southern News), with *Nanfang zhoumo* clearly pointing to the documentary's assumed 'political background'. (All articles appeared in November to December 2006 during the repeated airing of the documentary, and have been used here via the important widely-used internet portal *Xinlangwang* 新浪网 (ent.sina.com.cn) which is allowed to make published articles available online.)

79 This is also stressed by people involved in the making of the documentary, including one of the key planners, well-known journalist Mai Tianshu 麦天枢, in an interview for *Nanfang zhoumo* 南方周末 (Southern Weekend), that was meant to deflect the assumption of a 'political drive' behind the documentary (see Zhang Yi; 1 December 2006; see also Mai Tianshu; 14 January 2007).

80 For example, in the very popular *Tianya* 天涯 club BBS, an early article on the documentary attracted over 200 messages in three days, as the official *People's Daily Online* reported (*TV docu stimulates more open attitude to history, China, the world*; 26 November 2006). The entries have multiplied ever since (see www.tianya.cn. A search on *Daguo jueqi* rendered over 170,000 entries on 19 March 2012).

81 The latter article was received also by Chinese US specialists (see Zi Zhongjun 2007: 47).

82 See an interview with Zheng in 2004 in Zheng, Bijian (2005: 64) and Zheng's speech of 1997 in Zheng, Bijian (2005: 84). It might well be that Kahn had read these speeches published in English, though he does not refer to them.

83 Qian Chengdan started the book series in 2008 as a further means of transmitting historical knowledge in an easy-to-read manner for the general public. The author is a researcher at a naval institute. (Having become more self-assured in the meantime, a recent TV documentary series named *Zou xiang haiyang* 《走向海洋》 (Toward the Ocean) produced in 2011 by the State Oceanic Administration and the navy on Chinese 'maritime history' now even claims that China was, in fact, also historically a significant 'maritime power')!

84 Ren Xuean, as head of the project, Zhou Yan as main director and Qian Chengdan as chief academic advisor all stressed this point in various interviews. Ying Zhu, who interviewed Ren Xuean in 2009 for her book on CCTV, also states that he told her this (Zhu, Ying 2012: 114).

85 Many interviews with the makers of the documentary can be found on the website: http://www.sina.com.cn (*xinlangwang*).

86 This position was voiced by Zhuang Liwei 庄礼伟, a professor of South East Asian Studies at a university in Canton (see Zhuang Liwei; 8 December 2006).

87 Chang Ping was deputy editor of *Nandu zhoukan* 南都周刊 (Southern Metropolis Weekly) at the time. The paper had run a discussion on democracy and freedom in this context.

88 A similar assessment was conveyed by Qian Chengdan in a personal communication in 2008.

89   See, above all, the already noted reaction of German historian Winkler, who was appalled when told he was made part of a 'heroisation' of Bismarck – an image he had definitely not tried to convey in his interview with the documentary's film crew (see Winkler 2006).

90   Further single statements can be found on: http://www.sina.com.cn.

91   See above: he was one of the authors in the People's Press volume: *Qiangguo zhi jian* (2007).

92   On *Zou xiang gonghe* see Müller (2007b).

93   Zhu, Ying (2012: 108) states Ren Xuean presented her personally with a version with English subtitles, done by Singapore TV on request from former prime minister Lee Kwan Yew. (I have not seen this version.)

94   These licenses sold covered the People Press book *Qiangguo zhi jian* 强国之鉴 (The mirror of the powers), connected to the documentary's topic together with the book *Daguo jueqi* edited by Tang Jin (for both see above).

95   Yuan became a cause célèbre in 2006 when a critical article of his on 'historical distortions' in Chinese junior secondary school textbooks led to a temporary closing down of the newspaper supplement in which his article was printed: *Bingdian* 冰点 (Freezing Point).

96   The author is a cadre, fairly active on the Internet.

97   CCTV started its own documentary channel only in 2011 (cf. Chapter 1). For a discussion of the problems of documentary TV in the official media in China at the time of *Daguo jueqi* see the remarks of one of CCTV's documentary specialists: Chen Xiaoqing (1 February 2007).

98   A similar argument was put forward by the head of the Institute of Economic Management of Qinghua University, stressing the seriousness of the documentary and its historical depiction of the market economy: Qian Yingyi (28 November 2006).

99   See the very critical article on this series by Yu Qunying (7 September 2008).

100   For the Eurocentrism in Soviet historiography that influenced China, see above.

3 China's potential on display

The sequel documentary *Fuxing zhi lu* (The Road to Revival)

When the *Daguo jueqi* hype was still underway, CCTV quickly came out with a follow-up documentary: the six-part TV series *Fuxing zhi lu* 复兴之路 ('The Road to Revival'), made by more or less the same people who produced *Daguo jueqi*. It seems that the fact that *Daguo jueqi* did not include China in its line-up of 'great powers' called for such a complementary treatment of China: she was the emerging great power that in future would join 'the club', or rather displace those earlier members that can now no longer claim great power status. In this case, there was no political study session behind the production, but as will become obvious, the documentary nicely fitted the political agenda of the CCP, which would be propagated during the Seventeenth Party Congress in October 2007 and was part and parcel of a bigger project to market CCP politics via a 'standardised' reading of modern Chinese history.

TV, national politics, and the standardisation of history

The impression that the new documentary served to 'add' China to the list of 'great powers' is enforced by CCTV's Ren Xuean, again head of project as with *Daguo jueqi*. He stated that *Fuxing zhi lu* was produced in just ten months, starting in December 2006, i.e. as soon as *Daguo jueqi* was out on the market and proving successful. Obviously, the documentary format enables rapid production keeping it also in line with *Daguo jueqi* in format. As Ren Xuean spent four years on both,[1] this means that whereas *Daguo jueqi* was produced with quite some care and effort, *Fuxing zhi lu* was a comparatively hasty enterprise, which its producers – as its screening was to be linked to the Seventeenth Party Congress in October 2007 – were under pressure to get ready in time. This is also obvious to the viewer, since the series gives the impression of being composed of rather quickly assembled, readily available archival pieces as its main basis, is less careful in narrative design and visual arrangements, and (re)uses shots and several clippings from interviews obviously done in the context of the former series. The latter, in its final instalment, already provided several references to China regarding her relations with the 'great powers'. These materials were complemented with interviews done during a tour through China in a scaled-down imitation of the interview tours for *Daguo jueqi* (which also explains why the 'making of' in this case was not marketed in the same way, lacking the earlier documentary's 'exotic' qualities). In this case, four film teams were sent around all over China to do interviews and some on-the-spot filming (Fuxing zhi lu *shang de dianshiren*; 14 January 2008). Zhou Yan 周艳 was again one of the main directors to coordinate the filmic side of the documentary, as she had done already with *Daguo jueqi*. Quite tellingly, Ren Xuean expresses his surprise that these two series were 'so successful', since the information provided is basically what everybody knew from junior secondary school, especially with the second one on Chinese history (*Fuxing zhi lu* 2007/8, vol. 3: 371). He argued that their interpretative approach looking for 'key moments' in history (and his professional training in relating history through the medium of TV in an interesting and entertaining way) were decisive factors in keeping the public in front of the screen, although the avowed popularity of *Fuxing zhi lu* is actually less documented than that of *Daguo jueqi*. However, this shows an awareness of the advantages of the TV medium in getting history across to the audience which according to surveys, as already stated, conforms to the findings about where people today take their views on history from: other than school, mainly from TV.

The editor of the accompanying book series to both TV documentaries also highlighted the 'great success' of both TV series, on which the books, in turn, could capitalise. The longer series *Daguo jueqi* had run twice on TV immediately after coming out in November 2006, and the accompanying book series sold extremely well, leading to many reprints within months. Furthermore, many similar products were quickly sold by competing publishing houses. Thus, *Daguo jueqi* had created – as we have seen – a stir in the publishing market. And thus there was hope that *Fuxing zhi lu* could follow up, though it remains dubious whether the book version of the latter achieved high selling rates in the end.[2] To heighten *Fuxing zhi lu*'s appeal, it was calculated that reference to well-known public 'cases' disputed in Chinese society like the 'eight kings' of early Chinese privatisation moves in the 1980s whom many had envied for their sudden wealth would attract the readers'/ viewers' curiosity. In terms of visual appeal of the book version, some artwork by a minority painter, Yang Yan 杨彦, was added to the latter, though it is not very clear why he was chosen, but for the fact that he was well received in party circles. In fact, his paintings, predominantly landscapes, have no obvious connection to the topic.

For the book version, three authors were hired: Zhang Xiaoyu 章晓宇 (who wrote the script of the documentary and had already been involved in preparing the TV script of *Daguo jueqi* as we have seen, had also filmed in Russia and collaborated in the writing of several country volumes in the accompanying book series there), Chang Shiben 常仕本 and Gu Yaqi 顾亚奇. Chang had participated in *Daguo jueqi* as well, writing the script on the UK. The DVD versions of *Fuxing zhi lu* also mentions main director Zhou Yan who contributed to the script of the documentary as well, integrating, as with *Daguo jueqi*, the filmic concerns to the narrative. The whole project was supported, obviously, by the National People's Congress, which runs, as readers might be reminded, the publishing house that produced the accompanying books to both documentaries: China Democracy and

Legal System Press (Zhongguo minzhu fazhi chubanshe 中国民主法制出版社). For academic advice, a noted Qing historian – helping with nineteenth-century history – is named (Yan Chongnian 阎崇年) in the book version of *Fuxing zhi lu (Fuxing zhi lu* 2007/8, vol. 3: 377). The DVD version adds early twentieth-century history specialist and party member Jin Chongji 金冲及 and the two party historians and theorists Li Jie 李捷 and Li Zhongjie 李忠杰 as 'academic consultants' for the TV documentary. This focus on party-related historians and 'theorists' is in stark contrast to the high-profile academics of *Daguo jueqi*. In fact, the makers of the series admitted they deliberately asked for 'guidance' by party people, which betrays this series' foremost political function! Interestingly, however, as with *Daguo jueqi*, the book version presents only interviewed foreigners as 'specialists' consulted for the documentary in an appendix with photographs and short biographies, giving the documentary a more international 'scientific outlook'. Since, as stated above, there was only an 'internal Chinese' interview tour especially for *Fuxing zhi lu*, this means the series lived off the work done for *Daguo jueqi* in many respects. In fact, people interviewed for *Fuxing zhi lu* are partly those who appeared in *Daguo jueqi*, i.e. they might not always have realised they were being interviewed for something which would later be called *Fuxing zhi lu*.[3] Other (including foreign) interviewees appear only in *Fuxing zhi lu*, which leads to the conclusion that more foreigners had been interviewed during the tours for *Daguo jueqi* but that material would only be used for *Fuxing zhi lu*. As noted with *Daguo jueqi* above, in many cases there was a tendency to present foreign interviewees *not* specialised on China (speaking on their respective countries), whereas in *Fuxing zhi lu* mainly foreign China specialists were cited. This, in turn, suggests that *Fuxing zhi lu* was already on the minds of the producers earlier as a sequel production, and they had thus already prepared for it while working on *Daguo jueqi*.

All in all, one gets the impression that in spite of the staged appearance of a similarly 'scientific' enterprise on the level of *Daguo jueqi*, it was envisaged beforehand that *Fuxing zhi lu* would be used to 'add' China to the countries discussed in *Daguo jueqi*. However this would now be deliberately carried out with a more 'political' bent, using foreign interviewees only as a legitimisation device, but using party-related advisors to ensure conformity to political preferences (which are more pronounced for Chinese than for foreign history). The publisher for his part hoped to profit by serving Chinese nationalist pride in the aftermath of the *Daguo jueqi* hype.

In terms of intended 'message', the head of CCTV at the time, Zhao Huayong 赵化勇, explains *Fuxing zhi lu* as a tribute to the heightened importance that China has gained internationally in the meantime. Though a long-term global player, she has undergone a tragic and traumatic experience. In other words: she is now to become a great power again (a reference to her 'revival'), but not in a way that will be overbearing due to her own tumultuous past. Zhao hails China's comeback from Mao's (1893–1976) proclamation that 'China has stood up now' (in 1949) to her recent stunning economic development. In his summing-up of China's history during the last 100 years, the highlights were 1911 (the founding of the republic), 1949 (the founding of the PRC) and 1978 (the start of the reform and opening-up policy) – which corresponds to the periodisation of the first instalments in the documentary. (Interestingly, he does not mention 1921, the standard date of the founding of the CCP, as a key date.) And now, he proudly declares, China is again stunning the world by demonstrating that an old cultural nation can be so dynamic and creative (i.e. is ready for 'revival').[4]

For Zhao, China has now reached the climax since the humbling Opium Wars of the nineteenth century, by each generation building upon the former. To convey this, CCTV, as an enterprise with official responsibility for 'educating' the people, produced this series (as it produced *Daguo jueqi*). Herewith, Zhao openly acknowledges TV's 'mouthpiece' function as a 'public educator'. Zhao enumerates three basic aims for this presentation: to provide a comprehensive perspective (what did every phase in history leave us as lessons?); to provide a contemporary perspective in looking backward (how did we come to the present state?); and to provide a global perspective (what are the global implications of China's rise?)

In sum, the documentary is meant to combine historical and present concerns, taking in evaluations by Chinese and foreign experts. This, Zhao argues, is the first time that CCTV has evaluated modern Chinese society and history in toto, demonstrating that even such an old cultural nation as China does not 'grow old' (*Fuxing zhi lu* 2007/8, vol. 1: III). In this way, he claims that the documentary provides a comprehensive (and more or less authoritative) view on modern Chinese history.

To this more general evaluation of the head of CCTV, Luo Ming 罗明, now deputy head of CCTV and a long-term key figure in CCTV's producing big TV historical series like *Yongzheng wangchao* 雍正王朝 (Yongzheng dynasty) or *Zou xiang gonghe* 走向共和 (Towards the Republic), which are, however, not documentaries, adds that the documentary *Fuxing zhi lu* also wants to motivate the viewers to dedicate themselves more to China's further rise, stressing that the zenith is still ahead. In this way, he adds civic responsibility to the documentary's educational goal. He sees China's history as a mirror of options that might be used to learn for the future. In reflecting the problems that many people encountered in Chinese history, everyone, whether reformers or conservatives, whether keen on their own profit or on sacrificing themselves, whether thinkers or practitioners, should take up these lessons for China's future course. For Luo, the basic message is: China has already tried several times in history to follow foreign models, only to learn she had to rely on herself if she wanted to gain anything. Therefore, she needed to find her own way, as formulated in the motto of 'socialism with Chinese characteristics' (which, in fact, relativises the importance of 'foreign models', as presented in *Daguo jueqi*!). And the media have the task not only to document but also to actively create, i.e. to influence the viewers' perceptions. Thus, with Luo Ming's preface, the very nationalist background and strong political flavour of the whole enterprise becomes even more evident.[5]

This political background is betrayed also when the documentary is seen in the context of national politics: in mid-October 2007 (at the mid-term of the

Hu Jintao administration) the Seventeenth Party Congress convened in Beijing. Here, Hu Jintao held a programmatic opening speech, propagating more equal distribution of wealth, and integrating his well-known mottos 'scientific progress' and the 'harmonious society', both of which are cited in the documentary *Fuxing zhi lu*, which came out at that time. In fact, the documentary was aired just a few days before the opening of the Congress in TV during prime time (see below), and in the DVD version (*Fuxing zhi lu* 2007a) that came out afterwards the Congress itself is blended in – which again underlines the close relationship of the documentary with current politics. In fact, it suggests the documentary was made to promote the concepts of what was in the offing for the Congress.

Furthermore, the *Fuxing zhi lu* documentary was not an isolated media event, but has to be seen also in the context of an identically named exhibition in Beijing's Military Museum – which was serving as an alternative exhibition space to the Museum of the Chinese Revolution, then under reconstruction (now combined with the National Museum of Chinese History and called the National Museum). Both of them were connected to the Seventeenth Party Congress that was held in Beijing from 15–22 October 2007. Additionally, less than two weeks before the Congress opened, an Internet forum on the topic of 'revival' was launched which was officially inaugurated on 8 October. People could voice their political concerns and wishes for the upcoming party congress to communicate to the political leaders (*Yangshi guoji* Fuxing luntan *zhengshi shangxian*; 8 October 2007). The site is still hosted by CCTV.com and provides a forum of general discussion on cultural and political issues (*Fuxing luntan*; 2007–). This was a new way of inviting people to join political discussion, even if it might be more than doubtful whether it had any concrete effect on political decisions, which usually are already made starting a party congress. However, in terms of public marketing of politics, this party congress, which was the first to have an own website,(!) set a new standard.[6] And the cooperation and functionality of CCTV is notable, concerning the often-stressed 'semi-privatised' character of CCTV today. Obviously, this holds true for financial aspects more than for political ones. In short, even though there was no political study session behind *Fuxing zhi lu* as with *Daguo jueqi*, by its context it was nevertheless equally integrated into attempts at political communication between the party and the 'people'.

Following up the chronological evolution of these various media outlets more precisely, on 5–10 October the CCTV documentary series *Fuxing zhi lu* was broadcast on prime time every evening, thus to be completed shortly before the start of the congress. CCTV set up a special website on the series and connected issues. Here, the documentary can still be watched online (*Fuxing zhi lu* 2007b). The Internet forum referred to above was started during the airing as well. On 13 October, the exhibition opened, just two days before the party congress. It did not produce a catalogue but set up a website (hosted by CCTV!) where visitors could wander through it virtually (Fuxing zhi lu *daxing zhanlan*; n.d.). This exhibition was, nevertheless, officially organised not by CCTV, but by the Military Museum, and it was co-sponsored by the 'Publicity Department' (i.e. the

Propaganda Department)[7] of the Central Committee, the Ministries of Finances and of Culture, the General Political Department of the People's Liberation Army (PLA) and the Municipal Government of Beijing (see *Patriotic Exhibition Receives Strong Public Response*; 19 December 2007). This already shows the strong political and organisational links between these different agents, all in service to the party congress, and suggests the scope of it was to 'promote' the latter. Furthermore, the exhibition was also advertised on the Chinese military net as 'patriotic study material' (Zhang Yi and Liang Min; 2 November 2007). It was discussed on the Internet, with the Propaganda Department organising this event contemporaneously on the (official) platforms *Renminwang* 人民网 (People's net), *Xinhuawang* 新华网 (Xinhua net), *Yangshi guojiwang* 央视国际网 (CCTV International net), *Guangmingwang* 光明网 (Guangming net) and *Zhongqingwang* 中青网 (China Youth net). The forum chosen was the already-named 'strong power forum' (*qiangguo luntan* 强国论坛) which had been created in the context of the 1999 NATO bombings hitting the Chinese Belgrade Embassy, reminding one of the issue around the more 'aggressive' *qiangguo* vs the more 'honourable' *daguo* that we already pointed out in discussing *Daguo jueqi*. The outspoken aim was to 'discuss' the fact that Marxism, the CCP, and socialism were 'chosen' by history and the people. The people responsible for the exhibition, the deputy head of the Propaganda Department and other top cadres, were invited to underline this message in discussion; they used the opportunity to advocate their aims for the exhibition: to tell the unique story of the success of the CCP, which was China's only choice for a bright development: in modern history as it is today. A focus was to be on the time since 1978 and on how socialism guaranteed China's revival. To propagate the Seventeenth Party Congress, a substantial part of the exhibition was dedicated to the most modern developments, clearly marking the exhibition as one with political intentions (Fuxing zhi lu *daxing zhuti zhanlan wangshang tan*; 17 December 2007).

This great exhibition ran for several months and staged Chinese history – in parallel with the documentary – since 1840. It had a strong didactic flavour, and many school classes and other organised groups were shown around. Comparing it to the documentary, the division in sections was only 'shortened' to five vis-à-vis the six in the documentary, leaving merely two sections to PRC times vis-à-vis the four in the documentary (and instead dividing the pre-PRC phase into three sections vis-à-vis the two in the documentary). Thus, the first two parts of the exhibition as designed in 2007 were split up into the time of foreign encroachment and the time of the Chinese pre-communist liberation efforts, culminating in the founding of the party in 1921; the third and central part was assigned here to the guidance to liberation by the CCP, gloriously leading up to the founding of the PRC in 1949. The PRC phases following 1949 were subsumed here in only two parts: one on Mao's time with more ups than downs (evading 'problematic issues' like the Great Leap Forward, 1958–61 and the Great Famine in 1958–61, for example); and the unanimously positive and particularly stressed era since Deng Xiaoping 邓小平 (1904–1997) and the 'opening-up' (no mention of 4 June 1989, or of others such issues, of course). It ends on an upbeat note about how well people now live. In other words: the TV series divided communist times according to CCP 'leading generations' (Mao Zedong, Deng Xiaoping, Jiang Zemin, Hu Jintao – a technique of 'personalised' structuring that we will encounter again in the third documentary series to be discussed in this book: *Ju an si wei* and Soviet history); the exhibition, on the other hand, blended them into the part on founding the PRC (*jianguo daye* 建国大业) and the part on its development toward the future (*kaichuang weilai* 开创未来). Why there was this divergence between the contemporaneous TV documentary and the exhibition remains open to speculation, but it might be due to the somewhat contested historical interpretations behind the two simultaneous productions. In fact, the later restructuring of the exhibition (see below) demonstrated that there was further need to readjust its reading of history.

However, just as the *Fuxing* blog has become an institution ever since, the exhibition has also acquired an importance transcending the Seventeenth Party Congress. In March 2008 it was extended after some changes – already signalling that the presentation of modern Chinese history was all but uncontested – and this led to continuous reworking of the exhibition (Zhang Zongtang; 26 September 2009). The exhibition, which was originally intended to run provisionally for only some two months, was thus reopened for some further months as an 'official exhibition' (Zhou Yingfeng; 1 January 2008), and the media argued that it was well received by the public, citing some 'enthusiastic' public responses.[8] In March 2009 in tandem with the sessions at the National Congress of the People, the National Museum of Beijing being under reconstruction and expansion, the exhibition was shown internally at first only in some already finished exhibition halls (*Zhong-wai meiti canguan* Fuxing zhi lu *zhanlan*; 27 September 2009). Due to the sixtieth anniversary of the founding of the PRC, the exhibition was opened again to the public from 25 September to late November 2009, having again undergone several changes, not the least to update it with the last two years' political and other 'achievements', but also adding more artistic objects.[9] Finally, in the spring of 2011, it was shown again for an extended manner after the restructuring and expansion of the National Museum was completed; and it paralleled the Fourth Session of the Eleventh National Congress of the People (*Guojia bowuguan* Fuxing zhi lu *jiben chenlie fuzhan juxing*; 1 March 2011). Thus the exhibition, designed as a long-term project, has now finally become the definitive version of modern Chinese history.[10] As Li Changchun 李長春, an important politician specialised in propaganda work and member of the standing committee of the Politburo, had already voiced in 2009, the originally 'temporary' and 'thematic' exhibition was now to be *the* permanent exhibition on modern Chinese history.[11]

Some telling details about the background of these multiple rearrangements of the exhibition are disclosed by Ma Yingmin 马英民 of the National Museum: according to him, political guidelines were instrumental in all revisions of the exhibition. First, when the exhibition was designed for the Military Museum in 2007, the objectives were given as: following a red thread, focusing on certain key points, taking up a global perspective, and giving 'correct guidance' (Ma Yingmin

2009: 54–5). (There was, it may be noted, obviously no direct link to the parallel documentary of the same name, suggesting that both were designed somewhat apart from each other, which might explain the differences between them, even though both were linked latterly in the context of the Seventeenth Party Congress and by CCTV's hosting the website of the exhibition.) These objectives led to the periodisation placing the CCP's role in 'liberating China' in the middle of the exhibition, i.e. with the third part going up to 1949. When the exhibition was first moved to the National Museum in 2009, the sixtieth anniversary of the PRC was in the background. Major revision was called for, though the exhibition would only become fully accessible with the end of restructuring of the museum in March 2011. In 2009 the clearly voiced objectives included giving answers to the following questions (in fact, the so-called 'six whys' (*liuge wei shenme* 六个为什么)):[12] why do we need the CCP, why socialism, etc. and why *not* follow a Western path of democracy, multi-party-system, capitalism, division of powers, etc., and why do we have to keep to the path of opening-up and reform policies (a clear sign against 'leftist' critics) (Ma Yingmin 2009: 61). To this, the 'results' of the Seventeenth Party Congress of 2007 should now be integrated and the newest developments should be covered for the sixtieth anniversary of the PRC, for example, the Beijing Olympics of 2008. And in 2011 the final revision also had to consider that the former 'topical' exhibition was now a 'permanent' one, thus having to become more 'balanced' in its presentation of modern history. This meant more objects in the now more largely available exhibition space. In short, the exhibition was finally set as the 'standard' reading of modern Chinese history.

Besides the exhibition, another way of picking up the topic of 'The Road to Revival' was, again in 2009 on the occasion of the sixtieth anniversary of the PRC's founding, a huge epic with music, lyrics and ballet – a performance of roughly 2.5 hours, like the exhibition in five parts. However, here the time-splits were as follows: (1) 1840–1921, thus taking the founding of the CCP as the first 'break' (therewith covering the first two sections of the exhibition in just one part); (2) 1921–49, i.e. up to the founding of the PRC; (3) 1949–78, i.e. covering all pre-'reform era' developments in the PRC in one section, be it the more 'glorious parts' of the early PRC, or the more 'problematic' ones that followed; (4) 1978–2008 as the most pronounced and 'hailed' era of 'reform'; (5) 2009 and the anniversary. This means the division was yet different from the documentary and the exhibition, and the balance was shifted more to modern times, with the Olympics being the culmination of the fourth part and the present day making up an instalment on its own. In short, the epic, though in five parts as the exhibition, was in its more 'presentist' focus closer to the division in the six-part documentary series of 2007 than to the more 'historical' exhibition (though the key time breaks coincided more with the exhibition than the leadership generation periodisation of the documentary). The spectacle was staged at the Hall of the People from 20 September to 5 October 2009. It starred several famous artists and singers,[13] and was broadcast on 30 September 2009, on CCTV 1 on prime time as the official event to attune people to the anniversary on the following morning.[14]

The epic had a second round of shows in Beijing in early 2010.[15] (Its success was obviously also helped by the very moderate ticket prices; Chen and Ren; 8 February 2010.) In 2011 it finally toured the country as a contribution to the ninetieth anniversary of the CCP's founding and to the hundredth anniversary of the Xinhai Revolution (1911/12), which had ushered in the end of imperial rule in China.[16] Clearly, the message was to make people aware of the blessings they received by the party's guidance in modern history. The epic was turned also into a film as another '*Revival*' production,[17] which was, however, only relatively successful.[18]

The stage show was set in the tradition of huge anniversary celebrations with epics, as in 1964 on the fifteenth anniversary of the founding of the PRC with *The East is Red*, and 1984 at the thirty-fifth anniversary with *Songs of the Chinese Revolution*.[19] Thus the sixtieth anniversary was now celebrated with the epic *The Road to Revival*. These *Fuxing*-shows on the sixtieth anniversary, however, also received criticism from the leftist side, precisely because of their political thrust: on maoflag.net, a well-known site of party leftists, bloggers complained about the negative and cursory portrayal of the Cultural Revolution (1966–76), thus openly questioning this 'standardised' reading of history (*Dui* Fuxing zhi lu *de chensi he jueze*; 7 October 2009).[20] Others, however, saw the 'politicised' side of the epic to celebrate the PRC precisely as a sign of backwardness, reminding one of the 'last century', i.e. Maoist times.[21] In sum, 'The Road to Revival' as a broad political enterprise to 'standardise' Chinese history and settle the role of the CCP historically did not go unchallenged.

The above clearly shows that the topic of *Fuxing zhi lu* was of long-term importance for the marketing of CCP politics – and nation branding, with a view especially to the domestic audience;[22] and that all *Fuxing*-productions were extremely politicised and had to follow directives faithfully, although they also reflected in their divergence and continuous reworking the contested nature of historical evaluations.

The historical portrayal of modern China

The documentary *Fuxing zhi lu* thus was set against a larger context of *Fuxing*-productions. Nevertheless, it also had its distinctive features. Whereas the other productions were more straightforwardly concerned only with China, the documentary provides a look into attempts to profile China's potential for great power status in 2007 against the backdrop of Western experiences addressed in its predecessor documentary, *Daguo jueqi*. It is therefore especially concerned about presenting Chinese modern history in a 'global' perspective, also integrating foreigners' views in a more explicitly 'scientific' vein and by this sets itself apart – at least in appearance – from the primarily 'inner-Chinese' other *Fuxing*-productions. As we have seen above, for example, the periodisation was also not quite congruent with the other 'Revival' outlets. Therefore we turn now to take a closer look into the documentary's specific historical portrayal of modern Chinese history.

A Change after Thousands of Years (Qiannian Jubian 千年局变)

The introductory strip to all six instalments of the documentary starts with rain, snow, and storm, in the midst of which an old Chinese city gate, symbolising endurance under difficulties, appears. The music is a blend of Western and Chinese elements, soon shifting to familiar CCP 'sounds', with strings, brass and choir. This cues the viewer into a sentiment of 'elevation' when viewing socialist–realist sculptures (mainly from the stele of martyrs of the revolution on the Tian'anmen Square), while in the background, explosions remind one of the wars necessary to achieve the glorious aim, symbolised by balloons going up and birds flying through the sky. The Chinese flag is extended toward the Gate of Heavenly Peace, with Mao Zedong's portrait on it, thus making visually clear who was responsible for achieving this, ending with a rising sun, symbolising the 'rise' of China.

The narrative introduction, accompanied visually by the icons of Chineseness, the Yellow River and the Great Wall, starts off with praise of Chinese civilisation as an unbroken tradition situated at the 'East of the world', created by the 'diligent and daring' Chinese people (showing the Terracotta Army of the First Emperor of the third century BC). Compared with the previous documentary series *Daguo jueqi*, the male voice reading out the commentary comes with much more pathos, in a vein that Chinese viewers are accustomed to from other 'official' productions, and the visual cues in this instalment are on balance more 'action-like' than in the rather 'calm' *Daguo jueqi*. Thus, in terms of filmic language, the stance is less 'neutral' and 'scientific'. The Kangxi Emperor of the late seventeenth century is introduced to mark the climax of feudal greatness. But at the time he ascended the throne in China, things underwent dramatic changes in other parts of the globe. With Western capitalism spreading since the late fifteenth century (the topic of the documentary series *Daguo jueqi*, which is visually cited), the world had been drawn together, and no country could exist in isolation any longer. The late eighteenth century, when the Industrial Revolution, the independence of the US from Britain, and the French Revolution marked a new era, is described as a turning point. And these changes were to impact upon China also, which 'for 3,000 years' (which is remarkably more modest than the usual '5,000 years') had not seen such enormous changes. But now, the commentary argues, China would go through over 100 years of hardship to finally rise anew.

The storyline of the first instalment starts in Fujian where 140 years earlier a great wharf was founded by the Governor General Zuo Zongtang 左宗棠 (1812–85) in order to build up a naval defence in China. (Here the sea, a key topic in the 'rise' of a nation that has been familiar since the release of *Daguo jueqi*, is again introduced as the starting point in discussing China's destiny.) This wharf, in fact, was the biggest in the whole of Asia at the time. The reason for having it built was the first Opium War in 1840 – in China *the* key date dividing 'pre-modern' from 'modern' history. (This is visually stressed by an animated Chinese map, showing the British ships moving along the coast to set China afire at various points. Crucial dates such as the Opium War (1840) are continuously blended in transparently as a didactic orientation for the viewer.) The British had easily subdued Qing China by naval force in the war, but in this way, they also triggered China into modernisation, thus marking the war as decisive for future Chinese developments.

With this general assessment as a kind of introduction, the focus goes back to the Opium War itself and the reasons of the British to start it (again using shots from *Daguo jueqi*'s instalment on the UK): they simply had nothing to offer other than opium in exchange for the Chinese tea they desired. Chinese historian Niu Dayong 牛大勇 stresses the point that the British first attacked economically via the opium because of their trade disadvantage. But Western interviewee Hans Van de Ven, teaching in Britain, argues that from the British perspective of industrial-isation, China was simply economically backward, and thus turns the emphasis from British envy and selfishness to the civilising 'mission'. The commentary, however, sticks to the 'Chinese' perspective, arguing that the British had already colonised India because they needed markets for their products and resources, and their economic attack on China was simply in line with that logic. Thus they created addicts in order to make the Chinese dependent on opium – conveniently ignoring the fact that opium had been a 'Chinese product' as well and was all but unknown in China. However, the moralising tone is sustained with a dictum by Marx (1818–83): opium traffic was an *immoral* means to fill the British treasury. And Chinese historian and doyen of history at Beijing Normal University, Gong Shuduo 龚书铎, adds that it was not only the British merchants who profited from that trade, but the British State was involved via taxes as well (thus implicitly countering the argument that de facto the opium trade was done for most of the time on a private level). And British China expert Christopher Hughes self-critically agrees that the British way at the time to open markets was in fact by gunshots. (Notably, the interviewees here are set against very dark backgrounds mostly with historical photos, thus highlighting the faces but not where they were filmed, whereas in *Daguo jueqi* the location – whether at the interviewee's home or at the university with book shelves and other background detail – is shown to heighten the impression of 'being there'.)

The commentary then concentrates on the military side (time and again accompanied visually by feature film scenes), examining why the Chinese did not stand the test. Whereas it is admitted that the policy to wage war was very much contested in the British Parliament and decided by a small majority of five votes, the Qing felt very sure of themselves because of their military numerical strength, which was more than ten times that of the British. At this time, says Qian Chengdan, expert in English history and mastermind behind the *Daguo jueqi* documentary, the issue of China's being a backward agrarian country comes up again. (Some early film clips from the archives are included here to show daily life in the late Qing.) And this economic backwardness is combined with an attack on the ignorance of everything beyond the Chinese borders. Notably, even Lin Zexu 林则徐 (1785–1850), the 'usual hero' in the Chinese narrative on the Opium War, as the 'upright official' opposing the invaders, is criticised as being stuck in old beliefs by assuming that the Westerners would die unless they obtained tea and other products all from China alone! On the other hand, the British were much better informed and thus had a clear advantage in this obvious knowledge gap, realising, as a historian specialised in Qing times adds, that the Chinese military was in a deplorable state. In the end, the commentary briefly sums up in familiar textbook style, the final Treaty of Nanking 1842 led to the cession of Hong Kong, huge reparations and China's entering the 'half-colonial, half-feudal society' stage (as Mao famously defined it).

However, China did not learn anything from that experience, which was due to the government's policy of not allowing discussions of that topic, as a Chinese interviewee from People's University adds. Lin Zexu at least realised that he had been wrong, and assembled materials on Western countries, handing them to the scholar Wei Yuan 魏源 (1794–1857). Wei composed the work *Haiguo tuzhi* 海国图志 ('Illustrated Gazetteer of Maritime States'. of which a copy is shown) in the early 1840s as a manual on foreign countries; but nobody was interested in this information. In the end, Lin and Wei were both frustrated, and the 'chance' of 1840 went by unheeded. Only when things grew worse would the court finally move.

This aggravation was 'helped' by the other momentous event in Chinese history in the mid-nineteenth century: the Taiping 太平 Movement (1850–64), which is seen in typical textbook fashion as the culmination of many peasant unrests earlier. What, however, is not done in textbook fashion, is the argument that the Taiping, usually seen as a precursor to the CCP, engendered a first promotion of capitalism![23] However, the Taiping would only hold out for 14 years in China, but at the same time London boasted her industrial development via the world exposition in 1851, making up one-third of all industrial production worldwide (again accompanied by several shots taken over from *Daguo jueqi* for illustration). Thus, the gap between both countries had widened even since 1840. And before long the next attack would endanger China, according to another 'new' interviewee not appearing in *Daguo jueqi*: American China historian William Kirby: the Second Opium War (1856–60) and the final attack on Beijing in the aftermath. This is typically visualised by the destruction of the Old Summer Palace (*Yuanmingyuan* 圆明园) in 1860, focusing on the famous ruins of Western buildings that were originally built with Jesuit help between the reigns of Kangxi to Qianlong, which today are the usual cover for history textbooks talking about that period. This (Western) picture has become *the* symbol of Chinese 'shame'.[24] The commentary duly repeats the words, famous in China, of Victor Hugo (1802–85), who criticised the British and French looting troops for their uncivilised behaviour and adds the characterisation of this event as a 'deep scar' – in line with 'humiliation history' stressed repeatedly in China since the 1990s. This scar only finally made the court move to set out learning Western technologies, which it could already have done 20 years earlier.

In this context of modernisation, the armaments industry was the most important. However, as the Sino–Japanese War (1894/5) would show, this self-strengthening programme had not been thorough enough. As Japanese expert on modern Chinese history, Hazama Naoki 狹間直樹, is cited, the Japanese cleverly used their victory to extract from the Chinese a sum triple that of the annual revenues of the Qing and quadruple that of Japan, which meant that the Japanese financed much of their development in the following years using Chinese money. (Again, for illustration, many shots from *Daguo jueqi*'s instalment on Japan are reused.)

The crucial question for the Chinese, however, of how the great Qing Empire could ever lose against upstart neighbour Japan is explained by Li Wenhai 李文海, chairman of the Chinese Association of Historians, in again very textbook-like fashion, attributing it to China's 'corrupt society' and 'backward economy'. And these internal Chinese problems are then focused upon, demonstrating Chinese superstition and corruption with a positive counter-image of a Japan that was eager to learn. Whereas the Chinese would not use their first railway tracks for trains out of fear of disturbing the graves of imperial ancestors nearby, and thus allowed them to be used only for cars drawn by horses or mules, the Tenno would personally inaugurate new railways, and the Japanese public would respectfully take off their shoes when taking a look at the new trains' compartments. (This, again, is a link to the instalment of *Daguo jueqi* on Japan.)

Even worse, whereas in the West the Second Industrial Revolution was well under way and electricity changed people's lives tremendously, the Chinese would have their officials take exams in archery and the rigid *baguwen* 八股文 writing style. And those still clinging to the self-strengthening movement would confidently propose that China was basically 'better' than the West, needing only to adopt further technology while remaining true to her superior 'substance'. No wonder that Marx had also some negative things to say on China, predicting that she would come to a 'bad end', as long as she went ahead ignoring the rest of the world.

It was only people like Yan Fu 严复 (1854–1921), the commentary points out, who realised the dire need to learn about new things. With his translation of Thomas Henry Huxley's (1825–95) writings (of which the manuscript is shown), evolutionary thought became known in China and 'liberated' Chinese thought. And with this the narrative now turns to Sun Yat-sen (1866–1925) as embodying new thought: when he tried for change with his proposals in a peaceful way, he was turned down by the court – namely by Li Hongzhang 李鸿章 (1823–1901) who was also one of the dominating figures in the self-strengthening movement. Sun Yat-sen herefore turned to revolution, whereas 'another Cantonese', Kang Youwei 康有为 (1858–1927), tried the less extreme way of reform, believing China was not yet ripe for a republican system. With Kang, the narrative focuses at some length on the 1898 Reform Movement, which was spurred by the fear of China becoming a 'melon' split between foreigners (visualised by an animation of the famous late nineteenth-century map with the foreigners represented by animals grabbing Chinese territory, which is shown in every history textbook). The reform movement's endeavours for constitutionalism and national industrialisation are highlighted, flanked by Tan Sitong 谭嗣同 (1865–98), the 'textbook martyr' expected in this context, who was beheaded after the movement was crushed. In this way, the 1898 Movement comes across as fairly positive – in line with present-day Chinese scholarship, which detects some parallels of it with Chinese reforms since the 1980s. And American China historian Jonathan Spence adds that the nineteenth century was not only a time of 'shame' for China, but also one of reflection about how China could position herself in a more complex world. In short, the 1898 Movement is depicted as a window thrown open, though the only 'concrete' thing left over from it was the Imperial College (eventually becoming Beijing University, the institution that proved decisive in furthering the May Fourth Movement).

But the short-term aftermath of the crushed 1898 reform was the Boxers and the ensuing war, for which the reasons are not detailed, giving the (again fairly 'textbook-like') impression that the foreign Allies attacked out of the blue. Their behaviour in forcing people to fly Western flags is used again to enforce the image of humiliation and shame, which is characterised as 'previously unseen in the world'. (One may recall *Daguo jueqi* and the 'epochal' role assigned to the Boxer War in the US instalment there: it might also be pointed out here that the evalua-tion of the Boxers is still one of the 'hottest' topics in official historiography).[25] Only after the signing of the Boxer Protocol in 1901 – with its reparations from this period set at five times the annual revenue of the Qing, marking the climax of all 'unequal treaties' – did the Qing finally move and set upon their reform programme. This programme is admitted to have gone beyond what the 1898 reformers ever envisaged, but was 'deplorable' in its implementation – the commentary argues. As a Chinese interviewee adds, this only furthered the growing political opposition and therewith dug the dynasty's own grave. All this went down well with Sun Yat-sen's conviction that the Qing were so 'rotten' that even these last-minute pillars could not hold up the building any longer.

The narrative then switches to the end of the Qing and the revolutionaries, briefly sketching out Sun's 'Three People's Principles' (nationalism, democracy and welfare) and stressing that a lot of the revolution's 'martyrs' were in fact students returned from their studies abroad. The sacrifice is dramatised using the famous example of young Lin Juemin 林觉民 (1887–1911), who died shortly before the republic was established and who left behind a testament of dying willingly for the nation, addressed to his young wife and their expected baby. These (Guomindang) 'heroes', the commentary adds, will never be forgotten. (This obviously stretches out a hand to Taiwan and the Guomindang (GMD), and might be a reason for choosing the 'national' topic that was common to all political sides as the documentary's time divide – the toppling of imperial rule – rather than the founding of the CCP, for example.) With the establishment of the republic, the 'first republic in Asia' was born, as is proudly claimed. By demon-strating that the 'son of heaven' is just an imagined power, people realised that everything could be questioned, thereby 'liberating' the mind. This 'great legacy' is embodied in Sun Yat-sen, whose outstanding role in modern Chinese history is underlined. However, on a practical level, the 1911 Revolution was not yet a 'thorough' success. Thus, the instalment ends with the rhetorical question linking to the following one (and enticing the viewer to go on watching by this common device): who would 'really' liberate China from the fetters of feudalism to give her back her dignity? And how would the Chinese people's renaissance be achieved after such a tortuous path, to allow her to finally find the 'right' one?[26]

Momentous times (Zhengrong suiyue 峥嵘岁月)

To demonstrate the early republic's unfulfilled promise, the narrative of the second instalment takes the viewer on a quick tour through the initial years of the republic in conventional textbook fashion (and thus might 'update' viewers who had not watched the previous instalment). Although the emperor was dethroned and the queues were cut, the young republic was soon suffocated in the cradle by strongman Yuan Shikai 袁世凯 (1859–1916), who 'robbed the fruits of the revolution' – according to the oft-cited characterisation of a 1940s' booklet by communist propagandist Chen Boda 陳伯達 (1904–89) on him.[27] Thus, although nominally there were political parties, a parliament and a constitution, in reality Yuan and his Beiyang 北洋 warlords had all the say. Yuan's 'misdeeds', well known to viewers, are quickly reiterated: the murder of GMD politician Song Jiaoren 宋教仁 (1882–1913), and Yuan's signing the Twenty-One Demands of Japan in 1915, thus 'selling out' the republic. When he, the strongman, died in 1916, the whole republic virtually broke apart.

Against this background, the May Fourth Movement is now profiled and visually connected to the Gate of Heavenly Peace (Tian'anmen). Here, the 'orthodox' reading of the 1919 Versailles Peace Treaty's 'betrayal' of China's interests (by leaving Shandong to the Japanese) is accentuated, with a Chinese interviewee adding that Versailles showed that might still won over right. The protest movement of May Fourth, again, is presented all in familiar textbook fashion: it was 'patriotic' and represented 'all walks of life'. Chen Duxiu 陈独秀 (1879–1942) and the journal *Xin qingnian* 新青年 ('La Jeunesse' or New Youth) are recalled, together with Cai Yuanpei 蔡元培 (1868–1940), Li Dazhao 李大钊 (1888–1927), and Lu Xun 鲁迅 (1881–1936), and their quest for 'new thinking'. Interviewee Tu Wei-ming 杜维明 from Harvard, however, also spoke about the 'liberal' legacy of May Fourth that is usually skipped in Chinese textbooks (which rather focus on May Fourth as the cradle of the Communist Movement).

Political realities, the commentary continues, looked however more than dim: the warlords reigned with brutality and the foreigners, as ever, enjoyed their privileges. But noted intellectual Liang Qichao 梁启超 (1873–1929) had written from Europe on the West's bankruptcy following World War I, and thus the viewers' attention is drawn to the competing model newly risen on the international scene: the Soviet Union. (Again, some shots from *Daguo jueqi* are reused as illustration.) And this, the commentary claims, led to the Chinese intellectuals' growing interest in Marxism. Consequently, in many journals the October Revolution and Marxism were discussed, visually connected to the 'pioneer' and communist 'martyr' Li Dazhao who had published on these issues very early and whose grave, today a site of communist ceremonies, is shown.[28]

This links up directly to the recounting of the founding of the CCP, its commitment to anti-feudalism and anti-imperialism and the momentousness of its 'birth' – from which this instalment's title is derived – for Chinese future history. Although the party was tiny at the beginning, the commentary argues, it was bound to win since it had the 'support of the people'. As an example, a survey at

Beijing University of 1923 is cited that arguably showed the popularity of the Soviet model: when asked who the most important personality in the world was, the first ranked was Lenin (1870–1924)! US President Wilson (1856–1924) followed only at a great distance. And Sun Yat-sen, it is argued, also noted the CCP's importance which claimed influence on the Labour Movement since 1922. Thus as Zhang Lei 张磊, historian and head of the Sun Yat-sen Research Society stresses, Sun picked up the communist view to see the basis for revolution in the peasants and labourers now, thus insinuating (again in conventional PRC historiography fashion) that the CCP was the 'logical' continuation of Sun. Consequently, the first united front was created between Sun's GMD and the CCP.

However, Sun soon died. After his death in 1925, the Northern Expedition started with both parties, the GMD and the CCP still cooperating, but then came Chiang Kai-shek's (1887–1975) coup d'état and the ensuing purges of the Communists (betraying Sun's line). This, the commentary points out, cost the lives not only of 26,000 Communists, but also of 300,000 'people'. (Archival footing on executions is shown to stress the sacrifice and Chiang's brutality.) As an interviewed high cadre explains, again in textbook fashion, the CCP represented the 'broad' masses, whereas the right-wing GMD represented the capitalists, which meant that a break was, in fact, inevitable. And this would necessarily involve bloodshed, as Mao's famous phrase stated: 'Power grows out of the barrel of the gun'. In this way, the united front and its end are rationalised as following a historical 'logic'. The attack by Chiang, however, forced the CCP to change tactics: now they would rather take the cities by attacking from the countryside. In Mao's words to foreigners (in fact, to Edgar Snow, 1905–72): it was the GMD's aggression that 'forced' the originally peaceful CCP, including 'elementary school teachers' like himself, to take up arms. Therefore, they created their first Soviet Republic in a far-away corner of China in Jinggangshan 井冈山. (The narrative here is typically Mao-centred.) With the Zunyi 遵义 Conference 1935, Mao was arguably installed as leader, and the Long March then ended in Yan'an 延安, which attracted many idealists all over the country. (All these moves are shown as extending red arrows on a map.) These intellectuals were often not outright communists yet, but only in the CCP – the commentary emphatically states – did they perceive any hope for China's rise, thus explaining the attractiveness of communism to a broad range of people committed to the Chinese nation.

This 'hope' is then contrasted with 'realities' in the GMD urban context, which ignored the 'peasant problem'. The GMD levied thousands in taxes, exploited the populace, and created a monopoly in the economy and politics. In the global context, whereas the West went through Black Friday and the stock market depression, the Soviet Union set upon her spectacular economic rise. (Again, shots from *Daguo jueqi* are reused here.) But then World War II broke out. And in China, the Japanese had already started their aggression in 1931 with their invasion of Manchuria. In spite of Japanese aggression, however, the commentary complains, the GMD concentrated rather on fighting the Communists. The CCP, in turn, wanted to fight the Japanese as the 'common enemy', and thus it proposed another united front. But only after the CCP 'solved' (!) the Xi'an Incident in

1936 so as to guarantee peacefully the life of Chiang Kai-shek, who had been kidnapped by his own generals in exchange for his agreement to re-establish a united front, was the GMD finally recruited into the ranks of anti-Japanese resistance. Of course, the narrative stresses in a deliberate but common distortion of facts, that the 'main' contribution to anti-Japanese resistance remained with the CCP. As a nation, China could proudly claim that most of the Japanese losses in World War II were on her territory, but China, in turn, paid a high blood toll with more than ten times the losses of the Japanese! (Here, the figures are blended in for some seconds to accentuate them. However, even though this whole section on the 1930s and 1940s is very much conventional PRC historiography, one may note that – as in *Daguo jueqi* – the anti-Japanese war is dealt with surprisingly briefly and, again, the Nanking Massacre is not even mentioned!)

When the Japanese surrendered in 1945, this was, according to the commentary, the 'first complete victory of China'! In consequence, Taiwan came 'back' after half a century of Japanese colonisation, and China's international image rose. Historian Bu Ping 步平 concludes from this period that it was clearly the CCP that was finally able to unite the 'loose sand' (a stock phrase) of the Chinese people by guiding it through the anti-Japanese war, i.e. forged China into a nation worth its name.

However, the commentary cautions, major trouble was still ahead in the post-war scenario with the world split into two camps: the Soviet- and the US-led one. Although the GMD and CCP struck a deal in 1945 to stop infighting, the GMD was not ready in the end to give up her claims to monopoly and one party dictatorship – an ironic criticism seen from today's perspective. When even the consultative conference of 1946 to bind together the different political camps failed, the GMD's moves to 'provoke' civil war finally made the latter inevitable. In spite of the overpowering number of GMD troops, the CCP won. One of the decisive reasons for GMD failure is seen in the corruption and financial mismanagement that was advantageous only to people from the rich coastal areas. According to Western interviewee Ezra F. Vogel, the Communists are acknowledged to have been 'wise' instead by maintaining a high level of 'morals'. Even GMD high officials, the commentary claims, warned Chiang Kai-shek that he should change policies, but their advice went unheard. When Chiang wrote his book *China's Destiny* as a kind of political statement, he only wanted to push through with dictatorship and argued for one party, one ideology, and one leader – ironically exactly what the Communists would later realise. But this, the commentary argues, left many people dissatisfied. In accordance with Chinese textbooks, the writer Wen Yiduo 闻一多 (1899–46) is referred to as an example who tried to hold up May Fourth legacies against Chiang's dictatorial claims, and was consequently murdered on the latter's orders. Japanese China expert Mōri Kazuko 毛里和子 adds to this that people very much longed for democracy at the time, but any 'third way' was simply impossible. Thus, the only alternative to Chiang was Mao's CCP and its 'new democracy', which was based on Mao's thoughts canonised in 1945. (As a contrast to Chiang's book, Mao's various writings are shown, thus profiling both also visually as 'thinkers' as well as politicians.) Mao's thought, it is argued, had gone through a 'ripening process' in the Yan'an years through theoretical and empirical tests – in contrast to Chiang's. (In this context, the plurality of leading CCP figures is also shown: but for Mao himself, most prominently Zhu De 朱德 (1886–1976), Liu Shaoqi 刘少奇 (1898–1969), and Zhou Enlai 周恩来 (1898–1976), thus marking them as a leading 'generation'. In this way, the narrative takes a careful step back from a purely Mao-centred narrative – to suggest contrast with the 'one-man show' of Chiang in the GMD.) Notably, however, the presentation of land law implementation at Yan'an visually integrates peasant attacks on landlords, thus cautiously hinting at violence in this context, though not making it explicit in the commentary.

In sum, as China historian Hans Van de Ven evaluates the two competitors' performance, Chiang had lost the contest mainly in terms his of future vision, that is to say on an ideological level, since he provided nothing in this regard (whereas Mao had 'developed' and 'tested' his thoughts, as shown). The military defeat was only to be expected. (Again, casualty figures on the battles are provided. Notably, the viewer can deduce from them that more Chinese GMD troops were killed in the civil war than Japanese in China during the whole World War II!) In short, the people's opposition to Chiang and his military defeat together brought about an end to Chiang's rule over the mainland. To render his defeat more tragic, Chiang is even cited in a moment of self-criticism: 'we failed mainly because of ourselves'. (This statement of his, however, was less personally intended than the context here suggests – but it is often used in China to insinuate that Chiang finally realised his enemy's 'superiority'.)

In early 1949 a new consultative conference was set up, this time by the CCP (suggesting that the Communist Party was open to dialogue – in contrast with the GMD earlier), including Sun Yat-sen's widow Song Qingling 宋庆龄 (1893–1981); and also 'middle-of-the-roaders' were positive, thus demonstrating that the CCP reign was 'accepted' by a broad range of people. Mao's famous words, spoken at that conference, are repeated in his original voice: 'A quarter of mankind has now stood up.' And American China historian Jonathan Spence acknowledges that all this was achieved by great sacrifice, but claims that it was also a rich experience for mankind – again 'sustaining' as a 'foreign expert' the commentary's conclusions. With the inauguration ceremony of the People's Republic, this victory is declared as an outcome of the peculiar combination of China and Marxism. Again, Mao's famous words at that ceremony are presented in his original voice: 'The People's Republic of China and the Central People's Government are established today!'

With this triumph, the final part flashes backward to the Tian'anmen (linking back to the initial pictures of this instalment), which had seen the Boxers, May Fourth, and now the inauguration of the PRC. It also reviews the sacrifices made to achieve this final 'solution' to China's fate: the heroes of the anti-Japanese resistance, and of the civil war, and so on, ending with a picture of the revolutionary martyrs' stele to commemorate these sacrifices, which the consultative conference decided would be built the day before the PRC's inauguration ceremony was held. Mao personally penned the famous eulogy that was later inscribed on that stele to honour the contribution of these martyrs, without whom there would not have been a 'new China'.[29]

Clearly, this instalment represents a key juncture in the whole documentary, as it is the one to demonstrate the legitimacy of the CCP's rule, the Party being the 'true liberator' of China (being the obvious answer to the question raised at the end of the first instalment). Therefore, this instalment's narrative is especially close to conventional authoritative historical reading. What is special about it, however, is the fact that foreign experts' comments are employed repeatedly here to suggest to the Chinese audience that even foreigners 'share' this historical interpretation of the 'necessary' outcome of Communist rule. (This, obviously, is not to say that such a view fairly represents those experts, whose interview clippings have been used here as a legitimisation device.) In this way, developments in China are transmitted here in a fairly 'conventional' PRC way in terms of content, but in a more 'globalised' fashion in terms of presentation.

China's new birth (Zhongguo xinsheng 中国新生)

With the next instalment, the documentary now moves into China's Communist era. The first of October 1949 meant a completely new beginning for China, as the introduction underlines. One thing had already been achieved by this date: China had become a 'liberated' sovereign country. Now the main task was to regain honour and strength and create a better life for the populace. For the latter, the decisive achievement was to block the horrendous inflation of GMD times and to embark upon land reform.

When the Communists took over, there was no functioning railway system. The average wage was just two-thirds of the average in Asia and many people starved. In other words, the problems the CCP faced were the ones inherited from GMD mismanagement. And to these problems came those created by Cold War politics. This was the daunting task for the 'first generation of leaders around Mao' – notably toning down Mao's role here by the standard formulation of 'leading generations' of today, which from now on also form the basis on which the documentary's instalments are structured.

The storyline quite tellingly sets in with communist economic achievements, which are obviously seen as the major legitimisation for communist rule from an early twenty-first-century perspective: in 1953, the Chinese produced their own steel for the first time – exemplifying the symbolic role of heavy industry in communist 'success'. (The calm and relaxed music cues the viewer into feeling at ease with the new system.) But social reorganisation followed suit as well. Although Mao had realised already in Yan'an that light industry was also important for people's well-being, the global context in the early 1950s with the Cold War (illustrated by barbed wire and the building of the wall with a reference to Germany, but also with atomic explosions) was necessarily leading to a primary focus on heavy industry. As Harvard China historian William Kirby points out, China had been isolated by the US and thus had no access to foreign markets. Therefore, the topic of Sino–Soviet cooperation is introduced, climaxing in Mao's first visit to the Soviet Union. As a Chinese interviewee stresses, the Sino–Soviet Treaty of Friendship (1950) was extremely important for the internationally isolated PRC at the time. However, the Korean War (1950–3) then 'broke out' (typically, it was not mentioned that the communist North started it). The US quickly provided a guarantee for Taiwan, thus blocking easy Chinese reunification. The contribution of Chinese volunteers to the Korean War is emphasised (skipping over the disastrous results for them and accompanied by war songs of the time). Because of the 'victory' in the Korean War, China finally received international notice, and now experienced a period of domestic peace that allowed for development. The 'bad' role of the US in the war is even acknowledged by American Joseph Nye, formerly linked to the Clinton Administration and interviewed in *Daguo jueqi*, stating that in rolling back the North's attack it had been a mistake for the South Koreans together with the UN/US to cross the 38th parallel now from their side. (Nye is the first non-China specialist to appear in *Fuxing zhi lu* as an interviewee. Very probably this interview section was taken out of the interview done for *Daguo jueqi*.) That the Communist 'victory' in the Korean War, i.e. the re-establishment of the demarcation line, had been effectively achieved 'by China' whose steel output was one hundred and fortieth of US output, is not only seen as heroic but also as attributable to the socialist model of the Soviet Union. Arguably, the latter had achieved industrialisation so quickly mainly because of her planning system. It was therefore natural, as Shanghai-based Cold War historian Shen Zhihua 沈志华 argues (whom we will encounter again in Chapter 4), that China modelled herself on this example. Soviet economic help (showing Chinese workers, who eagerly learned from Soviet advisors) was very much appreciated in the early to mid-1950s, and the five-year plan model worked well in China, too. According to Harvard economist and China specialist John Quelch, for China this type of economy was 'fitting' at the time. And China, in fact, developed very quickly with many kinds of industries.

In the countryside, in turn, according to the narrative, the peasants themselves started the move toward greater collectivisation. Mao only 'picked it up' from the masses and realised it would fit the whole country – thus he shifted the responsibility for these measures to the people (as if it had not been state policies decreed from above). In 1952 the 'volunteer' collectivisation gained momentum in agriculture, to be followed by handicrafts and industry. British China expert Peter Nolan is also cited in support of the point that economic policies in the early 1950s (and late 1970s) were 'fitting' Chinese realities. Thus, it seems only logical that people dedicated themselves to work, as famous model steel worker Li Shaokui 李绍奎 (a Chinese version of Soviet miner Stakhanov introduced in *Daguo jueqi*'s instalment on the Soviet Union) is to illustrate. (This kind of praise for model workers comes across in the documentary as fairly old-fashioned.) Now, the intimation goes, the Chinese people are their own sovereign and are consequently motivated to work hard for their own benefit as a nation. The new 'sovereign status' is also expressed with the 'first broad elections in history' in 1953, for the National People's Congress, and the establishment of autonomous regions for minorities arguably demonstrated 'equal treatment' to ethnic plurality in the PRC. This point is underlined by the story of an Uyghur peasant (presumably because the Uyghurs are one of the most 'troublesome' minorities in China), who had been a slave but now had his own land to till. Out of gratitude the old man rode the whole way to Beijing from Xinjiang on his mule to thank Mao! As a friend of his recalls, the old man was a 'model worker', who finally made it to represent Xinjiang in the National People's Congress and managed to get a tractor for his village from Mao. In gratitude, a song was written which became very popular: *Salam Mao*. To the 'happy minorities', some foreigners who supported the young PRC are added: the Polish couple called Epstein, for example, declared how impressed they were to see that in China all 'struggled for one goal'. In sum, the presentation here is fairly unmitigated conventional PRC propaganda to suggest the 'Golden 1950s' in China, again including 'positive' foreigners' comments to sustain this.

Enthusiasm and euphoria are thus presented as the background to the economic achievements of the 1950s with their impressive first five-year plan, which set up heavy industry, producing mostly tractors and jet fighters, but also dams for hydroelectricity, steel and huge bridges, and thus going far beyond everything the 'old China' had achieved in the preceding 100 years. All planned objectives were exceeded, and socialist reconstruction was well under way. In 1956 Mao thus proudly declared that one should not simply copy the Soviet Union, which was too centralist, but should develop one's own way. By this, China's new self-consciousness is underlined.

As a Chinese expert evaluates the situation back then, the 'former class struggle' was now superseded by the people's growing demands for material well-being, which led to a forced policy of industrialisation, i.e. the Great Leap Forward (which is obviously a somewhat curious economic-'consumerist' argument for the clearly ideologically driven Great Leap). In 1957, Mao therefore forwarded his new theory of contradictions. In view of the pride and motivation that had grown out of the successes, new visions were now developed, which however went too far, being 'too enthusiastic' and too irrational, the commentary cautiously argues, in line with standard textbook wording. But this is immediately explained as something 'common' in the socialist camp at the time. Since the Soviet Union under Khrushchev (1894–1971) had declared that she wanted to catch up with the US, Mao, during his second visit to the Soviet Union (for the fortieth anniversary celebrations of the October Revolution, 1957), simply stuck to this line by arguing that China would similarly try to catch up with the UK – ironically in this way arguing for the Soviet Union, which objected to the Great Leap Forward (!), to have been responsible for this type of thinking.[30] US economist Stiglitz (again no China specialist and already an interviewee in *Daguo jueqi* but – judging from the filmed background – probably interviewed this time in China) is cited stating that this was simply too quick and too idealistic a movement for industrialisation. In agriculture, in turn, collectivisation was also speeded up to culminate in the People's Communes in too short a time. This 'confusion' in the economic system together with natural disasters, it is explained, made for the fact that grain production in 1960 fell back again to 1951 levels (thus circumnavigating the need to address the Great Famine that this entailed). The treatment of the Anti-Rightist Movement of 1957 is very elliptical as well: some rightists 'used' the occasion of the rectification campaign in the party to criticise the system itself, but the Anti-Rightist Movement was admittedly taken too far to check these criticisms. For example, the noted Chinese expert on population growth who advocated birth control (practised today) was at the time unjustly accused of aiming at China's dying out. Therefore, the strategy of presenting this whole period of 'problems' around the Anti-Rightist Campaign and the Great Leap Forward is basically to show that it grew mainly out of exaggerated enthusiasm only: deplorable for sure, but somehow understandable.

Adding to these 'incorrect' developments, the Soviet Union withdrew her experts 'out of the blue' in 1960. (Here, threatening music taken over from *Daguo jueqi* is used which, however, is here connected to 'external threat' only – Chinese 'crises' are significantly not marked as 'threatening' by audio cues!) China was thus suddenly 'deprived' of any foreign support and hampered in her development. On the other hand, also in the 1960s, China's neighbour Japan started her quick development (reusing again shots from *Daguo jueqi*, explaining why China now lagged behind so much). Adding to this, China lived through 'three years of natural calamities' – which is all that is said about what is probably the biggest famine in human history – to then move quickly on to economic 'recovery' between 1962 and 1965. This however did not last long, because 'some' people monopolised power, and Mao committed another 'grave error', fearing the recapitalisation of China which led to the Cultural Revolution. This was, the commentary argues, a 'wrong movement' used by Lin Biao (1907–71) and the 'Gang of Four' for their schemes, and it made China lag behind in economic, political, and scientific development. (The tragedy is expressed visually by zooming in on individuals looking into the camera with big questioning or sad eyes.) One example of these 'wrong' extremist positions is given in a village that had tried to motivate pupils assigned to help tearing out weeds by offering money, which was heavily criticised as 'destroying the souls' of these kids by such monetary incentives. A cadre is cited with the drastic remark that whoever channelled urine onto the ground of the collective was considered socialist, whoever did so onto private ground was considered a capitalist roader. By this, the whole period of the Cultural Revolution is presented as tragic and in any ideological respect as absurd.

With the party resolution of 1981 the whole period is officially summed up as a 'tragedy', but understandable at least as an outcome of searching for one's own way. Therefore, basically the history of the PRC up to then was still a success story ('too much enthusiasm'), not the least since during the time of the Cultural Revolution China nevertheless succeeded with the diplomatic coup of striking a deal with the US, that would prepare for China's getting out of her international isolation finally. Harvard expert in international relations, Akira Iriye, quite soberly notes Mao's realisation that he would not be able to stick to his Cultural Revolution while confronting both superpowers, the US and the Soviet Union, at the same time. The background to this diplomatic coup is presented with the meeting of Mao and his one-time US admirer, leftist journalist Edgar Snow, the ensuing ping-pong diplomacy and finally Kissinger and Nixon's (1913–94) visits to China. With the US opening up the international space, other Western countries were quick to establish relations with China, which greatly helped the latter after the Cultural Revolution. As Chinese scholar of international relations Wang Jisi 王缉思, an important figure sustaining the earlier *Daguo jueqi* documentary, remarks: from the viewpoint of the US, the Cultural Revolution was not really shocking, since China nevertheless presented the image of a fairly stable political entity to the outer world. Therefore, even during the Cultural Revolution, the seat for 'China' went finally to the PRC (in a way suggesting that the Cultural Revolution was in the end an internal problem of which foreigners were largely unaware at the time). Even Deng Xiaoping (who had his own difficulties during the Cultural Revolution) later remarked: we have to thank Mao for now being able to set upon the 'four modernisations'. Thus even the 'tragic' Cultural Revolution can be considered a stepping-stone on China's way up.

In fact, as the narration sums up, Mao's time produced several 'modernisation achievements', enumerating the atomic bomb (!), satellites, and computers, accompanied by photos of scientists and model workers. In short, the achievements of the Mao era lay in having provided China with the basics of national sovereignty, the political system under CCP leadership, a 'solution' to the minority question, industrialisation, and scientific progress. In view of this one should acknowledge that nobody can move out of his times, and some choices could be evaluated 'properly' only in hindsight – by this intending the 'problematic' sides of Mao-time China. The basic question since 1949, however, has remained the same all the way through: how to construct a socialist state. For tackling this, says the conclusion, the country needed another great leader to move China ahead.[31]

The great turn (Weida zhuanzhe 伟大转折)

This next leader is introduced by zooming in on a place where in 2007 (at the time of filming) preparations for the mega-event of the 2008 Beijing Olympics was underway: the Workers' Stadium. Thirty years earlier, a man who had vanished for two years was spotted there by the public during a soccer game: Deng Xiaoping. Foreign news reports of the time are cited describing the enthusiasm with which he was greeted by the audience, a US report ominously predicting his great future role in the Chinese economy. In fact, the preceding 10 years, i.e. the duration of the Cultural Revolution, had been largely a time of 'little advance', making for a widening gap between China and the surrounding developing countries, whether Japan or the 'four dragons' (which are not identified here more precisely).[32] It would therefore be Deng who changed China for the better (accompanied by romantic music), as the foreign press at the time had already prophesied.

After this introduction, the storyline sets in with 1976, immediately after Mao's death, with Hua Guofeng 华国锋 (1921–2008) (who notably is not even named but referred to only indirectly by the slogan of the 'two whatevers' he is associated with).[33] The question was whether to continue the Cultural Revolution policy as

Hua advocated, or to change course, as Deng wanted to. In 1977, Deng reinstated university exams and thereby gave academics a new breathing space in tandem with his counter-moves against the sanctifying dead Mao as Hua intended. Deng thus put forward the 'test of practice' motto in order to challenge Hua. Finally in 1978 Deng promoted reform openly (emphasised in the documentary by the use of his own voice). This speech laid the foundation for the opening-up and reform policy of the coming years – and side-lined Hua and his likes for good. He set up special economic zones as a testing ground, provoking Singapore's Lee Kwan Yew (who was to become a model for China with his authoritarian modernisation approach) to remark that the door Deng had opened could not be shut again. (Thus again, foreigners' comments on China are used as a legitimisation device.) Deng also visited the US, establishing the formal link between the two countries and thus bringing China visibly back onto the world's diplomatic stage. China now developed in the internationally changing context, with the US, the UK and Japan pushing their economies forward, Europe integrating economically and financially more and more, and on the other hand the Soviet Union struggling with ever greater economic problems, marking the 'threatening' alternative. Consequently, in 1982 the basic directions of the reforms were sketched out under Deng's label (again in his original voice) of 'socialism with Chinese characteristics', and the constitution was adapted. As an interviewed high cadre stresses, this was momentous, since the Cultural Revolution had destroyed all belief in law. Now the 'errors' of the Cultural Revolution were finally repaired, but still the whole process was not without problems, as the example of successful new entrepreneurs demonstrates. They were denounced as 'speculators' and thrown in jail by local cadres, until the party intervened to clarify the point that private accumulation of capital was now legal, and to 'save' and rehabilitate the entrepreneurs. (By this, internal party opposition to Deng's course is indirectly acknowledged.)

Deng even had to go to Shenzhen, one of the special economic zones, to encourage people to 'change their thoughts' while facing the opposition of some who still maintained that all this was simply capitalism. Deng, however, argued one 'never went back the same road', and Shenzhen's success demonstrated the 'correctness' of his economic policy. He even provoked his opponents by stating famously, as cited by interviewee Zheng Yongnian (teaching in Nottingham who had already been interviewed for *Daguo jueqi*), that to be socialist does not mean to be poor! A Japanese expert adds matter-of-factly that what Deng did was simply to experiment. However, these experiments also cost other segments in the economy dearly, namely the state enterprises that were not able to adapt to the market even though they had been an important instrument in earlier phases of the PRC's economy. By giving them more space and responsibility, they had a chance to modernise, and in case they went bankrupt (which often happened), this would now be regulated by insolvency law.

But the separation of politics and state enterprises was not yet complete. In 1984 the appraisal of goods markets as part of socialism was the next step towards a 'socialist market economy', and Deng himself admitted that what he proposed could be seen as 'heterodox'. Nevertheless, he went ahead, step by step, and new lifestyles followed suit.

The success in economics that this entailed is underlined by the success of some of China's new enterprises in taking over big shares of the market in competition with foreign firms. Outstanding among these was Lenovo, which snatched a huge market share away from IBM! In sum, China now turned into a global player. By 1986, with Feile Acoustics, China's first share issue was recorded at Wall Street (again reusing shots from *Daguo jueqi* in this context). John Phelan, head of the New York stock exchange, to whom Deng offered the first share, was reportedly enthusiastic to become the first foreign shareholder of a socialist enterprise!

In China as well, a stock market was established, though there were big problems in changing state enterprises into companies fit for the stock exchange. And nobody knew whether this would help privatisation and investment or would further social unrest. Nevertheless, the Shanghai stock exchange opened in 1986 with just two companies participating. (As a blended-in comment stresses, in the meantime numbers have grown substantially to 1,500. Such blended-in 'success stories' come up now more frequently, stepping up the 'didactic' flavour of the documentary.)

Outside of the economy, the second half of the 1980s also induced a spiritual 'reconstruction' – though the narrative keeps remarkably silent as to what that meant in practice. In any case, economy remained central, which was again the focus of the 1987 party congress. The goal was now set to achieve 'modernisation' by the middle of the twenty-first century. In order to adjust the ideology, 'leftist errors' were corrected by the new definition that China in fact was only in the 'beginning stadium of socialism'.

However, not everybody was satisfied with the reforms. For example, some social problems emerged along with price instability and the gap between set prices and market prices, which some used smartly to their personal benefit in order to deprive others. (Notably, the audio part changes during this section to disquieting sounds, underlining the critical state China was in at the time.) This unrest is implicitly connected to the public discontent of 1989, which is only hinted at. The 'political waves' of May/June 1989 were created by 'minor' internal but 'major' external influences, as the narrative only vaguely states, jumping then to the global scale, with blended-in comments listing quickly the changes in Eastern Europe, German reunification, and the Soviet Union's crumble without much further elaboration As a Chinese expert on Eastern Europe explains, some in the West assumed that also China would fall like the other socialist states in a big game of dominos. But Deng was convinced that Marxism was all but outdated for China, and therefore he declared it as a supreme goal to not get off track. (This, obviously, is to render comprehensible his heavy-handed dealing with the students' protest in 1989 as an action in defence of the Deng-style reform policies. A peaceful Tian'anmen Square is shown by night, cueing viewers to the conclusion that only this reaction to the crisis guaranteed peace in the end.)

On his Southern Tour in 1992, to which the narrative quickly turns, Deng visibly promoted his enduring economic reform policies, also arguing that if now 'discussions' set in, then nothing would be achieved but only time lost – thus again defending implicitly his forceful suppression of the students' protests. Using his original voice, his defence is underscored: there was no alternative to the way he stood for. The market concept was for him compatible with socialism, arguing that all socialism wanted was to set free the forces of productivity without exploitation. In short, as US China expert Stanley Rosen sums up this period under Deng Xiaoping, the years 1978 and 1992 were similarly key points for China's reforms (and hence 1989 is not a 'crucial date').

All in all, Deng's theories are presented as decisive for China. Where Sun Yat-sen had shown the way to fight imperialism and feudalism, and Mao had built up a new state, it was Deng who saved socialism (in spite of the Soviet crumble) by showing a way to become wealthy and strong through it![34]

Bridging the centuries (Shiji kuayue 世纪跨越)

At the close of the twentieth century, the introduction to the next instalment points out, the situation looked like this: a revolution in information technology was fully underway, global scientific progress had made leaps and Chinese society had changed very fast as well. At this historical juncture, it was Jiang Zemin 江泽民 (elected in the momentous June of 1989 as new general secretary) who led China's socialist market economy – which would, the commentary proudly states, stun the world and profoundly change the country. As Jiang declared at the official starting shot of the 'socialist market economy' in 1992 (again with original voice put in), establishing the 'correct' relation between the market and socialism was to be the key issue. He wanted to demonstrate not only that socialism was compatible with the market, but that it was actually the superior solution. In other words, economic performance should legitimise CCP rule, now that Communism was dissolving internationally.

The narrative quite tellingly starts with Pudong in Shanghai in 1992. (This skips over Jiang's first years as general secretary, leaving the 'problematic' time of 1989–92 to Deng's period of the previous instalment, which by taking the Southern Tour of 1992 as a turning point and as a break between instalments could end also on an upbeat note!) Pudong was to grow out of plain fields into a new financial centre. (In this way, Jiang, who is associated closely with Shanghai, is also 'positively' introduced as the 'reformer' who set Shanghai's spectacular rebirth since the 1990s on track.) And all over China, new enterprises were created (all identified with their outstanding 'creators', thus honouring entrepreneurs, who were now increasingly courted by Jiang), from steel production to new charter airplane companies to laser typesetting which also made Chinese characters compatible with the revolution in information technologies. 'Made in China' was now becoming a more and more attractive label globally, motivating also international big companies like Motorola to set up plants in China. In tandem, China's stock market exploded, leading to feverish activity at Shenzhen's stock exchange, which was established in 1992 and open to all. However, this entire buzz had also its drawbacks: inflation and overheating of the economy. Politics reacted, but now with economic and legal means (which is to show that finally China had changed her methods for dealing with crises to more 'modern' measures). And these measures made for a slowing down of inflation without hampering economic growth. As a – fairly explicit – Japanese expert soberly argues: politics simply had to follow the market.

But there were the losers as well, namely those working in the now inefficient state enterprises who were laid off. (Notably, no threatening music is accompanies the topic as with pre-socialist 'crises' or with crises in 'capitalist' countries such as in the documentary *Daguo jueqi*.) In common with those in the West, Chinese experts state, the main challenge was how to keep people on board with all these changes. The government tried to ease tensions by offering training for those laid off to learn new skills in order to find new jobs. (Thus, the 'sacrifice' of those laid off is acknowledged, but it is stressed as well that the government cared for them.) And restructuring was not done all at one stroke; however, this also wrought problems for the new entrepreneurs, who still had to put up with various restrictions. As one of them illustrates, his company went back and forth between collective and private ownership, depending on current tax regulations, which were usually in favour of collective ownership. Administrative problems also led to reorganisation of private ventures as state-connected ones at times because successful private enterprises were often 'sucked up' by local administration, thus hinting at corruption, though only on the 'lower level' of bureaucracy. Basically, the state was more concerned with the future of state-owned enterprises and only left space to the private ones without yet giving them much protection. However, China definitely had become richer in the meantime. Thus, when Deng Xiaoping, the architect of China's opening and reform policy, died in 1997, even the UN set her flags to mourning, as the commentary underlines; and in China, Jiang Zemin (again in original voice) recalled the importance of Deng for the progress that China had made in the meantime. Consequently, the party honoured him by writing his 'theories' into the party guidelines. Because of the earlier acknowledged definition of China's being only in the 'beginning stadium of socialism', now private enterprise could be claimed as also an ideologically acceptable part of the economy. Also, in the legal field, the slogan 'rule by law' was promoted.

In this context, the first village elections in 1997 were introduced (to parallel 'socialist market economy' with 'socialist democratisation'). Even in the cities, some local committees were now elected. However, in order to further people's participation, education was essential (visually integrating minority education), and thus education was to become a political focus, namely 'quality education'. When looking at where China was in 1997 (i.e. at Deng's death), she could claim to be number ten of the world's biggest trading countries and on the cusp of creating a middle-class wealthy society (an aim Deng had set out in the early reform years before the turn of the century). In this context, Hong Kong 'returned' to the 'motherland', and Macao soon after in 1999, as two major events profiling Jiang Zemin's era.

Even the Asian financial crisis of the same year, 1997, could not profoundly influence China's way to global importance; rather its efficient crisis management

earned her international respect. As a Chinese financial expert argues, the speculation which led to that crisis had been undertaken fully intentionally, and China
expert Peter Nolan from Cambridge adds that China was more concerned than
many noted. In fact, when Jiang Zemin went to the ASEAN summit, many feared
he might devalue the Chinese currency, but he did not, stating that China would
not add to the difficulties of her neighbours by such a measure. In sum, as China
expert Tim Wright from Sheffield acknowledges, China proved to be responsible
in dealing with the crisis.

The following year, 1998, again entailed many difficulties for China, this time
with several instances of huge flooding in the Yangzi region. But Jiang was able
to deal effectively with this natural crisis (presenting him once more with original
voice). This was also an occasion for the PLA to prove herself anew a 'friend of
the people' by involvement in managing the crisis management, an image that
after the bloody suppression of the student protests of 1989 had been severely
damaged.

There were many new opportunities and challenges in these years, namely the
spread of the Internet, and the challenge of global economics (again accompanied
by shots from *Daguo jueqi*, showing some capitals of the Western world), which
China now took up in her renewed attempt to join the World Trade Organisation
(WTO). As a Chinese expert argues, integration in world economics had many
advantages, namely going with more transparency in politics and rules. It is,
however, stressed that the world did not make it easy for China to join, asking
more of her than of other countries with a comparable status of wealth! This, it is
admitted, was because other countries were doubtful of the concept of the 'socialist
market economy' and the relation between state planning and market forces. In
addition, inside China, the joining of the WTO met with mixed feelings, since
many were worried about the consequences for Chinese enterprises in an open
competitive field. Internationally, however, the US under Clinton was very much
in favour of China joining, and thus Clinton and Jiang build up a 'strategic part-
nership', which was an important background to the final successful integration of
China in the WTO. As a Chinese expert points out, China had made enormous
steps forward since the reform and opening-up policy in exports and imports, and
had built up a huge reserve of foreign currency. She thus could also risk joining,
as she did in 2001; and the importance of this highlight of Jiang's era was emphasised by dating the decision of acceptance to the minute!

With this important move to integrate internationally, China had now regained
international status, pride, and responsibility. According to former British foreign
secretary Geoffrey Howe, already interviewed for *Daguo jueqi*, China had always
behaved very cautiously in the UN, but now she felt more confident and became
more active. And Russian economist Vladimir Mau, also interviewed for *Daguo
jueqi* as well, states that China proved extremely successful, demonstrating that a
'leap' could also be possible for countries lagging behind – probably meaning that
China should be taken as a model by the Russians.

This new confidence even spread to those seen before as the main problems:
the state enterprises. They (as far as they had survived) had gained through

restructuring and now were actually competitive on the world market. A host of new economic laws was released following China's admission to the WTO. Thus, at the turn of the century, China felt very confident, and also this was aided by the decision in the same year of 2001 that she would host the Olympics in 2008.

Again, as in previous instalments, several 'heroes' of the time are briefly introduced visually; this time, however, they were not model workers but mainly model cadres, featured in order to show what outstanding people the CCP could provide. And this party now decided, in 2002, to open up to more societal groups with Jiang Zemin's 'legacy', the 'Three Represents', which are introduced again via original voice. Now, with this 'progressive Marxist theory', the party represented not only peasants, workers, and soldiers, but all 'progressive productive forces', 'progressive culture', and the 'broad interest of the people' (i.e. including also entrepreneurs, and so on). This again became part of the party's statutes and is basically seen as a development of what Deng Xiaoping had already laid out.

In sum, at the end of the twentieth century, China was firmly on her way to a 'revival', in marked contrast to the beginning of that century with the Boxer War and China's 'mistreatment' by the foreigners. Now she was sitting on an equal footing in world organisations, showing her in the de facto exclusive security council of the UN. This image of the 'great statesmen' with Jiang in their midst is then linked to one of the 'third generation of leadership around Jiang Zemin' to demonstrate that nationally leaders have also become more 'integrated' (making for a shift from the largely 'one-man-centred' periods of Mao and Deng to collective leadership). Thus, the instalment ends on the positive note that China had finally regained her status in the world, and could set upon her revival in the twenty-first century, handing the torch from Jiang Zemin to his successor.[35]

Continue on the past to open up the future (Ji wang kai lai 继往开来)

The final part of the documentary now sets out to describe how the aim of a revival of China is going to be reached. This era is the one of Hu Jintao 胡锦涛, who is introduced with original voice, making a speech as the new general secretary and president in March 2003. The great challenge he faces is how to guide the fastest growing economy and biggest developing country into the future.

The storyline tellingly sets in with Hu Jintao visiting Xibaipo 西柏坡, i.e. the place from where Mao moved into Beijing to take up the leadership in China in 1949 (which might now indicate preparation for China's taking over the global lead by extension). The audience is reminded that Mao back then had stressed there that the Communists should not become overbearing, now that they were going to take over, and they should not lose their fighting spirit. (In this context, the commentary notably uses the expression *ju an si wei* 居安思危 (thinking of danger while dwelling in safety) which is also the title of the documentary series on the collapse of the Soviet Communist Party addressed in Chapter 4.) As a high cadre explains, the 'spirit of Xibaipo' consisted of 'serving the people'. Thus, this motto is obviously to characterise the leadership of Hu Jintao and his circle (the latter being given even more prominence than with Jiang Zemin, by this continuously retreating from a one-man-centred perspective).

This 'service' was immediately needed during the first crisis Hu's government had to face: SARS, which not only cost many lives of young and middle-aged people, but also was also a test for Hu's governing abilities. (Again, audio cues are only very carefully employed to create a short atmosphere of anxiety.) Finally, in summer of 2003 the 'fight against SARS was won' – reminding one by this expression of the Mao era's 'war against nature' rhetoric. And on top of this medical 'victory', China could now also boast of the first 'taikonaut', thus challenging the Soviet/Russian and US dominance in outer space. The astronaut Yang Liwei 杨利伟 is consequently charged with this 'victory' rhetoric, and duly replied that he went to the space for the party and his motherland! In sum, the commentary argues, the first year of Hu's government was full of 'victories', but nevertheless China remained humble – in the spirit of Xibaipo.

The 'scientific' handling of politics – another key slogan of his – is then introduced by referring to the newly institutionalised 'political study sessions' (of which the documentary *Daguo jueqi* had been an outcome). Also, a Chinese expert adds that the enormous hidden power of China had, in fact, to be tightly (and 'scientifically') controlled so as to be released only step by step (to prevent unpleasant results). That this could be successfully managed by the CCP is 'proven' by US professor Brantly Womack who is cited saying that nobody else would have been able to achieve such successes with China!

This, it is proudly highlighted, was possible in spite of great continuing poverty, especially in Western China. Ecology and natural resources are referred to as big problems, which, according to American expert Lester Brown who had also been interviewed already for *Daguo jueqi*, cannot be solved any longer just by one country alone. Therefore, Hu Jintao gave out as a new directive the motto of 'scientific development', which (in his original voice) is combined with the concept of 'sustainability'.

China had managed to keep a balance, US economist Joseph Stiglitz acknowledges, and needed always to consider the whole situation at every move. Thus, Hu's 'scientific development' aimed at a holistic, balanced, and sustainable development, with man at its centre. Consequently, when Hu stopped 30 ecologically problematic projects in 2005 (not mentioning the highly disputed Three Gorges Dam), he elicited positive reactions from Western countries. 'Scientific development' was also written into the five-year plan of 2006, in which eight out of 22 aims concerned resources and ecology.

But development of the poor West of China is definitely on the agenda, as the following is supposed to show. Whereas a noted American traveller had declared in the 1980s there would never be a train to Lhasa, in fact, the commentary proudly declares, that train was now running. Curiously, however, it is presented only as 'bringing advantages to the nomads'! (Given the sensitivity of the Tibet issue, the military advantages of the railway to Tibet are bound to be left out. However, the nomads, happy about better market access, are unwittingly comical. As an example, the documentary shows a small Tibetan factory producing walnut oil, which is now able to serve markets farther away.) With this railway, China even built the 'highest train tracks on earth', and thus started economic development for the Western regions as well, also constructing roads and airports there to improve infrastructure.

For profiling the 'balanced' policies on Hu's agenda further, the commentary points out that developmental focus is planned to shift also to the Northeast and other areas. For example, since 2006, in Tianjin a whole new area is already under construction. One region after another will be given special attention. And this will then build into the new 'harmonious society' – a motto that has been intensively discussed since 2005. This concept calls for the construction of a 'socialist economy, politics, culture and society'. As China expert from Britain, William Callahan, argues, this 'harmonious society' was, in fact, a very 'Chinese' idea, and a Chinese interviewee adds that it is designed to combine fast development with social welfare. The official explanation, in fact, is given in a deliberately Confucian-sounding fashion: to provide all Chinese with education, paid work, welfare for the sick and the old, and a home to live in.

As a concrete example of these new policies, the situation of migrant workers is addressed, for whom there would now be state allowances for tuition fees, assurances, medical help, and so on. The main issue, however, remains the peasants. For them, the grain tax was abolished. This step is praised as momentous because in 2006, for the first time in 2,600 years (!), peasants would not pay any more tax on grain. This memorable fact is illustrated by a peasant who made a *ding* 鼎 (an ancient Chinese sacrificial tripod), with an inscription that this had never happened under any dynasty in Chinese history – thus giving credit to this policy in a very pronouncedly traditionalist fashion, suggesting that the CCP is just another 'dynasty'!

In industrial production, 'made in China' is now a globally acknowledged label, but also domestically Chinese families enjoy it and live much better than they ever did before. This is illustrated by an old couple in Shanghai, who had noted down day after day their expenditures since 1957 – this again serves to underline the CCP's legitimacy to rule by the economic success it stood for. Whereas in 1977 (after the Cultural Revolution) the couple could afford a TV for the first time, ten years later by 1987 they could buy a fridge and a washing machine. In 1990 they did their first travelling, in 1994 they had their own telephone; in 1997 followed air conditioning; and in 2003 new furniture. By 2005 they bought various articles for improving health, in 2006 they financed the driving licence of their granddaughter and in 2007 they paid for her marriage. In short, the couple stated that day by day things visibly got better.

This is to illustrate that a middle-class wealthy society – a goal formulated already by Deng Xiaoping – now exists for many. To guarantee it for all, there needs to be a 'socialist legal system', the commentary argues. And thus, in 2007 (during the time the documentary was produced), the new property law was finally released. Since this law generated quite some discussion because of its explicit sanctioning of private ownership in an officially socialist country, a Chinese expert is cited who refers to an ancient proverb to the avail that people need security of property before they will do anything. American China specialist David Lampton sustains this by adding that nobody would want to invest if property were not legally protected. Thus, in the context of more law-based governance, the constitution now had to be amended, and property as well as 'human rights' guaranteed by the constitution. (Here, obviously, this recent major change in politics is defended in the documentary, again enlisting foreigners' argumentative 'help'.)

Furthermore, Hu Jintao encouraged scientific progress also by awarding various prizes for innovations. Such policies to push innovations led, for example, to a producer of special chips, 'CMOS chips', achieving a 70 per cent global share in this market segment. In the ensuing 15 years, it is assumed, China will grow from the biggest producing country into a globally important innovating country. The trend is illustrated in this instalment by a range of outstanding innovators, who take the place of the earlier model workers or cadres! By all this, Hu's agenda of eliciting innovative forces and guaranteeing them legal protection is promoted in the documentary.

In sum, whereas the Chinese Wall had expressed the earlier Chinese fears of what lay outside, now China has no need to fear anyone any longer, but invests her future in every single Chinese, the commentary emphatically argues. She is no longer the China of the government but the responsibility of every Chinese (which of course nicely fits with the patriotic education agenda). In a review of all those who had so far contributed to create present-day China – including the whole range presented in the earlier instalments, from the revolutionaries like Lin Juemin of Sun Yat-sen's 'Revolutionary Alliance' (see above), over 'model revolutionary' Lei Feng 雷锋 (1940–62) of Mao's time, to more recent 'heroes' – they are not only visually recalled, but they are named and enumerated to explicitly argue for the 'value system' that underpinned these successes, not forgetting to mention that without 'the people' all these heroes would, of course, have been nothing.

However, in order to grow from a global economic power into a global political great power (which is now finally revealed as the main aim this documentary's portrayal of modern Chinese history is going to serve), China has to base herself on culture; and this means 'classical' culture, as Harvard scholar Tu Wei-ming stresses – explaining, for example, the recent reappraisal (and political exploitation) of Confucianism. This value system has, it is argued, roots going back 5,000 years (!), and keeps the Chinese spirit up – which makes one wonder what the role of 'modern' socialism then might be. (As an audio background, famous young Chinese pianist Lang Lang 朗朗 is heard playing, insinuating that China has now also 'gone global' in terms of its culture.) Beijing University's most prestigious late Indologist and noted intellectual, Ji Xianlin 季羡林, sustains this argument for promoting culture in an interview, stating that a revival can be successful only when based on culture. Because, as the deputy minister of education adds, it is the value system that binds society together – to which end the enumeration of the earlier, though more recent, 'heroes' had also served.

This revival, however, is nothing to be feared, as the commentary cautiously points out with a view to the potential worries of other countries, since the Chinese have always been a 'peace-loving people' (arguably shown by their 'classical' culture). This thrust toward cooperation also in present times is also notably demonstrated by China's being host to a Chinese–African summit in 2006 commemorating 50 years of diplomatic relations between China and many African states, adding the remark that 'there were never that many leaders of state in China' at one time. (That the 'Africa strategy' is one of the priorities in Hu Jintao's foreign policy initiatives is not explicitly addressed but is, of course, in the background of this presentation.) In a style reminding one somewhat of the 1950s – when relations were established – the commentary claims that the president of South Africa wrote an enthusiastic article entitled 'I would have loved to be born on Beijing's Tian'anmen' to show China's 'attractiveness' to foreigners. Even experts from Japan (the great Asian 'rival') are cited as evaluating China's new global role and behaviour positively. The influential American International Relations scholar Joseph Nye, as well, acknowledges China's 'high soft power'. By this, Hu Jintao's record is also positively reflected upon in the aspect of values and culture as part of China's 'soft power' strategy.

Notably, the commentary argues – now with a view to the domestic audience – a revival will also need more 'socialist democracy', mentioning the existence of other parties (block parties) as well as local self-governing approaches. But in tandem with 'soft power', China – if needed – also now disposes of 'hard power' to 'defend peace' (showing the navy, the air force, and the army), an issue that was also raised when discussing what 'great power' means in *Daguo jueqi*. Consequently, China also needs a 'revolutionary', modern, and regular army to defend peace with a 'wall of steel'. This is the only reference, albeit a cautious one, to the military in the context of China's rise – and insinuates the Chinese viewer should feel assured that the government does not neglect that aspect either, just in case China's rise needs more 'hard defence'.

The party, in turn, has to remain ever 'creative' in the application of Marxism to the Chinese situation, the commentary warns, in order to stay in power and prevent corruption from within. That this 'creativeness' already works well is 'proved' not least by Hong Kong after ten years under Chinese rule – which is praised as a success story. And in this context, the 'not yet resolved reunification with Taiwan' is addressed unfailingly as the unfinished task (which, by insinuation, should be solved along Hong Kong model lines).

While the preparations for the 2008 Olympics are shown, the commentary assures the viewer that China has always moved ahead with the times. (In the DVD version finished in December 2007 Hu Jintao in his speech at the Seventeenth Party Congress was added, again with original voice; also added was the satellite that China sent into space in October 2007 after the TV series was broadcast for the first time.) In a kind of summary, the commentary concludes: China disposes of a glorious cultural heritage, has gone through hardships and now is going to rise. By having also experienced the flip side, she will, however, remain humble (the 'Xibaipo spirit'). On her way, she 'chose' Marxism, the CCP, and socialism. And only 'socialism with Chinese characteristics' can in fact hold together the diverse groups in society and provide them with one common ideal. In line with this obvious historical legitimisation function of the documentary for CCP rule, at the end the government's next political aims are proclaimed, which clearly mark this TV production as a 'political communication device'. Now the aim is set as to double GDP between 2000 and 2010, to triple it by 2020, the hundredth birthday of the CCP, and to be a mid-level developed country until the middle of the twenty-first century, the hundredth birthday of the PRC. All this, of course, will be only achieved 'under the guidance of the CCP', and only in this way will China have her revival. And, the commentary emphatically ends, this glory goes to socialism with Chinese characteristics and the Chinese people (returning visually to the stele of the revolutionary martyrs to remember those who have sacrificed themselves for this!).[36]

This whole last instalment of the documentary is clearly the most propaganda-like, using the occasion to communicate, explain, and market the policies and goals of Hu's government.

When considering the interviewees in this documentary in general, it is interesting to note that – but for the Chinese experts interviewed for *Daguo jueqi* – there is only a partial overlap, since, as already stated, foreigners presented as interviewees in *Daguo jueqi* usually had no connection with China, whereas foreigners presented as interviewees in *Fuxing zhi lu* were mostly China specialists. When considering the domestic interviewees, they were less purely 'academic', but included many high cadres, party school representatives, and some editors of official media, which goes well with our findings that the documentary is more openly 'political' than *Daguo jueqi*, with its primarily 'scientific' outlook. In terms of the audio part, *Fuxing zhi lu* is more text-centred than *Daguo jueqi* and thus comes with a heavily didactic flavour.

All in all, the documentary *Fuxing zhi lu* presents a view on modern Chinese history that is clearly in line with official narratives, serving as a legitimisation of CCP rule, and it is also used as an outlet for communicating current and envisaged future policies.

'Screening' China's 'revival'

The original TV documentary, aired in late 2007, was published shortly afterwards on DVD, together with a three-volume book series, which – as with *Daguo jueqi* – added some further information, illustrations and historical background to the script. This was all done by CCTV and published – as already mentioned – by the same publisher as the accompanying book series of *Daguo jueqi*: Zhongguo minzhu fazhi chubanshe 中国民主法制出版社, run by the National People's Congress (Zhao Buhui 2008). According to a SARFT article, the documentary was CCTV's first 'political piece' (*zhenglunpian* 政论片) to discuss the whole of modern Chinese history (Fuxing zhi lu *shang de dianshiren*; 14 January 2008).

CCTV itself also declared this documentary to be its first systematic programme on Chinese modern history. In an interview, Guo Zhenxi stated on the part of the producers, the difference between *Fuxing zhi lu* and *Daguo jueqi*, to which it was a 'sister piece', was that the content of *Fuxing zhi lu* was basically known to the audience. And now, following *Daguo jueqi*, was the 'ideal time' to discuss the 'revival of China'. In terms of emotions, Guo argued that the leading theme was 'anger' as to the period pre-1949, and then more 'mixed' feelings for the early PRC followed, and finally for the period post-1978 'excitement' abounds. When the interviewer asked why they did not start with China's 'great' times such as the Tang dynasty (618–906) or Genghis Khan (1162?–1227) but rather with the Opium War, Guo answered that they wanted to start precisely from the nadir, since the experience of shame would be a motivation for doing better in the future. (Here, however, one may add that this simply followed the line of argument set in the early 1990s by former president Jiang Zemin, who had called for building consciousness in Chinese history education via the remembering of shame!)[37] Furthermore, Guo clearly stated they set up the online forum *Fuxing zhi lu* to enable the topics raised by the documentary be discussed by a broader audience (Fuxing zhi lu – *Huishou guoqu, zhanwang weilai*; 10 October 2007), thus increasing the societal impact of the documentary.

In one of many interviews, head of project Ren Xuean also talked about similarities and differences between *Daguo jueqi* and *Fuxing zhi lu*. Whereas *Daguo jueqi* was a historical piece, relying heavily on historians as experts (with Qian Chengdan as the leading one), *Fuxing zhi lu* asked people with an expertise in Marxism and the CCP to act as advisors. This is – as we have seen – certainly a very telling option. Qian Chengdan on his part also rather stressed the differences between both documentaries: *Daguo jueqi* was more historical, *Fuxing zhi lu* more political. For *Daguo jueqi* he used, as we have seen, the term *lishi wenxian pian* 历史文献片 (historical document piece), for *Fuxing zhi lu: zhenglunpian* (political piece). And Ren explained that the basic thrust and aim of *Fuxing zhi lu* was to show what is specific about modern China: Sino–Marxism, the leadership of the CCP, and socialism with Chinese characteristics. And that this is the *necessary* option for China should become clear by watching *Fuxing zhi lu*. In short, he clearly acknowledged the primacy of politics. In fact, when asked whether he aimed at 'defining' history for the audience with this documentary, Ren responded cautiously that 'defining history' is the task of the Party alone! However, the 'party experts' on board guaranteed that the production would not go too far off mark. And Ren explained: though *Fuxing zhi lu* would not show anything new in terms of content, it provided, at last, a fresh explanation as to *why* the Chinese path was correct (Sun Ran 2007).

In an interview for the Chinese broadcasting and TV journal, however, Ren showed himself to the intended audience of this specialised publication as more self-confident. He argued even more assertively that they wanted to show their 'own view' of history in both documentaries *Daguo jueqi* and *Fuxing zhi lu*. Whereas, obviously, an openly acknowledged 'mouth-piece function' would not be a sensible marketing option with the Chinese audience, on the other hand one should not be too closely related to any particular political outlook. As an example of the continuously reworked exhibition that *Fuxing zhi lu* demonstrates, the 'set version' of modern history was all but uncontested in political circles, and thus the documentary could have run the risk of getting in between interpretative 'fronts'.

In this more 'technical' interview for TV specialists, Ren tried to steer clear from too much politics and referred rather to history theorist Hayden White and other theoretical approaches to visualising history, which he argued the production team pondered, though he admitted the Chinese audience 'does not like abstractions'. To make a 'story' out of history, he chose the techniques of focusing on topics, of dramatising them, and of estrangement to capture the audience with well-known content. To add something 'new', he wanted to show 'unknown' material to underline the basic points, such as the importance of the CCP in the *Fuxing* documentary. Especially with *Fuxing zhi lu*, he wanted to render history more lively and dynamic than in the more static *Daguo jueqi*. As methods, he explained, he used link over time, space, settings, ideas, and aesthetic moments. For all these points, he referred to some examples, though mostly from *Daguo jueqi*. He also argued that their techniques developed over the years, as *Daguo jueqi*'s early instalments were technically not as sophisticated as later ones, since TV techniques were developing quickly. They therefore increasingly used animation, particular angles or colours, and other cues. For example, in *Fuxing zhi lu*, the colours were purposefully brighter for the 'positive' era, since 1978. Also in *Daguo jueqi*, countries were associated with a dominant colour: for example, the early seafarer nations Portugal and Spain with blue, England with green, France with yellow, Japan with cherry blossom colours, and the US with strong colours. This shows that Ren and his crew tried to cue the audience and influence them in various ways (Ren Xuean 2008). In sum, for getting across the 'politicised' content, the technical repertoire of film was fully employed.

In another interview, Ren Xuean was confronted with the important question why, if *Daguo jueqi* and *Fuxing zhi lu* were so closely linked, the series on China did not use the word 'rise' (*jueqi*) but rather 'revival' (*fuxing*)? Ren tried to relativise the question, being certainly well aware of the contemporary political debate about the terms, stating that the goal of both was the same: wealth and power for the nation and individuals. Thus, with *fuxing*, the importance was not on the 're' (*fu*) part (indicating repetition), but on *xing*, meaning more or less 'rise' as well (and is, in fact, part of the traditional *xingshuai* model – see above, Chapter 2). He specified that to him this implied a rich, strong, democratic, civilised, peaceful, socialist, modern country that could be achieved by socialism with Chinese characteristics. This clearly echoed the message of the Seventeenth Party Congress. To achieve these goals, the Chinese people should learn self-confidence, since consciousness (in classical Marxist fashion) 'decides everything' (Ren Xuean; 2 November 2007).

It is interesting to note that the term 'rise' was avoided in the title of *Fuxing zhi lu*; in fact, the 're' (*fu*) element of the word *fuxing* implies that China is not 'newly rising', but just 'recovering' a status it had before the West humiliated it in the nineteenth century. (See the discussions of terms on the political scene, for example with Zheng Bijian, addressed in Chapter 2.) This means China's 'rise' was no 'threat' in view of regional or Western fears, but only a redressing of unjust historical developments. And the term 'rise' had been officially eclipsed in the meantime by 'peaceful development'. Thus, it was politically correct to avoid the potentially 'threatening' 'rise' (see also above in Chapter 2). China might even yet become a model for others still 'further behind' on the road to modernisation. In sum, the choice of terms certainly was not a casual one.

As we saw earlier, the book market already 'prepared' for the transition from the 'rise' topic to 'revival' as the key issue: Renmin chubanshe's volume on the 'The Road to Revival of Great Powers' (Zhang Xiaojing (ed.) 2007; thus blending the two documentaries' titles), and the sister volume on the downfall of great powers (Liu Jinghua (ed.) 2007), were signs of this shift. The first one also addressed China in its discussions of various nations rising (again), i.e. 'reviving' or 'rejuvenating' – as the translation of the term *fuxing* at times is rendered.[38] As the preface of 'Road to Revival of Great Powers' argues, blending in also Hu Jintao's stress on 'development', only 'developed countries' could be 'great powers', but not every developed country was necessarily 'great' (Zhang Xiaojing (ed.) 2007: 2). China had already missed three chances to assert herself as a great power: with the Ming-time Chinese maritime expeditions of Zheng He (1371–1433), which were discontinued, leaving the field of maritime expansion to Westerners who had lagged behind China in development before that age; in the late nineteenth century, when even upstart Japan could outdo China; and after World War II, when the Japanese had another spectacular comeback via economics, while China 'slept over' the 1960s and 1970s (i.e. was busy with its Cultural Revolution; Zhang Xiaojing (ed.) 2007: 3–5). Now she should be careful to use her chances well.

As a 2005 study on the 'peaceful rise' concept argues, *fuxing* in fact was the same as *jueqi*, with the only difference that *fuxing* referred to the 'comeback' of a historically great nation with a long, outstanding tradition, whereas *jueqi* rather focused on the developmental state that arises out of poverty (Peng Peng (ed.) 2005: 10). Although 'China's rise' had already been promoted in 1998 by International Studies scholar Yan Xuetong 阎学通 and again by Shanghai CASS scholar Huang Renwei 黄仁伟 in 2002, it now merged with the 'revival' of China (Peng Peng (ed.) 2005: 13–16).

Media reactions after the documentary's airing stressed the close connection to *Daguo jueqi*, marking this series as an extensive treatment of the 'missing tenth country' of the latter. Although the topic was a familiar one to the audience (it included the Chinese modern history that everybody did in school), the newness was to be seen in the way it integrated foreigners' views on China (in the interviews which, as we saw, are highlighted in the book version by leaving out the domestic interviewees in the list of 'experts') and by consciously setting China in a global perspective, due to its being integrated (at first by force) into the world by foreigners since 1840 (*Yangshi bochu* Daguo jueqi *jiemeipian*; 12 October 2007).) Official media like the 'People's Daily' (*Renmin ribao* 人民日报) came out in favour of the documentary, citing leading cadres with positive comments, though not going into much detail (see for example Sui Xiaofei; 18 October 2007). Others referred to renowned scholars who supported the series (Yu Du; December 2007).

A critical evaluation, however, was published by historian Zhang Lifan 章立凡 in *Nanfang dushibao* 南方都市报 (Southern Metropolis Daily). Whereas he could tolerate the *Daguo jueqi* series, *Fuxing zhi lu* was full of problems in his eyes. He wondered about the career of the term *fuxing* in China, noting its recurrence since 1949, for example in place or street names. Pointedly he argued that much of the vocabulary, including *fuxing*, in fact reminded one of the GMD and its dictatorial rule! The term suggests that China is somehow picking up on tradition. On the other hand, this series on modern Chinese history, calling itself a 'political piece', glossed over the 1950s to 1970s without analysing the problems in this historical phase. Citing Mao with irony, Zhang argued that internal factors are always primary to external ones. Therefore, all the praise the documentary heaps on the CCP does nothing to help the ever-existing internal problems and deficiencies in democracy and the legal system, the widening social gap, and so on. Measuring the PRC against its own claims, Zhang argued that it had *not* achieved what it aimed at in 1949. Whereas *Daguo jueqi* should rather be termed a 'piece on politics' – having a topic 'easier' to talk about since it was 'others'' history and what to learn from it – *Fuxing zhi lu* was in fact not matching this definition but was simply a 'propaganda piece' (Zhang Lifan; 2 November 2007). That overseas anti-CCP partisan journals such as 'Epoch Times' (*Dajiyuan* 大纪元) denounced the documentary as mere propaganda as well, is hardly surprising (see for example *Yangshi tui* Fuxing zhi lu; 6 October 2007).

In retrospect, Ren Xuean stressed in 2009 that the documentary had not yet lost its impact, as shown not least by the ongoing existence of the online forum of the same name, and the host of publications and productions all using *fuxing* in their titles ever since. This, he was convinced, was due to the topic's timeliness, and the interest of foreign countries into what China is up to. Since *Fuxing zhi lu* was aimed at directing China into the future and therefore not a mere historical piece, this explained why the relevance had not faded (Ren Xuean 2009). In fact, one may conclude by the many *fuxing*-productions still around that the *fuxing* topic was and is high on the agenda of marketing CCP politics by staging and 'screening' China's modern history in a particular way to argue for China's present and future global rise. As long as it stays on the political agenda in this way – and it has been already embraced officially also by China's next leading generation,[39] *Fuxing zhi lu* will continue to be relevant.

Notes

1 According to Ren Xuean in his afterword to the three-volume accompanying book series *Fuxing zhi lu* (2007/8, vol. 3: 370–2).
2 The afterword of the publisher is to be found in the book series *Fuxing zhi lu* (2007/8, vol. 3: 373–8).
3 For short biographies of these experts, see the book series *Fuxing zhi lu* (2007/8, vol. 3: 353–7).
4 The preface of Zhao Huayong to the three-volume book series *Fuxing zhi lu* (2007/8, vol. 1: I–III).
5 The preface of Luo Ming is in the three-volume book series *Fuxing zhi lu* (2007/8, vol. 1: IV–VI).
6 For details on the party congress, see its homepage: *Zhongguo gonchandang dishiqici quanguo daibiao dahui* (2007).

7 The English name was changed from 'Propaganda' to 'Publicity' when the former's negative connotation in English was realised, but the Chinese name (*Zhongyang xuanchuan bu* 中央宣传部) is still unchanged. In the following, I will stick to the 'translation', i.e. 'Propaganda Department'.

8 *Renmin ribao* boasted that the one million mark was already surpassed after 30 days (Jiang Shan and Xu Ke; 13 November 2007). Thus, the forum and the exhibition seemed to throng.

9 See for example *Guojia bowuguan* Fuxing zhi lu *dazhan ji jiang mianfei kaifang* (25 September 2009), and Zhongguo guojia bowuguan (1 March 2011), which looks back on the genesis of this exhibition.

10 See the official website of the National Museum: Zhongguo guojia bowuguan (1 March 2011).

11 See for details: Ma Yingmin (2009). On the museum that reopened in 2011 and the 'lack of concept' of its historical exhibitions, see the critical evaluation of German journalist Mark Siemons (2012), who addressed mainly the basement section on ancient China that was reopened in 2012. One may well argue that this 'lacks of concept' simply reflects the outcome of negotiating processes between widely diverging historical views of what China was, is, and shall become.

12 For a summary of the 'six whys', see *Jiedu 'liuge wei shenme'* (n.d.).

13 This is outlined in Road to Revival *premiered in Beijing* (22 September 2009). See also Liu Qiong (29 September 2009).

14 See *Daxing yinyue wudao shishi* Fuxing zhi lu (21 September 2009). The epic was also announced to English readers in the English-language Chinese newspaper *Global Times* on 22 September 2009 (see Road to Revival *opens in Beijing*; 22 September 2009).

15 Road to Revival *continues on stage of the National Center* (22 January 2010). See also '*Fuxing zhi lu* zaidu kaiyan' (20 February 2010), stating that it was to be staged at least 54 times in all, having started in January.

16 See Road to Revival *starts China tour* (3 March 2011), and '*Fuxing zhi lu* quanguo xunyan qihang' (21 February 2011).

17 Officially, the film was released only in May 2010 for the cinemas. 'Dianying *Fuxing zhi lu* quanguo fangying qidong' (15 May 2010).

18 It was one of the very few documentary features that earned something at the box office sales in 2010, though not earning back all of its investment ('Dianying jilupian, qidai hecai'; 8 April 2011; see also the *People's Daily Online* report: Low Box Offices Sales Plagued Chinese Documentaries in 2010: Report; 1 April 2011). (The report is based on an official 'report on the development of Chinese documentaries in 2010': '2010 nian Zhongguo jilupian fazhan yanjiu baogao'«2010 年中国纪录片发展研究报告».)

19 See, among others: Wu, Jia (23 September 2009).

20 Notably, as of early 2013 this leftist website seems to have become defunct. This might have to do with the political contestations going on in 2012 connected to the Bo Xilai 薄熙来 (born 1949) case when the leftists lost out. The website had also earlier been occasionally shut down when voicing dissent with current political options. (See Zhao, Yuezhi 2011: 228, who names an incident in 2007.)

21 Fuxing zhi lu *de quexian*, a blog entry for 3 October 2009.

22 See Barr (2012) on the function of nation branding for nation building. See also Stockmann (2011a) for short TV spots (PSAs, or Public Service Advertisements) for advertising state policies on certain issues.

23 Usually, with the Taiping, 'proto-communist' aspects, such as distribution of land to all, would be stressed.

24 On this, see for example, Broudehoux (2004: Chapter 3) and, above all, Callahan (2010).

25 The Boxer historiography issue was at the heart of the widely publicised conflict around Canton-based historian Yuan Weishi 袁伟时, who attacked the 'distorted' textbook presentations of this (and other events) in a 2006 article. This led to a temporary closing

down of the newspaper supplement in which his article was printed: *Bingdian* 冰点 (Freezing point). (For some brief remarks on Yuan, see also above in Chapter 2.)

26 The text of the script can be found in *Fuxing zhi lu* (2007/8, vol. 1: 298–313).

27 The full title reads: *Qieguo dadao Yuan Shikai* 窃國大盜袁世凱 (Great robber of the nation Yuan Shikai). The booklet has been reprinted several times since the mid-1940s. At the time, Chen was Mao's secretary.

28 Li's grave is today an important memorial site and used, for example, for ceremonies to pledge faithfulness to the Party.

29 The text of the script can be found in *Fuxing zhi lu* (2007/8, vol. 1: 314–29).

30 Though it is true that Khrushchev had provided examples for the rhetoric and aims of the Great Leap Forward, the measures undertaken in China were much more utopian and did not meet approval from the Soviets. Rather, they were one of the reasons for the Sino–Soviet split!

31 The text of the script can be found in *Fuxing zhi lu* (2007/8, vol. 2: 316–31).

32 This catchword often means Singapore, South Korea, Hong Kong, and Taiwan. At times, however, it refers to the first two together with Malaysia and Thailand or other combinations of Southeast Asian countries.

33 He is commonly identified with his slogan of the 'two whatevers': 'We will resolutely uphold whatever policy decisions Chairman Mao made, and unswervingly follow whatever instructions Chairman Mao gave.' That Hua is not named might be interpreted as unwillingness to give him too much personal prominence but rather to have him just represent an ideological line.

34 The text of the script can be found in *Fuxing zhi lu* (2007/8, vol. 2: 332–48).

35 The text of the script can be found in *Fuxing zhi lu* (2007/8, vol. 3: 308–23).

36 The text of the script can be found in *Fuxing zhi lu* (2007/8, vol. 3: 324–42).

37 See also Wang, Q. Edward (2010: 282). Jiang's 1991 directives for history education and the detailed new directives that followed on how to teach modern Chinese history in a way befitting 'Chinese sentiments/circumstances' (*guoqing* 国情), can be found in Kecheng jiaocai yanjiusuo (comp.) (2001: 607–36).

38 However, 'rejuvenation' is often used also as a translation for Chinese *zhenxing* 振兴 – a term popular some time ago as well with the slogan *zhenxing Zhonghua* 振兴中华 (rejuvenate China).

39 See Li Bin's (29 November 2012) report about Xi Jinping's 习近平 comments when visiting the *Fuxing* exhibition in late 2012. Xi combines the various slogans of 'revival' and 'rejuvenation' with his new term: the 'Chinese dream' (*Zhongguo meng* 中国梦, or *Zhongguo zhi meng* 中国之梦) to challenge the 'American dream'.

4 Soviet failure lessons for insiders

The party-educational documentary *Ju an si wei* (Alert to Danger while Dwelling in Safety)

The documentary series *Ju an si wei – Sugong wangdang de lishi jiaoxun* 居安思 危－苏共亡党的历史教训 (Alert to Danger while Dwelling in Safety: the historical lesson of the perishing of the Soviet Communist Party)[1] was not a CCTV production like the two earlier documentaries discussed in this book. This documentary was produced by the Chinese Academy of Social Sciences (CASS), which had set up a nationally funded special research group in 2000 under the (political) guidance of Li Shenming 李慎明, vice president of CASS, vice party secretary, and a party member since 1971 who earlier had had a career in the PLA.[2] He was also the chief responsible for the script of the documentary *Ju an si wei* (using the alias 'Xiao Li' 肖黎), aided by the publishing house connected to the Central Commission for Discipline Inspection of the CCP (*Zhongjiwei Zhongguo Fangzheng chubanshe* 中纪委中国方正出版社), the Jilin Publishing Company (*Jilin chuban jituan lianhe shezhi* 吉林出版集团联合摄制), and the TV art centre of the PLA academy (*Jiefangjun yishu xueyuan dianshi yishu zhongxin* 解放军艺术学院电视艺术中心).[3] This shows that the cadre-supervising party organisation and the army were involved in this documentary production as well as the 'scholarly' CASS, marking it as a piece of ideological importance that would then serve as mandatory study material for cadres. When it came out – more or less simultaneously with CCTV's great market success *Daguo jueqi* – it countered the latter's vision of foreign history as a model for the great public with an example of foreign history as a warning for the CCP cadres internally: the case of Soviet failure. This was in line with the tradition of using 'negative (teaching) materials' (*fanmian ziliao* 反面资料 or *fanmian jiaocai* 反面教材) for reference in ideological training as a part of internal party 'political communication' in the PRC, and it marked another possible use that 'foreign history' could be put to in China.

Documenting failure

In view of the fact that Soviet/Russian history is presented in a critical vein in this documentary, it is notable that Li Shenming, the cadre who was politically responsible for it, would receive an honorary PhD from the Russian Academy of Science in 2007 (though this might have been also due to his position in CASS as the corresponding institution in China).[4] He himself in any case argued that the documentary was 'well received' by 'the Russians' – or at least generated discussions on the topic in Russia.[5] Not being a historian himself, Li Shenming, however, obviously had to count on expertise of others. As one of the de facto authors of the documentary's script, Li Xiaoning 李小宁, reveals, he – not a historian either but also working in the political realm as a specialist on 'united front theory'[6] – was the one to write in the end the texts of instalments one to four and also of eight, whereas the other instalments were authored by Ge Youli 葛幼力 (from CASS, but with a more administrative than academic profile), Qiu Jian 邱建 (who had some credits in producing CCP videos) and Hao Yixing 郝一星 (mostly known as a translator).[7] (Notably, the authors of the instalments were not, however, part of the CASS project staff.[8]) Thus, none of the authors of the instalments (or Xiao Li alias Li Shenming who 'reworked' the whole) had historical expertise of their own. As basic reference they used the book *Sulian xingwang shigang* 苏联兴亡 史纲 (Historical outline of the rise and fall of the Soviet Union) (2004), co-edited by Chen Zhihua 陈之骅 who was also the responsible historian in the CASS project.[9] Chen Zhihua of the World History Department of CASS had studied in the Soviet Union in the 1950s and is considered a specialist in Soviet history. He therefore should be considered to be (at least indirectly) the principal provider of 'historical expertise'.

Li Xiaoning, the main 'real' author of the instalments of the documentary, disclosed some interesting details about its background, stating that it had already been planned in 2003 by himself and the head of the PLA academy's TV art centre, Li Quan 李荃, who would also be one of the two directors in charge of the realised documentary. Thus, as it seems, Li Xiaoning and Li Quan had first planned the documentary on their own, disconnected from the CASS project, intending to base it on publications by (Red Flag's) Huang Weiding 黄苇町 on the tenth anniversary of the end of the Soviet Union (i.e. in 2001). Huang, in turn, is a trained economist and a leading cadre in the Red Flag Publishing Company. He published *Sugong wangdang shinianji* 苏共亡党十年祭 (On the tenth anniversary of the CPSU's perishing) which appeared first in article form in 2001 and as a book in 2002, based on lectures he gave at the Party School of the Central Committee in Beijing (see Huang Weiding 2001).[10] Being no historian either, Huang viewed the Soviet collapse from the perspective of its political ramifications. However, Li Xiaoning adds, at the time they planned the documentary, i.e. in 2003, there was some 'uncertainty', including Huang's 'political approach',[11] which caused a momentary halt to these plans, and it was only in the context of the CASS project that the documentary could finally be realised. Whether the 'problems' were connected also to the contemporaneous shift from the Jiang Zemin administration to Hu Jintao's cannot be proven, but this assumption does not seem implausible when looking into Huang's work. Huang had been a strong supporter of Jiang's 'Three Represents' (*sange daibiao* 三个代表) – in fact, his party lectures, of which the reflections on the CPSU's demise were just a part, were 'to explain' Jiang's 'Three Represents' – and Huang was very critical of Stalin (1878–1953), to whom he attributed part of the guilt for the Soviet Union's demise, quite unlike the later *Ju an si wei* documentary. He even voiced some criticism of Lenin (including a reference to Lenin's having the tsar and his family shot, his 'purges' of dissidents, and the forced confiscation of grain – all topics largely evaded in the later documentary), and stressed the importance of 'keeping the people's hearts' for legitimate governance, pointing out the fate of Romania's Ceausescu (1918–89), who had faced execution after his fall (Huang Weiding 2001).[12] Obviously, this and similar examples of communist leaders being persecuted after their downfall because of their unpopularity are a hefty warning to the Chinese government to consider people's consent. Notably, the *Ju an si wei* documentary does not talk about such a possible outcome as it restricts itself basically to the Soviet Union and largely evades discussing Eastern Europe.[13] On the other hand, many of Huang's historiographical examples also figure in *Ju an si wei*, so it seems part of his work was kept as reference (maybe due to Li Xiaoning's main 'real' authorship), but the more 'liberal-critical' thrust of Huang's argumentation was shifted with Li Shenming's supervision, Chen Zhihua's book of 2004 as main reference and the CASS project to a more 'leftist' (and historiographically: a more pro-Stalin) stance.

The script of the documentary first provided by CASS, in turn, was originally titled *Sugong tuibian de lishi jiaoxun* 苏共蜕变的历史教训 (The historical lesson of the CPSU's moulting) but then renamed into 'The historical lesson of the perishing of the Soviet Communist Party'. There are no statements as to why the title was changed after the added proverb and motto 'Alert to Danger while Dwelling in Safety' used in party language increasingly in 2004,[14] but obviously the rather 'party-critical' rendering of the CPSU's 'moulting' was reshaped more 'tragically' and more in line with traditional historiography by fitting it into the frame of 'rise and fall' by the word 'perishing' (*wangdang* 亡党/'perishing of the party' in parallel to the established *wangguo* 亡国/'perishing of a nation'). Whether this was also due to the lingering influence of the work of Huang Weiding, who had used the term *wangdang*, or influenced by the contemporarily produced *Daguo jueqi*, which made the 'rise-and-fall' paradigm very popular, cannot be decided. Li Xiaoning, however, adds that the CASS's original text was not always politically 'adequate' either, and thus some 'changes' were introduced. This hints at contestations between different interpretations, probably even inside of the CASS group which was made up of a mixture of 'political' and 'historical' 'experts', as to what or who were 'guilty' in the end for the Soviet Union's failure. (However, one should stress there was not necessarily a simple line between the 'political' and the 'historical' experts, as chief historian Chen Zhihua seems mostly to agree with Li Shenming's 'leftist' reading.) The documentary's final script was in the end written in a few weeks and the documentary finished in June 2006 with some reworking of the commentary carried out until October of the same year.[15] Thus, *Ju an si wei* came out at more or less the same time as *Daguo jueqi*.

The intended audience for *Ju an si wei*, however, was party cadres, and the viewing was usually organised and compulsory. In fact, on the DVD collection cover it is declared that it was for 'inner-party reference' only and 'strictly forbidden' to put on public TV or the Internet. This might explain – together with the speed in final production – why so little attention was paid to make the documentary appealing in aesthetic and visual terms: it was not intended for a competitive market. However, the written version was soon publicly sold (and put on several websites, including governmental ones).[16] The credits also confirm the very 'ideological' bent: there are as many as eleven (!) named 'advisors' (all cadres, including Li Shenming with his real name) and nine people 'providing theory' (again including Li Shenming with his real name, but also historian Chen Zhihua and some academic staff from CASS besides 'political' people who all made up the project staff).[17] This demonstrates that the documentary was considered politically sensitive.

Ju an si wei consists mostly of an assembly of archival footage and some feature film scenes (i.e. the documentary is a compilation film).[18] Thus, no on-the-spot filming and no filmed interviews are integrated as with *Daguo jueqi* or *Fuxing zhi lu*, although the project members are said to have interviewed some Russian colleagues on several occasions, probably informally. Unlike the other two documentary series discussed in this book that went on public TV, the instalments are somewhat varying in length, between 20 and 40 minutes each, again bespeaking the non-market background.

Notable is the soundtrack. As there is no 'real' sound attached, besides the spoken commentary, pictures are accompanied by imported soundtrack, mostly either famous Russian folk music or war songs, or – more surprisingly – Western recent blockbuster soundtracks from *The Rock* (1996), *Troy* (2004), *Pearl Harbor* (2001) and *Pirates of the Caribbean* (2003)![19] Usually, Lenin (1870–1924) is connected to peaceful or heroic Russian folk songs, and Stalin (1878–1953) to more march-like music; Khrushchev (1894–1971), Brezhnev (1906–82) and Gorbachev (born 1931) have some sad and dark tracks in common, often taken from *Pirates of the Caribbean, The Rock*, or *Pearl Harbor*, especially, for Gorbachev, to insinuate death and destruction together with a dark foreboding track from *Troy*. These 'dark' tracks were crudely 'edited' to take out any parts that might sound more 'positive'. The identified tracks include: introduction of *The Rock*, where the soundtrack is associated with a general passing by a burial on a military cemetery where his wife is buried to remember his helplessness to prevent several people's death. 'The *Black Pearl*', i.e. a pirate ghost ship appearing, is taken from *Pirates of the Caribbean*. 'Blood ritual' from the same movie comes with undead pirates going to perform a dark ritual, whereas 'Underwater march' is associated with the undead pirate captain losing his immortality to die in a fight with the main character. 'Attack' is taken from *Pearl Harbor*, when the Japanese attack and sink the US battleship *Arizona*. 'December 7th' is from the same movie, describing the aftermath of the attack. 'Heart of a volunteer', again from *Pearl Harbor*, is associated with American volunteers who were taken prisoner and died while fighting the Japanese, even down to their bare hands. *Troy* provides another scary track: 'The Greek Army and its defeat', foreboding disaster. Only 'Tennessee' from *Pearl Harbor* is a calm tune that suggests some hope with a beautiful sunrise, notably used for the credits in the end, whereas the Russian folk music and war songs, including the famous 'Katyusha' (which was only composed in 1938 and was very popular during World War II), are related mostly to Lenin (who had been dead for many years when 'Katyusha' was composed!). As this use of soundtracks (and – in contrast to the other two documentaries discussed in this book – the telling absence of a responsible person in the production team for 'music') suggests, music is primarily used here to entertain and cue viewers into certain moods, being the only audio alternative to the spoken commentary while watching Soviet footage or feature film clips, intermingled with some present-day shots, probably taken from the news archives, while the overpowering commentary didactically provides continuous ideological 'explanation'. However, since the music is mostly taken from Western blockbusters, the aim seems to be to create a subconscious linkage between the ideological content and 'Westernised' or 'Hollywood-ised' feelings. Whereas Russian folk music and Soviet patriotic songs might appeal to the older generation of Chinese viewers still familiar with them, the Western blockbuster music might be chosen for keeping younger cadres at the screen: if not for filmic aesthetic qualities, then at least for the audio part, providing acoustic 'familiarity'. However, as Western music is employed mostly with the 'negatively' charged periods from Khrushchev onward, it also hints at estrangement between Soviet images and the Western soundtrack, whereas 'home-grown' Russian folk music provides a more coherent impression of the 'better times', when 'Soviets were still Soviets' (and not undermined by the West).

As with music, also the visual signifiers for the different leaders are fairly consonant: Lenin usually comes with archival footage, mostly connected to the revolution, holding speeches in front of cheering crowds and so forth accompanied by folk songs. Stalin is associated with images of industrialisation, the war and march-like music, whereas the following leaders are ever more negative, using archival footage as well, but accompanied by sinister tunes. Since material dating from after the Sino–Soviet-split obviously had to be taken from the (Soviet or Western) news, the images are rarely 'negative' in themselves, especially when taken from Soviet news which understandably presented their leaders positively at the time, making for an ever growing gap between image and soundtrack that the commentary does not successfully bridge, even though at times visual techniques as stills, slow motion or certain framings are introduced to provide somewhat different visual cues than those in the original. A case in point for these difficulties in dealing with footage 'from the wrong side' is Gorbachev, who appears as an easily chatting, smiling and fairly photogenic leader among the crowd, although the soundtrack and the commentary try to insinuate he was 'far from the masses' and a sinister fellow.

The whole documentary is very repetitive in the similar layout of each instalment, always going chronologically through all eras from Lenin to Gorbachev, though with a different thematic focus each time. This repetitiveness may also be intended to serve the hammering home effect of the 'historical lesson' to be learnt by the cadres. Visually, every instalment starts with a red map of the Soviet Union on which the later 'defected' republics then change colour (the 'colour revolution'), insinuating break-up as a key message.

Basically, whereas *Daguo jueqi* had served to present 'models' to emulate, this documentary served as an anti-model, especially focusing on the reasons for the Soviet Union's collapse. From the Chinese perspective, this was connected closely to China's 'different' reaction to 1989 events and what the historical alternative would have been.[20] (That the Chinese 'different reaction' was a factor in inducing the Soviet leaders *not* to react the same way, is the other side of the coin.)[21] And, one may add, the CCP succeeded in the sense that it did learn from the Soviet Union's fate *not* to discredit past communist history, undermining its legitimacy.[22]

As to Sino–Soviet relations and the portrayal of the Soviet leaders, clearly the Sino–Soviet split that occurred under Khrushchev made for a particularly bad image of the latter – though a few analysts in China also reflected positively on certain aspects of reform that distinguished him from his successor Brezhnev and his predecessor Stalin (possibly with a view to indirectly criticising Mao (1893–1976) who had strongly sided against Khrushchev).[23] As will also become obvious, Khrushchev's ideological tenet of having the party be the representative of 'all people' was not too far from Jiang Zemin's endeavours to broaden the party's base with his 'Three Represents' (for which Jiang, in fact, had been heftily criticised by party leftists as 'betraying communism'!).[24] Tellingly, the documentary portrays Khrushchev as a chief culprit – which underscores the 'leftist' thrust of the historical reading it provides.

With Gorbachev, things are even more complicated. In fact, at the time of his rule, Sino–Soviet contacts were re-established, and his reforms were seen at the time as fairly positive and consonant with the Chinese reforms that were underway (Shambaugh 2008: 56–7). But it was precisely his visit to China in spring 1989, the first Sino–Soviet summit in 30 years (!), which was used by the student protesters to gain publicity. They capitalised on the fact that many foreign journalists were present in Beijing to report on this historical event of Sino–Soviet rapprochement. Since they forced the Chinese leaders to receive Gorbachev through the back door before the eyes of the whole world, the leaders felt especially humiliated.

This 'unlucky' involvement of Gorbachev in the Chinese government's most serious humiliation and the ensuing crackdown, which destroyed at one stroke the whole positive image China had tried to build up internationally over the 1980s, influenced Gorbachev's official image in China negatively, although he himself was hesitant to criticise the 'Chinese solution' at the time for fear of hampering the newly established Sino–Soviet ties (Lukin 1991: 123–5)! When he also proved to be the Soviet Union's 'last' president (which corresponds perfectly well with the Chinese traditional historiographical pattern of describing the last emperor of a dynasty as wicked), his image as gravedigger was set, making for ignoring the actual Sino–Soviet improvement of ties under his rule due to the overpowering framework of betrayal and failure.

Historical portrayal of the Soviet Union

The documentary *Ju an si wei* is clearly designed as a didactic tool to demonstrate to the Chinese cadre audience the various dangers the CCP has to beware of.

Whereas the instalment on the Soviet Union in *Daguo jueqi* provided a somewhat 'marketised' view, this documentary shows which particular developments in the Soviet Union were seen as of relevance for today's Chinese cadres to 'negative learn from' in order to avoid a similar disastrous outcome.

Historical traces of the rise and fall of the Soviet Communist Party (Sugong xingshuai de lishi guiji 苏共兴衰的历史轨迹)

The very didactic vein of this documentary becomes obvious immediately in the preface to the whole, which is shown as running text in black and white and read, by the commentator without any underlying music. This preface outlines the basic question that is to drive this series: how could it happen that in the 1990s the Soviet Union, a state with a huge territory and a major world power (*daguo qiangguo* 大国强国),[25] simply dissolved without any foreign invasion or other great upheavals? This question is of course not simply one of historiographical concern. Rather, as British historian Toynbee is cited, the most important historical lessons can be drawn from the downfall of civilisations – thus making explicit the relevance of this 'historical lesson' as a warning for Chinese cadres – and thus marking this learning experience as distinct from the 'rise' examples in the documentaries discussed previously in this book.

As for the reasons why the Soviet Union dissolved, various explanations that have been forwarded are presented as the range of options (towards which the documentary then sets out to position itself): economic mismanagement, ossification of the 'Stalin model', ethnic conflicts, the arms race, Gorbachev's treason, foreign influences, and so on. But according to Mao, the commentary argues, there must be always one main contradiction in all these many facets. To define this 'main contradiction', the documentary cites Deng Xiaoping's 1992 evaluation of the Soviet Union's dissolution, where it is argued that the key problem lay inside the Communist Party itself, thus naming the party as the chief agent responsible for the whole state's faring. Jiang Zemin – whose cited intervention was slightly earlier than Deng's, but who is 'next' in the hierarchical and chronological leadership sequence and thus 'put in place' here – explained further that the changes in Eastern Europe did not symbolise the failure of scientific socialism but happened precisely because these countries had given up the way of socialism. And Hu Jintao, representing the 'wisdom' of the next generation of leaders, had already by 2000, i.e. before becoming the next party general secretary and president, denounced Gorbachev as the main driving force by following the footsteps of Khrushchev and dismissing the great tradition of Marxism–Leninism–Stalinism. This means that the documentary tries from the outset to enlist all leading generations of the CCP in suggesting they univocally shared the documentary's (de facto not uncontested) evaluation that basically it was human fault that made for the dissolution of the Soviet Union (a historiographical view closer to Chinese tradition than to Marxism): Gorbachev was the chief culprit, following up on Khrushchev, and helped by the degeneration of the CPSU. Clearly, this documentary directed at cadres was intended to drive home the lesson that the party and its ideology have to remain 'firm' to prevent any similar things happening (and a Gorbachev appearing) in China.[26]

After the title presentation, with a unified red Soviet map breaking up into the present map of Russia and the now independent ex-Soviet republics (accompanied by the track 'Fog bound' from *Pirates of the Caribbean*)[27], and with the visual markers of the Soviet 'leading generations' – Lenin, Stalin (both alone), Khrushchev, Brezhnev (both with entourage) and Gorbachev with Yeltsin (1931–2007) tellingly at his back – the first instalment as a kind of general assessment starts. It begins with a Soviet popular song well known to Chinese of the older generation at least, since it was also taught in the 1950s in Chinese schools, praising the capital, Moscow, with the Kremlin's starred roof – and the smoke of factories rising to the sky. In this way, an emotional attachment is created to allow the Chinese viewer to identify with the Soviet Union as in a way his second 'home'. It is also stressed that this was 'home' to Lenin, the great idol (who usually is accompanied by a patriotic folk song soundtrack in the whole series, such as the famous 'Katyusha'), and to the October Revolution 1917 (represented by Soviet feature film clips). And these two, Lenin and the October Revolution, are presented as remaining central also for China, despite any later Sino–Soviet split.

In this context of general time-spanning significance the documentary recalls how the Soviet Communist Party came into being: its roots lay in that particular historical moment when world capitalism was growing into imperialism. The first traces went back to 1898 in Minsk, but the 'real' founding came in 1900 with Lenin and Plekhanov (1856–1918) who designed the party statutes and started the publication organ *Iskra* (The Spark). In 1903 the faction of Lenin as the 'Bolshevists' emerged during internal-socialist debates, and with this Second Party Congress of the Russian Social Democratic Labour Party in Brussels and London the main ideological lines were fixed.

Jumping quickly to 1917, the documentary addresses the February Revolution that 'erupted' in that year and the new premier Kerensky (1881–1970) who continued Russia's fighting in the First World War while turning 'anti-revolutionary' at home; and points out that only Lenin evaluated the situation 'correctly' and promoted the slogan of handing all power to the soviets. Thus, in October,[28] 200,000 revolutionaries were ready finally to stage a real revolution in Petrograd. (For the visual part, mostly archival footage and feature film clips – only occasionally identified as such but being more readily available than archival footage for the early Soviet Union times – historical photographs and revolutionary paintings are used.)

Thus, the commentary stresses, the first socialist state on earth was born under the leadership of the Bolshevist Party. In spite of strong internal and external opposition, 'the heroic Soviet people' and the newly created 'Red Army' put down all of it: the internal rebellion by Kolchak (1874–1920) and Denikin (1872–1947), as well as the armed interference of 14 imperialist nations; and in 1922 the founding of the 'Union of Soviet Socialist Republics' was finally declared officially.

But the war conditions after the October Revolution hampered the beginnings, the commentary admits. Lenin was therefore forced to declare 'war-time communism' and later the 'New Economic Policy' (NEP) to deal with this challenge.[29] No wonder Lenin, who was actually the target of assassination attempts, was very exhausted by all this, which quasi necessarily led to his early death at the age of 54 in 1924, the insinuation goes.

After him, Stalin 'took over' (as if there had been no massive struggle for succession). Visually, illusion of an uncontested succession is created by showing Stalin weeping at the Lenin's deathbed, apparently knowing that he will 'take over the burden' of leadership. (Lest the message should not have come across, the succession line is also 'didactically' introduced to the Chinese viewer by a schematic presentation of 'leadership eras', with a big arrow pointing from Lenin to Stalin.) It was Stalin who would now build up the whole socialist system. Under Stalin, the commentary contends, socialism proved able to 'release the productive forces' and made for the Soviet Union's gigantic economic growth rates between 1929 and 1937, in marked difference from Western countries at the time. (Visually, whereas Lenin's era was represented by revolutionary images, Stalin's era is represented by footage on industrial production.) In this way, as in the other documentaries discussed in this book, the strong focus on alleged brilliant 'economic performance' as a legitimisation of Communist rule is stressed.

When Hitler (1889–1945) attacked the Soviet Union (no word on the Hitler–Stalin Pact 1939, of course), she had to make heavy sacrifices in defence, but due to her socialist system, the commentary argues, she could switch her economy to wartime needs and resist heroically. In spite of the Germans being close to Moscow in 1941, Stalin nevertheless would keep to the annual celebration of the October Revolution to encourage his people. The soldiers thus went directly from the parade to the front, filled with enthusiasm. During the whole 'war of defence', the commentary sums up, more than three million party members died, profiling the sacrifices the party itself had shouldered. And in 1945 the Soviet Union would march triumphantly into Berlin in her defeat of fascism.

However, the war had meant an almost total destruction of the Soviet economy, and the death of 27 million soldiers and civilians (thus acknowledging now also non-party members as victims). But the country would rise from the ashes, the commentary stresses, setting up a new five-year plan in 1946, constructing its own first atomic bomb in 1949 and again setting upon a way of impressive economic growth. Thus, when Stalin died in 1953 at 74, Mao is declared to have 'wept bitterly' just as Stalin is reported to have wept for Lenin – conveniently sidelining the fact that Mao was the only major communist leader not attending Stalin's funeral![30] In the final evaluation, Stalin, who had been general secretary of the party since 1923 (i.e. even at the lifetime of undisputed 'hero' Lenin), represented, according to the commentary, the glory of the Soviet Union surpassing all capitalists of his age by far! It was Stalin's Soviet Union that demonstrated to the world the abilities of socialism. Even Churchill (1874–1965), it is contended, admitted this, acknowledging that he made out of a Russia with a wooden plough a country with atomic weapons. (This evaluation by Churchill is, however, probably only legendary.) Thus, no one who lived through his age could deny his merits, although it is vaguely admitted that he was 'too much' bound on purging people, not 'democratic' enough and too heavy-handed. But all these faults pale in the face of his incredible merits!

After Stalin's death, the torch went to Khrushchev (who – as a bad figure in the documentary – is, of course, not shown at Stalin's side at the latter's funeral). Kruschev's 'secret speech' of 1956 in the context of the Twentieth Party Congress attacked the personality cult, i.e. Stalin and his legacy. In this, the commentary argues, Khrushchev went far beyond the mark and encouraged anti-Stalinist criticism all over the country. He even removed Stalin's remains from the Lenin mausoleum, tore down his statues and thus created 'unfavourable' moods. He furthermore denied some principles of socialism, which prompted Mao to remark Khruschchev had opted to drop the 'Stalin-knife' altogether – though the Sino–Soviet split at his time is not directly referred to in the documentary. (The soundtrack, which was for Lenin and Stalin either peaceful or heroic, changes with Khrushchev to disquieting rhythms.)

It was thus under Khrushchev that the 'children of the Twentieth Party Congress' (Gorbachev) would grow up,[31] i.e. those infected with the virus of unbelief in the party, who would later kill it step by step in the 1980s. (Visually, the following leader Brezhnev is introduced at the side of Khrushchev, and young Gorbachev and also Yeltsin are associated with 1980s' youth in 'decadent' fashion to show the evil long-term outcome of the Khrushchevian era.)

In relation to this, the era of Brezhnev (who replaced Khrushchev) is presented as slightly better (marked also by reappearance in the soundtrack of 'Katyusha' until the more problematic phases of his leadership are referred to. Basically, his great achievement is seen in the fact that he turned the Soviet Union into the second superpower of the world challenging the US. But the evaluation is mixed for other reasons: by this success he soon turned arrogant and hegemonic. He was too much bound on centralisation, the commentary argues, and caused economic stagnation by his efforts to keep the status quo. When he died in 1982 and both of his successors, Andropov (1914–84) and Chernenko (1911–85), did so in a short time as well, in 1985 it was finally Gorbachev who took on leadership.

Gorbachev, in turn, is introduced by his main catchwords: democratisation, *glasnost*, and pluralism of opinions to do away with the blockades to reform. Though this sounded nice, the commentary argues that the people never realised what he was really up to. This was partly revealed in 1988 when he stated that he wanted to hand the power back 'from the party to the soviets' – which meant the end of the party's monopoly. (He is the only one of the leaders 'cited' with text passages that probably demonstrate his personal responsibility for the political course.) In 1990 on the last party congress of the Soviet Communist Party he even spoke of a 'humanistic democratic socialism', which in practice translated into a system of multiple parties. This chance, the commentary suggests, was taken up immediately by the anti-communist forces which constituted themselves in several political parties to challenge the primacy of the Communist Party (while the soundtrack is cueing the viewer into a more depressed feeling, accompanying Soviet footage of the time).

Parallel to the dismantling of the Communist Party's monopoly, the party's (and national) disintegration gained momentum. By 1989 the Communist Party sections of the Baltic republics had opted for separation, and Gorbachev let them go. Then in 1991 by election most republics voted for staying together whereas six left. Thus, Gorbachev proposed a smaller union, but now leaving out the 'socialist' self-definition altogether.

Then Yeltsin, head of Russia, i.e. the biggest area among the republics, emerged to sideline Gorbachev, snatch real power and move towards simply dissolving the Soviet Union. In response, some leaders of the Soviet Union tried to pose opposition, but this last attempt to save socialism and the Soviet Union failed. One of the reasons was according to the Chinese commentary the lack of resolve in the communist rebels, the other that Gorbachev in the end also went over to Yeltsin's side. (This whole account of the attempted putsch in August 1991 remains very vague, however.) And it was still under Gorbachev's command when the bureaus of the Communist Party were shut down all over the country – thus marking him, the 'witness' of China's Tian'anmen Square protests in the spring of 1989, as the real responsible figure.

This meant that even after 74 years of rule and with the considerable number of 20 million members, the Soviet Communist Party was nevertheless finally destroyed. What, however, seemed to trouble the Chinese makers of the documentary series most was the obvious disinterest of 'the masses': nobody stood up to defend the Party, neither the cadres nor the people. In fact the closing down of the Communist Party bureaus occurred without major opposition voiced, though it is argued that some in Russia consider this today as in fact a 'tragedy' – a point that will be taken up in the end of the series in more detail. (The soundtrack sustains this tragic feeling.)

This ending of the Communist Party also meant the end of the whole state, since in the context of these events the Soviet Union was also dissolved, driving home the message that the fate of the Communist Party in China should be considered as tightly interwoven with the fate of China as a state as well. With Gorbachev's TV announcement of his resignation as president of the Soviet Union on 25 December 1991, the hammer and sickle flag was lowered (accompanied by burial music) and the Russian flag was raised instead (both dated to the minute!). The following day the Soviet Union was officially declared dissolved. (This tragic ending is underlined visually by recalling Lenin and Stalin, who look at the viewer questioning why their work has been destroyed.)

What happened after this 'tragedy' was a complete economic restructuring along US-proposed lines (a 'shock therapy'), which caused economic regression for the people and previously unseen criminality. (People queuing up in shops and police with criminals are shown, the music turning again to disquieting rhythms.) Even Yeltsin is reported to have acknowledged that Russia was the country with the highest rate of mafia activity in the world. Thus, to a Chinese audience, the risks in 'losing' the CCP are drastically outlined. The economic regression is said to have been even worse than during World War II! And life expectancy as well is alleged to have shrunk massively. Thus, the scope of the tragedy is highlighted, underlined also by Putin, who evaluated the end of the Soviet Union in similar regretful terms in 2005 (cited as text to underline its importance). Even Russian scholars are claimed to support the view that this threw Russia back in her development by 'decades'.

In this vein, the end of the first instalment sums up all the great achievements of the Soviet Communist Party since its beginnings, which were achieved with relatively few members. But then when membership grew, the party declined, which suggests that the problem lay mainly in its inner structures. This also reminds the Chinese cadres of the importance of 'quality' rather than of 'quantity', to prevent similar internal decay in the CCP. And thus it is plausible why the series concentrates on the party's various aspects, so as to explain why the CPSU and the whole country finally perished. (The final credits, shown after every instalment, are accompanied by the somewhat comforting but also meditative theme 'Tennessee' from *Pearl Harbor*, which suggests that another way – the Chinese one arguably – is nevertheless possible, if one pays heed to and ponders the 'negative lesson' of the CPSU.)

The basic theories and guidelines of the Soviet Communist Party
(Sugong de jiben lilun ji zhidao fangzhen 苏共的基本理论及指导方针)

After the general assessment in the first instalment, the documentary now turns to particular aspects of the CPSU, first its ideological baselines. In the fatherland of capitalism, the UK, the commentary emphatically starts, there was an opinion poll in 1999 about the most important thinkers of the world, which ranked Marx (1818–83) at the top, and Einstein (1879–1955) only second. When the BBC did a similar survey on the Internet, the result again rendered Marx as number one. (Ironically, Hegel (1770–1831) just made number 20.) This, it is suggested, should demonstrate that Marx is far from being outdated in the twenty-first century – and implicitly counters the argument that Marx belongs in the 'dustbin of history'. (The soundtrack here evolves from sad music taken from *The Rock* into a quicker, more upbeat 'chase' theme from the same movie.)

Marxism–Leninism is such a major force in society because it was the basis on which parties were built that stood up for the interests of the working class. With reference to the famous *Communist Manifesto* (1848) (which is shown with full pathos as solemnly emanating light!), the commentary argues that it marked the first time that class conflict between the workers and the capitalists was formulated as a principle, which then became the central, basic theory in communist parties. (Soviet film clips and footage are at times repeated from the first instalment as a link back.) And Lenin then took the step of adapting that basic idea for actual political needs, analysing imperialism and developing the additional notion of first instituting socialism in one country via a revolution. Furthermore, the commentary argues, it was Lenin who developed the particular idea of the dictatorship of the proletariat. (Lenin's crucial text passages are presented as blended-in script and read aloud. The heavily 'ideological' presentation in this instalment is very much text-centred and the music soundtrack accordingly reduced or toned-down.) By doing so, Lenin necessarily strengthened the means to exert that dictatorship: the party. Thus it was Lenin who adapted the basic Marxian ideas to societal practice. (As in the first instalment, Lenin's presentation is, if musically underscored, accompanied mostly by Russian folk songs.)

When the first socialist state was established Lenin again had to find new solutions to new problems, since there was no ready-made answer on how to build up a socialist system. (This part is accompanied by a slow theme from *Pirates of the Caribbean*, making for one of the relatively rare occasions where Western blockbuster music is used also for the 'good times', though for periods of difficult decisions.) His experiment was furthermore under constant attack by enemy forces, which also led to widespread hunger – thus giving rise to the argument that famine was not the fault of Lenin's experiments but of the fact that the Soviet Union was hampered from outside. Consequently Lenin had to deal with these challenges and instituted 'war-time communism', which meant confiscation of grain to feed the soldiers and workers, rationing goods, and so on, which is described as having been helpful in the war to remain in power. But on the other hand the peasants were dissatisfied. Therefore, in 1921 Lenin reoriented his policies and instituted the NEP. Instead of confiscation, now the tax system was reintroduced. And this turn to more pragmatic economic policies, the commentary suggests, eased the tensions.

Stalin at first kept to this policy, but when some people used it to make more profit by driving and manipulating prices to the effect that even bread had to be rationed in the cities in 1928, he started to reconsider economic policies. (Under Stalin, Russian folk songs keep a link to Lenin but are in a more march-like version.) Stalin rejected the approach of Trotsky (1879–1940, named here for the first time and appearing vaguely as Stalin's rival), who was fixed upon getting the world revolution started in the West that he thought would help the Russians in their own development in turn. Stalin saw this as an underestimation of Russian capabilities, which did not need the West. He wanted to catch up with the West by relying on the Soviet Union's own forces. To guarantee no one would ever again interfere in these experiments, he put the focus on quick development and on military defence, i.e. on heavy industry. Instead of importing goods from the West, the Soviet Union should produce everything herself. This was the basic thrust of his spectacular industrialisation programme. To achieve these aims, Stalin ordered the means of production to be nationalised and set up a planned economy and cooperatives all through the country. With this system he could lay the foundations for victory over fascism and an economic rise after the war.

With his 'Stalin model', however, he deviated at some points from dialectic materialism, due to the times and also because he was too fixed on taking decisions all alone – which drives home the message to the viewer that 'collective leadership', as has become the CCP's mantra after Mao's time, is the better alternative. Stalin therefore evaluated the situation wrongly when he thought that socialism had already been realised fully, when he aimed at doing away with money to exchange goods instead, or when he one-sidedly focused upon heavy industry, neglecting light industry and agriculture. (The soundtrack here provides a sad track from *Pearl Harbor*: 'Heart of a volunteer'.) This makes for a rather mixed assessment by the documentary of the Stalinist economic policies, which has also to be seen against the Chinese discussions on economic policies that certainly deviate from dialectic materialism, but had to be pushed through against the opposition of Stalinist factions. (In fact, it seems that the evaluation of Stalinist economic policies is one of the issues contested even between the makers of the documentary, as Li Shenming, for one, would continuously defend the 'Stalin model'.)

When Khrushchev took over (accompanied by dark music taken from *Pirates of the Caribbean*: 'Underwater march'), he went against Stalin and Lenin altogether and thus betrayed Marxism–Leninism. For example, he argued that the state represented not just the workers but the whole nation – thus doing away with class distinctions in practice. Therefore he also attacked the basic idea of the dictatorship of the proletariat. But, the Chinese commentary stresses, as long as there are class conflicts, the state cannot cover all classes! (This is notable given the 'Three Represents' of Jiang Zemin, which opened the CCP to 'all progressive forces in society', assuming their existence in all 'classes', which suggests that the documentary *Ju an si wei* was in tendency critical of this 'theory'.) This meant that Khrushchev invited people into the party who did not represent the workers' interests. In other words: he was not cautious enough to prevent a restoration of capitalism. Even though he undertook some economic reforms, he still was fixed upon heavy industry and arms production, and did not end the overly centralised economic policy making which made for very low efficiency. In sum, the commentary stresses, the aim that Khrushchev set in 1961 (at the high-time of Sino–Soviet disagreement), i.e. to become a communist society within 20 years, was totally unrealistic from the outset. (Here, one may recall Deng Xiaoping's later 'adjustment' of 'theory' to argue for China's being only in the beginning stadium of socialism – after similar Chinese ambitions to find a short cut to communism under Mao, even overtaking the Soviets, though 'class' remained fundamental to Mao.)

These 'errors' of Khrushchev were in part corrected by Brezhnev, who admitted in 1967 on the fiftieth anniversary of the Soviet Union that Soviet society still was characterised by class, and needed the dictatorship of the proletariat. (His era presentation is accompanied by themes from *Pirates of the Caribbean*.) Brezhnev also realised and stated that the Soviet Union was yet to 'develop socialism' against 'communist' utopian short-term aims of Khrushchev. But Brezhnev had also his drawbacks: he clung too much to the letter, and proved uncreative in adapting Marxist categories to social practice. Although he managed to challenge the US on the military field, he soon turned to imperialist means himself (the so-called Brezhnev Doctrine of 1968), playing out his superpower role without constraint, thus going against Marxism–Leninism (hinting at Chinese fears at the time of Soviet intervention and hegemony as witnessed by Eastern Europe and Afghanistan). And because of Brezhnev's obsession with the status quo, the commentary argues, the Soviet Union slept through new developments such as the rise of information technologies. Thus, he made for the economy to lag behind more and more, leading to a slow-down in economic growth. Had he taken up reforms in the spirit of Marxism–Leninism adequately (as China did, the implication goes), he might have prevented the ensuing developments and the Soviet socialist system could have survived. (Visually, this part juxtaposes icons of socialist realism and American-style fast food to insinuate Brezhnev's 'in-between' position.)

When Gorbachev took over (accompanied by sinister music from *Troy*: 'The Greek Army and its defeat', and presenting him by stills as a 'culprit' to be considered in detail), at first (in 1986–8) the economy recovered but then great crises set in, first in agriculture, then in the industrial sector. To solve this Gorbachev wrongly blamed the party and the social system as the causes of these crises, and in time he moved even farther from Marxism–Leninism than Khrushchev had done. Gorbachev was on the one hand a product of his times, but, the commentary argues, he had also a personal responsibility for what happened. He quite consciously moved to capitalist positions and betrayed socialism, as is proven by his (later!) statement to the avail that Marxism was simply a theory that did not work in practice. (From here onwards, the underlying music is the track 'Attack' from *Pearl Harbor*, describing the attack and its sad aftermath.) When he came out with a book in 1987 on *perestroika* (also translated immediately into Chinese, i.e. in the same year also, as the book cover shown demonstrates), he promoted his key ideas such as *glasnost* and humanistic socialism, which in fact, the commentary states, showed him actually as a social democrat. When in 1988 he approved of the Khrushchevian idea of the state representing 'all', he was ready to debunk the whole idea of the dictatorship of the proletariat. In 1990 he stated that Marxism–Leninism was in fact a very 'limited' theory, and later in his memoirs (also translated into Chinese in 2002) said he in fact wanted to lay power into constitutional hands which, in practice, meant a Western parliamentary multi-party system. (The footage showing an easily chatting Gorbachev on the international or domestic stage is countered by the sad tunes from *Pearl Harbor*.) The slogan he used ('all power to the soviets') cleverly recalled Lenin, the commentary argues, but the intention of the latter in 1917 was to get power for the Bolshevists, whereas Gorbachev had the opposite intention. By opening up power to be allotted via elections, people like Yeltsin and dissident Sakharov (1921–89) could become influential. And for all his constitutional talk, it was Gorbachev who went against the constitution when he proposed a new alliance of those Soviet republics that had voted for staying together (and allowed those who had opted out to go).

In 1990 economy was down, the state was in debt and staple goods were short. In spite of some economic growth it was the huge debt of state that Gorbachev had accumulated which drove inflation and thus made for the economic crisis. Thus, if economic crisis was the main factor in the crumbling of the Soviet Union, Gorbachev's economic policy had added substantially to it. In his belief in Western capitalist methods, the commentary points out, he took privatisation and neo-liberalism as an all-round remedy to check the crisis. In 1991 liberalist economist Yavlinsky drew up a reform programme together with Harvard economists that was to transform the Soviet economy into a Western-style market economy and democracy. The idea was to have the economy undergo 500 days of shock therapy to emerge as a market economy. In this context, privatisation was enforced at high speed. When Lenin had instituted the NEP, the commentary concludes, he had in mind to end up with socialism. With Gorbachev, the intention was precisely the reverse. In sum, Lenin's legacy was betrayed first by Khrushchev, then by Gorbachev. And the latter was the worst since Yeltsin at least would openly advocate capitalism, whereas Gorbachev concealed his stance by the more pleasant-sounding term of 'humanistic socialism'.

The ideological work of the Soviet Communist Party (Sugong de yishi xingtai gongzuo 苏共的意识形态工作)

Building on the discussion of ideological baselines, the documentary now focuses on how ideology is transmitted, starting from a particular event of ideological clash: in 1988, a public letter in the newspaper *Sovetskaya Rossiya* (Soviet Russia) by a woman lecturer, entitled 'I cannot give up my principles', caused a public stir: the author attacked the ongoing mood of 'reflecting on history' under Gorbachev as nothing more than a drive for Westernisation and a blackening of Soviet history. This letter, the Chinese commentary argues, was immediately picked up by the so-called reformers as representing the 'conservatives'. Gorbachev quickly called an emergency meeting and used the occasion to replace steadfast Leninist Ligachev in the Politburo with reformer Yakovlev (1923–2005) who launched a counter-attack on *Pravda* (The Truth) against the woman lecturer, calling her a 'Stalinist'.

With this heightened attack against the Soviet system from the side of the highest political circles, ideological work necessarily crumbled. Gorbachev even made Yakovlev, one of the first Soviet students ever to have studied in the US, head of the Propaganda Department. In this way Yakovlev, who 'hated socialism' (underlined by threatening music cueing the viewer into anxiety and showing a Chinese translation of one of his books),[32] could destroy it from within, arguing the October Revolution had interrupted Russia's way to democracy and one should go back to that point to take up this thread anew! His adoration for capitalism could play full force because Gorbachev had given him this chance, which means the latter was personally responsible. All this started, in fact, with Gorbachev's *glasnost* slogan put forward in 1986. The term had already been used by Lenin, but again, the Chinese commentary stresses, Gorbachev had cleverly reoriented the concept which with Lenin had meant to take in public sentiment. (Such ideological 'clarifications' are presented in black and white script in a very didactic fashion.) Gorbachev (accompanied by gangster-like music), used it instead to induce the media to become more 'independent'. In course of time the term connoted 'democratisation'. As soon as open criticism was permitted, the anti-Soviet forces gained momentum. But Gorbachev himself, the commentary adds, was partial, being 'democratic' only towards the critics but not towards the defenders of the Soviet legacy. In combining *glasnost* with a 'reflection on history', he put all Soviet history on trial. Again this turned against Stalin, greatly exaggerating the number of his alleged 'victims'. Stalin was now even accused of 'errors' at the beginning of World War II, and victory in the war was no longer connected to the Communist Party. (One might add here that it was only in these years under Gorbachev that an investigation into the secret pact between Hitler and Stalin was undertaken, arguing for the existence of this pact – which greatly damaged Stalin's 'anti-fascist' image.) In consequence, the Chinese commentary stresses, criticism of Stalin turned into criticism of the system, and it even extended backwards to a criticism of Lenin. That the compulsory subject of Marxism–Leninism in schools was also abolished in this context only completed the picture.

Public media now started moving towards capitalist positions, and more and more a 'clandestine press' appeared. Some made a real profit out of these 'underground' publications, and people like Solzhenitsyn (1918–2008) with his *The Gulag Archipelago* and other anti-Stalinist authors dominated public opinion. Following the appearance of all these underground publications, the state quite tellingly reacted by legalising them in 1990. In this way, the Communist Party lost its ideological guiding function. Consequently, some openly advocated capitalism, whereas others wanted even to go back to the tsar! As a Soviet writer put it: what the enemy had lacked in the 1940s as a weapon to subdue the Soviet Union, was now there: malicious media. And these included not only newspapers and journals but also TV, which started to put on critical programmes. Oppositional forces agitated against censorship and used the new possibility of elections to do anti-Soviet propaganda. This led to many people's losing trust in the state, and starting to change sides. (Obviously, this is a clear call for close political surveillance of the Chinese media by the CCP.)

In 1988, the so-called Soviet reformers came forward with a manifesto criticising Stalin and the Soviet system and arguing for Westernisation. These people quickly made a career, for example Popov, Yeltsin and Sakharov. Yegor Gaidar was to be the central figure in economic reform, and these people together with the mafia simply buried socialism, because now the basic ideology was no longer Marxism–Leninism. And this sealed the CPSU's fate.

In sum, whereas in the beginning of the Soviet Union, revolutionary ideals and a heroic fight in the war had been driving the people to act, now all this was declared a lie, which explains the question raised earlier in the documentary series why nobody defended the Soviet Union: they now all believed this new 'propaganda' (conveniently sidelining the fact that if that was the case, then Soviet education to 'believe in propaganda' worked now only against the system that had created it). Therefore, the commentary concludes as a basic lesson to be derived from all this, ideological work is of central importance.

The party style of the Soviet Communist Party (Sugong de dangfeng 苏共的党风)

The documentary now moves to the issue of work style and therewith to human agency closer to home for the watching cadres. Presenting a statue of Lenin in front of the revolutionary headquarters of the October Revolution, again a particular event is taken as a starting point: as the Chinese viewer is reminded, every child in Chinese elementary school of the 1950s and 1960s heard the story of Lenin and the guard, which illustrated that Lenin was not haughty but praised the guard who had refused him entry before showing his papers just like everybody else for his sincere working attitude. This shows that Lenin's style took into consideration the people he dedicated his life to. He was able to motivate the people to join the revolution with the prospects of peace, land and bread, and attracted them to work together for the common goal.

With the founding of the Soviet Union, finally the people became the sovereign of state, and Lenin saw to it that everybody was seen working (i.e. that no one could just live off his privileges). For example he 'took up' the idea of 'voluntary work' by some cadres, and instituted a manual workday on Saturdays when cadres also would do manual labour. (Needless to say, Chinese communists in the early days of the PRC were already copying this gesture.) The rationale (stressed by citations of his speeches in script) was that the party is simply a part of the people. Therefore, the basic problem was to keep the contact with the masses. Also, without them the war could not have been won. Consequently, for example Lenin gave orders that every administrative body had to be open to the public seven days a week, and carefully register every complaint. He himself daily received a number of visitors. As a US journalist (Albert R. Williams) is cited: Lenin's bureau was the greatest reception room of the world. In sum, Lenin's style was oriented towards 'serving' the masses.

With Stalin, the style, it is admitted, changed somewhat, but he, too, has to be credited for great achievements from which everybody still benefits today, such as the underground in Moscow. If without Lenin there had not been a socialist revolution, without Stalin there would not have been a socialist great power. His 'steel' will made for socialist industrialisation and victory in the war. He even sent his own 'beloved' son to the German front, and when he was taken prisoner by the Germans who offered to exchange him, a 'simple soldier', for the German field marshal Paulus held prisoner by the Soviets, Stalin refused the 'unequal deal', rather having his son die in a concentration camp. (It might not be needed to stress here that this is a legendary, but very typically 'moralised' rendering of the facts: Stalin never cared about his eldest son – born to his first wife, with whom relations were strained.) By this discipline and personal 'sacrifice', the Chinese commentary argues, he secured the respect of his people.

Stalin is presented as personally living a frugal life, having only two uniforms and two civilian sets of clothes and leaving behind just half a month's worker's pay at his death. As he himself often liked to refer to Greek hero Antaios, whose strength was derived from his mother Earth, Gaia, the commentary adds the only danger a great hero could run into was to lose contact with his 'mother', in this case with the masses. Therefore, Stalin only failed when he lost that nurturing contact. In other words: the party must ensure never to lose that contact to prevent disaster.

Consequently, it is argued, Stalin's 'problems' were connected to his loosening contact with the masses after 1928, i.e. his coming into unchallenged power. (This early date is interesting as it actually undermines the impression given elsewhere in the documentary that Stalin only 'lost contact' in his 'later years' and therefore should be evaluated positively for most of his time. The soundtrack provides again a sad theme from *Pearl Harbor*.) Above all, he lost contact with the countryside, which he would not visit any more (which goes to explain why he had particular problems in realising problems in the agrarian sector). And the party, it is argued, was instrumental in building up a personality cult around him (as if he had had no role in that) hence isolating him even more. (This means whereas he had some responsibility, the party was responsible as well by distancing him from the masses.) Therefore, he gradually lost touch, like Antaios from Gaia, his mother Earth.

This tendency of loosening bonds grew worse under Khrushchev (who is presented here walking in with comrades in hats and coats like gangsters, with disquieting sounds, and later accompanied by dark music taken from 'Blood ritual' in *Pirates of the Caribbean*). Although he voiced his opposition to the personality cult around Stalin, he did no better; he concentrated power and finally furthered a personality cult around himself. This overbearing attitude led to his being removed from power, although he could not understand why those people that had always applauded him and his policies were now disposing of him as if they had had no role in the policies now criticised. In fact, the commentary suggests that this atmosphere and the party's style of encouraging only applause necessarily made for such an outcome. And Brezhnev was even worse. In his conservative 'no reforms' mode he widened the gap between the party style and the masses. As then editor-in-chief of the *Pravda* commented in his memoirs, Brezhnev was always using the same set phrases on capitalism being doomed and the great achievements at home in a purely formal way, without any creativity. His personal arrogance and vanity damaged the party style even more. Given the fact that he shared with Lenin the name 'Ilyich', he encouraged the talk of the 'two Ilyichs', having Lenin and himself glorified during the sixtieth anniversary of the October Revolution, i.e. 1977. Since he was fond of ceremony and medals, he made for being decorated with dozens of medals so that at his funeral there were 44 people needed to carry them all. (The accompanying music is, quite fittingly, the sad opening theme from *The Rock*, describing a burial.)

Brezhnev is also presented as very vain, greedy and corrupt, having promoted the party secretary of Azerbaijan when the latter presented him with his bust in gold. Seeing such behaviour, the commentary concludes, it was small wonder that corruption grew exponentially in the party and that people were no longer motivated to enter the party because of lofty ideals but rather joined up out of hope for some profit. And in larger society, economic and political problems abounded.

With Gorbachev (again introduced with disquieting sounds), the party completely lost its link to the masses, according to the commentary. Even though he toured the country, he talked above the people's heads and was only a rhetorician. (In this, the presentation is less than convincing, since the footage shows continually an easy-chatting Gorbachev among the people. At times, as with Khrushchev earlier, the technique of stills or slow motion is used to introduce a visual element of estrangement.) The distance was also growing more pronounced between him and the party, since many cadres were not properly informed before-hand but had to collect from the news or the newspapers whatever new policies Gorbachev had voiced somewhere. (Here, it seems, Gorbachev is envied for his medial 'appeal'.) He thus lived out a very personalised style, becoming totally subjective. For example, he single-handedly attacked the vodka-drinking habits that were so popular, earning him the nickname 'secretary mineral water'. (Again, this sequence is very unconvincing, given the fact that the CCP often drives similar 'good manners' or 'anti-drugs' campaigns, as every watching cadre knows all too well.) As one-time secretary of his, Valery Boldin (author of *Ten Years that Shook the World: the Gorbachev Era as Witnessed by his Chief of Staff*), is cited from his memoirs, he was fond of Western 'enlightened despotism' concepts and loved to read for hours Western positive evaluations of himself instead of taking up the files that he should have worked through. Another important Soviet leading figure, Nikolai Ryzhkov, is referred to as evidence that Gorbachev talked only to himself and did not consult others. Believing his elaborations would bring success by themselves, the accusation goes, he did not investigate any facts, making for the real problems to grow and grow. And he did not cling to his ideals: whereas he declared that the party meant everything to him before he came to power, his later actions suggested that the opposite was true. This image is reinforced by his ex-secretary: Gorbachev changed like a chameleon. (In this way, it is hoped the hard-to-avoid visual 'positive' image would be undermined by suggesting he had, in fact, 'two faces'. The accompanying music is 'December 7th' from *Pearl Harbor*, describing the aftermath of the attack.)

By Gorbachev's individual style many party members felt alienaated and many left the party for good (underlined didactically by coloured graphs showing a decline in membership, and blended-in numbers). In face of all the economic and social problems, trust in the party continued to decline, so that in 1990, according to Ryzhkov, the party was almost dead. (The underlying music is again the sad 'Underwater march' from *Pirates of the Caribbean*.) Although Gorbachev later self-critically admitted that he had been too aloof from the masses, he had not only committed an 'error', as he termed it, but – according to the Chinese commentary – outright betrayal. For all his talk of humanitarianism and democracy, he had led the people to lose all trust in the party. And thus it is no wonder the people, who no longer felt represented by this party, did not care for its demise. When, as a last attempt to rescue the Soviet Union the putsch was put down, many 'real' commu-nists were desperate, and some tragically resorted to suicide because all they had fought for in the past was now destroyed.

The privileged stratum of the Soviet Communist Party (Sugong de tequan jieceng 苏共的特权阶层)

The approach of the documentary now zooms in on the leading cadres' lifestyle and the delicate problem of corruption. In this instalment, the storyline begins again with a concrete event: in 1988 in front of a shop in Moscow a huge crowd gathered because this particular shop, which had sold luxury products only to the privileged – or, as the populace said, the 'communist aristocrats' – was going to be closed. The institution of such special places for privileged cadres, the commentary explains, was invented under Brezhnev and would eventually contribute to the party's downfall. Blending in a sequence from Eisenstein (1898–1948) and Aleksandrov's (1903–83) famous film *October* (1928) on the October Revolution, this rush for luxury goods is contrasted with the times of Lenin when a slice of bread was treasured. In that film a 'true story' was referred to, where an obviously uncorrupted cadre responsible for grain collection was himself so underfed that he fell unconscious from hunger. It was only when seeing this dramatic proof of utter unselfishness and dedication that Lenin decided to set up special canteens for cadres so that they at least were fed enough to work. But from this 'sensible measure' to guarantee the ability to work, slowly there developed the idea of privileges.

Only a tiny minority of high cadres was entitled to frequent these later shops, however, buying French brandy, Scotch whisky, and so on. This was a far cry not only from Lenin but also from Stalin, who had insisted on strict cadre discipline. 'Privileges' in these earlier times consisted rather of the cadres' special sacrifices for the people, as the commentary declares with pathos. Khrushchev was the leader who started with material privileges; however, due to the fact that he frequently had cadres replaced, there was not yet a fixed class to profit from them. Thus, it was only under Brezhnev (introduced in a mafia-like appearance with threatening sounds), who wanted a fixed loyal body of cadres, that the system of privileges was instituted, reducing the incentive to work efficiently for those already on the job they most probably would hold for a long time, if not a lifetime. And anyone who could do so tried to prove his loyalty in order to enter the ever-swelling bureaucratic body to get a share of these privileges. As Gorbachev-rival and 'orthodox Marxist' Ligachev is quite unconvincingly cited from his memoirs, cadres were even reprimanded if they wanted to step back freely from their privileges for not endangering the comfort of everybody else.[33]

This system included also privileges for children of higher cadres (and here clearly a Chinese viewer's association would go to the similar case of Chinese so-called 'princelings'). For example, Brezhnev's son-in-law and his son both made spectacular careers in a short time. His daughter accumulated great riches, though she was very probably involved in smuggling activities. (Visually, these 'cases' are introduced by black and white photos with a spotlight, or film clips with a reduced aperture, giving the impression of a detective's perspective.) Even though some of their criminal dealings were reported, none of those involved was ever put to trial. Brezhnev's secretary for domestic affairs enriched himself as well, and these unhealthy tendencies grew even worse during the later period of his rule. When in 1980 a great scandal over undeclared caviar sold to the West shook the Soviet Union, it was discovered that Brezhnev's relatives and politicians he relied on were involved. Brezhnev reacted by personally intervening to block any legal consequences (illustrated by citing him in speech bubbles). He also distributed positions against bribery, and when even his closest political allies argued this should be stopped since it might severely hamper the image of socialism, he would not accept it, clinging to the status quo. This made for a widening gap between the party and the people who would now usually talk of a 'them' against an 'us'. (Underlining the importance of the whole problem of privileges and corruption, this instalment is again heavily text-centred with a soundtrack reduced mainly to the spoken commentary.)

However, the commentary argues, Western reports that the whole Communist Party was corrupt were exaggerated and only malign propaganda, since this pertained only to a small range of cadres (thus absolving the 'normal' cadres). Furthermore, one should distinguish between a 'sensible' difference in allotment and 'privileges' (whatever that might mean in practice); and one should distinguish illegal ways of seeking gains, going outright against party discipline and law, from 'privileges'. (Here, it seems, the commentary is somewhat retreating to argue that there must not be complete egalitarianism, as if the strong criticism of high-cadre privileges in the Soviet Union might be taken up too literally by the Chinese viewing cadres. To hammer home the 'conclusion' and mark its importance, it is didactically presented in yellow script.)

Under Gorbachev, finally, the privileged cadres formed into a new bourgeoisie that even intended to make their own children inherit their privileges and wealth. With shots taken of Gorbachev's huge luxurious dacha it is argued that this was the true background to the drive for capitalism: it would make it easier to keep wealth for future generations as well. Formerly privileges had at least been only for the present generation. Now it was logical that the emerging new bourgeoisie argued for the reinstitution of private ownership against socialism. (This, in other words, means that the whole 'reform' endeavours under Gorbachev were only a cover-up for legalising personal wealth and inheritance. This is notable with a view to the fact that China herself, at the time of the production of this documentary, was preparing for the strongly debated new property law that was to be passed in 2007, and the documentary might be interpreted as a 'leftist' indirect comment.)

During Gorbachev's time in office state enterprises were often simply economically 'transformed' in the sense they were treated as personal belongings by their managers, and most of the newly rich had quite tellingly been party cadres before. Thus, the commentary suggests, these high cadres were the chief gravediggers of the Soviet Union, and many also kept their economically favoured positions after the collapse of that state.

On the other hand, according to an American economist cited in the documentary, the social gap in the Soviet Union was much smaller than in capitalist countries. Therefore, that class which wanted to achieve and keep more wealth in the Soviet Union logically opted for doing away with socialism, which challenged their newly acquired status. The people, in turn, understandably perceived the party as representing the interests of the high cadres only. And thus, given the lack of resolve against privileges, the party suffered from a progressive disease, which also made for the fact that in the end nobody cared for it – again explaining the startling fact that at the end of the Soviet Union and the Communist Party hardly anybody stood up for them.

The organisational line of the Soviet Communist Party (Sugong de zuzhi luxian 苏共的组织路线)

From this focus on personal shortcomings such as corruption, the documentary moves on to more structural issues. In 1918, Lenin had to confront the fact that no country was willing to recognise the new state of the Soviet Union diplomatically. Being a skilled strategist, he thus opted for setting up a separate peace treaty with enemy Germany, which, however, in the beginning was very unpopular with his party. The vote for this move was therefore very close. Bukharin especially voiced opposition, and Lenin, it is argued, was very much for 'fair play' (!), winning others over by persuasion and accepting voices of dissent before such important decisions as legitimate. In this way, he proved himself an ideal model of how to act out 'democratic centralism'. (The underlying music is another of the rare occasions where Lenin is linked with soundtrack taken from *Pirates of the Caribbean*, though consisting of more spirited parts, as the message is a 'positive' one.)

This idea of democratic centralism was to be a guiding organisational principle by which Lenin could realise his famous statement: give me a revolutionary organisation and I will turn over all of Russia. The commentary explains that the idea of democratic centralism itself goes back to Marx and Engels (1820–95), was fixed by the Bolsheviks in 1905 and written into the party statutes in 1906. In 1920 it eventually became a normative part of the Comintern also.

During Lenin's lifetime, the Central Committee was to be very small, all had equally one vote, and decisions were taken by majority votes. In other words: basically all had equal rights, and leading positions in the party were also only allotted via voting. In turn, those in office had to report on their work. On the other hand, when oppositional parties were dissolved (by this, de facto, admitting there were 'limits' to Lenin's 'democratic' attitude),[34] Lenin would argue that the points of criticism they had embodied should be taken up seriously. However, he made clear that after majority decisions had been taken, they had to be carried out swiftly and strictly to prevent any 'anarchism'. The basic guideline was therefore Lenin's motto: discuss and criticise freely, but act as one.

It was only due to foreign intervention and other external pressure that Lenin 'had to' focus more on discipline and centralism (than on democracy, by this again admitting Lenin's democratic outlook was qualified). During the Civil War he was forced to act as a commander and this meant that internal party democracy was hampered. To guarantee success, Lenin conceived of party-surveying organs (also graphically explained in a didactic vein), though they were to consist of only a very few people. (Notably, there is no word about the larger societal 'surveying body', the infamous Cheka and later KGB! It is only in this section that some mild criticism is voiced even of Lenin, though it is explained by the 'needs of the time'. Most of this section on Lenin's time is presented with spirited Russian folk music in the background, cueing the viewer into positive feelings about this potentially unsettling topic.)

Stalin, like Lenin, the commentary boldly states had been 'open to criticism' in the beginning. For example, it is contended that in 1936 the constitution was only passed after months of 'debates', and even in the face of Nazi aggression, party sessions went on relentlessly! (This 'democratic' rendering of Stalin in the 1930s – in view of his massive terror, already at its height at the time – is quite breathtaking.)

However, from 1934 onward Stalin's position in the party was unchallenged (which, in turn, is one of the few hints in the documentary to the fact that Stalin had ever faced any challenge to his supremacy), and he became more and more 'self-confident', the commentary more cautiously adds. (Only here the music changes from the bucolic mode to a more anxiety-raising and sad one taken from 'Underwater march' in *Pirates of the Caribbean* and then 'December 7th' from *Pearl Harbor*). In fact, he no longer convened the National Congress, and often only dictated the new policies orally – thus more or less contradicting the above 'democratic' image. However, as one of his trusted generals, Georgy Zhukov (1896–1974), accounts in his memoirs (published in Chinese translation in 1991), Stalin did call and consult a smaller circle of people quite regularly.

As for surveillance, it is argued that it changed 'only with Stalin' from a counter-check on the party to an instrument of control of the people, namely to eradicate opposition, which, it is admitted, was very 'unpopular' with the people (again presenting the official surveillance system graphically in parallel to Lenin's times). (This is one of the rare instances that the Great Purges of the 1930s are alluded to, though without going into detail.) In effect, the commentary only states, this led to everybody's simply fawning over Stalin. Since Stalin was too heavy-handed and attacked 'some' people 'wrongly', no one dared to speak up any longer.

With Khrushchev and Brezhnev, the attitude of deciding all by oneself changed to one of deciding 'by a few'. (This might explain why in the introduction to every instalment of the documentary, Khrushchev and the following leaders are all presented with an entourage, whereas the 'canonised' first two leaders, Lenin and Stalin, are single, marking their overpowering personalities.) But there was no real internal party democracy during these eras. For example, when a critical high-ranking railway engineer argued against Brezhnev's personality cult, he was simply expelled from the party. (Again, a sad extract from 'Heart of a volunteer' from *Pearl Harbor* underscores the commentary's message). In the earlier phase, Brezhnev had paid more attention to the party organisation, but later he suspended this and simply decided within a small circle. Failing in this way to listen to the 'wisdom' of the broader masses, he often took wrong decisions, for example the invasion in Afghanistan (1979–89), which was not popular at all with the people. In fact, that invasion would cost many Soviet lives (and was strongly criticised by the Chinese at the time).

Gorbachev tried to correct this, but went to the other extreme of 'democratisation' instead: he argued that if one did not agree with a decision one had not to execute it. This, according to the commentary, led to fatal consequences: capitalist liberalisation (which is explained as a 'fake' 'absolute freedom' since it is in reality a cover-up of giving capital free reign). In fact, Gorbachev soon moved to cancel the whole concept of democratic centralism in all the party statutes. In this way, he moved factually towards extreme subjectivism and did not take into account any longer.

Even Stalin had said that basically internal party decisions were to be taken by vote, and that after decisions are taken, the decisive factor is the cadres (who implement them). However, by Stalin's later years the system had degenerated into formalism and the control of cadres had become inefficient as well. (Again, the 'Underwater march' from *Pirates of the Caribbean* is in the background.)

Khrushchev therefore was able to climb the ladder in this system, having endeared himself to Stalin and his wife (which is a rare hint at Stalin's having helped Khrushchev to his position), and similarly Gorbachev came up by feigning loyalty to Brezhnev, knowing well this was the only criterion by which Brezhnev who liked to rely on friends and alliances of earlier days judged people. (These personal connections are stressed visually by showing Khrushchev and Gorbachev in their younger years together with their respective predecessors while the soundtrack blends sections of 'Blood ritual' from *Pirates of the Caribbean* and of 'Heart of a volunteer' from *Pearl Harbor*.) When Gorbachev came to power, he simply cancelled democratic centralism as a guiding principle, dismissed all those cadres not of his opinion and took in his own trusted followers. In this way he almost completely revamped the higher cadre stratum, and he also changed the editorial staff of many leading publishing organs, which was the death bell ringing for the Soviet Union. In consequence, the commentary concludes that due to Gorbachev's wrong cadre recruitment line, the cadres were profoundly confused about the organisational line, the party's image degenerated, and the people lost their trust altogether.

The leading circle of the Soviet Communist Party (Sugong de lingdao jituan 苏共的领导集团)

The documentary now shifts its attention to the decisive people driving all this: as Lenin already had realised, a class can only govern when it is organised well and has a potent leadership. This means that personal leadership capability plays a crucial role: it must not only be able to organise but must also continuously 'develop' Marxism further, though staying loyal to socialism, class conflict, and the dictatorship of the proletariat as the obvious baseline for any communist party. In short, the most central problem of the Soviet Communist Party was its leadership. According to Lenin, it is the party that guides the class by authority and experience. And this party, in the end, had become unchallenged in its power by being the only party to rule (i.e. being in the best position to keep this role, which would only be lost if the leadership was incapable).

All in all, there had been five 'generations' of leaders (thus stressing for the first time there were more leaders than just the one pivotal person per era as referred to in the previous instalments, and going well with Chinese present-day argumentation of 'collective leading generations'). At the time of Lenin (1870–1924), there were also Sverdlov (1885–1919), Kamenev (1883–1936), Zinoviev (1883–1936), Trotsky (1879–1940), Bukharin (1888–1938), and Stalin (1878–1953), all born between 1870 and 1885. (Here, notably, communists who for a long time had been ostracised from Soviet – and in consequence also PRC – historical memory such as Kamenev, Zinoviev, Trotsky, and Bukharin are presented, but without going into detail about what happened to them after Lenin's death. They are presented didactically with individual photos, as are all of the main members of the following leading circles.)

The generation of Stalin's leadership followed, including Molotov (1890–1986), Zhdanov (1896–1948), Kaganovich (1893–1991), Malenkov (1902–88), Khrushchev (1894–1971), and Mikoyan (1895–1978), who were born between 1890 and 1902. Thus, even a Stalin is 'put in place' in a larger leadership circle!

The third generation around Khrushchev consisted of Mikoyan again, Brezhnev (1906–82), Kosygin (1904–80), Podgorny (1903–83), Suslov (1902–82), and Gromyko (1909–89), born in the first decade of the twentieth century.

The fourth one around Brezhnev included Kosygin, Suslov, and Gromyko again, Chernenko (1911–85), Andropov (1914–84), and Ustinov (1908–84), born 'between 1910 and 1920'.[35] (The ensuing short period of Andropov and Chernenko is again skipped as not amounting to a 'generation', thus making for a little break in argumentation with the earlier generations where the successor is usually already presented as part of the circle of his predecessor, suggesting an 'organic' evolvement of the leading generations.)

The last one around Gorbachev (born 1931) included Ligachev (born 1920), Ryzhkov (born 1929), Yakovlev (1923–2005), Yeltsin (1931–2007), and Shevardnadze (born 1928). These men had all grown up after Stalin and mostly shared a Khrushchevian view. It was, the commentary insists, the latter (but for Ligachev) that would bring the Soviet Union down.

Of all these, of course, it was Lenin who was the exemplary leader (introduced by calm and peaceful music, and with him once again returning to the pivotal-person-per-era mode. Born in 1870 into a family of intellectuals, he very early became a revolutionary and often went to jail for his activities. He was not only a good Marxist, the commentary claims, but also someone able to 'correctly judge' the historical situation. For example, in early 1917 when there existed two rival regimes, there was some wavering among the Bolsheviks about what to do. Lenin, at the time still in exile, warned against any compromises with the capitalists as represented by the rival regime (i.e. led by Kerensky). Kamenev and Zinoviev, however, were in favour of collaboration with the provisional government. To argue against this, Lenin wrote his famous 'letters from afar'. When he voiced his strategic 'April theses', he made a strong point for an immediate social revolution. However, in the beginning many in the party were not convinced. As Molotov is cited with his memoirs, nearly all objected, not realising that while they were still talking of a democratic revolution, Lenin was already talking of a socialist one. When Lenin explained his views at length, the situation began to change and in the end he 'convinced' them.

This demonstrates that Lenin was capable of applying Marxism 'creatively' to the historical situation in Russia. Although he was the supreme authority, the commentary argues, he nevertheless clung to collective leadership and would not ignore the necessity of discussions with the others. He was thus also capable of taking on valuable suggestions forwarded by them. (Archival footage of and film clips on Lenin are accompanied again with a mix of music from *Pirates of the Caribbean* and Russian folklore.)

When he died, there were several possible candidates to succeed him: Trotsky, Bukharin, Zinoviev, and Stalin. (This is the first time the documentary explicitly admits that there existed rivals to Stalin, though remaining vague about the in-fighting around Lenin's succession.) As 'most of the CPSU judged it', the commentary argues, Trotsky had no clear visions for the Soviet Union, especially since he thought one could not build up socialism in Russia. Bukharin was considered weak in organisational skills, Zinoviev was outstanding in neither ideology nor organisation. Thus, the conclusion goes, the party understandably turned to Stalin, who had 'many deficiencies' but was determined and capable.

Like Lenin, Stalin had become a revolutionary early on as well. (Remarkably, there is no word about his childhood, which is usually the focus in Western studies, particularly to explain his later cruelty by the abusive treatment he endured as a child. Furthermore, whereas with Lenin the region of birth is named, with him there is no mention of his ethnic identity as being not a Russian but a Georgian!) He is presented as someone who – unlike Lenin – had never left Russia but had similarly undergone the 'revolutionary baptism' of several prison terms. According to the commentary, he was an 'outstanding Marxist' and gave everything to the country and its people. He was furthermore especially skilled in organising and paid for these activities with imprisonment during the October Revolution and during the Civil War. Being able to speak in a way that even ordinary people could follow, he could organise them well and was ready to sacrifice everything for his objectives. In short, he showed himself a born leader.

The problem with his leadership style was that he tended to concentrate 'too much' power on himself. Although he himself is said to have been no friend of personality cults, he did not do full justice to democratic centralism, the commentary cautiously states (by this referring back to the previous instalment). To those who held different opinions, he often was 'steely' and cruel. (Images of troubled party members underscore this impression of uneasiness.) Thus, the apparent unanimity in the party (shown by ever-applauding cadres at party events) was different from Lenin's time: for Lenin the collective was paramount, but with Stalin people agreed out of obedience to him.

Still, but for this fault, the merits he accumulated were outweighing this by far! Therefore, it is claimed, on the commemoration of what would have been Stalin's eightieth birthday in 1959, even someone like Churchill would honour him posthumously as an outstanding person. (This, again, seems to be a legend, as there is nothing in Churchill's collected speeches to this avail!)[36]

After Stalin, at first there was a collective leadership again, but then Khrushchev did away with everybody else as an 'anti-party clique' (which included Kaganovich, Malenkov and Molotov who, in fact, had tried to overthrow Khrushchev, not agreeing to his forced de-Stalinisation policy: a background which is, of course, left out in the documentary, thus insinuating he simply wanted to brush aside all others). Khrushchev came from a peasant family and was a 'complicated' person, as the commentary terms it. He knew 'near to nothing' of Marxism, and as sacked Molotov was later to state (in revenge), he took many wrong decisions precisely because he had no idea about it. For example, it was totally 'absurd' to claim the Soviet Union could arrive in 20 years at the communist society, as Khrushchev did in 1961 (at the time of the Sino–Soviet split) – an ideological position already criticised earlier in the documentary. It was precisely then, the commentary argues, that the country 'drifted away from Marxism'. (This comment is notable in the sense that, given the 'leftist' bent of the documentary, Khrushchev is here attacked for voicing policies in line with Mao's 'leftist' Great Leap Forward rhetoric.[37] The Chinese 'Great Leap Forward' of the late 1950s was, as might be reminded, historically one of the reasons for the Sino–Soviet split.)[38]

Khrushchev furthermore criticised Stalin mercilessly, though being simply a 'turncoat' himself, having praised Stalin in the latter's lifetime without ends, and letting himself be made into an object of personality cult as well. Basically, the Chinese commentary argues, he had 'no theory' but did things out of his moods. Consequently, his 'reforms' did not prove effective. For example, he ordered land to be turned into fields that was not suitable for agriculture at all. When he tried to decentralise, the party lost its guiding role and the result was an uncontrolled fragmentation of responsibilities. Namely his notorious aim to arrive at communism in a short time was totally utopian. Thus, the leading echelon of the party decided to step in, take him by surprise and demote him in 1964. (This, again, is a notable presentation as it seems a 'madman' had to be stopped who voiced policies that remind Chinese viewers of Great Leap Forward to Cultural Revolution experiences.)

Then Brezhnev took over who was born into a Russian worker's family in the Ukraine. Here it is argued – somewhat contradicting earlier instalments – that it was him to finally end the 'one person decides' mode of his two predecessors. On the one hand he is presented as a mere apparatchik, on the other it is acknowledged that he was able to stabilise the system. Basically, the people lived better under his rule, but there were also drawbacks: he was very 'conservative' which led to stagnation. This proved problematic especially in the second half of his long rule. 'Serve the people' was only lip service to him. He liked the Western style of living and had not much contact with the people. Since he overslept important reform needs, he was historically instrumental in bringing down the system in the end. But at the time, it is admitted, people were fairly satisfied: they lived better than before; the Soviet Union was apparently stabile and strong so that people in Russia today usually think of his reign as the best!

Gorbachev, born into a (Russian-Ukrainian) peasant family in the Northern Caucasus, and his clique, finally, had grown up under Khrushchev and had lost all faith by the latter's de-Stalinisation, as Gorbachev disclosed later in 2001 in a radio interview. In a book on Communism and Buddhism (*Moral Lessons of the Twentieth Century*, London: I.B. Tauris) with Ikeda Daisaku 池田大作, the leading figure of the Japanese lay Buddhist organisation Sōka gakkai 創価学会 which is involved in

Japanese politics via the party Kōmeitō 公明党, Gorbachev admitted not long after the end of the Soviet Union in 1993 (when he was invited by Ikeda to Tokyo) he had become critical even of Lenin and Marx. According to Gorbachev then, communism was simply 'impossible to realise'. (The book has been published in English in 2005 and translated into Chinese in the same year.) By this, the Chinese viewer is supposed to conclude that Gorbachev surely thought so already earlier.

In 1988, when still the leader of the Soviet Union, he pushed for 'unlimited democracy' and by this even 'informal' (*bu zhengshi* 不正式) groups were now allowed to set up a political party in the new multi-party system he created. His argument that the Communist Party should 'share' the power with the 'soviets' was in fact just Western-style democracy. Quickly, many 'informal' groups turned into oppositional parties, and free labour unions sprang up. This simply meant a complete overthrow of the system and the loss of power of central party organs.

It even came to the point that 'people like Sakharov and Popov' aimed at changing the constitution, the commentary stresses. The move for a multi-party system was especially pushed by Yeltsin, and Gorbachev consented to delete the leading role of the Communist Party from the constitution. (Somewhat differently from earlier instalments it is argued here that the driving force was Yeltsin, and Gorbachev only was giving in to him. The change in the constitution is visually emphasised by showing the text passage in question in Chinese translation.) This was the end of the secured basis of the Communist Party's leading role. By Gorbachev's dividing state and party in this move, he also now became the first elected 'president' of the Soviet Union. Gorbachev argued that elections would heighten the legitimacy also of the Communist Party, but this was only to shield his actual destruction of it by putting it on an equal footing with other societal groups. (This statement, of course, means that the party is acknowledged as 'endangered' in a free competitive field.)

Yeltsin then feigned to deal with corruption and malpractice only to attack orthodox high cadres, namely Ligachev. In 1987 he still encountered such strong opposition that it was Yeltsin who had to step down. But Gorbachev intervened to 'keep him' and had him elected by a very close vote as head of the Russian Soviet. In 1990 Yeltsin even left the Communist Party, and when in 1991 the president of the Russian Federation was elected, Yeltsin outdid the candidate of Gorbachev and Ryzhkov. As president, Yeltsin then prohibited further activities of political parties in state organs, mass organisations or basic industry, intending the Communist Party. Evidently, when even the (ex) leaders of a party do not sustain the party any longer, the conclusion goes, no wonder it is doomed. (Choral music cues the viewer here into a meditative mood.)

The reaction of the Soviet Communist Party to the Western world's Westernisation and splitting strategy (Sugong dui xifang shijie xihua, fenhua zhanlüe de yingdui 苏共对西方世界西化，分化战略的应对*)*

The last instalment now takes up the role of foreign influence in the Soviet demise, notably starting with a reference to a book by ex-US president Nixon (1913–94), titled *1999: Victory without War* (New York, NY: Simon and Schuster). Nixon argued in this book of 1988 (translated into Chinese already in 1989!) that there was a basic rivalry at work between the Western system ('we want a free world') and the Soviet one ('they want communism') which was fought out not by arms but ideology. In fact, in his prognosis he was right in another sense already earlier than in 1999: in the early 1990s communism had faltered there altogether, i.e. had 'lost without war'. All the time of her existence, the Western world had been against the Soviet Union, but at the times of Lenin the Soviet people was strong enough to resist. With Stalin, the communist flag was raised high and the West gave up its hope to put the Soviet Union down by force, the commentary contends. Therefore the West invented the undermining strategy of 'peaceful evolution'.[39] This was especially stepped up at the time of Khrushchev to Westernise and split the Soviet Union. (The soundtrack, again, provides – quite fittingly here – the 'Attack' from *Pearl Harbor*.) After Nixon came into power in the US, he went for a 'balance of power diplomacy'. And he tried to put forward a campaign in the realms of 'values' (freedom, democracy and so on). With US president Reagan (1911–2004), the strategy turned toward throwing Marx into the dustbin of history, whereas Gorbachev on his part was convinced that for the survival of mankind the two superpowers had somehow to come to an agreement. By this, however, he obscured the real ongoing competition between the two systems. Observing Gorbachev's attitude, the West thought time now was ripe, and Gorbachev, in fact, simply gave in.

The first strategy the West took up was to infiltrate the media, the commentary argues, demonstrating again the high importance the Chinese endow the media with. With Radio Free Europe and Radio Liberty the US pointed broadcasting channels towards the Soviet Union. Adding the BBC and the Deutsche Welle (German wave) the whole range of Eastern European communist countries was to be targeted. In fact, as Reagan stated, broadcasting stations were a fairly economic and effective way to discredit the Soviet Union. This discrediting was done with regard to history as well as with actual problems, instigating discontent. (Visually, this discontent is shown by Western media images describing communism as built on skulls, by the dismantling of the Berlin Wall and by the tearing down of Lenin's statues.) The CIA, for one, directly sponsored several programmes critical of Lenin and Stalin and full of praise for Gorbachev's Western lifestyle to win over the Soviet populace.

In fact, lifestyle was seen by the West as an ideal way of undermining Soviet morals. The idea, according to the CIA director, was that if 'they' sing 'our' songs, they will also 'think like us'. With this the West mainly targeted the youth, and Gorbachev had no patriotism to set up against this malign influence. (This explains, by contrast, why China has stepped up 'patriotic education' in the early 1990s). Instead, Gorbachev called upon the youth to 'look around'. He even gave up technical disturbance of Western broadcasting – which is a technical 'counter-measure' common also in China and 'legitimated' here – and even actively imported Western journals. No wonder around 1990 the country was brimming with an anti-socialist mood. In this way, the US definition of propaganda had proven true: to make people think they do what you want out of their own volition.

The second Western strategy was to attack via the economy. After World War II the West had laid an embargo on all communist countries. When Gorbachev was in power, seemingly receptive to the West's overturns, the West quickly backed him in reform endeavours that in reality hurt the economic development of the Soviet Union, leading to Gorbachev's ever-growing dependence on Western 'help'. (The soundtrack underscores this with the sad 'Underwater march' from *Pirates of the Caribbean*.) With the so-called Harvard Plan, the whole economy was uprooted, and the West, having successfully made the Soviet Union dependant, threatened it would withdraw all help if Gorbachev did not comply.

At the time Nixon openly stated in his 1988 book the US wanted to destroy communism, Gorbachev was cleverly turned into a marionette for the West's agenda, though in fact he hardly received any real help but was only lauded loudly and received the Nobel Prize, while his wife was extremely well-paid by the US for authoring a book. By this it is argued, Gorbachev was corrupted and this personal gain was one of the driving forces for his behaviour.

The third strategy of the West was 'human rights' – again a topic of salience to the Chinese. (The music accompanying this section is taken from 'Attack' in *Pearl Harbor* and sad tracks from *The Rock*.) The West argued all the time, socialism trod upon human rights. Oppositional forces were therefore supported with money, but also ideologically. US president Carter (born 1924), e.g. received Solzhenitsyn and wrote to Sakharov. When the US caught some Soviet spies, they smartly treated them for Russian dissidents like Aleksandr Ginzburg (1936–2002), making the Soviets lose face. The West spent a lot of money on convening 'human rights' conferences, the commentary points out, supporting Russian dissidents. Although the dissidents had become fewer under Brezhnev, under Gorbachev they multiplied again. And Gorbachev feared the West, thus helping them de facto. For example, when Sakharov stood finally for an election and was not voted in for the National Congress, Gorbachev nominated him personally, and thus Sakharov was able to get 'socialism' and the CPSU's monopoly cancelled in the constitution – as already stated earlier and stressed here again as a crucial step to legalise the retreat from the most basic principles of a socialist state in the Soviet Union. In other words, Gorbachev encouraged the opposition, legalised oppositional parties and let them take over power regionally. (The soundtrack underscores this with sad tunes from *The Rock*.)

The fourth strategy the West used was to instigate ethnic conflicts in the multi-ethnic Soviet Union – again a point very salient to the Chinese, and visually under-lined by focusing on central Asian Muslims which would remind the Chinese viewer of the north-western region of Xinjiang. For example, the US 'instigated' the Baltic independence movements by declaring the US had 'never accepted' the Soviet 'occupation'. When the secession was under way, the US ambassador in Moscow came out in favour, and US president Bush senior personally pressured Gorbachev into accepting secession. He effectively threatened to withdraw all economic help, and therefore Gorbachev ordered the Soviet troops to retreat. (The accompanying music is the sad track 'Heart of a volunteer' from *Pearl Harbor.*) With the Baltic States as the first dominos fallen, the dissolution of the Soviet Union gained speed (visualised by the map with the three Baltic countries having changed colours).

The fifth Western strategy, however, was the most decisive (underscored by scary music): to support the inner enemies in the Soviet Communist Party itself. Thus, e.g. the US ambassador lent his support to Yeltsin because the latter worked against the interests of the party and wanted to split it up. (Yeltsin is again introduced with threatening sounds and shots suggesting his 'dangerousness', soliciting antipathy.) And when Yeltsin clashed finally with Gorbachev, the US backed up Yeltsin and honoured him greatly on a visit to the US. Basically the US wanted the two, Yeltsin and Gorbachev, to work side by side. When Yeltsin moved towards the final dissolution of the Soviet Union, the first he informed about his aim were the US. And at the eve of the putsch attempt to save the Soviet Union, reformer Popov called the US ambassador that something was underway. Thus, Western countries and Japan immediately blocked all money and sided with Yeltsin to prevent the putsch's success. At this juncture, also Gorbachev sided with Yeltsin. The moment (which went through all the media of the world at the time) when Yeltsin spoke in front of the tanks of the putschists was the funeral of socialism and the Communist Party, the commentary concludes.

In sum, many factors had led to the end of the Soviet Union, but the most decisive one was inner decay. This evaluation – it is stated – is even shared today in Russia. (Here, the version on DVD and the written version slightly differ, basically the DVD having a coda. It seems this was added in view of the recent Russian moves under Putin to re-evaluate the Soviet Union and Stalin which was not yet in full swing when the basis for the written version, i.e. Chen Zhihua's edited book of 2004, was fixed. The written version, in fact, ended with a 2002 reference, whereas the DVD version refers to events up to 2005.) Even one-time critics, it is argued, reconsidered their stance after the turn of the twenty-first century like Aleksandr Zinoviev (1922–2006) whose book on the 'tragedy' of Soviet Communism (*Russkaya tragediya*, Moscow: Algoritm) is shown in Chinese translation (published in 2004). Thus, the commentary asks for thinking about it again (visually underscored by the map changing colours). In a black and white written coda (of which the reading out is accompanied with Stalin-reminding march-like songs), it is argued that the majority of the present-day Russian popu-lace according to opinion polls in 2005 feels proud of the Soviet Union's history and her achievements and especially disdains the era under Yeltsin. With presi-dent Putin taking office in 2001, the evaluation of the Soviet Union and Stalin was reconsidered also on an official level. The core textbook on the history of the CPSU (later called the 'short course') widely disseminated since Stalin's times was reprinted, and positive evaluations on Stalin were published. Even one-time harsh critics like Solzhenitsyn or some of those responsible for the break-up of the state are said to have come to realise they 'wronged their country' back then. Hopefully, the commentary paternalistically suggests from a Chinese perspective which is the positive counterexample intended, also the home of Lenin and the October Revolution will sooner or later get back again on the 'right' track after having provided mankind with the negative example of break-up. This, then, is the final lesson Chinese cadres should retrieve from the history of the Soviet Communist Party.

Learning from others' disasters: research, communist anxieties, and cadre education

Reception in the case of *Ju an si wei* was different from the other two documentaries presented in this book, since the series was intended for 'internal party use only'. But for the more stereotype comments by the people responsible for its production who naturally stressed how well it was received, even letting smokers forget their cigarettes, asking to watch all in one time (Li Shenming; 4 August 2009), there was only occasional reference in the public media. Given the fact that the documentary was distributed on DVDs, one might argue it is no 'TV' series in the classical sense. As a format, however, it is serialised – which is one of the key distinguishing features of a 'TV documentary' from 'documentary film'. In fact, although the final label appearing on the DVDs is *dangnei cankaopian* 党内参考片 (inner-party reference piece), the producers refer to it often as a *dianshipian* 电视片 ('TV piece'; Li Xiaoning 1 December 2006), and this self-labelling also appears in the documentary itself, arguably because of its format, although it did not go to public TV. Other terms that come up in the discussion of the piece include *zhenglunpian* 政论片 (political piece) and, above all, *jiaoyu cankaopian* 教育参考片 (educational reference piece).[40] Either way, the DVDs could be bought in China – though with a stamped-on 'secret',[41] and came with a booklet by 'chief' historian Chen Zhihua, providing a chronology of the Soviet Union and some screen-shots showing the decisive people. These screen-shots include various canonised photos of official Soviet history.[42] (This focus on people bespeaks the key interest of the documentary in human agency, notwithstanding all denial by Li Shenming and other producers later against critics.) The documentary also soon found its way on the Internet. The text of the commentary was publicly available anyway. Nevertheless, especially for the first time the documentary was considered 'sensitive'. In the meantime things have somewhat relaxed and in the context of the twentieth anniversary of the Soviet Union's dissolution 2011, the documentary was referred to again. Its historical reading, however, is still all but uncontested (see below).

Internationally, only very few comments on the documentary appeared in English,[43] and they were mostly by Chinese living or writing in the US. As the blog comment 'Think of danger' on the Blood & Treasure website concludes – referring to English posts on the blog of Sun Bin who had posted also on *Daguo jueqi* – it was no coincidence that *Ju an si wei* was more or less simultaneous with *Daguo jueqi*: the first for the cadres, the other for 'the masses'. While *Daguo jueqi* promotes that the people should feel as 'part of a kind of developmental matrix under the guidance of a wise, open and forward looking leadership', *Ju an si wei* is 'to promote discipline within the party' ('Think of danger'; 15 December 2006).[44]

Public reactions by and in Chinese, in turn, can be found, above all, in blogs: on the 'international' YouTube at the time still available also in China (and of course also to Chinese overseas), the instalments are commented in a variety of ways. Interestingly, here quite often the Russian/Soviet 'infringement' on 'Chinese' territory – not discussed in the documentary itself – is referred to, marking some of these Chinese comments as fairly chauvinist. There is no uniform reaction, but leftist/Maoist positions appear as do positions close to Social democracy or Taiwanese anti-communist comments. But all are critical in one way or other.[45]

Another video portal, run in this case in China, is Youku.com 优酷. Here, it is little surprise that comments are favourable, and the occasional criticism is quickly 'addressed' to switch the discussion into a more 'orthodox' fashion. (As is well known, there are paid contributors to blogs, the so-called *wumaodang* 五毛党 'fifty-cent party', whose task is to keep discussion threads within desired limits.[46]) Here, also, threads are obviously not archived fully, but occasionally posts seem to have been deleted for some reason. What remains on Youku.com are mostly posts that praise the documentary series as 'realist', 'informative', a 'lesson', 'worth watching', and so on. Only the discussion of the fourth instalment on the party style (and in part the one on the sixth dealing with the organisational line) is rather negative, pointing out the discrepancy in internal logic which attacked Gorbachev (who seems to have some sympathisers in China[47] – as to be noted in various posts) first for being too much away from office to tour his country and talk, and then that he was 'aloof from' the masses – in fact a point that became obvious in our discussion of the documentary series itself, i.e. that Gorbachev comes across fairly sympathetic in the pictures, and the commentary is at complete variance.[48-]

The documentary, however, has to be seen in the larger context of Chinese reflections on the breakdown of the communist bloc.[49] Reflections had been called for already by Jiang Zemin in 1996. They set the tone for the political line: Gorbachev's adoption of a 'humanistic and democratic socialism' was the crucial issue for Soviet failure to the 'orthodox' commentators, but also his economic mismanagement, as stressed by the reformers. And to this, Jiang's own 'Three Represents' should provide a viable alternative (Munro 2008: 42–3). As Shambaugh has summarised the Chinese assessments of Soviet failure, key factors discussed may be divided into the four categories of economy, politics, society and culture, and international impact.[50]

On the scholarly side, according to Shanghai-based historian Shen Zhihua 沈志华,[51] three books were marking the terrain of discussion in China before his time of writing (2009): Zhou Shangwen 周尚文, Ye Shuzong 叶书宗 and Wang Side's 王斯德 co-edited *Sulian xingwangshi* 苏联兴亡史 (History of the rise and fall of the Soviet Union) of 1993; influential Lu Nanquan 陆南全 *et al.*'s edited *Sulian xingwangshi lun* 苏联兴亡史论 (On the history of the rise and fall of the Soviet Union) of 2002; and the above referred-to book edited by Chen Zhihua 陈之骅: *Sulian xingwang shigang* 苏联兴亡史纲 (Historical outline of the rise and fall of the Soviet Union) of 2004 on which the documentary *Ju an si wei* is based. However, Shen stresses in this brief review of existing scholarship, these books were either focused on events (the safest way to get a sensitive historical topic started when political evaluation is not yet 'settled', one may conclude, as was feasible for the 1993 book), or more generally preoccupied with 'historical issues' (as was Lu Nanquan with his cautiously reformist bent),[52] or with basic historical developments (i.e. political interpretation as is more 'orthodox' Chen Zhihua).[53] Neither, however, used the newly opened Soviet archives which Shen himself had worked upon with his group. Based on this meticulous archival work, published after seven years in 2002,[54] Shen went on to lead another project on the Soviet Union's rise and fall which produced three volumes published in 2009: *Yige daguo de jueqi yu bengkui* 一个大国的崛起于崩溃 ('The rise and collapse of a superpower') – notably evoking with the title the association of the famous documentary series *Daguo jueqi*!

Undoubtedly, Shen Zhihua's edited volumes are the most scholarly contribution to the subject, but interestingly similar 'projects' on the fall of the Soviet Union or the CPSU were contemporaneously done also elsewhere, though on a smaller scale. For example, in Nanjing Wang Lixin 王立新 wrote the nationally sponsored *Sugong xingwanglun* 苏共兴亡论 (On the rise and fall of the CPSU) (2007), and at CASS Liu Shuang 刘爽 came out with *Sulian jieti de shixue chanshi* 苏联解体的史学阐释 ('On the disintegration of the Soviet Union from a historical perspective') in 2009 as a doctoral thesis grown out of his work in the CASS project behind *Ju an si wei*. Both however are no match to Shen Zhihua's endeavour. In fact, some of Shen's researchers were among those who attacked *Ju an si wei* as unscholarly.[55] But Li Shenming, the responsible for *Ju an si wei*, rebuffed criticism in his 2009 published introductory essay on his historical 'interpretation',[56] which – as we have seen – is 'leftist' in bent, enriching his argumentative repertoire with the economic crisis then under way in the West. To this one may add that in the same year, 2009, the Party History Press also came out with a three volumes work on Sino–Soviet relations, however restricting itself only to the 'good times' of 1917 to 1949, written by Xue Xiantian 薛衔天 (the second volume co-authored by Korean Kim Donggil 金东吉). Xue is again from CASS and Kim, now at Beijing University, did his PhD there. Interestingly, this work was again growing out of a nationally funded project which, however, had started in 1996 (i.e. the year when Jiang Zemin had called for 'reflections' on the Soviet Union), as Xue writes in his afterword, and had originally been planned to cover the whole time span up to 1991. This means that after 13 (!) years only the part up to 1949 had been realised. The group of scholars had, in fact, broken up.[57] Obviously, the topic was and is still far from being unproblematic and an issue of contention.

In 2011, due to the twentieth anniversary of the CPSU's demise (and the ninetieth birthday of the CCP), the two sides clashed again when Li Shenming (in fact together with Chen Zhihua) edited a whole book sustaining the views of *Ju an si wei* as the final publication of the CASS project (of which the documentary had been, as might be remembered, the 'mid-term' output). These views consisted in a nutshell in his conviction that the fate of the CPSU and the disintegration of the Soviet Union was not due to the 'Stalin model'[58] – a term to him 'anti-communist' in bent though used by Chinese scholars not subscribing to his view[59] – or even socialism as such, but in the backsliding and final betrayal of Khrushchev to Gorbachev vis-à-vis Marxism, socialism and the 'masses'. Thus, the key message to learn from Soviet experience – he underlines, by this reiterating the message of the documentary – is to give high priority to 'thought work' in the CCP, to assure faithfulness of top cadres to Marxism, to the rule of the proletariat represented by the CCP alone, to democratic centralism and inner-party control, while being vigilant against inner or outer enemies' schemes to Westernise or split up China.[60] (The latter point had gained salience by Peter Schweizer's book *Victory: The Reagan Administration's Secret Strategy That Hastened the Collapse of the Soviet Union*).[61] In other words: the Soviet Union failed because it gave up Stalinism, and for China ideological training for cadres is the paramount task for preserving the party and national unity.

Obviously, this (hardliner) view and its implications for China did not go well with everybody. Even though discussion had been 'tamed' in 2006/7 by the context of the documentary being an internal piece, inner-party critics immediately voiced alternative 'historical readings'. In fact, from the outset Li Shenming marked the message of the documentary series as in opposition to other current readings of the causes of the Soviet Union's collapse: that it was – in the end – a 'utopia', that it was flawed early on, that it mismanaged economy, that it channelled too much funds into the arms race, that it broke up because of inter-ethnic conflicts, or more basically, that its political and economic system ('Stalin model') and the Soviet socialist model as such was a failure (Li Shenming; 4 August 2009).[62] As we have seen, especially the point of the problematic heritage of Stalinism had been an issue for Red Flag's Huang Weiding who was associated with former president Jiang Zemin and who had been the key reference at the *tenth* anniversary of the Soviet Union's demise back in 2001. Now, for the *twentieth* anniversary in 2011, Li Shenming tried to take over the 'power of definition' to shift this evaluation, although there were also inner-party sceptics like Jiang Yue 姜跃 (presently professor at the Party School of the Central Committee in Beijing) who had experienced the changes in the Soviet Union personally as an 'exchange student' and pointedly cautioned to not glorify the Soviet Union. If socialism was not 'developed', she warned, China could very well be endangered, too (Jiang Yue 2011).[63] However, Li Shenming also received support, including well-known elderly 'expert' on the Soviet Union at People's University, Zhou Xincheng 周新城, who has written himself on the 'tragedy' of the Soviet Union's end and basically repeated what Chen Zhihua had voiced about the book he and Li Shenming had edited on occasion of the twentieth anniversary of the Soviet Union's end.[64] In sum, the historical reading of the Soviet Union's demise remained a hot and politically contested issue up to the present.

One of the most prominent criticisms of the documentary series itself, based on the text of the commentary which had been published in the journal *Kexue shehuizhuyi* 科学社会主义 (Scientific socialism) from late 2006 to early 2007, was voiced immediately by two professors at the Department of International Strategy of the Party School of the Central Committee in Beijing: Zuo Fengrong 左凤荣 and Jiang Changwu 姜长斌, published in *Dangdai shijie shehuizhuyi wenti* 当代世界社会主义问题 ('Issues of Contemporary World Socialism') in early 2007. As stated above, Zuo was a collaborator of Shen Zhihua's 2009 volumes on the rise and fall of the Soviet Union and had been interviewed for *Daguo jueqi* on Russian history. Zuo and her colleague Jiang concentrate on the 'information' or 'message' the commentary provides, i.e. they do not comment on visual or audio aspects, but on the ideological implications. That their criticism is not voiced purely from the 'scholarly' side is corroborated by the fact that occasionally they use the term 'correct' (*zhengque* 正确) to label ideological positions, which, however, are at variance with the positions held by the documentary series. Their criticism is an inner-party one, and it is notable that proponents of a different ideological line were often connected to the Party School of the Central Committee in Beijing.[65]

The main thrust of Zuo/Jiang's criticism is against the positive evaluation of Stalinism – which clearly is the 'hot potato' of the whole political contest and of more than historiographical concern. Their criticism moves not through the single instalments but chronologically through the 'generations' of leaders to challenge the documentary's reading. Already for the era of Lenin they point out various distortions in the presentation, e.g. that the February Revolution in 1917 was not 'led' by the Bolsheviks at all as the documentary argues, but in fact erupted spontaneously out of unpolitical protests against rising bread prices and was then furthered by a variety of political groups, whereas the leaders of the Bolsheviks returned to Russia only later. The attack on the Winter Palace as described in the documentary was more than exaggerated, and in general the documentary followed, according to Zuo/Jiang, always blindly the later versions of Stalin on 1917, lambasting his own role which in fact was very minor, which only served to suggest his 'natural' succession of Lenin. In fact, Zuo/Jiang stress, Lenin had warned against Stalin, who simply got forcefully rid of his rivals to become the new leader (thus enlisting the relatively undisputed 'hero' Lenin to their 'Stalin-critical' camp).

Stalin emerges in Zuo and Jiang's view as a ruthless dictator who did mostly harm to his people. In this, Zuo and Jiang's reading has much in common with Western views on the Stalinist era. They accuse the documentary of glossing over the enforced collectivisation and poverty of the populace that paid for the hailed industrialisation, which focused on heavy industry rather than on consumer goods, and – above all – the monstrous Stalinist 'purges'. That 'chief executioner' Beria (1899–1953) is hardly mentioned at all is – according to them – more than telling. Since much of the argumentation on legitimacy of rule, be it in the other already discussed documentary series *Daguo jueqi* or *Fuxing zhi lu*, be it in general in the CCP's endeavour to show it is the best government for China, is focused on economy, the criticism points out that in economic terms the Soviet Union under Stalin lagged even behind the tsarist times and – though growing – led to an ever greater divide between the Western 'capitalist' countries and the Soviet Union. Thus, even in economic terms, Stalinism was a failure! Referring to Deng Xiaoping, Zuo and Jiang stress that Lenin's NEP was the 'right way', unfortunately given up under Stalin, concluding that much of what happened after Stalin was due to his disastrous legacy. With an implicit reference to *Daguo jueqi*'s instalment on the Soviet Union, they argue the reports of Westerners sympathetic to the Soviet Union were quite disillusioned after seeing the realities in Stalinist Russia, like the ones of Romain Rolland (1866–1944) and André Gide (1869–1951). (These Western reports are, however, not addressed in the documentary *Ju an si wei* but only in *Daguo jueqi*!)

In short, though Stalin did make his country into the second superpower, he made pay his populace dearly. Even the underground of Moscow so much praised in the documentary was in fact built by forced labour, and also in international affairs China should have no reason to feel sympathy with Stalin, since he was, according to Zuo/Jiang, the Soviet leader most disadvantageous for China, including the territory he snapped away from China (a point very often stressed with the Western 'imperialists' and thus reflecting particularly badly on Stalin).[66] Therefore, the contention in the documentary that Mao cried when he heard of Stalin's death is not only not proven but even implausible. And finally the documentary series' assessment that Stalin as a person was very modest[67] and stuck to personal poverty is contrasted with his daughter's remark that he did not need money because he had everything anyway, including several dachas. Thus, Zuo and Jiang insinuate, the problem of corruption did not arise with de-Stalinisation, but was already part of the system earlier!

The documentary's depiction of the times after Stalin is equally problematic, according to Zuo and Jiang: neither was Khrushchev totally against Stalin, in fact continuing several aspects like personality cult, nor was his 'secret speech' a single-handed move, having been approved beforehand by several top cadres. And his ideological 'error', as pointed out by the documentary, to argue for the CPSU being the party of 'all the people', was not 'anti-Marxist' at all, but the logical consequence of his assuming the Soviet Union to have realised socialism. Without 'class enemies' left, 'all the people' were now represented. (Here, one may read between the lines a positive reference by Zuo and Jiang to Jiang Zemin's 'Three Represents' to 'broaden' the party basis.) And in consequence also the 'dictatorship of the proletariat' was not mentioned any longer, since this is an instrument which, according to Marx, serves to facilitate the process for attaining socialism by keeping down the 'class enemies'. But these, according to Khrushchev's interpretation, were already inexistent.

Finally with the other 'culprit' of the series, Gorbachev, Zuo/Jiang argue that to simply call him a 'traitor' does not make clear anything: had he not been elected general secretary? Many decisions he took were approved by the party's leading circles. Thus, he was not 'responsible' as a single person for many decisions like the changes in article six in the constitution which had guaranteed the monopoly of rule for the CPSU, and the dictatorship of the proletariat was done away with anyway even earlier since there were no 'class enemies' any longer.

For the part of the present assessment of the Soviet Union in Russia, the documentary series had referred to Russian Communist Party leader Zyuganov who had voiced nostalgia for the Soviet Union and Stalin in particular. Zuo/Jiang state that this presumed Russian 'Stalin-renaissance' is in fact inexistent. Rather there is simply more interest in the era which generates more relevant publications, but the assessment of it is more than mixed, and the references referred to in the documentary are biased, unscientific and rather motivated by nostalgia for the power lost than for socialism. In other words, the driving force for any positive evaluation of the Soviet Union in present-day Russia is rather chauvinism! Looking to the development of the Communist Party in Russia, it does not thrive at all. And even though Putin voiced some regret over the dissolution of the Soviet Union, he nevertheless is basically set upon getting ahead and into the world, not on turning back history's wheel (Zuo and Jiang 2007).[68]

From this one can see that Zuo/Jiang's criticism depicts the documentary series (and Li Shenming and Chen Zhihua's point of view as its basis) as outdated, uninformed, leftist in thrust, and sets it against the reformist course of opening up China and developing its economy in a global context.

The documentary *Ju an si wei* obviously was to replace Huang Weiding's earlier book in cadre education which had been set before as a 'study material', as can be gleaned from smaller party journals.[69] Therefore, one may assume, the documentary, which – as we have seen – kept some influence from Huang Weiding's view by Li Xiaoning's main 'real' authorship but was 'reworked' afterwards according to Li Shenming and Chen Zhihua's opinion – re-fixed what the cadres had studied earlier.

A 'report' on a reaction to the documentary by a young cadre born in the 1980s may suffice to illustrate how these young cadres without a personal 'historical memory' of the Soviet Union's fall were influenced by the documentary to 'know' something about the reasons for this historical development. As this young cadre summarised the 'lesson' he had received from watching the documentary, the key message he took away was to keep the close bond between party and the 'masses', e.g. in terms of the problem of corruption, and to behave pragmatically: not good or bad is the question, but whether something is adequate for the moment and place. In other words: the argument of the Chinese characteristics (Kuang Wenzhang 2008). In this way, by the Soviet example the documentary pointed out potential dangers to beware of, but on the other hand it assured cadres of China's being different and on the right track already.

As mentioned, the interpretation of the fate of the Soviet Union became virulent again in 2011 at the twentieth anniversary of its end, being also the year of the ninetieth birthday celebrations for the CCP. Again, the main official 'lesson' to be derived was declared for the cadres as to keep 'vigilant' and to keep 'close to the masses' (see Chen Yuanzhang 2011). And the Fourth Congress of the Central Committee of the Seventeenth Party Congress in 2009 had also referred to the catchword of being 'alert to danger while dwelling in safety' which had been a topic already in 2004 at the Fourth Plenum of the Sixteenth Party Congress which concentrated on the party's capacity in governance ('Quandang bixu ju an si wei' 2009).[70]

In sum, the negative 'lesson' of the Soviet Union remains salient in the eyes of Chinese policy makers up to the present day and it is seen as important to above all brief cadres on the issue lest they should draw the 'wrong' conclusions. For achieving this, besides the 'usual' ways of reaching cadres with party documents and other written directives, academic research along the lines of officially sponsored projects is seen as a useful legitimising back-up, and the TV documentary format adds to this the visual and audio dimensions. In this multiple way, it is hoped, the lesson will be received by its intended primary audience: the cadres, who then should carry it on subsequently as multipliers to the broader public in an approach to 'political communication' yet different from the other two documentaries discussed in this book.

Notes

1 In the 2011 final publication in book form of the project of which the documentary series was the mid-term output, the title of this Chinese-language book very close to the documentary's title is rendered in its English subtitle as 'Be Vigilant on Possible Danger in Peace Time. 20 Years' Reflections on Soviet Communist Party's Decline' (sic) (see Li Shenming (ed.) and Chen Zhihua (co-ed.) 2011). I prefer a more literal translation of the title, giving credit also to 'safety' (rather than 'peace', both meanings covered by *an* 安) being the opposite of 'danger', and 'perishing' being semantically more accurate than 'decline' for Chinese *wang* 亡, which means something is getting lost or is dying.

2 For his biography, see *Li Shenming tongzhi jianli* (2011). As of March 2013 he has just been re-elected member of the Standing Committee of the National People's Congress.

3 See annotations to the preface of *Ju an si wei*, seen at http://www.chinaelections.org/NewsInfo.asp?NewsID=99228 (a website unfortunately defunct as of 2012) (*Ju an si wei – Sugong wangdang de lishi jiaoxun (jieshuoci)* 2006). (Chinaelections.org is a Chinese-language website run by the US–American Carter Center, but with editors mostly inside China and officially collaborating with the Chinese government.) In the 'official' printed version of the commentary in *Kexue shehuizhuyi* (see Li Shenming *et al.* 2006/7), these annotations are not included, but the cooperating agencies are also named on the cover of the DVD collection and appear in the credits.

4 The year 2007 was 'China year' in Russia and Li Shenming was head of the Chinese delegation of CASS.

5 Li Shenming (4 August 2009) contends it was 'well received'. (Though this website is now defunct – see also below – the text is basically identical to the introduction to the final 2011 book publication of the project behind the documentary: Li Shenming (ed.) and Chen Zhihua (co-ed.) 2011). Chen Zhihua also states in his 2011 assessment of this book, which came out on the occasion of the twentieth anniversary of the Soviet Union's end, that the documentary had been 'received' in Russia and Vietnam and had led to 'further discussions' in Russia (see Chen Zhihua; 14 March 2011).

6 He has a personal blog, providing also some information about himself: Li Xiaoning (2006?). He teaches at the Central Academy for Socialism which is a 'party school' for the 'democratic parties', i.e. nominally independent parties 'cooperating' with the CCP.

7 See Li Xiaoning's addendum to the documentary's online text on the website of the Shiyan Technical Institute in Hubei: Li Xiaoning (1 December 2006). The information in brackets on the singular co-authors, who are not very well known, has been assembled from various internet sites.

8 For a list of project members, see the afterword of Li Shenming in the final project publication of 2011: Li Shenming (ed.) and Chen Zhihua (co-ed.) (2011: 520).

9 For a brief summary of this background, see Chen Zhihua (14 March 2011).

10 On his lectures, which were mainly on Jiang Zemin's 'Three Represents', but also covered the topic of the CPSU's demise, and the ensuing book, which combined this article with several other 'reports', see Huang Weiding (2003). For a short presentation

of the organisational system of party schools of which this one in Beijing is the 'head' institution, see Shambaugh (2008: 143–51). The centrality of the party school system for cadre formation has been challenged only recently (see Chin 2011).

11 Notably, Huang revised his book in a new edition in 2004 (see Huang Weiding 2004).

12 In the 2004 revised edition of his book, in contrast, criticism of Lenin and Stalin was toned down; but the main thrust the importance of a close relationship between party leaders and the people was retained. Huang's main argument of potential danger to CCP rule was then rather shifted to the uncontested issue of corruption.

13 For a brief summary of Chinese reactions to Eastern European developments after 1989, see Shambaugh (2008: 45–53). From a contrary angle, the Chinese discussions on the 'remaining socialist brother' Cuba aim to reflect positively on the Chinese way of reform as the superior alternative (see Cheng, Yinghong 2012).

14 The proverb has its origin in the pre-imperial Spring and Autumn period (from the eighth to the fifth century BC), admonishing any ruler to prepare for war when there is not yet the prospect of one. In 2004, the Fourth Plenum of the Sixteenth Party Congress referred to this proverbial expression as a back-drop to why governance should be ameliorated (cf. Shambaugh 2008: 126).

15 See the already referred-to annotations to the preface of *Ju an si wei* in: *Ju an si wei – Sugong wangdang de lishi jiaoxun (jieshuoci)* (2006) at http://www.chinaelections. org/NewsInfo.asp?NewsID=99228 (which is unfortunately a now-defunct website). In the 'official' printed version of the commentary in *Kexue shehuizhuyi* (see Li Shenming *et al.* 2006/7), these annotations are, as stated, not included.

16 That the written version was soon publicly sold is confirmed, for example, by a review of the final book publication of the CASS project in 2011: Zhang Lei (2011: 5). (This article stresses, by the way, that with recent US disclosures about politics versus the Soviet Union – which, in fact, are not so 'recent' disclosures at all – the strategic 'under-mining' influence of the US has become obvious, thus arguing for the salience of *Ju an si wei*'s historical reading which sees the malign manoeuvring of the US as one crucial factor in the Soviet demise.) (As of March 2013, it is notable that the governmental websites which had put on the text of *Ju an si wei* – see below – have now been blocked. It could well be that this has to do with the political turmoil in 2012 connected to the Bo Xilai 薄熙来 (born 1949) case, which led to the ousting of some 'leftist' politicians.)

17 This becomes clear when comparing the list of 'theory-providing people' on the DVD collection cover and the list of project members provided in Li Shenming and Chen Zhihua's 2011 book on the twentieth anniversary of Soviet demise, which marked the 'end of project' (see Li Shenming's afterword in Li Shenming (ed.) and Chen Zhihua (co-ed.) 2011: 520).

18 On Soviet feature films and their impact in the PRC see Chen, Tina Mai (2010). For the genre of compilation film documentaries, see Chapter 5.

19 Thanks are due to my student Florian Richter who identified the various tracks and to whom this section is indebted.

20 Cf. Brady (2008: 175–8). See also Shambaugh (2008: Chapter 4).

21 On this, see Lukin (1991) and Tucker (1995/6).

22 Cf. here Brady (2008: p. 186) and, above all, Shambaugh (2008: Chapters 4, 6, and 7).

23 See Shambaugh (2008: 60–1 and 66–7). Notably, since the late 1970s when research on the Soviet Union was again possible in China and in the context of China's moves toward 'reform', the evaluation of Brezhnev was largely negative, whereas Andropov and Gorbachev were seen as closer to Chinese policies, suggesting that an amelioration of bilateral ties might be possible. Against this negative view on Brezhnev, Khrushchev appeared as problematic, but relatively more positive – and one may add that Liu Shaoqi (1898–1969) had been reviled as 'China's Khrushchev' at the high time of the Cultural Revolution. Thus, when Liu was cautiously 're-evaluated' after the Cultural Revolution, Khrushchev's image also became somewhat 'better' than in Mao's time. See Rozman (1987) on Chinese views of the Soviet Union between 1978 and 1985.

24 Jiang, of course, stressed that his idea was not identical to Khrushchev's as only 'progressive' elements would be considered for party membership, not everybody. For the leftist criticism of Jiang's 'theory', cf. Lee (2010: 274–5).

25 In view of what we have discussed earlier, it is interesting to note that with this terminology there is a telling ambivalence toward the Soviet Union, whether it should be evaluated primarily as an honourable 'great power' (*daguo*) or rather as an 'aggressive' one (*qiangguo*). One could assume that for the times of Lenin and Stalin it rather counts as a *daguo*, whereas later it would rather be subsumed under the *qiangguo* label.

26 The preface and the whole script have been published in the journal *Kexue shehuizhuyi* (Scientific socialism) in three instalments: 2006 nos. 5 and 6, and 2007 no. 1 (see Li Shenming *et al.* 2006/7). They are or were also available at various websites, e.g. of the Shiyan Polytechnical Institute: http://www.syzy.com.cn/baicao/nhf/zxyd/200612/20061201143112.html (*Ju an si wei – Sugong wangdang de lishi jiaoxun (jieshuoci)*; 11 December 2006); or at http://www.chinaelections.org/NewsInfo.asp?NewsID=99228 (*Ju an si wei – Sugong wangdang de lishi jiaoxun (jieshuoci)*; 2006). (As of 2012 the latter website, as already stated, is not working any longer, but the website of the governmental Hunan Information and Technology Commission put it on as well: www.hnii.gov.cn/ – which as of March 2013 seems to be defunct now however, too. On a non-governmental platform, the whole is also to be found on http://www.docin.com/p–289491747.html etc.) The series itself has been distributed 'internally' on DVDs (*Ju an si wei – Sugong wangdang de lishi jiaoxun* 2006).

27 Again, I am indebted here to my student Florian Richter for identifying the movie soundtrack clips.

28 The lack of precision can be seen here, since even in junior secondary school pupils would be briefly confronted with the issue of diverging calendars.

29 These two concepts are not explained in detail but come up time and again in the series later. One may therefore assume the intended audience, i.e. the cadres, were supposed to know sufficiently about them, though in later instalments some more explanation is provided.

30 It is interesting to note that in spite of the known difficult relationship between the two men, Mao is presented here as emotionally deeply affected.

31 This expression is taken from a comment Gorbachev made in a radio interview in Radio Mayak in March 2001, and is cited in the penultimate instalment of the documentary.

32 It is interesting to note that Chinese translations of Soviet reformers' books have mostly appeared since the mid/late 1990s, i.e. after Jiang Zemin's call to consider the Soviet experience, to the early 2000s. Only some of Gorbachev's works had been translated by the late 1980s.

33 Ligachev is cited to the avail that he did not want to use a luxury limousine but was 'forced to'.

34 This issue is only vaguely described. In fact it had to do with the Kronstadt Mutiny in 1921 and anarchist opposition to the Communist Party.

35 Here, obviously, the didacticism of the documentary leads it to distort even simple facts such as dates of birth (not provided in detail but with collective time-frames to suggest a neat chronological 'generational' explanation of every leadership group as 'born 1890–1902; 1902–1910; 1910–1920; grown up under Khrushchev'. Contrasting them here with the individual birth dates de facto not completely in accord with these time frames, the typically forced nature of argumentation should be evident).

36 Interestingly, the 1988 open letter of protest by the communist woman lecturer cited above in an earlier instalment which was in turn used by Gorbachev and the reformers to denounce the 'Stalinists', referred to this legend. (However, there is no precise reference given for Churchill's alleged 'praise', which is more than telling.)

37 Khrushchev had, in fact, declared to the communist international community in 1957 he wanted to catch up with and even overtake the West in terms of material well-being

of the populace (prompting Mao into declaring similar 'catch-up' aims for China, namely with steel production) and instituted reforms in various sectors, but soon had to acknowledge that the aim of catching up in a few years was not realistic. His various reform endeavours, however, though at times miscalculated, were less utopian than the Chinese 'Great Leap Forward' (which was not supported by the Soviets at all): although he largely failed with agrarian reforms, the industrial production grew and led to a heightened standard of living. His ideological proposition of being able to arrive quickly at communism was, however, given up after his demise.

38 For a recent assessment cf. Lüthi (2008) who details the mounting differences between the Soviets and the Chinese at the time, reconstructed mostly from archival materials.

39 This term was first introduced by George Kennan (1904–2005), US ambassador to the Soviet Union, in 1947. US secretary of state, John Foster Dulles (1888–1959), made it famous in the 1950s. In China, this 'mischievous' US 'strategy' was pointed out as a major threat after the crumble of the Soviet Union, leading to a revamping of history education to counter potential similar devices (cf. Wang, Zheng 2008: 790).

40 See, e.g. the discussion of the documentary series in the journal *Makesizhuyi yanjiu* 马克思主义研究 ('Studies on Marxism'): Liu Shuchun (2006).

41 Probably for this reason foreigners at the time were not allowed to buy it even though the price could be checked on the Internet. (I thank a Chinese friend for doing so in my stead.)

42 For Soviet 'official' photography (and its 'reworking' of photographs), see, e.g. King (1997).

43 From the academic side, Shambaugh (2008: 42) names it but does not discuss it. Guan (2010: 507–8) addresses it only briefly in one paragraph, though underlining the fact that it was highly influential in China.

44 The Blood&Treasure website has a strong focus on China but does not provide direct clues as to who runs it.

45 See *Ju an si wei – Sugong wangdang de lishi jiaoxun* (2007) on YouTube.com.

46 On the 'fifty cent party' (*wumaodang* 五毛党) see, e.g. Bristow (16 December 2008). The practice was initiated in 2004 (see Wu Nan; 15 May 2008).

47 On the development of Chinese assessments of Gorbachev and his policies, see Rozman (2010a).

48 See *Shipin: Jilupian* Ju an si wei – Sugong wangdang de lishi jiaoxun *diyi ji* (n.d.) on Youku.com for the first instalment. The other instalments are linked on the right.

49 See Marsh's (2003) summary of Chinese reflections on the Soviet experience, and, above all, Shambaugh (2008: Chapter 4), who details various inner-party articles on the issue but does not mention Chen Zhihua and – strikingly – even hardly names Huang Weiding in spite of the latter's influence on cadre education on the topic after 2001. Shambaugh provides, however, a useful periodisation of Chinese analyses of Soviet reforms and collapse, going from scepticism and support in the late 1980s through suspicion and shock during the crucial phase 1989–91 to a systemic study and 'conclusion' as to how to assess it (Shambaugh 2008: 55). Another very useful overview on Chinese literature and research projects on the end of the Soviet Union up to 2006 is provided by Beijing University's Guan Guihai (2010: 506–7), though he names only projects undertaken in Beijing. For a more politically interested approach as to how the Soviet experience might influence Chinese prospects for more democracy, see Munro (2008), who bases himself also on interviews with Sovietologists in China. Munro presents also some Chinese books on Soviet history on pp. 47–51 of his article, focusing on publications by Chen Zhihua (co-ed.) (2004) – the book on which the *Ju an si wei* documentary is based – and Xu Xin *et al.* (2001), an earlier work by Xing Guangcheng of 1998 and one by Lu Nanquan of 2002. Here, I will briefly address Chen and Lu as the 'newer ones' among these four and add others.

50 See the list of factors in Shambaugh (2008: 62–3).

51 Shen is based at East China Normal University and specialised in Soviet and Cold War history. For the following see Shen Zhihua (ed.) (2009). (Shen is not named by Shambaugh, but his work in the field has been extremely important since the 1990s.)

52 Lu's edited book is briefly discussed by Munro (2008: 50–1) and his views in Shambaugh (2008: 55, 64 and 66).

53 For the above, see Shen Zhihua (ed.) (2009: 6).

54 This work is titled *Sulian lishi dang'an xuanbian* 苏联历史档案选编 (Collection from the Soviet historical archives) and amounts to 34 volumes.

55 Zuo Fengrong (who had been also interviewed in *Daguo jueqi* about Catherine the Great), together with her colleague Jiang Changwu (2007); for details see below.

56 See Li Shenming (4 August 2009) who had first published this on the 'xj71.com' website (in the meantime taken off, as it seems). In 2011 it reappeared – mostly identical – as the introduction to the final book of the project behind the *Ju an si wei* documentary (Li Shenming (ed.) and Chen Zhihua (co-ed.) 2011). The 'xj71.com' website is under the supervision of the Beijing Municipal Propaganda Bureau.

57 See Xue's introduction in Xue and Kim (2009).

58 This expression was, according to Li Shenming, taken over from British historian Hugh Seton-Watson (1879–1951). Therefore he considers it an 'anti-communist' term which should not be applied in Chinese. In any case it is understood as the highly centralised political and economic system set up under Stalin, whereas 'Stalin*ism*' 斯大林主义 in Chinese refers to Stalin's ideological contributions. The term 'Stalin model' implies a separation from the historical person and times of Stalin to describe a type of system in place also elsewhere, e.g. in the PRC.

59 This, evidently, means that in his eyes those scholars are in tendency 'anti-communist'!

60 See Li Shenming (4 August 2009), abstract; and Li Shenming (ed.) and Chen Zhihua (co-ed.) (2011), introduction. See also his interview which is integrated in the article by Zhang Lei who reviewed the latter book (Zhang Lei 2011: 8).

61 Strangely, the review article of Zhang Lei (2011: 7) declares Schweizer's contention as 'new in 2007'. Schweizer's book was already out in 1994 and has been available in Chinese translation since 2001! Again, evidently, interpretations are forced and politically motivated.

62 These alternative readings are also enumerated in the introduction of the *Ju an si wei* documentary in the first instalment (see above).

63 Jiang was an exchange student from 1988 to 1993, i.e. lived through the whole process of Soviet demise. In 2011 she lectured at the central party school on the 'lessons' of failure of the CPSU to remain the ruling party. By enumerating daily problems in the Soviet Union such as the lack of commodity goods, she insinuates that China has to stick to 'reforms' if she is to evade a similar fate.

64 For Zhou's sustaining comment see Zhou Xincheng (2011). (The journal *Zhonghuahun* (China's spirit) in which Zhou's article appeared is a mouthpiece of 'elder cadres'.) Chen Zhihua's presentation of the book Li Shenming and he himself co-edited has been posted on the website of CASS: Chen Zhihua (14 March 2011).

65 As we have seen, Huang Weiding had voiced his evaluation of the Soviet Union at lectures there, Jiang Yue is now teaching there, and Zuo/Jiang do so as well.

66 Zuo/Jiang refer to territorial claims in the Ussuri–Amur regions, the independence of Outer Mongolia with the help of Stalin, and Stalin's declared intention to 'take back' whatever Russia had 'lost' in the Far East during the Russo–Japanese War of 1904/5 which was de facto accepted at the Yalta Conference in 1945.

67 This deliberately created self-image has been termed by Stalin cult specialist Jan Plamper 'immodest modesty' (Plamper 2012: 123–35).

68 For Russian shifts in history writing, see Merridale (2003) and Zajda and Zajda (2003).

69 See Chen Xiao (2005) – a typical piece of officially required 'written report' to the political lessons studied.

70 For the importance of the 2004 plenum, see Shambaugh (2008: 124–8).

5 Framing visions of China and the world

The state, documentary, and history in comparative perspective

The three cases of Chinese documentaries looked at above provide interesting insights into the changing context Chinese politics and the media are operating in in recent years and how this influences historical representations: while on the side of the state obviously political considerations of how to modernise China without endangering the CCP's ruling position are paramount, the ever greater integration of China into global developments challenges also received ways of handling history and opens up new spaces for discussing history. These developments are actively taken up by the state as well as by the media and the public, though not necessarily with the same aims in mind. Trying at an 'updated' version of 'using the past to serve the present', historical documentaries are employed to discuss questions of political legitimacy and of developmental strategies offered by the Chinese state, but historical reading by the public has at times its own dynamics, is in the plural and does not necessarily conform to the state's intentions. In either case, the framing of the others' history is clearly linked to the central question about the national Self, but whereas the state's official history views, also transmitted in world history classes in school (cf. Müller 2011b), is focused on this 'self-serving' side, the public at times used it also as a window on 'alternative' historical ways. Thus, the reception side was a mixture of nationalism and the tourist gaze. The media on their part use their own manoeuvring space, and scientific historiography is another player coming in, again with very different 'voices',[1] complicating a simple binary relationship between the state's desired historiographical view transmitted on various levels and in multiple ways, and its supposed 'receiving' public. Therefore, more general questions, including the workings of the media in historical representations and the implications of formats, but also their role vis-à-vis other forms of memory culture, have to be discussed in more detail and have also to be considered in a comparative view, as will be done later in this chapter, to situate our Chinese documentaries in a meaningful way.

History on screen: Chinese uses and global challenges

For China, one of the outcomes of recent developments due to the country's greater global integration is reconfigurations of its own history and a greater awareness of other countries' histories; changes in format likings with the fad for documentaries is another. In terms of content, the three Chinese documentaries have shown which elements in the history of other nations are seen as favourable and worth copying by China, how the potential of China herself is evaluated when reflecting upon the CCP leadership and which are the potential dangers China/the CCP should beware of. The whole historical depiction is driven by this 'practical need', i.e. contrary to the public's first-hand expectations (or reading) there is not the primary goal of more information on chosen other countries. Nevertheless, the popularity of the first case *Daguo jueqi* on Western countries and Japan shows many people were very interested in knowing more about them and simply 'used' it that way. This is underlined by the high selling rates of the host of side publications on foreign history and the whole hype surrounding the series. That on the 'sender side' this was to serve a larger agenda, is testified by the 'prolongation' with case two, adding China to the frame with *Fuxing zhi lu*. Though this might have gone well with current nationalism and neatly fits into the state's long-term political interpretation of history, the second series is much more propaganda-like, blasting the 'merits' and 'wise' decisions of every leading generation in the PRC. Thus, for the Chinese viewer, there was little new in content, and the visual and narrative quality was no match to *Daguo jueqi*, but the integration of foreign (China) experts who are usually cited with positive comments on the Chinese performance was a new feature and intended to show China's new 'global' integration – and to serve as an additional legitimisation device for CCP policies. Though not officially admitted, it seems clear from the comparatively limited discussion the documentary series elicited that it lagged far behind *Daguo jueqi* in popularity nevertheless. However, as the accompanying exhibition, which was promoted strongly by the state, shuttling lots of school classes etc. to visit it in the huge military museum in Beijing, demonstrated, it was central to the state's agenda and finally evolved into *the* set version of modern Chinese history by installing the reworked exhibition (of which we followed-up the various changes) as the permanent exhibition on modern Chinese history in the National Museum. Thus, even though the documentary itself might not have attracted patriotic enthusiasm to a degree hoped for at first, the important role of the various *Fuxing*-productions we addressed in chapter three for the political agenda is obvious, including the epic and film and their connection to crucial events like the 2009 festivities of the PRC's sixtieth anniversary. They therefore are of high political long-term relevance. Seen in this context, the documentary gains its particular salience.

The third case was different in that it was at first not public, but an educational cadre piece of politically correct thinking about the perishing of the Soviet Union. This sets it apart from the first two aimed at 'public education' via TV – and further side productions. Nevertheless, several connections are there with *Daguo jueqi* which included a part on the Soviet Union as well. Thus, the third one also explains the basic thrust that particular *Daguo jueqi* instalment had to have in the background, though skipping over most of the problematic features there. *Ju an si wei* provides us therefore with a more in-depth view on the 'system's' take on the

Soviet road and how to avoid this fate for China in her rise.[2] In a way, it makes explicit what is more implicit in the first two.

With format, the choosing of interview-added documentary in the case of *Daguo jueqi* and *Fuxing zhi lu* is notable to diversify the exclusive 'voice of God' commentary style prevalent in earlier documentaries – not only in China (and also still used in the case of *Ju an si wei*). Today's Chinese TV makers are well aware of international competitors and new genre developments and try to introduce new features here and there without necessarily challenging the basic auctorial approach. Thus, more 'traditional' *approaches* (as in *Ju an si wei*, even though the use of the 'compilation film' documentary format – see below – and the content of 'Soviet history', including also post-Sino–Soviet split times, is not 'traditional', neither is the sound track with Hollywood blockbusters!) coexist with more modern ones (as in *Daguo jueqi*). The choosing of the documentary format suggests the whole enterprise is designed to cue viewers into accepting contents as more 'truthful' and done with more 'expertise' than earlier historical propaganda films with re-enactments clearly not 'real' – and very probably reflects also the awareness that today's viewers do not buy into conventional propaganda films as easily as they might have earlier, due to more globalised 'viewing experiences'. The trend toward the documentary format goes well also with the *lao zhaopian* ('old photos') fad mentioned earlier in Chapter 1 which not only takes part in opening up 'alternative windows' on history by using 'private' or otherwise 'alternative' materials, but also has another important aspect: it capitalises on the fact that pictures/photos insinuate they 'do not lie', but 'document, as it is/was'. The scientific experts, in turn, 'know' what the connecting sense between the documents shown 'is' and provide the 'correct' reading. (On these authentication strategies, see below). Even if there is not always information for the viewer about where the pictures and film sequences shown in our documentaries are taken from, in the first two cases, mainly in the first, it is notable that even the production process, which includes a lot of location shooting, to a degree has become a selling asset in itself (as is also very common in the West: 'the making of'). This, again, is a device to authenticate what is shown. But in that case this is to serve also tourist curiosity: how did the Chinese camera teams fare in foreign countries? How does one film there? That 'foreignness' as such is appealing bespeaks the fact that most Chinese 'experts' coming up in the documentaries do not figure in the book versions which – as we saw – tend to focus on the foreign ones, providing only the latter's photos. Obviously, this again is supposed to heighten credibility or to serve as a legitimisation device (i.e.: 'if even foreigners say so . . .'). Interestingly, the original sense of what is said in a non-Chinese-language interview is occasionally altered somewhat in the Chinese translation, but since the original voice is mostly there (if at times cut short), those able to understand the particular language may at least countercheck. However, as some interviewees had commented later on the interview situation, the interviews were conducted with an 'envisaged answer' already in mind and did not really like to take up different views expressed by the 'experts'. In fact, some directors writing on the production process admitted this, too, since the basic narrative (and historical reading) had been fixed before they went abroad. Thus, cutting was a crucial device to retain of the interviews what 'fitted in', and eliminate what did not.

This is also the reason that while it is true, as Chu states, that documentaries are now designed in a less 'dogmatic' and more 'polyphonic' way than they used to be during Mao's life-time, the final editing and cut is decisive in what gets across to the viewer in the end. Some 'polyphony' during production might simply disappear at the cutting stage for whatever reason. However, polyphony should not only be sought in narrative or 'voice', as Chu points out with reference to Bakhtin's studies on novels (Chu, Yingchi 2007: 27),[3] but may emerge precisely in the contrast between 'official' narrative and other elements present only in the filmic genre, namely images and sound, which renders film more complex than literature. For this, the documentaries presented above have provided several nice examples, for example charging music with the task to debunk seemingly sympathetic figures because the only available footage came 'from the wrong side', or compensating for 'lack of narrative' in the script (e.g. with Japanese war atrocities) by a quick sequence of iconic pictures (which could easily be introduced in a late production stage after the script was finished to satisfy potential demands/ criticisms having come up in the meantime). Thus, beyond the 'literary-narrative' side, production procedures and the many individuals involved have to be considered when evaluating a documentary. (In this sense, Chu is perfectly right that a narrow focus on a film's 'text' only is not enough; Chu, Yingchi 2007: 86.) The final decision as to let it go to, or stay on, the screen in whatever fashion remains in any case the 'emergency brake' and circumscribes the limits of 'polyphony'.

Basically, history representation on screen in the People's Republic started from Lenin's view that film is an ideal educational and propagandistic tool and should 'reflect reality' while being full of 'Communist spirit'.[4] Lenin had paralleled it with the party's newspaper in function, i.e. what the newspaper provided in print, films should provide in images. Decisive was content, not form. Obviously, the basic tenet to 'reflect reality' meant something different to Lenin than to the modern average reader, since joined with the equally basic tenet of 'Communist spirit' (as opposed to 'counter-revolutionary'). In other words, also in the PRC only those things should be shown as 'reflecting reality' that were conducive to produce good communists. This meant in practice, e.g., the concentration on topics like the military or exemplary personalities which show the *wu* 武 ('military') and the *wen* 文 ('cultural-civilised') side of communist victory (and of selected aspects of 'Chinese tradition'). To this, the geographical documentary popular since the Japanese co-productions of the 1980s adds the 'national pride' moment, focusing on symbols of Chineseness like the Yangzi, the Great Wall or the Yellow River, going also well with emerging inbound tourism. Thus, politics, nationalism, and identity are firmly entrenched also in the Chinese documentary tradition. However, global documentary developments have not been without reverberations in China and have introduced new challenges. Therefore, the question remains as to how the very recent examples of Chinese historical documentaries presented in this book relate in a more general vein to global developments and to functions of the documentary in society? More precisely: what role do documentaries play in the context of other modes to bring history to the public? How do they deal with key problems raised by putting history on screen in general, and in the documentary format in particular? And how about the particular notions of the national 'Self' and the foreign 'Other' that emerge?

Memory culture, functions of history in society, and the power of images

The appearance of history on screen has to be set into the context of the cacophony of representational modes in which history comes to the public. These include, e.g. museums, memorials, theatre, children's books or cartoons and films, but also interactive modes like re-enactments, for example in the case of medieval markets popular in the West or other events like re-enactments of historical battles, historical guided city tours, computer games and so on.[5] (Some of these modes are recently coming up in China as well.) History on screen is therefore a part of – as called in the West – 'public history' (Robert Kelley), 'popular history' or 'applied history', though the terms 'public'/'popular' history – formulated with a view to Western civil societies – are ambiguous in the Chinese context.[6]

History on screen in TV is therefore one of several agents in 'memory culture' to construct identity,[7] and of 'history culture' (Rüsen) which focuses on history consciousness in a society.[8] In this, at the most simple level two aspects are involved: the sender with his intentions/agenda, and the receiver and his 'use' (de Certeau) of what is presented to him. This binary conception is however, as said above, too simplistic, as it skips the medium itself and the additional 'players' coming in, but the more pressing problem is that it is, above all, the receiver side and its 'use' that is still largely elusive. Reception studies are very scarce and mostly boil down to checking viewing quotas with TV (or tickets sold for cinema). In China, polling is normally done by special agencies for prescribed uses and therefore only partly helpful to gain insights.[9] The use of blog entries, which is another way to locate 'public response', is tricky as well, because it is difficult to assess anonymous reactions and in how far they are representative,[10] apart from the problem of possibly 'sponsored' entries.

In the European context, the empirical work of Bodo von Borries has been fairly exceptional in the field, though not on TV but rather on history consciousness and the 'effectiveness' of history education in an attempt to look into history culture. In a large project he has used questionnaires to investigate into European youths' history consciousness and reception of history education, targeting 15-year-old students in 27 mostly European countries in 1995. Although his studies are restricted to youths, they nevertheless imply that nationally different educational systems and 'memory cultures' have an impact on history consciousness in a given society, and that in highly modernised, secularised and individualised societies there is usually less 'interest' in history than in 'traditional, religiously-bound and collectively thinking' ones.[11] If we look to East Asia, however, we might rather question the ubiquity of this phenomenon, pointing out that modernisation is not necessarily a 'history-killer': it is especially well-off, relatively young urban middle class people who engage in history and consume history on screen in China (and arguably also in other East Asian countries). And whereas Pierre Nora has suggested that the nation-state-linked memory has nowadays given way to the 'modern' individualised, psychological memory (Nora 1989; cf. also Greene 2001: 246), this, too, seems to hold true primarily for modern Western societies. In the PRC – as in the Soviet Union some time ago – the nation-state and collective 'authoritarian' memory building obviously held/ still holds on.

This nation-state-linked memory is, in fact, basic to the PRC's history views which in spite of Chinese subscription to a 'Marxist' historiographical view follow the dominant narrative suggesting 'men make history' – in line with Soviet historiography since its shift under Stalin from structures to 'great men' – as can be seen in our three documentaries.[12] This view, focusing on outstanding figures in a model-to-emulate paradigm, falls – to use Nietzsche's term – in the category of 'monumental history' which goes well with the use the documentaries are put to:[13] to reflect in one way or other on the nation-state, the exemplary, and past achievements for emulation in the future. This holds true also for history education in school. Notably, although the Chinese official guidelines for history textbooks in schools have reasserted the importance of 'Marxist' categories (economic structures, social classes, developmental laws etc.) since the 1980s, the details of curricular requirements betray the lingering importance of the 'great men' Stalinist model, as I have shown elsewhere (Müller 2011b). Thus, the exemplary approach – which also fits well the Chinese pre-communist historiographical tradition – pervades history representations in the PRC on many levels.

History representations provided by our documentaries do relate back to school history education (though not necessarily always sustaining it) as this is the 'prefiguration' (Ricoeur) which viewers 'bring with them' when watching, but we need to consider also the relationship to scientific historiography as a further factor of influence. This relationship is not unilateral in the sense that documentaries only 'feed on' scientific historiography, simply adapting it to their own mode, but, as we saw, historians also try to use non-school representations on their own to diffuse, modify or challenge received historical 'knowledge' in a less 'authoritative/normative' genre than textbooks.[14] In our cases, especially with the more 'scientific' *Daguo jueqi*, chief historian Qian Chengdan attempted to 'update' historical knowledge of the audience via the documentary. Popular renderings of historical topics therefore may diffuse also scholarly historiography, which means there is some overlap between both in practice, although conceptually they remain distinct. To differentiate between the modes of scientific historiography on the one hand and other forms of history representations on the other, Rolf Schörken has suggested to distinguish between 'reconstruction' as the aim of scientific historiography, and – referring to Paul Ricoeur's terminology – 'refiguration' as to what happens when history is represented in other forms, though not denying the interaction between both (cf. Schörken 1995: 12).[15] This characterises the different basic thrust in both modes. When history is represented in society, it serves multiple functions, which, according to Schörken, may be divided into political legitimisation, social upgrading and surrogates for experience.[16] Clearly in our three Chinese documentaries the political legitimisation is paramount for the sender side, though social upgrading (to a lesser extent) and surrogates for experience (to a greater extent) are certainly present as well, mainly with *Daguo jueqi*, for the receiver side and its interest in other countries' histories.

Besides these more functional aspects of history representations in society, on a more general and theoretical level, the interaction between images and historiography and the use and function of images for and in writing history is important to evaluate the specific role of documentaries in 'history culture'. This relationship between images and historiography has been reflected upon in historical studies quite extensively. For example, Peter Burke has elaborated on the use of images as historical 'sources', detailing the fallacies of various genres, but arguing also for the potential and need of taking visual sources into account.[17] Gerhard Paul situates this into the general 'visual' or 'pictorial turn' historical studies have undergone, arguing for the special constitution and the added value for the historian by integrating visual sources (Paul (ed.) 2006).[18] However, one of the pitfalls is the fact that many widely disseminated images come from propaganda sources and have to be decoded before they might be used as to avoid falling prey to the suggested perspective.[19] This means when reusing archival visual material, e.g. in a documentary, one has to be aware they are not simply 'raw' material – a point we will come back to. This has become obvious also in our Chinese cases when the commentary 'struggled' with the footage. Rosenstone, doyen of history on screen studies in the West, has proposed a general classification of history put on screen as 'history as drama', 'as document' and 'as experiment' (Rosenstone 2001).[20] At first glance, with our Chinese documentaries we are dealing with the second, but we will discuss the relations between historical dramatisation and the documentary character below, as the classification is not that clear-cut in practice.

In terms of effect, history on screen has a strong and sometimes long-lasting influence on viewers by its advantage vis-à-vis texts of coming along with powerful images. Some of these might remain permanently in people's heads when thinking of a historical subject or person: the face or scene one once saw on screen is easily identifiable in memory with the historical subject it represented. (In fact, some studies on history images suggest the strong impression left by history film actors' faces, which tend to suppress the impression by portraits etc.[21]) The power of images is, for example, dramatically clear when images even reconfigure memories of eyewitnesses. An impressive example is provided by Christoph Hamann who found that even drawings by survivors of the Nazi concentration camp Birkenau – who obviously knew the place – later took over the *wrong* interpretation of perspective on the camp's entrance gate in a well-known photograph which was mistaken as a view from *outside* (with train tracks seemingly converging and – suggestively – leading to the 'end') but was in fact showing the gate from *inside* (and the final section of the train tracks there; see Hamann 2006: 291). This is a striking illustration of the 'power of images' – in a *wrong* but easily convincing interpretation more compelling than in reality – overtaking even personal experience. This means history on screen has a psychological edge over texts in memory building. It is therefore of high significance for a society's memory culture. And by repeating certain 'fetish images' of an event or person, the media often contribute to cement certain views,[22] which – turned around – also means they are good allies of propaganda making and have also in the past served well the propagation of official history views. Here, China is no exception.

By the agency of the state, certain views on history can be promoted, excluding other readings, which leads to myth and legend building (Keil 2009: 35–6). By this, historical films (and documentaries) take actively part in history politics, working as 'mytho-motors' (Riederer 2006: 101), and thus influence a society in practice. In our Chinese cases this clearly was intended as an outcome. The public, on its part used to these myths and thus being 'prefigured' in its historical views,[23] reacts typically negative to anyone questioning 'established truths': a reflex of 'protection of vested interests', as historian Winkler put it (Winkler 2004: 11). This might be seen in some reactions of the Chinese public as well: we want to be reassured in what we assume we know already (e.g. from school education). For attracting audiences, documentaries therefore usually conform to the views prevalent among the audience. For example, as we saw with *Daguo jueqi* mainly, in presenting other countries they will pick up stereotypes (or what might be assumed to be known by the audience, e.g. by school education – I would add) about these countries (Kilborn and Izod 1997: 39),[24] and add 'iconic' pictures to satisfy the assumed quest of the public for a 'recognition effect'. This 'conformity' to assumed public expectations is, however, structurally not different from Western practices, and is the more pronounced the more the market has to be considered. It limits also the possibilities of introducing too much 'divergent' reading which needs to draw on the scholarly image of 'experts' to be taken up by the public as 'credible'.

Besides intentions coupled with a production, obviously the medium's specificity and technical workings are important as well to fully comprehend and evaluate outcomes: when putting history on screen, a shift occurs during the process from the historical expertise of those involved in the project's original conception to considerations of film people about what at all can be shown (which should not be equated with the usual and simple criticism of 'vulgarisation').[25] Obviously, only what is visually representable can be shown, and only by the commentary function may one keep interpretative and narrative threads. That this potentially leads to tensions has been addressed also in our Chinese cases in reflections on the production.

For the technical side of filming, the medium comes into play in a double function: film as storage medium on the one hand, and as dissemination/circulation medium on the other (cf. Hoffmann 2009: 135).[26] This means with regard to history on screen, it functions as a 'source' *and* as a way of historiography. When looking at it from the receiver's side, a third function is its potential to cue.[27] In this way, the media become part of cultural memory of a society in their own right and add to other ways of memory-building. Historian O'Connor has therefore called for film analysis to start with gathering information about content, production and reception, and then move on to look at film as either a) a vehicle for historical representation; b) as a material source for social and cultural history; c) documentary footage as source of historical evidence; or d) the history of the audiovisual media as industry and art (cf. Guynn 2006: 13).[28] In our Chinese cases, we have taken up this call in so far as we have first assembled information about content, production and reception, and then looked at the documentary as a vehicle for historical representation and partly as a material source for Chinese contemporary social and cultural history, whereas the other two aspects did not concern us here.

By its specificity, film furthermore obviously differs from written historiography by integrating (graphically or spoken) language, image and sound (Guynn 2006: 69). Already on the level of 'authorship', in contrast to the historiographer writing a narrative, the filmmaker is 'author' twice and with different functions: at the stage of filming and again at the stage of editing.[29] On another level, since film and TV appeal to emotions, one has to consider that aspect specifically as a central feature also in historical films or TV productions (Bösch 2006: 318; see also Bösch and Borutta (eds.) 2006),[30] which sets them apart from written historiography, too. This emotional involvement in film/TV is provoked not only by visual, but also by audio means (cf. Korte and Paletschek 2009a: 33), the music being the 'unnoticed instrument of narrational manipulation' – as Guynn has put it (Guynn 2006: 76), of which *Ju an si wei* was an excellent example. Therefore, we have tried to pay attention to this usually 'unnoticed manipulation' in our discussion of the single documentaries above.

Even if the genre separation between film and TV has become increasingly blurred, with the specificity of TV remaining only in seriality, historical documentaries are nowadays mostly shown on TV, with the British and American productions leading the field in the West.[31] The BBC, for example, was the first to use eyewitnesses which became a typical feature of Western documentaries on recent history.[32] Our Chinese official documentaries, instead, (still) prefer the less 'personal' educative device of commentary and academic interviewees, adding to the general air of 'objectiveness', which obviously is intended to be transmitted to the audience. Also other new genres developed in the UK like the historical docusoap which transported reality TV to historical topics (e.g. *The 1900 House* where a modern British family tries to live as in 1900), are not yet diffused in China, although reality TV has made some inroads. Again, the 'personal' factor seems to be the problematic issue as seen from the authorities' side, as reality TV precisely markets its supposed 'spontaneity' and thus 'authenticity'. This, however, would imply the 'unpredictability' of the filmed people's live actions. Not surprisingly, in China existing 'reality TV' is therefore usually (and admittedly) scripted (Berg 2011).[33]

In sum, as for the dissemination of history views in society, TV has been called *the* institution in the West (Wolfrum 2003: 36), and even if not all formats popular in the West are also popular in China, one may argue that in terms of the importance of TV for the dissemination of history views there is no big difference to the West. It has become *the* medium there as well, outdoing scientific historiography for sure (which therefore at times tries to actively 'use' it now), but even rivalling mandatory school history education in societal influence. This is due to the medium's specificities which go beyond the written and include visual and audio aspects, to its easy availability, and to its leisure context. Therefore, to understand the influence and particularity of TV history in the broader societal context, its relation to memory culture, to other modes of societal historical representations, to scientific historiography, and its specific technical workings had to be addressed.

A key question that remains in the wings when talking about the influence of TV representations of history on viewers is 'authenticity': what does it mean in a given context? Medial authenticity might be different from authenticity to the historian (Wirtz 2008a: 23).[34] 'Authenticity' is mainly defined here by what the public accepts as such, i.e. what concerns us is rather the maintenance of an 'illusion of authenticity'.[35] Quite tellingly – as historian Martin Zimmermann has concluded from his experience participating in the making of a historical documentary – in production 'fictionalisation' is of utmost importance, whereas in marketing 'authenticity' is upheld (Zimmermann 2008: 153–8).[36] This tension between fictionalisation so as to create a compelling storyline and the expectation of historical 'authenticity' on behalf of the viewer, above all in the case of a 'documentary', can be sensed also in our Chinese cases, although the fictionalisation part is not openly acknowledged by the producers. The key question to authenticity in the context of images (and – by extension – film) is therefore, as Wortmann has argued, not so much an ontological (or technical) one, but one of cultural practices and assumptions which translate into the *use* of images which 'read' them in one way or other, and this holds true for a medieval panel as much as for a nineteenth century photograph or a digital image (Wortmann 2006).[37] In short, what is of interest to us here is not how 'authentic' our Chinese documentaries 'are', but the question of which *strategies of authentication* they use and how they are received and evaluated by the viewers. This, however, presupposes a look into the specificities of the documentary genre as such.

Framing by format: the documentary genre

Documentaries in general have been a rather rare genre in early film history around the globe, and those produced were often attached to propaganda (Downing 2001: 294; see also Lersch 2009: 173–4). In British documentary, the tradition established since the 1920s/30s by Grierson, one of the 'founding fathers' of the documentary movement, was based on the intention to involve citizens in society by providing educational enlightenment (Kilborn and Izod 1997: 6 and 19). Consequently, from Grierson onward, documentaries were often sponsored by state institutions. The same, of course, holds true for the other paradigmatic tradition: the Soviet documentary. Thus, since the 1920s/30s all over the world documentaries were used by governments to promote a sense of participatory citizenship (Nichols 2001: 98), even if 'contents' of the respective citizenship concept differed. This demonstrates that the Chinese political background to the documentaries we addressed here is per se not unique.

Documentaries – famously defined by Grierson as 'the creative treatment of actuality'[38] – are usually set against 'fiction films' as a form of 'non-fiction', or – in a shorthand definition by Nichols: fiction is orientated to *a* world, non-fiction to *the* world.[39] Basically, early ethnographers turning to the film medium like Margaret Mead conceived of documentaries as a way to avoid the fallacies of fictionalisation which Mead associated with editing and mise-en-scène (Guynn 2006: 1). This explains also, why in marketing fictionalisation is no asset and is explicitly rejected for a 'documentary'.

Documentaries, however, do not simply chronicle 'the world out there', but willy-nilly do transform it. But there is a kind of 'contractual agreement between filmmaker and audience' (Kilborn and Izod 1997: 4) that the raw material is collected from the socio-historical world, and this 'authenticates' the documentary. In sum, at closer scrutiny, documentaries are always framing world views as well, in spite of the gesture they come with and the expectations they raise in viewers to 'faithfully show' the things they present. To cite film scholar Bill Nichols: 'As digital media make all too apparent, fidelity lies in the mind of the beholder as much as it lies in the relationship between a camera and what comes before it' (Nichols 2001: xii). This goes well with what we observed above: decisive is the acceptance of 'authenticity' on the part of the viewer, as documentaries in themselves do not only 'document' indexically (to use Charles Peirce's term) or 'reproduce'. They, instead, try to persuade the viewer to 'adopt a given perspective' (Nichols 2001: xiv), as is evident also from our three examples of Chinese documentaries.

In their claim to 'authenticity', documentaries draw on the 'remarkable power of the photographic image' (Nichols 2001: 3) (and, one may add, the audio tape) to record situations and events, even though we know that it is possible to alter them at any production stage. (Already in photo history there are notorious examples of alteration making unwanted figures 'disappear', be it in Stalinist Russia or in Maoist China.)[40] Documentaries only seem to not involve in what they film: people supposedly behave 'normally' and are just watched by the 'fly at the wall', even though we know that the presence of a cameraman will not go unnoticed. Documentaries certainly do present indexically the world in a way, but by shaping it from a distinct perspective, they represent it. A documentary is therefore more than mere footage,[41] – though, in fact, I would argue that the problem goes even further in so far as this entails the question of what 'footage' exactly implies. Arguably, there is no 'innocent' 'raw' material as such. Strangely, most film studies seem to take 'footage' as such a given 'raw' material which is then worked upon, i.e. 'edited'. A similar problem exists already with photography and the distinction between a 'private' or 'occasional' shot and the professional (or artistic) photo. Here, at best, there is again a distinction in degree, not in kind. With 'footage', some scholars seem to identify them with 'newsreel' mainly, but clearly, cameramen for news are professionals and news programmes are following conventions as well (for this, one may just think of the problems *Ju an si wei* was confronted with when using the Soviet news coverage of Gorbachev and so on). Whether an 'amateur' video is more 'authentic' is also simply a matter of good faith, an assumption. In sum, I see here the distinction rather as in the degree of consciousness (or the presence or absence of a posterior edit), not in kind, since obviously also unedited 'footage' provides some perspective and selects what is filmed and what not.

Most clearly and directly, documentaries intervene with a particular view by commentary (and interviews as voices of authority). They follow a certain logic to make some point. To cite again Nichols: 'The logic organising a documentary film supports an underlying argument, assertion, or claim about the historical world that gives the genre its sense of particularity' (Nichols 2001: 27). For example, cuts between totally different shots do not appear disruptive because the different shots are argumentatively linked. Nichols calls this 'evidentiary editing' (vis-à-vis continuity editing) (Nichols 2001: 29–30). This editing dominated all three of our Chinese documentaries. Others, drawing the line somewhat differently, term the two main editing approaches: the 'constructivist' editing which makes meaning emerge from the 'contrasts, echoes and reverberations *between* shots';[42] and the 'fly-on-the-wall' account, which aims at providing the impression of 'being there' (Kilborn and Izod 1997: 206). In either perspective, the Chinese cases are of the former variety. Furthermore, via stylistic means of rhythm, pace etc., meaning is produced as well (Kilborn and Izod 1997: 207). In our documentaries, we encountered such stylistic devices, not only, e.g. with contrasting shots between successful Stalinist industrialisation and American social misery during the Great Depression, but also when a slow-motion pace underlines the dubiousness of post-Stalin Soviet leaders or a close-up on a picture with special light effects evokes typical criminals' photos, insinuating we are presented with a historical 'culprit'. (The audio track, of course, adds to this by cueing viewers into certain reception modes.)

Since documentaries tend to show metonymically, i.e. part for the whole, audiences assume that what is shown is somehow representative. This, however, might induce 'distorted' evaluations. For example, the Chinese government objected strongly to a Western documentary on 'Chinese orphanages' which showed to a Western public some 'horror' cases, not so much negating the evidence in itself but precisely on the grounds that this would be taken as 'representative' by the viewers.[43] Turned around, however, this also demonstrates the possible 'educational' uses of a documentary to cue viewers into believing in the representativeness of what is shown, and if this is 'positive' with regard to Chinese policies, viewers are cued into sustaining the government.

Furthermore, 'a great deal of persuasiveness stems from the sound track' (Nichols 2001: 30), – another point we encountered with our examples which is usually underestimated in scholarship on (Chinese) film or TV, being mainly concerned with narrative and visual issues. In Nichols' seminal categorisation of six documentary modes (poetic, expository, observational, participatory, reflexive, performative), our Chinese examples would count as 'expository', which also is the mode with the greatest affinity to historical topics. As he notes: 'The notion of the "history lesson" functions as a frequent characteristic of documentary' (Nichols 2001: 39) – and was present in all our three Chinese cases. (As mentioned earlier, Chu has argued to add the 'dogmatic' mode for the Chinese case to Nichols' list to cover also the specific context of 'Maoist' film production, which, however, sets China apart from the rest of the world and does not even address the relationship to the Soviet example so influential in China in any depth. In a comparative view, I therefore would like to stick to the more 'general' modes of Nichols and address the specific Chinese context of production separately).[44] The 'expository mode' gives precedence to the commentary, uses images rather as illustrative and is by trend didactic. This type, as Nichols describes it, usually adds to knowledge but does not challenge the underlying categories; frequently, it calls also on the viewer's 'common sense'. But 'common sense' is (in part – I would qualify) historically relative which makes for why things convincing at one time (or place – I would add) might not be so at another (Nichols 2001: 107 and 109). Certainly, our documentaries, even if at times providing unconventional views, as in *Daguo jueqi*, did not challenge underlying categories, but precisely were intended to sustain them.

The voice of a documentary which transports to us its argument uses many means: but for the voice-of-God (unseen) or voice-of-authority (seen) commentaries, both of which we encountered in our examples with the spoken commentary and the interviewees, there are also other means: when to cut or edit, what to juxtapose, and how to frame a shot; whether to record synchronous sound or to add additional sound, including the spoken commentary, later; whether to adhere to an accurate chronology; whether to use archival footage; and finally, which mode to rely on to organise the film (i.e. the expository in our cases). Documentaries follow rhetorical agendas for convincing viewers by the so-called 'three Cs': being credible, convincing and compelling (Nichols 2001: 51). Interviewees, e.g. guarantee by their professional or personal trustworthiness: they sustain credibility. The solemn intonation by a male commentator's voice is a classical convention in documentaries in the West – and is dominant also in China. Commentary is the most instrumental device as it may work towards guiding 'correct' or desired perceptions, since images do not simply speak for themselves: it is there to convince us. Documentaries furthermore couple 'evidence' *and* emotion by selecting and arranging images and sounds to compel us. All of this then becomes part of the 'triangle of communication' between filmmaker, film and audience.[45] But whether receivers 'use' this in the way the producer side intended it or opt differently, is an open question, as audiences have their own reception dynamics. As we saw with glimpses into discussions about our Chinese cases, reception was certainly not uniform.

At closer scrutiny, 'evidence' is, in fact, not 'compelling' in itself and therefore also 'relative', as Nichols has forcefully argued elsewhere: a first-hand impression of a (casually filmed) scene of four (white) policemen beating a (black) victim (Rodney King) came to be reinterpreted by clever attorneys of the policemen as a 'self-defence' which even convinced the jury in the end (Nichols 1993: 188–90). Thus, a 'documenting image' is obviously *not* 'speaking for itself', but by analytical techniques like 'reframing; repetition; reversed, slowed or arrested movements' the tape could be made into 'defamiliarising' what was shown. Thus, 'the "human" response elicited from most viewers [. . .] could be wrung out of the "legal" spectator through multiple exposure and through constant recourse to a rationalised and reconstructed version of the event', as Renov (1993: 9) phrases it. For our cases, this means that documentaries can also work *consciously* with defamiliarising techniques to prevent easy identification between viewer and images and create a distance between them to elicit acceptance for an interpretation provided by the commentary clearly at variance with a first-glance impression (even if the outcome, e.g. in *Ju an si wei* with Gorbachev, might be termed unsuccessful).

Moving on to how TV as a medium influences the development and making of documentaries, we have to pay attention to the particular TV context, i.e. whereas cinema documentaries are made for reception by more 'committed' people who decide to buy tickets, the TV and its multi-channel competitive surrounding compel producers to consider a potentially zapping viewer, who consumes domestically with also many other possible distractions present. 'Factual entertainment' is therefore the main concern with TV documentaries (and, we may add, compels producers to present an intriguing storyline). In short, TV documentaries are under pressure to attract continuously. Today's multi-channel environment also means that TV has no longer the 'integrative function, once claimed for' to bind the nation together,[46] and this holds true also for China, although CCTV remains the dominating agent on the TV market, and official regulations on prime time mandatory use of Chinese productions help propaganda-like series as *Fuxing zhi lu* to be aired. *Daguo jueqi* offered a case where a documentary successfully attracted high viewing rates on its own in a competitive environment and obviously provided this 'factual entertainment' to keep audiences at the screen.

For sure, institutions like broadcasters or the government with its political needs have framed documentaries everywhere. In line with the state's sponsorship, this meant TV documentaries were prodded by the Public Broadcasting Service (PBS) in many countries. This, however, led also to certain formatting standards which framed TV documentaries. With 'deregulation' and privatisation of the media in many regions of the world, documentaries now are set in a context of channel branding to compete with other channels, making also for specialised niche channels or slots devoted to documentaries. Since the 1990s, in the West cable and satellite channels multiplied the terrestrial offer of TV options, thus also allowing for channels specialising in documentaries (Kilborn and Izod 1997: 165–6 and 178–9). In Chapter 1, we have seen something similar happening in China, e.g. with the Shanghai Documentary Channel, and CCTV setting up its own documentary channel on 1 January 2011. In fact, the Chinese state has declared its active interest in developing documentaries as a key part of building up its soft power,[47] thus trying to keep the traditional bond between documentaries and government interest also in the times of increasing privatisation.

Now, if documentary is a 'non-fiction' genre as opposed to feature film, how do viewers recognise they are watching a non-fiction? To mark off a documentary as such is done in part by supra/meta-textual devices: calling it thus, putting it on a time slot were people know they have to expect a documentary and so on.

Documentaries may be attached to a feature of the same topic, or may capitalise on an anniversary. A crucial feature for a documentary is scheduling, which tells much about the targeted audience. Clustering and zoning documentaries in 'roped-off' schedule sections is therefore one way of promoting documentaries. And the selling of an additional book series including the 'how it was made' is a well-known device of promotion. As film scholars Kilborn and Izod argue, 'sched-uler's calculation is that viewers will have had their interest stimulated by their exposure to additional media outlets'.[48] We have seen something similar, for example, with *Daguo jueqi* with its supplementing media outlets, and *Fuxing zhi lu*. But there are also historically generated conventions on how to do a documen-tary to highlight the documentaries' particularity. One standard feature is the stance of dispassionate objectivity. Nichols once identified it as a 'discourse of sobriety',[49] which belongs to the standard repertoire of what we have termed above 'strategies of authentication' to cue the viewer into accepting what is shown as credible. However – different from an ideal-type pure news format – documen-taries do provide some interpretation: they always argue something, as we have seen. Recognition of this specific format therefore works also via formal conven-tions: presenting an argument, taking up typical documentary subjects etc. However, with reality TV on the one hand, and more use of 'fiction' elements (e.g. re-enactments) on the other, the boundary between documentary and fiction has become ever more blurred in recent times,[50] the genre of 'docudramas' being but one outcome of this development. At closer scrutiny, genre-crossing commonal-ities between fiction and documentaries are present also in the conventional docu-mentary format: not only fiction films give pride of place to main characters, but this might well be the case in documentaries as well (cf. *Ju an si wei*, always repeating the same people's sequence: from Lenin and Stalin through Khrushchev and Brezhnev to Gorbachev and Yeltsin). This, again, demonstrates that the boundaries between 'fiction and faction' are not that sharp (see also below).

Something expected from a documentary which renders it 'authentic' is verisi-militude. This verisimilitude, however, is not only achieved via the audience's own experiences (some they might not have), but also according to other accounts against which they measure what they see: e.g. a murder will be judged as 'veri-simile' not against personal experience, but against other 'viewing experiences'. What seems 'realistic' is therefore partly depending on audiences, i.e. will not be the same always and everywhere (Kilborn and Izod 1997: 34). In historical contexts – we may add – 'experiences' obviously cannot be personal, so one might infer from the above that verisimilitude will be judged by the viewer rather by confronting it with his/her received knowledge. The same holds true for foreign countries if one has not visited them: viewers will judge verisimilitude according to their 'viewing experiences' in other contexts. Of course there are also certain filmic devices to enhance a realist impression: location shooting, presented talk from the scene or interviews. Some of these have been used also in our Chinese cases. On the other hand, in terms of filmic devices, whereas feature films will give artistic expression using lighting and so on, a documentary may not employ these devices which would jeopardise a 'realist' impression (Kilborn and Izod

1997: 35–6). Therefore, outright cues provided by an obvious mise-en-scène have to be avoided to not disturb the viewer's impression that he is watching a documentary. All this, however, is the description of an 'ideal-type' documentary, and – I would like to argue – the range of 'tolerance' vis-à-vis genre-external elements might differ over place, time and viewing generations. Looking at our Chinese examples, we did detect some devices of mise-en-scène like special lighting, suggesting they are not considered by their producers as detrimental to the holding-up of an 'illusion of authenticity' but rather as serving to sustain the commentary's interpretation, i.e. to drive home certain points.[51] If 'ideal-type' documentaries are considered a conscious sequencing of 'documents' (cf. Rosen 1993: 72), and viewers as convinced by default that what they see 'authentically' reflects what was there, some provocative documentaries have exposed how easy it is by re-contextualisation to completely change meanings,[52] consciously misleading the viewers. This is possible because, as Nichols observes, 'our willingness to agree with what is said relies to a surprisingly large extent on rhetorical suasion and documentary convention' (Nichols 1993: 178). Therefore, rhetoric and conventions are crucial for guiding reception. For example, one of the conventions of academic interviews is iconic authentication by bookshelves in the background to heighten credibility of what is said, another location shots to provide a sense of being there.[53] Such techniques were present also in our Chinese cases and count as part of their authentication strategies to suggest to the viewer he is watching a credible 'non-fiction' historical documentary.

Viewers, in turn, today potentially know that in the present-day digital world it has become extremely easy to manipulate images, which jeopardises the notion of 'any firm indexical bond between signifier and signified' (Kilborn and Izod 1997: 11). However, I doubt normal lay audiences, consuming TV in their leisure time, look at documentaries with such a critical eye. They rather like to believe in the fact that what they see must have been there because of the 'promise' of old photography: based on a chemical process and thus being 'mechanical' – the 'indexical bond' (Peirce).[54] Therefore, if there is no cue to doubt the 'authenticity' of what is shown, there is no incentive to question it. Documentary conventions and (skilled) rhetorical suasion thus may achieve their aims without much difficulty, at least with less critical viewers. In the end, the 'effect' a documentary has on whom, is not easy to measure. In any case, audience is now in the plural. As some reception studies suggest, reception and produced meaning in the course of reception may differ according to audiences.[55] In fact, as has been observed for Britain, even programming directors often rather follow guesses of what the audience(s) might want, following the somewhat circular rationale that established modes that sold probably will engender similar products, without any evidence that audiences want this or that (cf. Williams 2008: 19). As we saw with *Daguo jueqi*s' sequel *Fuxing zhi lu*, to follow up on a success story by simply replicating the basic design is not necessarily leading to a similar success with the audience. What, however, is obvious from the Chinese TV market is that in historical representations the documentary format has gained in popularity with the viewers, and the boom of certain genres at certain times suggests changes in representational aesthetics (Lersch 2009: 176–7). This, in turn, also corroborates the fact that globalisation does not simply mean homogenisation, but rather that national cultures in general and local developments at specific times impact on formats and their likings (cf. Chan 2010: 203). We will therefore turn to this genre of historical documentaries now in more detail.

Historical documentaries and their discursive strategies

Looking at the specific genre of historical documentaries with the general observations on the documentary format in mind, they may be distinguished from historical *films* by their discursive strategies: the historical *documentary* relies on documents: archival images, testimonies, historical texts, contemporary shots of historical sites, interviews with eyewitnesses or historians. In 'compilation film' documentaries a voice-over commentary connects and arranges the documents/archival images used – if this is not left to interviewed historians. The historical *film*, in turn, amounts to a 'configuration' (Ricoeur) by using all resources of mise-en-scène to create a fictional doubling (cf. Guynn 2006: 143–4).

Given its public and economic context, history on screen necessarily has to take into consideration also the public's preferences: with contents, presentation and formats. To conform to viewers' expectations (and keep them at the screen), history on screen should be presented as entertaining, but at the same time – to 'market' its specialty – convince viewers of historical 'authenticity'. For the latter, as we have seen, documentaries are particularly suited (Bordwell and Thompson 1997: 42–6). For example, a device used to authenticate a more fictional rendering of a historical topic in a historical film, is to have a 'documentary' and internet information etc. accompany the film, to enrich the productions with more 'true' (credible) information (Wirtz 2008a: 20). However, as Borries tested with his own students of history didactics, although they theoretically favour documentaries as the 'more authentic' form, feature films were consumed much more in practice (Borries 2007: 187–9).[56] Even if the reasons are not stated, one may assume they were perceived as 'less demanding' in consumption. This, however, might be time-, group- and place-specific to some extent, since the new 'fad' for documentaries in China suggests there are ups and downs of format likings which to a great extent also hinge on the topics and uses. Arguably, the more important a topic seems to the receiver (and sender), the stronger the quest for a 'credible' format, and here documentaries have an edge over other formats.

Historical documentaries use to compile old newsreel (or other archival) footage as source material. If they are mainly based on this, they may be termed 'compilation film' documentaries, assembling different previously shot materials and re-contextualising them (Kuehl 2008: 31).[57] Of our three Chinese cases, *Ju an si wei* (and *Fuxing zhi lu* in part) belongs to this 'compilation film' documentary genre. As Chu has noted, compilation film has historically peaked twice in the PRC: once for budgetary constraints in the early 1960s, and once for political reasons after the Cultural Revolution, then focusing on individual communist leaders to reassess PRC history (and rehabilitate party figures vilified in the Cultural Revolution) (Chu, Yingchi 2007: 81–3). With a view to the genesis of this genre in the West, from the outset the compilation film followed a market-driven or ideological agenda and was historically closely associated with war, as practitioner Kuehl underlines. Although our Chinese examples are not focused on war, war documentaries are undoubtedly well represented on the market and very popular in China as well. (In fact, some of the very earliest Chinese documentaries already were on war-related topics, and in communist documentary film war was a primary subject matter.)[58] The documentary that set the tone in the West was the publicly funded *The Great War* on the fiftieth anniversary of World War I, i.e. in 1964. However, it freely associated 'original' 'footage' (often not actually original but re-contextualised different historical footage units/archive films) with features (Downing 2001: 295; see also Downing 2004: 9), thus being not 'purely' documentary. Our Chinese examples showed a similar tendency, especially with *Ju an si wei* combining Soviet film clips with (at times staged) 'footage', only occasionally disclosing to the viewer the feature film background of certain sequences. In the mid 1970s, *The World at War* on World War II by commercial Thames Television set a new standard in the West: it combined the 'classic' make-up features of a historical documentary as it is understood until today: archival film, interviews with eyewitnesses or experts ('talking heads') and location shooting.

In the case of historical events for which no archival footage was available, producers had to be creative in adding location shooting, reenactment, old photos etc. (Downing 2001: 295 and 297). These devices have been the most controversial ones since they go beyond the 'purely' documentary level and the question is in how far the audience is made aware of the distinction. In more recent productions, some documentary filmmakers have been deliberately 'liberal' in using CGI (computer-generated imagery) to even change existing archival material which, however, provokes again questions of ethics: is it acceptable to blur the real and the fictional in a 'documentary' on purpose and add fictitious elements even where 'not necessary' (cf. Williams 2008: 10)?[59] Or is this, if not openly acknowledged, a conscious (mischievous) misleading of the audience?

In terms of how a historical documentary should be made, there has therefore been a long discussion in the West: vis-à-vis the seemingly 'objective' classical documentary which compiles 'original' footage, integrates de facto re-enactments or parts of history film sources to fill in gaps, uses photos and interviews with eyewitnesses and/or experts, bridging all by the voice-over commentary (as with our Chinese cases), other modern forms which openly acknowledge 're-enactments' as such are sometimes evaluated in recent scholarship as 'safer' since they precisely do not insinuate an 'objectivity' not there. Whereas docudramas admittedly combine fact and fiction and are an openly hybrid genre (Steinle 2009: 149), 'classical' documentaries with their promise of being devoid of fictitious elements might, in fact, be more 'misleading' in this sense and have been a favourite tool for propagandists, because here commentary is everything. The fact that filmed 'objects' must have been 'there' is used as an authentication method vis-à-vis the audience (Keilbach 2009: 154–5), to which the commentary then adds interpretation. In such conventional productions the images, however, only illustrate but precisely do not authenticate the commentary – which is then 'free' to add its own reading. This is the usual mode we encountered also in our Chinese examples. Some 'filmic super-signs' might even travel between different films/documentaries (cf. Korte and Paletschek 2009a: 38), which helps also with identification on part of the viewer who 'meets' with what he assumes to know already (his 'prefiguration'), but they, again, only illustrate and are of no specific argumentative value. Rather, they are used as cues. By repeating the ever same images in TV, a kind of image canonisation is achieved (Lersch and Viehoff 2009: 97), often joining in with 'iconic images' diffused in other media as well. All this can be found also in the Chinese documentaries we examined. They therefore largely qualify for the conventional type of historical documentary. Thus, whereas TV in the West has basically moved now from the explanatory to the narrative mode, as documentary filmmaker Fischer argues,[60] in China the explanatory (or 'dogmatical' – if we are to use Chu's term) mode is still strong and very marked in our three cases, in spite of the differences between them. Certainly, *Ju an si wei* is in this sense the most 'conventional' of all and *Daguo jueqi* the most 'modern'.

Developments of the historical documentary in the 'trend-setting' Anglophone world outlined above have therefore not been without influence on China in the last two or three decades, and we have encountered many devices like location shooting, old photos and even the use of CGI also in our Chinese cases of historical documentaries. The paradigmatic *World at War* format was, however, not the only one in the Western historical documentary tradition: it paralleled another 'classic' form: the presenter-led one (Downing 2004: 10). Presenter-led historical documentaries have been accused for prescribing values and homogenising history views into dominant trends (e.g. marginalising other voices) and being too personal (Williams 2008: 13). In China, the presenter-led mode, though appearing on TV with other types of programmes, is not dominant in the context of historical documentaries as in the West, namely in the British tradition, being perceived as 'individualistic', whereas history should be 'objective' – conforming to Marxist historiographical basic convictions of what 'objective' intends. As was mentioned earlier, Lenin had his particular views on what 'reflecting reality' means, which is connected to this issue of 'objectivity'. And, of course, it goes along with the contention of Marxism being 'scientific'. 'Objectivity' is precisely what is suggested by the typical unseen commentator/narrator in Chinese documentaries (and the academic interviewees). However, with the format of TV lectures, personal 'explanations' of history have become popular also in China recently. This, however, is rather like an educational lecture close to school-style with the aim of making history more 'accessible' to a general audience, not claiming to present 'unconventional' 'personal' readings, and does not come along in the documentary mode.[61] Thus, as we saw already with the reluctance to use eyewitnesses or forms of reality TV, officially, 'personalised-individualised' history views are not favoured in China where history is predominantly considered as connected to the nation and interpretative authority remains fundamentally with the state.

Apart from the comparative historical development of the genre 'historical documentary' as sketched out above, its specificities should be considered as well when trying to account for possible outcomes and effects it provokes. For evaluating historical representations on screen, Pierre Sorlin reminded us already in 1980 in his seminal chapter 'How to look at an "historical" film' (Sorlin 1980, reprinted in Landy (ed.) 2001), that we have always to bear in mind how films (or documentaries in our case) are produced: not only is the footage deliberately chosen from the 'raw' materials and pasted together, but soundtracks are often totally independent and fixed to these images. Thus, what appears to the viewer as a coherent impression is in fact the result of two different steps in production. (As I argued above, what remains to be clarified here is what 'footage' actually means, since it implies a differentiation between 'raw' footage – as if this were 'innocent' – and consciously filmed parts). Further, we must be careful to the copies' own histories (as with any textual histories). But more than that: we have to realise a film (or documentary) is team work and thus the outcome of negotiation processes (Sorlin 2001: 28–9, 38–9, 42). This means that any reading has to account for the much more multi-faceted production process of a historical documentary vis-à-vis a historical text. Thus, also for evaluating the outcome of a historical documentary, the way it is practically made is crucial and must be considered (Kuehl 1988b; Watt 1988).[62] For this, accounts of practitioners like Thomas Balzer on how a TV documentary is done, step by step, are very helpful to consider factors also relevant for our Chinese productions. First of all, a topic is chosen that promises to sell. This implies it must be able to elicit response and must be 'emotionalisable'. There must be key figures, side figures, changes, aims and a red thread – like in any narrative. If recent times are involved, eyewitnesses can be integrated. Cutting is a crucial phase. Old films, in turn, might be edited to accord to modern viewing habits (e.g. quicker cuts) or they might be topicalised precisely in the way they were made (Balzer 2009: 145, 147, 150). Of crucial importance is further the audio part. And in general, all aspects valid for any film of course pertain also to historical representations on screen concerning the narrative structure, the mise-en-scène or film editing (cf. Bordwell and Thompson 1997).

If recent historical issues are taken up, this usually is connected to their being potentially linked to the present. In our Chinese cases, recent historical issues were mainly addressed in *Fuxing zhi lu*, but obviously also the discussion of earlier times was connected to the present, following the well-known motto of 'using the past to serve the present'. Often for the decision to produce a documentary, round anniversaries are taken up, which have the advantage of being foreseeable and 'preparable'. This holds true for the West as for China. Topics are also chosen that are moralisable (Große Kracht 2009: 21), and this implies they are personalisable. In our Chinese cases as well, a moralisation and partly a personalisation is ever present. Though the timing of our three documentary series was originally not related to some anniversary, many other Chinese productions are coming out specifically for such occasions, and in other ways external factors are integrated also in our cases, most obviously with *Fuxing zhi lu* and the Seventeenth Party Congress.

Historical documentaries are particularly confronted with the problem of sources – as we saw also in our Chinese case, e.g. when on Soviet history there are only Soviet official news images available which the Chinese – *faute de mieux* – tend to subvert by music and commentary; archival material which is not there, cannot be shown. This raises the problem of the fragmentary, selective and necessarily partisan character of materials: only things thought worth by someone were produced or conserved.[63] In other words: with archival footage, one has to be careful since this is usually what earlier generations/film makers (or their 'masters') wanted the world to remember (Brauburger 2009: 205). As has been exemplified with the early Soviet film *The Fall of the Romanov Dynasty* by Esther Shub who had only 'imperial' footage at hand to write 'revolutionary history', one needs to subvert the available material by means of contrast, be it visual (see above: e.g. by contrasting shots) or by the audio part, to wring out another meaning (Guynn 2006: 149; Nichols 2001: 75). This Soviet/tsarist case is an interesting parallel to our case of *Ju an si wei* subverting Soviet footage.

Another way of dealing with shortage of sources is the highly contested practice of assembling image material from somewhere else and putting it in a new context.[64] Alternatively – one may add – 'documents' might have been staged from the outset. For example 'archival footage' on the October Revolution or on World War I turned out to be (unacknowledged) re-enactments as nobody was there to film when things happened. In photo history, this is well known: many famous pictures have been staged as there was nobody there at the time 'historical events' took place. But one wanted to 'document' them nevertheless, if afterwards.[65] For re-contextualised images, the seemingly 'historical footage' on World War I is a good example which was, in fact, mostly filmed manoeuvres, not the war itself (where it was difficult to film; cf. Lersch 2009: 172), but by the commentary and context was suggested to be precisely that. As documentary filmmaker and critic of this practice, Jerry Kuehl, has shown, 'similar' footage is often used in totally different contexts (for example the ever same filmed sinking ship appears in various documentaries as supposedly different ships in a 'one stands for all' fashion).[66] This has to be borne in mind when watching, e.g. the Soviet 'original footage' which, in fact, often blends staged historical scenes and stills of Soviet films (only partly disclosing this to the viewer). And these are re-used in *Ju an si wei*, often without further comment. Joshua Rubinstein's elaboration on 'World War II – Soviet style' and his critical reading of Soviet footage on World War II should therefore be borne in mind when considering *Ju an si wei* (see Rubinstein 1988). In both cases, the whole works rather on 'associative' illustration by 'similar' footage (cf. Lersch 2009: 172), but leaving the viewer who assumes he sees what he is told to see, in the dark about it. For older topics where there is no archival footage available, historical paintings are often used for illustration. With digital technical means, images can be also artificially historicised,[67] again potentially misleading the viewer. All these devices were, e.g., used in

Daguo jueqi, as we saw. They are employed to illustrate and entertain, though in dissonance with the aim of maintaining the illusion of 'authenticity' in those cases where manipulation is obvious. As stated above, it seems the Chinese producers did assume that this would be tolerated by their audience, who would rather appreciate the entertainment factor.

With interviews as another common feature in historical documentaries besides archival footage or images, they are done with the aim to produce answers that fit for being broadcast. If one considers the production circumstances, given the technical complexity always involving at least three people, i.e. reporter, camera-man and audio expert besides the interviewee, and an interview setting with big lamps, there is no intimacy as might be possible with oral history interviews, even if the viewer of the documentary will not realise this difference as the circumstances are not visible to him. The 'talking heads' might be used – in parallel to the use of images – as either mere illustration or with argumentative value. By showing them full-face, images can be emotionalised (cf. Keilbach 2009: 157–8), as is often done with eyewitnesses. If, instead, 'scholarliness' and 'objectiveness' are to be stressed, as with interviewed academics, bookshelves in the background are the conventional device, as described above. In our Chinese cases, interviewed scholars, especially foreign ones, are very obviously there to primarily authenticate the documentary, usually playing a minor role vis-à-vis the commentary for argumentation, as we have seen. Interestingly, with the predominantly foreign interviewees in *Daguo jueqi* the studio or scholarly home abroad was shown as a device of location shooting, whereas the (predominantly Chinese) interviewees in *Fuxing zhi lu* were set in a more 'anonymous' context, going well with that documentary's focus on a 'political' (essentialised) reading of history. Furthermore, documentaries are under pressure to shorten interviews down to manageable sizes (thus making it often impossible for the interviewees to develop longer arguments).[68] This problem we encountered also in the two interview-added Chinese examples: at times almost nothing of importance remains of the statement. This, however, does not matter to the producers of our Chinese documentaries as the commentary anyway is to shoulder the main function of presenting the desired historical reading, employing interviews as well as archival footage rather to illustrate and authenticate than to 'prove'.

But the problem of sources or with interviewees is not the only one that necessitates 'creativity' on the part of the documentary filmmaker. Rosenstone, as already mentioned, has proposed a general classification of modes of historical representation on screen: 'history as drama', 'as document' and 'as experiment'. According to Rosenstone's systematisation, we are obviously dealing with the second when talking about documentaries. The documentary, mixing original footage and contemporary 'talking heads', is considered a 'window' on the past – and present (by the modern commentator). However, Rosenstone admits that documentary and drama are, in fact, linked in various ways: both tell a story (of progress usually), both concentrate on individuals, offer history as of just one closed, completed and simple nature, as emotional and dramatic; both give us the 'look' of the past with buildings etc. and show history as a process assembling many aspects (Rosenstone 2001: 52, 54, 55–7). In fact, even though at first glance our Chinese documentaries present history 'as document', there are many dramatic elements in: key figures, heroes as culprits, success and failure, and the pervasive narrative of progress.

Rosenstone suggests, however, that in the zone of overlap between document and drama a distinction in quality can be made between 'false' and 'true' inventions which relates back also to the ethical questions mentioned above: inventions are simply unavoidable in history on screen, but they should not contradict/violate historical scientific knowledge (Rosenstone 2001: 62–4).[69] In a more radical vein, Hoffmann has argued the overlap is in fact very substantial, as narrative pattern pervades drama as well as document. Thus, as in historiography (à la Hayden White), a distinction between fictional and documentary is not that helpful as it might seem (Hoffmann 2009: 138),[70] though one might still argue, as some critics maintain, that there is a line of distinction between 'construction' on the one hand and 'fictionalisation' on the other (Urmersbach 2009: 108). Kuehl – himself a documentary filmmaker – also argues forcefully for the 'pure' historical documentary and rejects need and legitimacy of the recently more popular docudramas, suggesting the proposed added value in 'understanding' is in fact no understanding of the historical facts but only of the film's message. To his view, the basic difference is that only the pure historical documentary can make any truth claims (Kuehl 1988a: 109). Still, one might well argue the difference is more in degree than in kind as 'truth claims' can only be valid relatively. And for being acknowledged or not, the viewer must be convinced of the 'truth claims'. This is why, as mentioned above, suasion into believing in 'authenticity' is the real main issue, if we want to look into effects of a documentary.

In sum, historical documentaries have their genre specificities and format conventions, but the distinction between 'fiction and faction' is only a relative one, as there is par force a narrative structure, and this automatically involves a perspective as to how to assemble image or sound materials. Historical documentaries are therefore mainly distinct in their discursive strategy. In any case, with historical subjects problems of sources and interpretation are more pronounced than with other documentary subjects, given the simple fact that history is gone by, unchangeable and not repeatable (only reenactable). One therefore has to live and work with those traces left over, if one is to reconstruct earlier times. However, reconstruction is not the only possible agenda behind historical documentaries; rather the relevance of historical topics for present-day issues often drives their production, assuming this will make them sell on the market. And this holds true for China as for the West. It therefore has now become usual also in China to promote history in many linked-up modes: exhibitions accompanied by internet forums and films etc., as we have seen. In short, the marketing has become fairly similar. And, due to international flows of products, marketing, and international programme exchange, history on screen has long been inscribed into global connections (Riederer 2006: 101 and 103). In our Chinese cases, at least for *Daguo jueqi* this holds true. The popularity of historical documentaries in China in recent years, in turn, connected to the contents of foreign vis-à-vis Chinese history – in our examples with the aim of addressing

China's rise directly or indirectly – suggests this format is seen as particularly pertinent to discuss historical issues of present-day relevance to China in today's globalised world.

National Self and Others' history in a 'globally rising' China

The final issue we need to look into for evaluating our three Chinese examples of historical documentaries is the way they conceive of the Chinese Self and the foreign Others in a historical perspective and what ends this is going to serve. The concepts of 'Self and Other' have been widely discussed in scholarship and often are immediately linked to post-modern/post-colonial approaches.[71] Whereas Said's orientalism with its constructions of Self and Other comes to mind first, historian Edward Wang has proposed to use Lacan's three-partite scheme of 'Self', 'Other' and 'other' in its post-colonial reading for understanding Chinese world historiography. In this understanding, the 'great Other' as 'opposing the Self' and the mirror-of-I 'other', i.e. a 'mere reflection of the Self' in terms of an I-to-be, are differentiated (Wang, Q. Edward 2003: 328–9). However, from the discussion on the three documentaries presented in this book, I doubt the distinction is always clear between Other and other, as – in fact – the supposedly opposing 'Other' reveals itself as also 'reflecting the Self'. In other words, the 'Other' is of interest only through the lens of the Self and not 'as such', even though one might argue that where the Chinese transmitted official history view offers the mirror-of-I 'other', the public is partly in search of the opposing/really different 'Other', and the marketing very much lives on this 'Othering' anyway. This, however, is in itself not specific to the case of China. Therefore, I would rather argue that there are different *types* of connecting Self and Other which might be taken up by the very same people in different contexts or by different people vis-à-vis the same 'object'.

In our three examples, the Others' history is clearly and from the outset framed to be linked to the Chinese Self. In it, the potential of and the dangers for the national Self are mirrored. Behind this is the unchallenged and deeply engrained belief in history's providing 'lessons' ('*magistra vitae*') – or (to use the Chinese expression) 'to use history as a mirror' to guide future behaviour. Thus, historical documentaries are logically and intrinsically connected to education for further action and – in consequence – politics, at least from the viewpoint of the state. The media and the audience link Others' history and the Chinese Self, too, but the *type* of connection is not necessarily restricted to education and politics as the state wants to have it. For the general audience, entertainment and curiosity are important factors as well. Others are different, and one wants to understand or enjoy the 'exotic'. Tellingly, although occasionally there are ill-feelings towards especially the US or Japan, empirical studies suggest people tend to distinguish between the present-day political role of these countries and their general (or historical) role.[72] This means the very same people change evaluations according to contexts.[73] Nevertheless, although one might never be sure with internet comments whether the authors were hired to write (the 'fifty-cent party'),[74] or whether they express their 'true' feelings as parts of the so-called 'new opinion class',[75] it seems from the traceable reactions to our documentaries that many Chinese are sustaining the view that China will and has to rise and therefore basically go with the intentions behind the documentaries to consider Others' history in this regard. On the government's side, current policies are more easily and quickly transmitted visually, since reworking of schoolbooks would take much longer. Most of the contents and evaluations we encountered do not challenge schoolbook versions anyway, but provide more detail and integrate more explicit political guidelines, e.g. when *Fuxing zhi lu* includes speeches of Hu Jintao at the party's congress. In this way, historical documentaries can be used as a quick 'update' on the 'slower' textbooks – by the authorities or by professional historians.

Even though Others' history is used for a basically nationalist agenda in our cases, therefore picking up only those 'Others' that are 'useful' in a 'model or warning' paradigm, and not addressing other 'Others' (Latin America, e.g. which is considered to be 'lagging behind' China as a potential competitor in the 'rising' race, though occasionally Brazil has been named in China as a 'comparable country'; or the 'tiger states' which could have been interesting models as well – but maybe of less prestige than the historically 'established' countries),[76] the Self has shifted as well: Chinese history is now part of world history (Shambaugh 2008: Chapter 1). This, however, entails also challenges to the intention of sustaining a 'particularistic' 'Chinese way'. If there are 'general laws' regulating the ups and downs of nations (which might be concluded from the 'model' cases in *Daguo jueqi*), 'Chinese characteristics' can be nothing more than a localised version of universal trends. This conclusion, obviously, is not intended by the Chinese state. But the logical fallacy opens up a space for diverging reception. It is precisely this space that critical historians and history consumers use, though most viewers might go with the intentions from 'above'. As especially *Ju an si wei* profiles, it is of crucial importance to the Chinese state to demonstrate that a fall of the CCP is not a 'universal law' after the crumbling of socialism in the Soviet Union and Eastern Europe. Therefore, the 'Chinese characteristics' are to be marketed as the only 'true heirs' to Marxism–Leninism, updating it to a version compatible with modernity. To show this, *Fuxing zhi lu* was designed to demonstrate how and why the 'Chinese way' is different. By this, the CCP hopes to 'co-opt' history of foreign Others and the national Self into service to help China rise globally.

In lieu of conclusion: the 'added value' of studying historical documentaries in China

Now, as the era Hu Jintao is drawing to a close, the historical documentaries looked at in this volume and their connection to politics of the state provide a window on the agenda of Hu's regime and how it was communicated to the populace and the cadres. On the other hand, they showed that the impact and reception do not necessarily go in tandem with the intentions the producers attached to the projects, even though the general importance of TV for establishing people's views of history is unquestionable.[77] This is also why TV productions are particularly strictly monitored. Furthermore, we saw that documentaries as a format became now a way favoured by the state as well as by the audience to relate to history, due to their perceived 'credibility'. These assumptions are more or less similar to conceptions of historical documentaries in the West, but the appropriation by the state of this format goes well beyond what might be found in any Western country today. The 'tolerance' towards deviations from the 'ideal type' 'pure' documentary, in turn, bespeaks the somewhat different 'viewing habits' of the Chinese audience,[78] having grown up with a normative view on history with a 'guided' reception provided by textbooks in school or commentary in film. 'Democratised' history is still in the making.

Documentaries are declared by the Chinese government as part of its 'soft power' build-up (see, e.g. 'Dianying jilupian, qidai hecai'; 8 April 2011). In fact, the concept of 'soft power' is one part of what officially is named 'peaceful development' (or earlier: China's 'peaceful rise' – see Chapters 2 and 3), the other being the (officially purely defensive) military build-up as the 'strong country' (*qiangguo* 强国) side to finally achieve 'great power' (*daguo* 大国) status. As we have seen, these terms have always been contested, depending on which international standing was vied for. Thus, historical documentaries take part also in delineating foreign policies and in guiding perceptions of Self and Others.[79] Western scholarship on China's new nation branding and soft power attempts should therefore pay attention also to the documentary genre.[80]

A look into this genre may furthermore enrich studies on Chinese nationalism which has received a boost in recent years as well.[81] And it may enrich discussions on propaganda, the media and state–society relations (see Chapter 1) which tend to concentrate on the print media, even though TV is proven to be the most widely disseminated medium.[82] Documentaries and their reception are therefore one further window into the complicated state-society relation in present-day China, which Reilly has summarised as a 'cyclical' relationship entailing elements of tolerance, responsiveness, persuasion, and repression on the part of the state. With our documentaries, persuasion is paramount, and they are employed to add to regime stability by providing historical 'explanations' and (anti)models by today's 'smart' state. They demonstrate on the part of the state that the 'age of propaganda' and 'ideologies' is not gone by as the CCP realises well that economic performance is not enough to sustain legitimacy. Therefore, the issue of nationalism is also linked to China's international status as a 'performance criteria that is better suited to the modern age' (Zhang, Xiaoling 2011: 11). However, in society's 'use' these documentaries might be read in a variety of ways. Here, the filmic genre provides more fissures than any print source, being an ensemble of text, image and sound. The specificities of the genre provide new chances for suasion and cues not present in these usually studied print sources (see above in this chapter), but they provide also more possible ruptures between the different elements involved, opening up spaces of divergence.

Another field of interest the documentaries addressed in this book contribute to is the question of the Soviet example and how and why China differs (see Chapter 4).[83] The 'negative example' is an important backdrop to the 'positive' formulated policies of the CCP. Again, up to now documentaries have not been included in pertaining studies,[84] but they add to the 'theoretical' discussion important new perspectives by using and reframing Soviet visual materials. For the attentive Chinese viewer, they are also a possible window on Soviet self-representation at a particular time, aside from the Chinese commentary interpreting them 'correctly' for him.

Finally – and to my mind most importantly – historical documentaries also add to an understanding of how historical consciousness is generated in present-day China which is not only defined by school history education any longer. Therefore, to evaluate the creation and construction of images of national Self and foreign Other in a historical perspective, studies on history textbooks should consider also the extra-scholastic environment, as already pupils often watch historical representations in public media and confront their classroom lectures with them. Therefore, in today's medial context, the monopoly of school education on socialising the younger generation into certain values has been challenged. This is not to deny the enduring importance of school history education for the average historical consciousness in the Chinese populace, but additional medial influences, especially if they are entertaining, and the specific advantage of the audiovisual, have the potential to stick with people more than any textbook or classroom lecture. They therefore are a potent factor in real life.

Notes

1 As we saw mainly with *Ju an si wei*, there are at times widely diverging readings in Chinese 'scientific historiography', let alone the range of views of Western, Russian, or Japanese historians interviewed.

2 As we have seen, there are different opinions on the evaluation of the Soviet Union's 'historical lesson' even inside the CCP, but the fact that this documentary was set as an obligatory study material for cadres marks it as the 'official' normative reading – at least for the time being.

3 The reference is to Bakhtin's studies on Dostoevsky.

4 Lenin's views were recorded by Lunacharsky in his memoirs. According to him, Lenin is said to have voiced his classic statement in 1922 that 'of all the arts the most important to us is cinema' (Wade (ed.) 1993: 332) – a saying that became a kind of 'standard' in the Soviet Union's view on film, together with his opinion that film should 'reflect reality' and be imbued with 'Communist spirit' (see [Lenin] 1922, note 1). In China, a whole booklet on the *Party's View on Film* was published at the beginning of the PRC with the Soviet leaders' pertaining utterances in translation as a must-read for filmmakers (cf. Chu, Yingchi 2007: 55). (The book was compiled by Soviet film director and scholar N. A. Lebedev.)

5 The range of modes and their specificity have recently become a 'hot' issue especially in German academia: see, e.g., Hardtwig and Schug (eds) (2009); Horn and Sauer (eds) (2009); Korte and Paletschek (eds) (2009b); Meyer (ed.) (2009) and the earlier work by Schörken (1995).

6 For the problematic nature of the term 'public/popular history' widely used in Western academics in the case of China, see Müller (2011a).

7   For a recent discussion of the concept of 'memory culture' popular since the 1990s, see Aleida Assmann (1999/2009 and 2006) who has been together with her husband Jan Assmann a dominating figure in academic discourse in this field. See also Erll and Wodianka (2008) on memory and film more specifically; Erll and Rigney (2012) on cultural memory and mediation more generally; and Erll (2005/2011) for a German-language critical synopsis of different approaches to and aspects of memory culture. For a very condensed form in English, see the introduction by Erll to Erll and Nünning (eds) (2008).

8   The concept of 'history culture' ('Geschichtskultur') has been worked out especially by Jörn Rüsen and Bernd Schönemann. For a brief assessment, see Korte and Paletschek (2009a: 10–11). This concept has now been largely sidelined by 'memory culture'. For a short overview and comparison of terms, see Wolfrum (2010).

9   Cf. Reilly's brief remarks on polling as an information source for politicians (Reilly 2012: 36). In appendix two of his book, Reilly ponders the question in how far Chinese polls might be reliable, being cautiously optimistic (as is, by the way, Stockmann 2013), though admitting they are not 'unproblematic'. Obviously, polls are elicited (and paid) by someone, are framed and designed to serve the client's need and are at times publicly reported, at times not, in China like everywhere, although in China the political context circumscribes what can be asked and reported clearly more than in many other countries. 'Unlicensed' polling, in turn, may run into problems. For the ideological ambivalence with regard to random polling, long seen as 'bourgeois' by the Communists who preferred 'typical investigations', see Thornton (2011: 254–5).

10 It has been noted not only in China that people who use to speak out (especially anonymously) on the internet tend to hold extreme views as others are less eager to find ways to express themselves (cf. Shirk 2011a: 27). In fact, as Zhao Yuezhi (2011) has pointed out, in China 'new' and 'old' 'leftists' often like to turn to the internet (as do 'rightist' chauvinists).

11 This broad – and certainly not unproblematic – categorisation into civilisational 'types' is proposed by Borries (see Borries 2000: 332).

12 For the impact of this Stalinist shift in historiography on Soviet film see Devlin (2008).

13 For the category of 'monumental history', cf. Landy (ed.) (2001) 'Introduction', p. 3 – referring to Nietzsche: 'Vom Nutzen und Nachtheil der Historie für das Leben'. The other two forms are, according to Nietzsche, the antiquarian and the critical.

14 Some Chinese scholars openly stated that there is a big chance in TV history as one could reach many more people with TV history than with any classroom lecture.

15 Ricoeur enumerated three modes of mimesis: prefiguration (i.e. what the reader 'brings with him' to a text before he has read it), configuration (i.e. what makes a sensible whole out of the parts he reads) and refiguration (i.e. the interaction between his own experience and the text).

16 For more details, see Schörken (1995: Chapter 4).

17 See especially Peter Burke's book on eyewitnessing (Burke 2001).

18 Paul has also edited a two-volume monumental work (Paul (ed.) 2008/9) on the twentieth century as a 'century of images'. (For the concept behind this, see Paul 2009.)

19 This point has been raised often (see, e.g. Krauss 2006: 68). However, 'suggestions' only work well with people 'predisposed' to take them up as it is equally true that one and the same photo might be interpreted or evaluated differently by different people (cf. Erll 2005/2011: 160). The 'reading' of a photo is therefore guided by intra-visual *and* context elements (labelling, social conventions or else).

20 He proposed this already in the early 1990s.

21 See Borries (2007: 209), who refers to empirical studies on the influence of fictional representations on historical memory and history culture.

22 The expression 'fetish image' I have taken from Guynn (2006: 166). Other terms often used include 'iconic pictures'.

23 The importance of 'prefiguration' is stressed, e.g., by Erll and Wodianka (2008).

24 In fact, Kilborn and Izod argue that the expository mode is especially akin to the use of stereotypes (Kilborn and Izod 1997: 61).

25 This argument of 'vulgarisation' has been a long-term debate between historians and film people (see, e.g. Schörken 1995: 153).

26 These categories were introduced originally by Harold A. Innis.

27 Cf. Erll who has enlarged the conventional understanding of two functions of media with a third: they store, they circulate *and* they cue (see Erll 2005: 137–40; 2011: 151–4).

28 O'Connor has been mostly interested in the latter two.

29 Cf. Guynn (2006: 74), referring to André Gaudreault.

30 More generally: Smith who stresses, however, that films only can 'invite' certain emotions by cueing viewers into moods, but the individual is, of course, the site were the invitation is accepted, modified or rejected (Smith 2003: 12).

31 Cf. Korte and Paletschek (2009a: 34–5). A convenient collection of articles from British practitioners is David Cannadine (ed.) (2004).

32 This was done 1964 for the first time in the context of the famous documentary on World War I: *The Great War* (see Korte and Paletschek 2009a: 35); cf. also Steinle (2009).

33 Berg discusses the example of a Chinese web-based reality show (of non-historical content).

34 For a discussion of authenticity as a concept cf. also Knaller and Müller (eds) (2006).

35 For such a receiver-defined understanding of 'authenticity' see Wirtz (2008b: 195). Thus, I leave here other approaches to authenticity aside which, e.g. in philosophy are more concerned with ethics, most famously Charles Taylor's (1991) work. For the maintenance of an 'illusion of authenticity', see Zimmermann (2008: 141) and Pirker *et al.* (eds) (2010: 11–30).

36 Zimmermann is a specialist in ancient history and took part in a documentary on Troy.

37 Wortmann is a specialist in media studies.

38 Grierson in 1966, here cited after Kilborn and Izod (1997: 12).

39 Nichols in 1991, here taken from Renov (1993: 194, note 6).

40 For the Soviet Union, which was the model for the Chinese communists, see the numerous examples in King (1997).

41 Cf. on this: Nichols (2001: 36–8).

42 In film history, a famous example is Esther Shub's Soviet re-use of tsarist footage, working with contrasting shots to subvert the footage 'from the wrong side' – see also below.

43 This interesting case is mentioned by Kilborn and Izod (1997: 212).

44 Chu enumerates a whole list of features, ranging from film politics and ideological control over predominance of the colour red to controlled film criticism (see Chu, Yingchi 2007: 86). However, many of these features might be found also in the Soviet Union (which provided the basic model anyway, even if 'Maoist' policies added to it) and in other communist countries – and in historical comparison probably not even only in countries with a communist regime.

45 For several of the points, see Nichols (2001: 46, 51, 55, 57, 61, 65).

46 On the above points, see Kilborn and Izod (1997: x, 25, 228).

47 See, e.g. 'Dianying jilupian, qidai hecai' (8 April 2011), or the *People's Daily Online* report of 1 April 2011: *Low Box Offices Sales Plagues Chinese Documentaries in 2010: Report.* See also *China's total investment in documentary films last year reached 500 Million Yuan ($76.3 Million)* (8 April 2011). Here the head of publicity and management of SARFT is cited with these aims in a Xinhua interview. (There are Chinese annual reports on the development of documentaries since 2009, also called the 'blue book of documentaries'.) See the article on the report of 2010, posted on 27 April 2011: *Dazao hao jilupian zhezhang 'guojia mingpian'.*

48 Kilborn and Izod (1997: 219; see also pp. 215, 220, 224–5).

49 According to Kilborn and Izod (1997: 125). See also on the above Kilborn and Izod (1997: 31).
50 For more on this, see Kilborn and Izod (1997: 125–134 and 6).
51 As Chu, Yingchi (2007: 17) has pointed out, reenactment and staging were favourites of 'dogmatic' film culture in China before 1977, i.e. (older) viewers are probably used to such fictionalising devices and might feel less 'irritated' by them in documentaries than other audiences.
52 See Nichols' (1993) thought-provoking article (esp. pp. 177–8) in which he had also referred to the (not intentionally filmed – see above) Rodney King case.
53 This point has frequently been stressed. See, e.g. Nichols (1993: 178).
54 On this, see Kilborn and Izod (1997: 27).
55 This is also conceded by Kilborn and Izod (1997: 229). For the parallel case of journal consumption, Stockmann (2013) has shown this for China.
56 Even though this was not a 'representative' study in the sociological-methodological sense, Borries' casual multiple checks with students over the years suggest a general trend.
57 Kuehl is referring here to the classic study of Jay Leyda: *Films Beget Films* (1964).
58 Cf. on this: Chu, Yingchi (2007: 42 and 75–6).
59 Williams, however, points out that this might enhance the appeal of TV history.
60 See Fischer's account on the recent developments in German historical TV documentary (Fischer 2009: 193–4).
61 In fact, when TV lectures that were done not only on Chinese history but also on classical literature ventured to leave the 'official' reading, they ran into trouble, as the example of an attempted unconventional interpretation of the Chinese famous novel *Dream of the Red Chamber* by a renowned fiction writer illustrates. (Zhu, Ying 2012: 157–9).
62 Both articles have been reprinted by Alan Rosenthal from the book edited by Paul Smith (1976) *The Historian and Film*, Cambridge: Cambridge University Press.
63 This point is raised by many scholars (see, e.g. Guynn 2006: 133).
64 For some nice examples in the parallel case of photography see Haus der Geschichte (ed.) (1998), Jaubert (1986) or specifically on the Soviet Union – the reference for similar Chinese practices – King (1997).
65 Various excellent examples can be found in the two volumes edited by Paul (2008/9).
66 See Kuehl (2008) and also Downing (2001: 296–7).
67 This is pointed out by Keilbach (2009: 157 and 159).
68 Cf. Schörken (1995: 155). The other extreme would be to turn interviews of experts into simply filmed radio discussions.
69 Thus, a documentary should make its special 'mark', e.g. with precision in costumes and other details (see Steinle 2009: 148).
70 Cf. Hayden White: the narrative structure is the same. Guynn (2006) has expressed similar views.
71 For a different approach from an international studies perspective, pertaining to China, see Katzenstein (ed.) (2012c), including Katzenstein (2012a) and – in a comparative perspective – Katzenstein (2012b).
72 See, e.g. Shi *et al.* (2011) on the 'bifurcated images of the US' and the impact of the media. See also Stockmann (2011b) on the image of the US, and on the image of Japan Stockmann (2010) and Reilly (2012). Shirk (2011b) considers the broader implications of the media's role for Chinese foreign policy. Her assessments have been in part challenged by Reilly (2012).
73 As opinion polls also suggest, the image of a country changes very much according to the question asked. E.g. when asked where it is best to live, the US will be named first, but in a 'like/dislike' question, Russia will be ranked higher (cf. the *Pew Research Global Attitudes Project*, searchable at www.pewglobal.org).

74 Cf. Bristow (16 December 2008) and Shirk (2011a: 14). More recently, the Chinese official newspaper *China Daily* has tried to counter this 'accusation' of manipulating 'public opinion' in its English edition contending that also in the West anti-Chinese comments were 'paid' (see Li, Hongmei; 23 May 2011).

75 This term has been introduced by the '2010 Society Blue Paper' of CASS (see Reilly 2012: 221).

76 Shambaugh (2008: Chapter 5) briefly reflects on the examples of other non-communist party-states, namely Singapore, and shows Chinese discussions on their model were going on as well.

77 See *Lishi jiaoyu ruhe kaolü gongzhong kouwei* (7 December 2006), referring to polls.

78 Cf. Chu, Yingchi (2007: 33), who sums up Chinese research on differences between Western and Chinese documentary which concludes that the Chinese documentaries distinguish themselves by a focus on education, social morality, narrative closure and careful framing, whereas the Western ones focus on the real, individual values, fragmentation and dynamic presentation.

79 Reilly (2012: 184) refers to a survey in 2008 showing the public takes its information on Japan mainly from TV, including all varieties of 'serious' and 'entertaining' TV genres.

80 For recent scholarship on Chinese soft power and nation branding, see, e.g. Kurlantzick (2007); Li, Mingjiang (ed.) (2009); Barr (2012); Ramo (2007); Wang, Jing (2008). Zhao, Yuezhi (2008: 181) also briefly touches upon the subject of soft power in connection to Chinese media. See also Callahan (2010: 10) on the 'reverse' side of humiliation history and the ensuing 'structure of feeling' in China's national aesthetic. Shambaugh and Xiao (2012: 39–40) very briefly address *Daguo jueqi* in their overview of Chinese domestic foreign policy debates.

81 See, e.g. the influential work by Peter Hays Gries (2004), but also Zhao, Suisheng (2004), Callahan (2006) and the dispute in *The China Quarterly* between Gries *et al.* (2011) and Neil J. Diamant (2012).

82 This desideratum has recently been pointed out again by Reilly (2012: 184). Reilly, focusing on the case of Sino–Japanese relations, briefly addresses the use of documentaries in 2006 to influence popular negative sentiments towards Japan for the better.

83 This issue has been addressed in the West, e.g. by Shambaugh (2008) and Rozman (1987 and 2010b). See also the recent edited volume on the Soviet legacy in China by Bernstein and Li (eds) (2010). In China, the issue is obviously of key concern to all in the field of Soviet and communist studies.

84 Shambaugh (2008), for one, refers to *Ju an si wei* only in passing.

Bibliography

'Action plan for patriotic education' (2006) (Chinese original: 23 August 1994), trans. Ming, Qiang and Fairbrother, Gregory P., *Chinese Education and Society*, vol. 39, no. 2: 7–18.

Agnew, Vanessa (2007) 'History's affective turn: Historical reenactment and its work in the present', *Rethinking History*, vol. 11, no. 3: 299–312.

Ap, John (2003) 'An assessment of theme park development in China', in Lew, Alan A., Yu, Lawrence, Ap, John and Guangru, Zhang (eds) *Tourism in China*, New York and London: Haworth Hospitality Press, pp. 195–214.

Assmann, Aleida (1999; 4th edn 2009) *Erinnerungsräume. Formen und Wandlungen des kulturellen Gedächtnisses*, München: C.H. Beck.

— (2006) *Der lange Schatten der Vergangenheit. Erinnerungskultur und Geschichtspolitik*, München: C.H. Beck.

Bai, Ruoyun (2005) *Media Commercialization, Entertainment, and the Party-State: The Political Economy of Contemporary Chinese Television Entertainment Culture*. Online. Available HTTP: <http://www.sino.uni-heidelberg.de/cgibin/webkat_imperia/regsrch. pl?wert=media+commercialization,+entertainment,+and+the+party\\xC2Dstate&recnu ms=5912&index=3:&db=dachs> (last accessed 7 February 2013).

— (2007a) *Anticorruption Television Dramas: Between Propaganda and Popular Culture in Globalizing China*, PhD thesis, Urbana, IL: University of Illinois.

— (2007b) 'TV dramas in China. Implications of the globalization', in Kops, Manfred and Ollig, Stefan (eds) *Internationalization of the Chinese TV Sector*, Berlin and Münster: LIT, pp. 75–97.

Bai Wangang 白万纲 (2007) *Daguo de jueqi* 大国的崛起 ('Rise to leading power'), Beijing: Zhongguo shehui chubanshe.

Balzer, Thomas (2009) 'Die Fernsehdokumentation – ein Werkstattbericht', in Horn, Sabine and Sauer, Michael (eds) *Geschichte und Öffentlichkeit: Orte – Medien – Institutionen*, Göttingen: Vandenhoeck & Ruprecht, pp. 144–52.

Barmé, Geremie R. (1999) *In the Red: On Contemporary Chinese Culture*, New York: Columbia University Press.

Barr, Michael (2012) 'Nation branding as nation building: China's image campaign', *East Asia*, vol. 29, no. 1: 81–94.

Berg, Daria (2011) 'A new spectacle in China's mediasphere: A cultural reading of a web-based reality show from Shanghai', *The China Quarterly*, vol. 205 (March): 133–51.

Bernstein, Thomas P. and Li, Hua-Yu (eds) (2010) *China Learns from the Soviet Union, 1949–Present*, Lanham, MD: Lexington Books.

Berry, Chris (2008) 'Shanghai television's documentary channel: Chinese television as public space', in Zhu, Ying and Berry, Chris (eds) *TV China*, Bloomington, IN: Indiana University Press, pp. 71–89.

— (ed.) (2010) *The New Chinese Documentary Film Movement. For the Public Record*, Hong Kong: Hong Kong University Press.

— (2010) 'New documentary in China. Public space, public television', in Berry, Chris and Kim, Soyoung (eds) *Electronic Elsewheres. Media, Technology, and the Experience of Social Space*, Minneapolis, MN: Minnesota University Press, pp. 95–116.

Berry, Chris and Farquhar, Mary (2006) *China on Screen. Cinema and Nation*, New York: Columbia University Press.

Bordwell, David and Thompson, Kristin (1997) *Film Art. An Introduction*, 5th edn, New York: The McGraw-Hill Companies.

Borries, Bodo von (2000) 'Nationale Geschichtskulturen und jugendliche Geschichts-vorstellungen im europäischen Vergleich', in Mütter, Bernd, Schönemann, Bernd and Uffelmann, Uwe (eds) *Geschichtskultur. Theorie – Empirie – Pragmatik*, Weinheim: Deutscher Studien Verlag, pp. 307–35.

— (2007) 'Historischer "Spielfilm" und "Dokumentation". Bemerkungen zu Beispielen', in Kühberger, Christoph, Lübke, Christian and Tertberger, Thomas (eds) *Wahre Geschichte – Geschichte als Ware: Die Verantwortung der historischen Forschung für Wissenschaft und Gesellschaft*, Rahden/Westfalen: Verlag Marie Leidorf, pp. 187–212.

Bösch, Frank (2006) 'Holokaust mit "K". Audiovisuelle Narrative in neueren Fernseh-dokumentationen', in Paul, Gerhard (ed.) *Visual History. Ein Studienbuch*, Göttingen: Vandenhoeck & Ruprecht, pp. 317–32.

Bösch, Frank and Borutta, Manuel (eds) (2006) *Die Massen bewegen. Medien und Emotionen in der Moderne*, Frankfurt am Main: Campus.

Brady, Anne-Marie (2008) *Marketing Dictatorship. Propaganda and Thought Work in Contemporary China*, Lanham, MD: Rowman & Littlefield.

— (ed.) (2012) *China's Thought Management*, London: Routledge.

Brauburger, Stefan (2009) 'Fiktionalität oder Fakten: Welche Zukunft hat die zeitgeschicht-liche Dokumentation?', in Korte, Barbara and Paletschek, Sylvia (eds) *History goes Pop. Zur Repräsentation von Geschichte in populären Medien und Genres*, Bielefeld: transcript Verlag, pp. 203–13.

Bristow, Michael (16 December 2008) *China's Internet 'spin doctors'*. Online. Available HTTP: <http://news.bbc.co.uk/2/hi/7783640.stm> (last accessed 8 February 2013).

Broudehoux, Anne-Marie (2004) *The Making and Selling of Post-Mao Beijing*, London and New York: Routledge.

Burgoyne, Robert (2008) *The Hollywood Historical Film*, Malden. MA: Wiley-Blackwell.

Burke, Peter (2001) *Eyewitnessing. The Use of Evidence as Historical Evidence*, London: Reaction Books.

Callahan, William A. (2006) 'History, identity, and security: Producing and consuming nationalism in China', *Critical Asian Studies*, vol. 38, no. 2: 179–208.

— (2010) *China. The Pessoptimist Nation*, Oxford: Oxford University Press.

Cannadine, David (ed.) (2004) *History and the Media*, Basingstoke: Palgrave Macmillan.

CCTV 6 (2007) *Huashuo shijie lishi* 话说世界历史 (World history retold) [a TV documentary in 100 episodes], 4 vols, Beijing: Xiandai chubanshe.

Certeau, Michel de (1984) *The Practice of Everyday Life*, Berkeley, CA: University of California Press.

Chan, Joseph M. (2010) 'Cultural globalization and Chinese television: A case of hybridization', in Curtin, Michael and Shah, Hemant (eds) *Reorienting Global Communication. Indian and Chinese Media beyond Borders*, Urbana, IL: University of Illinois Press, pp. 201–19.

Chang Ping 长平 (8 December 2006) *Tamen weihe bu xihuan yi minzhu ziyou jiedu daguo jueqi* 他们为何不喜欢以民主自由解读大国崛起 (Why do they not want to read the rise of the great powers via democracy and freedom?) (Originally on *Nanfang xinwenwang* 南方新闻网 (Southern News Net).) Online. Available HTTP: <http://ent.sina.com.cn/r/m/2006-12-08/17081362357.html> (last accessed 8 February 2013).

— (28 December 2006) *You geren duli cai you daguo jueqi* 有个人独立才有大国崛起 ('Only via the independence of the individual may a great power rise'). (Originally in *Wenzhaibao* 文摘报 (Digest).) Online. Available HTTP: <http://theory.gmw.cn/2006-12/28/content_523622.htm> (last accessed 8 February 2013).

Chen, Fong-ching and Jin, Guantao (1997) *From Youthful Manuscripts to River Elegy. The Chinese Popular Cultural Movement and Political Transformation, 1979–1989*, Hong Kong: Chinese University Press.

Chen, Peiqing and Liu, Haigui (2010) 'Radio broadcasting: Deregulation and development', in Scotton, James F. and Hachten, William A. (eds) *New Media, New China*, Chichester: Wiley-Blackwell, pp. 74–82.

Chen, Tina Mai (2010) 'Film and gender in Sino–Soviet cultural exchange, 1949–1969', in Bernstein, Thomas P. and Li Huayu (eds) *China Learns from the Soviet Union, 1949–Present*, Lanham, MD: Lexington Books, pp. 421–45.

Chen Xiao 陈肖 (2005) 'Ju an si wei: Baochi dang yu renmin qunzhong de xuerou lianxi – Chongdu *Sugong wangdang shinianji*' 居安思危. 保持党与人民群众的血肉联系。重读《苏共亡党十年祭》(Alert to danger while dwelling in safety: Preserving the intimate bond between the party and the masses of the people: A second reading of *On the Tenth Anniversary of the CPSU's Perishing*), *Bengbu dangxiao xuebao* 蚌埠党校学报 (Bulletin of the Bengbu Party Academy), vol. 1: 11–12.

Chen Xiao 陈晓 and Zhang Hong 张宏 (2005) *Dianshiju zhipian guanli. Cong xiangmu cehua dao shichang yingxiao* 电视剧制片管理。从项目策划到市场营销 ('Management of TV series production. From programme planning to marketing'), Beijing: Beijing daxue chubanshe.

Chen Xiaolü 陈晓律 (ed.) (2004) *15 shiji yilai shijie zhuyao fada guojia fazhan lichen* 15 世纪以来世界主要发达国家发展历程 (The course of development of major advanced countries in the world since the fifteenth century), Chongqing: Chongqing chubanshe.

Chen, Xiaomei (1992) 'Occidentalism as counterdiscourse: He Shang in post-Mao China', *Critical Inquiry*, vol. 18, no. 4: 686–712.

[Chen Xiaoqing] 陈晓卿 (1 February 2007) *Chen Xiaoqing: Jilupian hai mei dao gaochao* 陈晓卿。纪录片还没到高潮 (Chen Xiaoqing: The documentary is not yet at its peak). (Originally in *Xinjingbao* 新京报 ('Beijing News').) Online. Available HTTP: <http://culture.gmw.cn/2007-02/01/content_544585.htm> (last accessed 8 February 2013).

Chen Xingxing 陈星星 and Ren Shanshan 任姗姗 (8 February 2010) 'Dahuitang-ban fanxiang yianglie. Dajuyuan-ban zaichuang huihuang. Kan *Fuxing zhi lu* ruhe "yizhi"' 大会堂版反响强烈。大剧院版再创辉煌。看《复兴之路》如何 '移植' (Powerful reactions to the Great Hall version. The National Opera-version creates again glory. Looking at how *Road to Revival* was 'transplanted'), *Renmin ribao* 人民日报 ('People's Daily'): 12.

Chen Yuanzhang 陈远章 (2011) 'Ju an si wei – You dang xing dang' 居安思危.忧党兴党 (Alert to danger while dwelling in safety: Worrying about the party and making the party rise), *Xinxiang pinglun* 新湘评论 (The Xinxiang Critic), no. 15: 50–2.

Chen Zhihua 陈之骅 (co-ed.) (2004) *Sulian xingwang shigang* 苏联兴亡史纲 (Historical outline of the rise and fall of the Soviet Union), Beijing: Zhongguo shehui kexue chubanshe.

— (14 March 2011) *Ju an si wei – Sugong wangdang 20nian de sikao* 《居安思危——苏共亡党 20 年的思考》 (Alert to danger while dwelling in safety: A reflection on the twentieth anniversary of the perishing of the CPSU). Online. Available HTTP: <http://www.cssn.cn/news/148953.htm> (last accessed 4 June 2012).

Cheng, Yinghong (2012) 'The "socialist other": Cuba in Chinese ideological debates since the 1980s', *The China Quarterly*, vol. 209 (March): 198–216.

Chin, Gregory T. (2011) 'Innovation and preservation: Remaking China's national leadership training system', *The China Quarterly*, vol. 205 (March): 18–39.

China's total investment in documentary films last year reached 500 million yuan ($76.3 million) (8 April 2011). Online. Available HTTP: <http://www.europe-asia-documentary.com/2011/04/chinas-total-investment-in-documentary-films-last-year-reached-500-million-yuan-763-million/> (last accessed 10 March 2013).

Chu, Godwin C. and Ju, Yanan (1993) *The Great Wall in Ruins. Communication and Cultural Change in China*, Albany, NY: SUNY.

Chu, Yingchi (2007) *Chinese Documentaries. From Dogma to Polyphony*, London and New York: Routledge.

Chua, Beng Huat and Iwabuchi, Kōichi (eds) (2008) *East Asian Pop Culture. Analysing the Korean Wave*, Hong Kong: Hong Kong University Press.

Cippitelli, Claudia (ed.) (2009) *Fernsehen macht Geschichte. Vergangenheit als TV-Ereignis*. Baden-Baden: Nomos.

Cooper-Chen, Anne and Liang, Yu Leon (2010) 'Television: Entertainment', in Scotton, James F. and Hachten, William A. (eds) *New Media, New China*, Chichester: Wiley-Blackwell, pp. 83–97.

Croizier, Ralph (1990) 'World history in the People's Republic of China', *Journal of World History*, vol. 1, no. 2: 151–69.

Curtin, Michael (2007) *Playing to the World's Biggest Audience: The Globalization of Chinese Film and TV*, Berkeley, CA: University of California Press.

— (2012) 'Symposium. Chinese media and globalization', *Chinese Journal of Communication*, vol. 5, no. 1: 1–9.

Daguo jueqi 《大国崛起》 (The Rise of the Great Powers) (2006). 12 TV episodes. Beijing: CCTV. 6 DVDs.

Daguo jueqi: *12 ji daxing dianzi jilupian* 《大国崛起》。十二集大型电视纪录片 (*The Rise of the Great Powers*: A 12-part big-format TV-documentary) (2007), 3 vols, Beijing: Zhongguo minzhu fazhi chubanshe.

Daguo jueqi *jueqi yingping. Yangshi tashang huanqiu wenming zhi lu* 《大国崛起》 崛起荧屏.央视踏上环球文明之路 (*The Rise of the Great Powers* rises the screens. CCTV treads the path of global civilizations) (29 November 2006). (Originally in *Shenghuo ribao* 生活日报 (Life Daily).) Online. Available HTTP: <http://ent.sina.com.cn/v/2006-11-29/03261348356.html> (last accessed 8 February 2013).

Daguo jueqi *nongsuo 500 nian shijieshi. Tanxun 9 daguo bufa* 《大国崛起》 浓缩500 年世界史 探寻 9 大国步伐 (*The Rise of the Great Powers* condenses 500 years of world history. Enquiry into the steps of nine great powers) (4 December 2006). Online. Available HTTP: <http://ent.sina.com.cn/v/2006-12-04/09551354853.html> (last accessed 9 February 2013).

Daguo jueqi *xilie congshu* 《大国崛起》 系列丛书 (Collection series *The Rise of the Great Powers*) (2006), 8 vols, Beijing: Zhongguo minzhu fazhi chubanshe.

Daguo jueqi *zai xi gaochao. Hao jilupian rang ren kanle you kan* 《大国崛起》 再掀高潮。好纪录片让人看了又看 (*The Rise of the Great Powers* creates a further wave. A good documentary moves people to look at it repeatedly) (5 December 2006). (Originally in *Jiefang ribao* 解放日报 ('Jiefang Daily').) Online. Available HTTP: <http://ent.sina.com.cn/v/2006-12-05/09561356606.html> (last accessed 9 February 2013).

Dang Guoying 党国英 (27 November 2006) *Pinglun: Cong* Daguo jueqi *kann daguo zenyang cai neng jueqi* 评论: 从: 《大国崛起》 看大国怎样才能崛起 (Discussion: How may a great power achieve a rise as seen from *The Rise of the Great Powers*). (Originally on *Guoji zaixian* 国际在线 (International Online).) Online. Available HTTP: <http://ent.sina.com.cn/r/m/2006-11-27/09241344662.html> (last accessed 9 February 2013).

Daxing yinyue wudao shishi Fuxing zhi lu 大型音乐舞蹈史诗 《复兴之路》 (Large-scale music and dance epic *Road to Revival*) (21 September 2009). Online. Available HTTP: <http://news.cctv.com/special/fxzl2009/01/index.shtml> (last accessed 9 February 2013).

Dazao hao jilupian zhezhang 'guojia mingpian'. Zhongguo jilupian fazhan zhanlüe luntan zongshu 打造好纪录片这张'国家名片'——中国纪录片发展战略论坛综述 (Design the documentary well, this 'name card of the nation'. Summary of a discussion on the strategy to develop Chinese documentary) (27 April 2011). Online. Available HTTP: <http://www.cssn.cn/news/158096.htm> (last accessed 9 February 2013).

Denton, Kirk A. (2005) 'Museums, memorial sites and exhibitionary culture in the People's Republic of China', *The China Quarterly*, vol. 183 (Fall): 565–86.

— (2007) 'Horror and atrocity: Memory of Japanese imperialism in Chinese museums', in Lee, Ching Kwan and Yang, Guobin (eds) *Re-envisioning the Chinese Revolution. The Politics and Poetics of Collective Memories in Reform China*, Stanford, CA: Stanford University Press, pp. 245–86.

Devlin, Judith (2008) 'Recreating "history" on film: Stalin and the Russian feature film, 1937–1939', in Nicholas, Siân, O'Malley, Tom and Williams, Kevin (eds) *Reconstructing the Past. History in the Mass Media 1890–2005*, London: Routledge, pp. 29–48.

Diamant, Neil J. (2012) 'Response. On caffé lattes, nationalism and legitimate critique: A reply to Gries, Zhang, Crowson and Cai', *The China Quarterly*, vol. 210 (June): 494–9.

'Dianying *Fuxing zhi lu* quanguo fangying qidong' 电影《复兴之路》全国放映启动 (The film *Road to Revival* is now released nationally) (15 May 2010), *Renmin ribao* 人民日报 ('People's Daily'): 4.

'Dianying jilupian, qidai hecai' 电影纪录片, 期待喝彩 (Feature documentaries, waiting for applause) (8 April 2011), *Renmin ribao* 人民日报 ('People's Daily'): 12.

Ding, Sheng (2008) *The Dragon's Hidden Wings. How China Rises with its Soft Power*, Lanham, MD: Lexington Books.

Dirlik, Arif (2002) 'History without a center? Reflections on eurocentrism', in Fuchs, Eckhardt and Stuchtey, Benedikt (eds) *Across Cultural Borders. Historiography in Global Perspective*, Lanham, MD: Rowman & Littlefield, pp. 247–84.

— (2003) 'Confounding metaphors, inventions of the world: What is world history for?', in Stuchtey, Benedikt and Fuchs, Eckhardt (eds) *Writing World History, 1800–2000*, Oxford: Oxford University Press, pp. 91–133.

Donald, Stephanie H., Keane, Michael and Hong, Yin (eds) (2002) *Media in China: Consumption, Content and Crisis*, London: Routledge.

Downing, Taylor (2001) 'History on television: The making of "Cold War", 1998', in Landy, Marcia (ed.) *The Historical Film. History and Memory in Media*, New

Brunswick: Rutgers University Press, pp. 294–302; originally printed in *Historical Journal of Film, Radio and Television* (1998), vol. 18, no. 3: 325–32.

— (2004) 'Bringing the past to the small screen', in Cannadine, David (ed.) *History and the Media*, Basingstoke: Palgrave Macmillan, pp. 7–19.

Dui Fuxing zhi lu *de chensi he jueze* 对 《复兴之路》 的沉思和抉择 (Reflection and judgement on *Road to Revival*) (7 October 2009). Online. Available HTTP: <http://www.maoflag.net/?action-viewthread-tid-590521> (last accessed 28 February 2012). (As of March 2013, this website seems defunct.)

Duihua Daguo jueqi *Guo Zhenxi: Guanzhong jianyi chongbo 12bian* 对话《大国崛起》 郭振玺。 观众建议重播 12 遍 (Talking about *The Rise of the Great Powers* with Guo Zhenxi: The audience requested to air it again a dozen times) (1 December 2006). (Originally in *Dongfang zaobao* 东方早报 ('Oriental Morning Post').) Online. Available HTTP: <http://ent.sina.com.cn/v/m/2006-12-01/07421351055.html> (last accessed 9 February 2013).

Duihua Qian Chengdan: Wo zai Zhongnanhai kaijiang daguo lishi xingshuai 对话钱乘旦。 我在中南海开讲大国历史兴衰 (A talk with Qian Chengdan: When I lectured on the historical rise and fall of the Great Powers at Zhongnanhai) (4 December 2003). Online. Available HTTP: <http://news.sina.com.cn/c/2003-12-04/08382279497.shtml> (last accessed 10 March 2013).

Edgerton, Gary and Rose, Brian (eds) (2005) *Thinking Outside the Box: A Contemporary Television Genre*, Lexington, MD: University Press of Kentucky.

Erll, Astrid (2005; 2nd enlarged edn 2011) *Kollektives Gedächtnis und Erinnerungskulturen. Eine Einführung*, Stuttgart and Weimar: Verlag J.B. Metzler.

— (ed.) (2008) *Film und kulturelle Erinnerung. Plurimediale Konstellationen*, Berlin: De Gruyter.

Erll, Astrid and Nünning, Ansgar (eds) (2008) *Cultural Memory Studies. An International and Interdisciplinary Handbook*, Berlin and New York: De Gruyter.

Erll, Astrid and Rigney, Ann (2012) 'Introduction: Cultural memory and its dynamics', in Erll, Astrid and Rigney, Ann (eds) *Mediation, Remediation, and the Dynamics of Cultural Memory*, Berlin and Boston: De Gruyter, pp. 1–11.

Erll, Astrid and Wodianka, Stephanie (2008) 'Einleitung: Phänomenologie und Methodologie des "Erinnerungsfilms"', in Erll, Astrid and Wodianka, Stephanie (eds.) *Film und kulturelle Erinnerung. Plurimediale Konstellationen*, Berlin and New York: De Gruyter, pp. 1–20.

Fang Fang 方方 (2003) *Zhongguo jilupian fazhanshi* 中国纪录片发展史 (A history of the development of the Chinese documentary), Beijing: Zhongguo xiju chubanshe.

Fischer, Thomas (2009) 'Ereignis und Erlebnis: Entstehung und Merkmale des zeitgenössischen dokumentarischen Geschichtsfernsehens', in Korte, Barbara and Paletschek, Sylvia (eds) *History goes Pop. Zur Repräsentation von Geschichte in populären Medien und Genres*, Bielefeld: transcript Verlag, pp. 191–202.

Fischer, Thomas and Wirtz, Rainer (eds) (2008) *Alles authentisch? Popularisierung der Geschichte im Fernsehen*, Konstanz: UVK Verlagsgesellschaft.

French, David and Richards, Michael (eds) (2000) *Television in Contemporary Asia*, New Delhi: Sage.

Frevert, Ute and Braungart, Wolfgang (eds) (2004) *Sprachen des Politischen. Medien und Medialität in der Geschichte*, Göttingen: Vandenhoek & Ruprecht.

Friedberg, Aaron L. (2011) *A Contest for Supremacy. China, America, and the Struggle for Mastery in Asia*. New York: W.W. Norton and Company.

Fuxing luntan 复兴论坛 (Revival Forum) (2007–). Online. Available HTTP: <http://fuxing.bbs.cctv.com> (last accessed 9 February 2013).

Fuxing zhi lu 《复兴之路》 (The Road to Revival) (2007a), 6 DVDs, Beijing: CCTV.

Fuxing zhi lu 《复兴之路》 (The Road to Revival) (2007b). [CCTV website on the documentary.] Online. Available HTTP: <http://finance.cctv.com/special/C19478/01/> (last accessed 9 February 2013).

Fuxing zhi lu 《复兴之路》 (The Road to Revival) (2007/8), 3 vols, Beijing: Zhongguo minzhu fazhi chubanshe.

Fuxing zhi lu 复兴之路 ('The Road of Rejuvenation') (n.d.). National Museum of China website. Online. Available HTTP: <http://fuxing.chnmuseum.cn/> (last accessed 5 June 2012).

Fuxing zhi lu *daxing zhanlan* 《复兴之路》 大型展览 (*The Road to Revival* large-scale exhibition) (n.d.). [CCTV website.] Online. Available HTTP: <http://museum.cctv.com/special/fuxingzhilu/1/index.shtml> (last accessed 9 February 2013).

Fuxing zhi lu *daxing zhuti zhanlan wangshang tan* 《复兴之路》 大型主题展览网上谈 (Discussing the large-scale thematic exhibition *The Road to Revival* on the net) (17 December 2007). Online. Available HTTP: <http://www.people.com.cn/GB/32306/54155/57487/6665638.html> (last accessed 9 February 2013).

Fuxing zhi lu *de quexian* 《复兴之路》 的缺陷 (Deficiencies of *The Road to Revival*) (3 October 2009). Online. Available HTTP: <http://blog.sciencenet.cn/home.php?mod=space&uid=2237&do=blog&id=259500> (last accessed 9 February 2013).

Fuxing zhi lu – *Huishou guoqu, zhanwang weilai* 《复兴之路》 。回首过去, 展望未来 (*The Road to Revival*. Looking back to the past, looking forward to the future) (10 October 2007). Online. Available HTTP: <http://finance.cctv.com/special/C19478/20071010/113742.shtml> (last accessed 9 February 2013).

'*Fuxing zhi lu* quanguo xunyan qihang' 《复兴之路》 全国巡演起航 (*The Road to Revival*'s tour of the country starts) (21 February 2011), *Jiefang ribao* 解放日报 ('Jiefang Daily'): 2.

Fuxing zhi lu *shang de dianshiren* 《复兴之路》 上的电视人 (*The Road to Revival*'s TV people) (14 January 2008). Online. Available HTTP: <http://www.sarft.gov.cn/articles/20080114143607400366.html> (last accessed 14 January 2008). (The website is defunct now.)

'*Fuxing zhi lu* zaidu kaiyan' 《复兴之路》 再度开演 (*The Road to Revival* again on stage) (20 February 2010), *Renmin ribao* 人民日报 ('People's Daily'): 4.

Glaser, Bonnie and Medeiros, Evan (2007) 'The changing ecology of foreign policy-making in China: The ascension and demise of the theory of "peaceful rise" ', *The China Quarterly*, vol. 190 (June): 291–310.

Goldsmith, Jack and Wu, Tim (2006) *Who Controls the Internet? Illusions of a Borderless World*, Oxford: Oxford University Press.

Greene, Naomi (2001) 'Empire as myth and memory', in Landy, Marcia (ed.) *The Historical Film. History and Memory in Media*, New Brunswick, NJ: Rutgers University Press, pp. 235–48.

Gries, Peter Hays (2004) *China's New Nationalism. Pride, Politics, and Diplomacy*, Berkeley, CA: University of California Press.

Gries, Peter Hays, Zhang, Qingmin, Crowson, Michael H. and Cai, Huajian (2011) Patriotism, nationalism and China's US policy: Structures and consequences of Chinese national identity, *The China Quarterly*, vol. 205 (March): 1–17.

Groot, Jerome de (2009) *Consuming History. Historians and Heritage in Contemporary Popular Culture*, London: Routledge.

Große Kracht, Klaus (2009) 'Kontroverse Zeitgeschichte. Historiker im öffentlichen Meinungsstreit', in Horn, Sabine and Sauer, Michael (eds) *Geschichte und Öffentlichkeit. Orte – Medien – Institutionen*, Göttingen: Vandenhoeck & Ruprecht, pp. 15–23.

Guan, Guihai (2010) 'The influence of the collapse of the Soviet Union on China's political choices', in Bernstein, Thomas P. and Li, Huayu (eds) *China Learns from the Soviet Union, 1949–Present*, Lanham, MD: Lexington Books, pp. 505–15.

Guo, Sujian (ed.) (2006) *China's 'Peaceful Rise' in the 21st Century. Domestic and International Conditions*, Aldershot: Ashgate.

Guo Zhenzhi 郭镇之 (1997) *Zhongguo dianshi shi* 中国电视史 (History of Chinese TV), Beijing: Wenhua yishu chubanshe.

Guojia bowuguan Fuxing zhi lu *dazhan ji jiang mianfei kaifang* 国家博物馆 《复兴之路》 大展即将免费开放 (The great exhibition in the National Museum, *The Road to Revival*, will be opened for free) (25 September 2009). (Originally in *Beijing Qingnianbao* 北京青年报 (Beijing Youth Daily).) Online. Available HTTP: <http://yule.sohu.com/20090925/n266985619.shtml> (last accessed 9 February 2013).

Guojia bowuguan Fuxing zhi lu *jiben chenlie fuzhan juxing Li Changchun chuxi* 国家博物馆 《复兴之路》 基本陈列复展举行 李长春出席 (The basic permanent exhibition *The Road to Revival* is reopening in the National Museum with Li Changchun presiding) (1 March 2011). (Originally on *Zhongguo gongchandang xinwenwang* 中国共产党新闻网 (CCP news net).) Online. Available HTTP: <http://cpc.people.com.cn/GB/64093/64094/14035244.htm>l (last accessed 9 February 2013).

Guynn, William (2006) *Writing History in Film*, New York: Routledge.

Hamann, Christoph (2006) 'Fluchtpunkt Birkenau', in Paul, Gerhard (ed.) *Visual History. Ein Studienbuch*, Göttingen: Vandenhoeck & Ruprecht, pp. 283–302.

Hanawa, Yukiko and Hoaglund, Linda (1997) 'Interview with Christine Choy and Nancy Tong, filmmakers (*In the Name of the Emperor*)', *Positions*, vol. 5, no. 3: 811–33.

Hardtwig, Wolfgang and Schug, Alexander (eds) (2009) *History Sells!* Stuttgart: Steiner.

Hartmann, Robert (16 March 2007) *China Rising: Back to the Future, Asia Times*. Online. Available HTTP: <http://www.atimes.com/atimes/China/IC16Ad01.html> (last accessed 20 February 2013)

Haus der Geschichte der Bundesrepublik (ed.) (1998) *Bilder, die lügen*, Bonn: Bouvier.

He Suliu 何苏六 (2005) *Zhongguo dianshi jilupian shilun* 中国电视纪录片史论 (A study on the history of China's TV documentary), Beijing: Zhongguo chuanbo daxue chubanshe.

Hevia, James L. (2007) 'Remembering the century of humiliation: The Yuanming Gardens and Dagu Forts Museums', in Jager, Sheila Miyoshi and Mitter, Rana (eds) *Ruptured Histories. War, Memory, and the Post-Cold War in Asia*, Cambridge, MA and London: Harvard University Press, pp. 192–208.

Hoffmann, Hilde (2009) 'Geschichte und Film – Film und Geschichte', in Horn, Sabine and Sauer, Michael (eds) *Geschichte und Öffentlichkeit. Orte – Medien – Institutionen*, Göttingen: Vandenhoeck & Ruprecht, pp. 135–43.

Hohenberger, Eva and Keilbach, Judith (eds) (2003) *Die Gegenwart der Vergangenheit. Dokumentarfilm, Fernsehen und Geschichte*, Berlin: Vorwerk 8.

Hong, Junhao (2007) 'The historical development of program exchange in the TV sector', in Kops, Manfred and Ollig, Stefan (eds) *Internationalization of the Chinese TV Sector*, Berlin and Münster: LIT, pp. 25–40.

— (2011) 'From the world's largest propaganda machine to a multipurposed global news agency: Factors in and implications of Xinhua's transformation since 1978', *Political Communication*, vol. 28, no. 3: 377–93.

Hong, Junhao, Lü, Yanmei and Zou, William (2008) 'CCTV in the reform years: A new model for China's television?', in Zhu, Ying and Berry, Chris (eds) *TV China: A Reader on New Media*, Bloomington, IN: Indiana University Press, pp. 40–55.

Horn, Sabine and Sauer, Michael (eds) (2009) *Geschichte und Öffentlichkeit. Orte – Medien – Institutionen*, Göttingen: Vandenhoeck & Ruprecht.

Hsiung, Ping-chen (2004) 'Moving the world according to a shifted "I": World history texts in Republican China and post-war Taiwan', *Berliner China-Hefte*, vol. 26: 38–52.

Hu Zhengrong 胡正荣 (2000) *Meijie guanli yanjiu. Guangbo dianshi guanli chuangxin tixi* 媒介管理研究。广播电视管理创新体系 (Media management studies: The innovative system of broadcasting media management), Beijing: Beijing guangbo xueyuan chubanshe.

Hu Zongshan 胡宗山 (2006) *Zhongguo de heping jueqi. Lilun, lishi yu zhanlüe* 中国的和平崛起。理论, 历史与战略 ('China's peaceful rise: Theory, history, and strategy'), Beijing: Shijie zhishi chubanshe.

Huang Huilin 黄会林 (ed.) (2005) *Zhongguo dianshiju mingpian jiedu jiaocheng* 中国电视剧名片解读教程 (Course on understanding famous Chinese TV dramas), Beijing: Beijing Shifan daxue chubanshe.

Huang Weiding 黄苇町 (2001) 'Sugong wangdang shinianji' 苏共亡党十年祭 (On the tenth anniversary of the CPSU's perishing), *Juece yu xinxi* 决策与信息 ('Decision & Information'), no. 10: 58–63.

— (2003) 'Jiqu lishi jiaoxun, jianchi zhizheng wei min: Wo xie *Sugong wangdang shinianji*' 汲取历史教训, 坚持执政为民。我写 《苏共亡党十年祭》 (Drawing historical lessons, keeping to a governance for the people. About my *On the Tenth Anniversary of the CPSU's Perishing*), *Jinqiu* 金秋 (Golden autumn), no. 12: 4–5.

— (2004; 2nd revised edn) *Sugong wangdang shinianji* 苏共亡党十年祭 (On the tenth anniversary of the CPSU's perishing), (1st edn 2002), Nanchang: Jiangxi gaoxiao chubanshe.

Hughes-Warrington, Marnie (2009) *The History on Film Reader*, London: Routledge.

Jager, Sheila Miyoshi and Mitter, Rana (eds) (2007) *Ruptured Histories. War, Memory, and the Post-Cold War in Asia*, Cambridge, MA, and London: Harvard University Press.

Jaubert, Alain (1986) *Le commissariat aux archives*, Paris: Éditions Bernard Barrault.

Jiang Shan 江山 and Xu Ke 许可 (13 November 2007) '*Fuxing zhi lu* zhanlan yinglai di yi bai wan ming guanzhong' 《复兴之路》 展览迎来第 一 百万名观众 (*The Road to Revival* welcomes its one millionth visitor), *Renmin ribao* ('People's Daily'): 2.

Jiang Yue 姜跃 (2011) 'Yuedu Sulian (zhi yi)' 阅读苏联 （之一) (Reading the Soviet Union (1)), *Zhongguo dangzheng ganbu luntan* 中国党政干部论坛 ('Chinese Cadres Tribune'), vol. 8: 49–51.

Jiedu 'liuge wei shenme' 解读 《六个为什么》 (Explanation of the 'six whys') (n.d.). Online. Available HTTP: <http://news.cctv.com/special/lgwsm/01/> (last accessed 20 February 2013).

Ju an si wei – Sugong wangdang de lishi jiaoxun 居安思危——苏共亡党的历史教训 (Alert to danger while dwelling in safety – The historical lesson of the perishing of the Soviet Communist Party) (2006), 8 installments, 8 DVDs, Beijing: Zhongguo jiwei Zhongguo fangzheng chubanshe.

Ju an si wei – Sugong wangdang de lishi jiaoxun 居安思危——苏共亡党的历史教训 (Alert to danger while dwelling in safety – The historical lesson of the perishing of the Soviet Communist Party) (2007). Online. Available HTTP: <http://www.youtube.com/watch?v=JPXLoJyLVzY> (last accessed 10 March, 2013).

Ju an si wei – Sugong wangdang de lishi jiaoxun (jieshuoci) 居安思危——苏共亡党的历史教训 (解说词) (*Alert to danger while dwelling in safety – The historical lesson of the perishing of the Soviet Communist Party* (commentary)) (11 December 2006). Online. Available HTTP: <http://www.syzy.com.cn/baicao/nhf/zxyd/200612/20061201143112.html> (last accessed 20 February 2013).

Ju an si wei – Sugong wangdang de lishi jiaoxun (jieshuoci) 《居安思危——苏共亡党的历史教训》 解说词 (*Alert to danger while dwelling in safety – The historical lesson of the perishing of the Soviet Communist Party* (commentary)) (2006). Online. Available HTTP: <http://www.chinaelections.org/NewsInfo.asp?NewsID=99228> (last accessed 3 March 2009). (As of 2012, this website seems defunct.)

Kahn, Joseph (8 December 2006) *China opens public discussion of its rising power.* Online. Available HTTP: <http://www.nytimes.com/2006/12/08/world/asia/08iht-china.3830388.html> (last accessed 20 February 2013).

— (9 December 2006) *China, shy giant, shows signs of shedding its false modesty.* Online. Available HTTP: <http://www.nytimes.com/2006/12/09/world/asia/09china.html> (last accessed 20 February 2013).

Katzenstein, Peter (2012a) 'China's rise: Rupture, return, or recombination?', in Katzenstein, Peter (ed.) *Sinicization and the Rise of China. Civilizational Processes beyond East and West*, London and New York: Routledge, pp. 1–38.

— (2012b) 'Sinicization in comparative perspective', in Katzenstein, Peter (ed.) *Sinicization and the Rise of China. Civilizational Processes beyond East and West*, London and New York: Routledge, pp. 209–41.

— (ed.) (2012c) *Sinicization and the Rise of China. Civilizational Processes beyond East and West*, London and New York: Routledge.

Keane, Michael (2003) 'Civil society, regulatory space and cultural authority in China's television industry', in Kitley, Philip (ed.) *Television, Regulation and Civil Society in Asia*, London: RoutledgeCurzon, pp. 69–187.

— (2007) *Created in China. The Great New Leap Forward*, London: Routledge.

— (2008) 'From national preoccupation to overseas aspiration', in Zhu, Ying, Keane, Michael and Bai, Ruoyun (eds) *TV Drama in China*, Hong Kong: Hong Kong University Press, pp. 145–56.

Keane, Michael, Fung, Anthony Y. H. and Moran, Albert (2007) *New Television, Globalisation, and the East Asian Cultural Imagination*, Hong Kong: Hong Kong University Press.

Kecheng jiaocai yanjiusuo 课程教材研究所 (Institute for curricular teaching materials) (comp.) (2001) *20 shiji Zhongguo zhongxiaoxue kecheng biaozhun, jiaoxue dagang huibian. Lishi juan* 20 世纪中国中小学课程标准，教学大纲汇编。历史卷 (Collected twentieth-century curriculum standards and teaching outlines for Chinese secondary and primary school: History), Beijing: Renmin jiaoyu.

Keil, Lars-Broder (2009) 'Fiktionen im Geschichtsbewusstsein. Wie Legenden und Mythen das Bild von der vergangenen Wirklichkeit beeinflussen können', in Horn, Sabine and Sauer, Michael (eds) (2009) *Geschichte und Öffentlichkeit. Orte – Medien – Institutionen*, Göttingen: Vandenhoeck & Ruprecht, pp. 32–9.

Keilbach, Judith (2009) 'Geschichte im Fernsehen', in Horn, Sabine and Sauer, Michael (eds) *Geschichte und Öffentlichkeit. Orte – Medien – Institutionen*, Göttingen: Vandenhoeck & Ruprecht, pp. 153–60.

Kennedy, Paul M. (1987) *The Rise and Fall of the Great Powers. Economic Change and Military Conflict from 1500 to 2000*, New York: Random House.

Kilborn, Richard and Izod, John (1997) *An Introduction to Television Documentary*, Manchester: Manchester University Press.

King, David (1997) *The Commissar Vanishes. The Falsification of Photographs and Art in Stalin's Russia*, New York: Metropolitan Books.

Kitley, Philip (ed.) (2003) *Television, Regulation and Civil Society in Asia*, London: RoutledgeCurzon.

Knaller, Susanne and Müller, Harro (eds) (2006) *Authentizität. Diskussion eines ästhetischen Begriffs*, München: Wilhelm Fink.

Kong Hanbing 孔寒冰 (8 December 2006) Daguo jueqi *tiaozhan guoren beiqing lishiguan* 《大国崛起》 挑战国人悲情历史观 (*The Rise of the Great Powers* challenges the pessimistic historical view of our people). (Originally in *Huanqiu shibao* 环球时报 ('Global Times').) Online. Available HTTP: <http://ent.sina.com.cn/r/m/2006-12-08/17061362356.html> (last accessed 21 February 2013).

Kops, Manfred and Ollig, Stefan (eds) (2007) *Internationalization of the Chinese TV Sector*, Berlin and Münster: LIT.

Korte, Barbara and Paletschek, Sylvia (2009a) 'Geschichte in populären Medien und Genres: vom Historischen Roman zum Computerspiel', in Korte, Barbarqa and Paletschek, Sylvia (eds) *History goes Pop. Zur Repräsentation von Geschichte in populären Medien und Genres*, Bielefeld: transcript Verlag, pp. 9–60.

—— (2009b) (eds) *History goes Pop. Zur Repräsentation von Geschichte in populären Medien und Genres*, Bielefeld: transcript Verlag.

Koselleck, Reinhart (1967) 'Historia magistra vitae: über die Auflösung des Topos im Horizont neuzeitlich bewegter Geschichte', in Braun, Hermann and Riedel, Manfred (eds) *Natur und Geschichte. Karl Löwith zum 70. Geburtstag*, Stuttgart: Kohlhammer, pp. 196–218.

Kramer, Stefan (2004) *Vom Eigenen und Fremden: Fernsehen und kulturelles Selbstverständnis in der Volksrepublik China*, Bielefeld: transcript Verlag.

—— (2006) *Das chinesische Fernsehpublikum. Zur Rezeption und Reproduktion eines neuen Mediums*, Bielefeld: transcript Verlag.

Krauss, Marita (2006) 'Kleine Welten. Alltagsfotografie – die Anschaulichkeit einer "privaten Praxis" ', in Paul, Gerhard (ed.) *Visual History. Ein Studienbuch*, Göttingen: Vandenhoeck & Ruprecht, pp. 57–75.

Kuang Wenzhang 邝文彰 (2008) 'Ju an si wei; Jian tan Sulian gongchandang kuatai de yuanyin ji lishi jiaoxun' 居安思危.浅谈苏联共产党垮台的原因及历史教训 (Alert to danger while dwelling in safety: A simple discussion of the reasons and lessons of the CPSU's downfall), *Jingguan wenyuan* 警官文苑 (Literary Garden of the Police), vol. 2: 44–6.

Kuehl, Jerry (1988a) 'Truth claims', in Rosenthal, Alan (ed.) *New Challenges for Documentary*, Berkeley, CA: University of California Press, pp. 103–9.

—— (1988b) 'History on the public screen, II', in Rosenthal, Alan (ed.) *New Challenges for Documentary*, Berkeley, CA: University of California Press, pp. 444–53 (originally printed in Smith, Paul (ed.) (1976) *The Historian and Film*, Cambridge: Cambridge University Press, pp. 177–85).

—— (2008) 'Visual history traduced. A century of compilation films', *Journal of War and Culture Studies*, vol. 1, no. 1: 31–7.

Kurlantzick, Joshua (2007) *Charm Offensive. How China's Soft Power is Transforming the World*, New Haven, CT, and London: Yale University Press.

Lai, Hongyi (2012) 'Introduction. The soft power concept and a rising China' in Lai, Hongyi and Lu, Yiyi (eds) *China's Soft Power and International Relations*, London and New York: Routledge, pp. 1–20.

Lai, Hongyi and Lu, Yiyi (eds) (2012) *China's Soft Power and International Relations*, London and New York: Routledge.

Lall, Marie and Vickers, Edward (eds) (2009) *Education as a Political Tool in Asia*, London: Routledge.

Landy, Marcia (ed.) (2001) *The Historical Film. History and Memory in Media*, New Brunswick, NJ: Rutgers University Press.

Lee, Chin-Chuan (2003) *Chinese Media, Global Contexts*, London: Routledge.

— (2010) ' "Bound to rise": Chinese media discourses on the new global order', in Curtin, Michael and Shah, Hemant (eds) *Reorienting Global Communication. Indian and Chinese Media beyond Borders*, Urbana, IL: University of Illinois Press, pp. 260–83.

Lei, Ya-Wen (2011) 'The political consequences of the rise of the Internet: Political beliefs and practices of Chinese netizens', *Political Communication*, vol. 28, no. 3: 291–322.

[Lenin], Vladimir Ilyich (1922) 'Directives on the film business', trans. Isaacs, Bernard, in *Lenin Collected Works* (1971), vol. 42, Moscow: Progress Publishers, pp. 388b–89a. Online. Available HTTP: <http://www.marxists.org/archive/lenin/works/1922/jan/17.htm> (last accessed 1 March 2013).

Lersch, Edgar (2009) 'Zur Entwicklung dokumentarischer Formen der Geschichtsvermittlung im öffentlich-rechtlichen Fernsehen der Bundesrepublik', in Korte, Barbara and Paletschek, Sylvia (eds) *History goes Pop. Zur Repräsentation von Geschichte in populären Medien und Genres*, Bielefeld: transcript Verlag, pp. 167–90.

Lersch, Edgar and Viehoff, Reinhold (2009) 'Folgenlose Unterhaltung oder kunstvoller Wissenstransfer?', in Hardtwig, Wolfgang and Schug, Alexander (eds) *History Sells!*, Stuttgart: Steiner, pp. 91–105.

Li Bin 李斌 (29 November 2012) *Xi Jinping: Cheng qian qi hou. Ji wang kai lai. Jixu chaozhe Zhonghua minzu weida fuxing mubiao fenyong qianjin* 习近平: 承前启后。继往开来。 继续朝着中华民族伟大复兴目标奋勇前进 (Xi Jinping: Follow up on the past to enlighten the future. Continue earlier traditions to open up for the coming times. Keep moving forward courageously toward the goal of the Chinese nation's great revival) Online. Available HTTP: <http://news.xinhuanet.com/politics/2012-11/29/c_113852724.htm> (last accessed 30 March 2013).

Li, Fan (2011) 'New curriculum reform and history textbook compilation in contemporary China', in Müller, Gotelind (ed.) *Designing History in East Asian Textbooks. Shifting Images of 'Self' and 'Other' between Identity Politics and Transnational Aspirations*, London: Routledge, pp. 137–46.

Li, Fan and Wang, Xiaojing (2008) 'Reinterpreting late Qing history in historical movies and television dramas: The case of the 1898 reform', in Richter, Steffi (ed.) *Contested Views of a Common Past. Revisions of History in Contemporary East Asia*, Frankfurt am Main and New York: Campus, pp. 339–49.

Li, Hongmei (23 May 2011) *Let go of 'WuMaoDang' and 'fifty-cent party'*. Online. Available HTTP: <http://english.peopledaily.com.cn/90002/96417/7388336.html> (last accessed 16 March 2013).

Li, Mingjiang (ed.) (2009) *Soft Power. China's Emerging Strategy in International Politics*, Lanham, MD: Rowman & Littlefield.

Li Shenming 李慎明 (4 August 2009) *Sugong de tuihua bianzhi shi Sulian jieti de genben yuanyin: Zhuanzhu* Ju an si wei – Sugong xing shuai yu Sulian xingwang *xulun* 苏共的蜕化变质是苏联解体的根本原因——专著 《居安思危——苏共兴衰与苏联兴亡》绪论 (The moulting of the Soviet Communist Party was the fundamental reason for the disintegration of the Soviet Union: Introduction to the specialist work *Alert to Danger while Dwelling in Safety: The Rise and Fall of the Soviet Communist Party and the Rise and Perishing of the Soviet Union*). Online. Available HTTP: <http://www.xj71.

com/?action-viewnews-itemid-104755-page-1> (last accessed 15 August 2010). (As of 2012, this website seems defunct.)

Li Shenming *et al.* (2006/7) *Ju an si wei – Sugong wangdang de lishi jiaoxun.* 8ji DVD jiaoyu cankaopian jieshuoci 居安思危——苏共亡党的历史教训。 8 集 DVD 教育参考片解说词 (*Alert to danger while dwelling in safety: The historical lesson of the perishing of the Soviet Communist Party.* Commentary of this 8-DVD educational piece'), in *Kexue shehuizhuyi* 科学社会主义 (Scientific Socialism), part 1 (2006), no. 5, pp. 111–20; part 2 (2006), no. 6, pp. 111–20; part 3 (2007), no. 1, pp. 139–52.

Li Shenming (ed.) and Chen Zhihua 陈之骅 (co-ed.) (2011) *Ju an si wei – Sugong wangdang 20nian de sikao* 居安思危——苏共亡党 20 年的思考 (Be vigilant on possible danger in peace time. 20 years' reflections on Soviet Communist Party's decline), Beijing: Shehui kexue wenxian chubanshe.

Li Shenming tongzhi jianli 李慎明同志简历 (Short biography of comrade Li Shenming) (2011). Online. Available HTTP: <http://myy.cass.cn/news/378057.htm> (last accessed 15 March 2013).

Li Xiaoning 李小宁 (2006?) Personal Blog. Online. Available HTTP: <http://id.bokee.com/showInfo.b?username=lixiaoning1953.bokee.com> (last accessed 28 September 2011).

— (1 December 2006) *Guanyu baji dianshipian* Ju an si wei *de chuangzuo guocheng* 关于八集屯视片居安思危的创作过程 (On the production process of the TV piece in 8 instalments *Alert to Danger while Dwelling in Safety*). Online. Available HTTP: <http://www.syzy.com.cn/baicao/nhf/zxyd/200612/20061201143112.html> (last accessed 28 September 2011).

Li, Xiaoping (2001) *Significant Changes in the Chinese Television Industry and their Impact in the PRC: An Insider's Perspective.* Online. Available HTTP: <http://www.sino.uni-heidelberg.de/archive/documents/media/lixiaoping011015.pdf> (last accessed 21 February 2013).

Liebman, Benjamin L. (2011) 'The media and the courts: Towards competitive super-vision?', *The China Quarterly*, vol. 208: 833–50.

Lin Fengchun 林逢春 (2007) 'Ling yizhong jueqi liliang: Ruan shili' 另一种崛起力量。－软实力 (Another power for rising: Soft power), *Juece yu xinxi* 决策与信息 ('The Friend of the Head (Financial Observation)'), no. 5: 74–6.

Lishi jiaoyu ruhe kaolü gongzhong kouwei 历史教育如何考虑公众口味 (How history education might take into consideration the audience's tastes) (7 December 2006). Online. Available HTTP: <http://www.gmw.cn/01gmbr/2006-12/07/content_518811.htm> (last accessed 21 February 2013).

Littrup, Leif (1989) 'World history with Chinese characteristics', *Culture and History*, vol. 5: 39–64.

Liu Jinghua 刘景华 (ed.) (2007) *Daguo shuailuo zhi jian* 大国衰落之鉴 (The mirror of the downfall of great powers), Beijing: Renmin chubanshe.

Liu Qiong 刘琼 (29 September 2009) 'Weida de fuxing, zhuangli de shipian. Daxing yinyue wudao shishi *Fuxing zhi lu* bianchuang jishi' 伟大的复兴。 壮丽的诗篇。大型音乐舞蹈史诗《复兴之路》 编创纪实 (Great revival. Wonderful epic. Record of the making of the large-scale music-and-dance epic *The Road to Revival*), *Renmin ribao* 人民日报 ('People's Daily'): 11.

Liu Shuang 刘爽 (2009) *Sulian jieti de shixue chanshi* 苏联解体的史学阐释 ('On the disintegration of the Soviet Union from a historical perspective'), Beijing: Zhongguo shehui kexue chubanshe.

Liu Shuchun 刘淑春 (2006) 'Baji DVD jiaoyu cankaopian *Ju an si wei – Sugong wang-dang de lishi jiaoxun* bitan' 8 集 DVD 教育参考片《居安思危—苏共亡党的历史教训》笔谈 (Discussion of the 8-part DVD educational reference piece *Alert to Danger while Dwelling in Safety – the Historical Lesson of the CPSU's Perishing*), *Makesizhuyi yanjiu* 马克思主义研究 ('Studies on Marxism'), no. 10: 16–30.

Liu Tao 刘涛 (2007) *Zhongguo jueqi ce. Yi lishi de yanguang he quanqiu de shiye jiedu tongxiang fuxing zhi lu de zhongguo ce* 中国崛起策. 以历史的眼光和全球的视野解读通向复兴之路的中国策 (The strategy for China's rise. Investigation into a Chinese strategy towards revival with a historical view and global perspective), Beijing: Xinhua chubanshe.

Liu Xiliang 刘习良 (ed.) (2007) *Zhongguo dianshishi* 中国电视史 (A history of Chinese TV), Zhongguo guangbo dianshi chubanshe.

Lochman, Tomas, Späth, Thomas and Solomon, Jon (eds) (2008) *Antike im Kino. Auf dem Weg zu einer Kulturgeschichte des Antikenfilms*, Basel: Verlag der Skulpturhalle.

Lou Hejun 娄和军 (2007) '*Daguo jueqi* heyi jueqi?' 《大国崛起》何以崛起? (Why does *The Rise of the Great Powers* rise?), *Shitingjie* 视听界 ('Broadcasting Realm'), no. 1: 76–8.

Low box offices sales plagues Chinese documentaries in 2010: Report (1 April 2011). Online. Available HTTP: <http://english.peopledaily.com.cn/90001/90782/7337054.html> (last accessed 22 February 2013).

Lu Fen 陆芬 and Li Jia 李佳 (3 January 2007) *2007nian Yi Zhongtian-men de shu yao jixu rexiao ma* 2007 年 一种天们的书要继续热销马 (2007: Will books by the likes of Yi Zhongtian continue to be bestsellers?). (Originally in *Zhonghua dushubao* 中华读书报 ('China Reading Weekly').) Online. Available HTTP: <http://reader.gmw.cn/2007-01/03/conten_531433.htm> (last accessed 22 February 2013).

Lu, Yiyi (2007) 'The collective study sessions of the Politburo: A multipurpose tool of China's central leadership', in China Policy Institute, University of Nottingham (ed.) *Briefing Series*, vol. 27, no. 10: 13 pp.

Lukin, Alexander (1991) 'The initial Soviet reaction to the events in China in 1989 and the prospects for Sino–Soviet relations', *The China Quarterly*, vol. 125: 119–36.

Lull, James (1991) *China Turned on. Television, Reform, and Resistance*, London: Routledge.

Lüthi, Lorenz M. (2008) *The Sino–Soviet Split. Cold War in the Communist World*, Princeton, NJ, and Oxford: Princeton University Press.

Ma Shiling 马世领 (3 January 2007) *Jiexi zhongyang jiti xuexi zhidu de liuge mima: xian xuefa er hou zhiguo* 解析中央集体学习制度的 6 个密码: 先学法而后治国 (Decipher the six codes of the collective study system: Study the methods first before governing the country). Online. Available HTTP: <http://politics.people.com.cn/GB/1026/5429770.html> (last accessed 28 March 2012).

Ma Yingmin 马英民 (2009) 'Zai xian Zhonghua minzu fuxing de zhuangwei huajuan. Daxing zhuti zhanlan *Fuxing zhi lu* cong Zhongguo renmin geming junshi bowuguan dao Zhongguo guojia bowuguan' 再现中华民族复兴的壮伟画卷. 大型主题展览《复兴之路》从中国人民革命军事博物馆到中国国家博物馆 (Re-exhibition of impressive scrolls on the revival of the Chinese people. The large-scale thematic exhibition *The Road to Revival* from the Revolutionary Military Museum of the Chinese People to the Chinese National Museum), *Zhongguo bowuguan* 中国博物馆 ('Chinese Museum'), no. 1: 50–66.

[Mai Tianshu] 麦天枢 (14 January 2007) *Mai Tianshu tan* Daguo jueqi: *Weihu shehui anquan shi zui gao zhengzhi* 麦天枢谈《大国崛起》: 维护社会安全是最高政治

(Mai Tianshu discusses *The Rise of the Great Powers*: To protect social security is the highest politics). Online. Available HTTP: <http://teacher.cersp.com/edumedia/rise/200701/206.html> (last accessed 22 February 2013).

Marsh, Christopher (2003) 'Learning from your comrade's mistakes: The impact of Soviet past on China's future', *Communist and Post-Communist Studies*, vol. 36, no. 3: 259–72.

Martin, Dorothea (1990) *The Making of a Sino–Marxist World View: Perceptions and Interpretations of World History in the People's Republic of China*, Armonk, NY: Sharpe.

— (1998) 'World history in China', *World History Bulletin*, vol. 14, no. 1: 6–8.

Merridale, Catherine (2003) 'Redisigning history in contemporary Russia', *Journal of Contemporary History*, vol. 38, no. 1: 13–28.

Meyer, Erik (ed.) (2009) *Erinnerungskultur 2.0. Kommemorative Kommunikation in digitalen Medien*. Frankfurt and New York: Campus Verlag.

Miao, Di (2011) 'Between propaganda and commercials: Chinese television today', in Shirk, Susan L. (ed.) *Changing Media, Changing China*, Oxford and New York: Oxford University Press, pp. 91–114.

Mierzejewski, Dominik (2012) 'The quandary of China's soft-power rhetoric. The "peaceful rise" concept and internal debate', in Lai, Hongyi and Lu, Yiyi (eds) *China's Soft Power and International Relations*, London and New York: Routledge, pp. 64–82.

Mitter, Rana (2000) 'Behind the scenes at the museum: Nationalism, history and memory in the Beijing War of Resistance Museum, 1987–1997', *The China Quarterly*, vol. 161 (March): 279–93.

Mou, Yi, Atkin, David and Fu, Hanlong (2011) Predicting political discussion in a censored virtual environment, *Political Communication*, vol. 28, no. 3: 341–56.

Müller(-Saini), Gotelind (2006–) *Representations of History in Chinese Film and TV*. Online. Available HTTP: <www.sino.uni-heidelberg.de/representations> (last accessed 22 February 2013).

— (2007a) 'Historical consciousness in the PR China between education and consumption: Intersecting collective and individual narratives of identity', in Ackermann, Peter and White, Bruce (eds) *Strategies of Belonging: Individual and Collective Construction of Narrative Continuity*, Erlangen: Lehrstuhl für Japanologie, pp. 71–9.

— (2007b) *Representing History in Chinese Media: The TV Drama* Zou Xiang Gonghe *(Towards the Republic)*, Berlin: LIT.

— (2008) 'Wie sag ich's meinem Kinde? Strategien zur Vermittlung eines normativen Geschichtsbilds in zeitgenössischen chinesischen Schulbüchern', in Chaniotis, Angelos, Kropp, Amina and Steinhoff, Christine (eds) *Überzeugungsstrategien*, Heidelberg: Springer, pp. 189–206.

— (2011a) 'Intervention: Some thoughts on the problem of "popular/public history" in China', *Rethinking History*, vol. 15, no 2: 229–39.

— (2011b) 'Teaching "the others' history" in Chinese schools: The state, cultural asymmetries, and shifting images of Europe (1900 to today)', in Müller, Gotelind (ed.) *Designing History in East Asian Textbooks. Shifting Images of 'Self' and 'Other' between Identity Politics and Transnational Aspirations*, London: Routledge, pp. 32–59.

— (ed.) (2011c) *Designing History in East Asian Textbooks. Shifting Images of 'Self' and 'Other' between Identity Politics and Transnational Aspirations*, London: Routledge.

Munro, Neil (2008) 'Democracy postponed: Chinese learning from the Soviet collapse', *China Aktuell*, no. 4: 31–61.

Nakajima, Seio (2010) 'Film as cultural politics', in Hsing, You-tien and Lee, Ching Kwan (eds) *Reclaiming Chinese Society. The New Social Activism*, London and New York: Routledge, pp. 159–83.

Nathan, Andrew J. and Scobell, Andrew (2012) *China's Search for Security*, New York: Columbia University Press.

Nau, Henry R. and Ollapally, Deepa M. (eds) (2012) *Worldviews of Aspiring Powers. Domestic Foreign Policy Debates in China, India, Iran, Japan, and Russia*, New York: Oxford University Press.

Neder, Christina (1996) *Flußelegie: Chinas Identitätskrise. Die Debatte um die chinesische Fernsehserie* Heshang *1988–1994*, Dortmund: Projekt Verlag.

Nicholas, Siân, O'Malley, Tom and Williams, Kevin (eds) (2008) *Reconstructing the Past. History in the Mass Media 1890–2005*, London: Routledge.

Nichols, Bill (1991) *Representing Reality. Issues and Concepts in Documentary*, Bloomington, IN: Indiana University Press.

— (1993) ' "Getting to know you . . .": Knowledge, power, and the body', in Renov, Michael (ed.) *Theorizing Documentary*, New York: Routledge, pp. 174–91.

— (2001) *Introduction to Documentary*, Bloomington, IN: Indiana University Press.

Niedenführ, Matthias (2008) 'Revising and televising the past in East Asia: "History soaps" in Mainland China', in Richter, Steffi (ed.) *Contested Views of a Common Past. Revisions of History in Contemporary East Asia*, Frankfurt am Main and New York: Campus, pp. 351–70.

Nora, Pierre (1989) 'Between memory and history. Les lieux de mémoire', *Representations*, vol. 26 (Spring): 7–24.

Nye, Joseph (1990) *Bound to Lead. The Changing Nature of American Power*, New York: Basic Books.

— (2004) *Soft Power. The Means to Success in World Politics*, New York: Public Affairs.

Patriotic Exhibition Receives Strong Public Response (19 December 2007). Online. Available HTTP: <http://www.cctv.com/english/20071219/101617.shtml> (last accessed 22 February 2013).

Paul, Gerhard (2009) 'Das Jahrhundert der Bilder. Die visuelle Geschichte und der Bildkanon des kulturellen Gedächtnisses', in Paul, Gerhard (ed.) *Das Jahrhundert der Bilder. 1900–1949* [vol. 1], Göttingen: Vandenhoeck & Ruprecht, pp. 14–39.

— (ed.) (2006) *Visual History. Ein Studienbuch*, Göttingen: Vandenhoeck & Ruprecht.

— (ed.) (2008/9) *Das Jahrhundert der Bilder*, 2 vols, Göttingen: Vandenhoeck & Ruprecht.

Peng Peng 彭澎 (ed.) (2005) *Heping jueqi lun. Zhongguo chongsu daguo zhi lu* 和平崛起轮。中国重塑大国之路 ('Peaceful rising theory: The path of China becoming a Great Power'), Guangzhou: Guangdong renmin chubanshe.

Pew Research Global Attitudes Project (n.d.). Online. Available HTTP: <http://www.pewglobal.org> (last accessed 10 March, 2013).

Pickowicz, Paul and Zhang, Yingjin (eds) (2006) *From Underground to Independent: Alternative Film Culture in Contemporary China*, Lanham, MD: Rowman & Littlefield.

Pinglun: Daguo jueqi, heqi shengcai? 评论:《大国崛起》,和气生财? (Discussion: *The Rise of a Great Power*: Peacefully making business?) (11 December 2006). (Originally in *Guoji zaixian* 国际在线 (International online).) Online. Available HTTP: <http://ent.sina.com.cn/r/m/2006-12-11/08591364128.html> (last accessed 22 February 2013).

Pirker, Eva U., Rüdiger, Mark, Klein, Christa, Leiendecker, Thorsten, Oesterle, Carolyn and Sénécheau, Miriam (eds) (2010) *Echte Geschichte. Authentizitätsfiktionen in populären Geschichtskulturen*, Bielefeld: transcript Verlag.

Plamper, Jan (2012) *The Stalin Cult. A Study in the Alchemy of Power*, New Haven, CT, and London: Yale University Press.

Qi Shirong 齐世荣 (ed.) (2005a) *15 shiji yilai shijie jiu qiang de lishi yanbian* 15 世纪以来世界九强的历史演变 (The historical evolution of the nine world powers since the fifteenth century), Guangzhou: Guangdong renmin chubanshe.

— (ed.) (2005b) *Qiangguo xingshuaishi congshu* 强国兴衰史丛书 (The history of the rise and fall of the powers series), 7 vols, Xi'an: San qin chubanshe.

Qian Chengdan (2001) *Shijie jin-xiandai shi de zhuxian shi xiandaihua* 世界近现代史的主线是现代化 (Modernisation is the main thread of modern world history), Lishi *jiaoxue* 历史教学 ('History Teaching'), no. 2: 5–10.

— (7 December 2006) *Zhidu gouzao duiyu guojia feichang zhongyao* 制度构造对于国家非常重要 (The systemic structure is very important for a nation). (Originally in *Xinjingbao* 新京报 中国正在深入地了解世界 新浪娱乐 ('Beijing News').) Online. Available HTTP: <http://culture.gmw.cn/2006-12/07/content_519160.htm> (last accessed 22 February 2013).

— (29 December 2006) *Zhongguo zhengzai shenrudi liaojie shijie* 中国正在深入地了解世界 (China is about to understand more deeply the world now). (Originally on *Xinlang Yule* 新浪娱乐 (sina entertainment).) Online. Available HTTP: <http://ent.sina.com.cn/v/2006-12-29/17341391623.html> (last accessed 22 February 2013).

Qian, Gang and Bandurski, David (2011) 'China's emerging public sphere: The impact of media commercialization, professionalism, and the Internet in an era of transition', in Shirk, Susan L. (ed.) (2011) *Changing Media, Changing China*, Oxford and New York: Oxford University Press, pp. 38–76.

Qian Yingyi 钱颖– (28 November 2006) *Qinghua daxue Qian Yingyi: Fuzao huanjing xia de yibu yansu jilupian* 清华大学钱颖 –.浮躁环境下 一 部严肃纪录片 (Qian Yingyi of Qinghua University: a serious documentary in an unserious surrounding). (Originally on *Xinlang Yule* 新浪娱乐 (sina entertainment).) Online. Available HTTP: <http://ent.sina.com.cn/v/2006-11-28/18001347505.html> (last accessed 22 February 2013).

Qiangguo zhi jian Bawei yangshi Daguo jueqi *zhuanjia zhi shendu jiedu* 强国之鉴。八位央视 《大国崛起》专家之深度解读 (The mirror of the powers. A deep reading of eight specialists of the CCTV *The Rise of the Great Powers*) (2007).

'Quandang bixu ju an si wei' 全党必须居安思危 (The whole party must be alert to danger when dwelling in safety) (2009), *Xin Chongqing* 新重庆 (New Chongqing), no. 10: 1.

Ramo, Joshua Cooper (2004) *The Beijing Consensus*, London: The Foreign Policy Centre. Online. Available HTTP: <http://fpc.org.uk/fsblob/244.pdf> (last accessed 18 December 2012).

— (2007) *Brand China* (淡色中国), London: Foreign Policy Centre.

Reilly, James (2012) *Strong Society, Smart State. The Rise of Public Opinion in China's Japan Policy*, New York: Columbia University Press.

[Ren Xuean] 任学安 (30 November 2006) Daguo jueqi *zong biandao Ren Xuean: Lishi buke jiandanhua* 《大国崛起》 总编导任学安。 历史不可简单化 (*The Rise of the Great Powers*: Chief editor Ren Xuean: History is not to be simplified). (Originally in *Nanfang Zhoumo* 南方周末 (Southern Weekend).) Online. Available HTTP: <http://news.sina.com.cn/c/cul/2006-11-30/112711663429.shtml> (last accessed 22 February 2013).

— (2 November 2007) Fuxing zhi lu *zongbiandao Ren Xuean: Women yinggai xuehui zixin* 《复兴之路》 总编导任学安。 我们应该学会自信 (*The Road to Revival*'s chief editor Ren Xuean: We should learn self-confidence). (Originally in *Jiefang ribao* 解放日报 ('Jiefang Daily').).) Online. Available HTTP: <http://big5.xinhuanet.com/gate/big5/news.xinhuanet.com/politics/2007-11/02/content_6996018.htm> (last accessed 22 February 2013).

— (2008) 'Yong jilupian de yufa zhongxian lishi. Jiantan yingshi shixue zai *Daguo jueqi, Fuxing zhi lu* zhong de shijian' 用纪录片的语法重现历史。兼谈影视史学在《大国崛起》《复兴之路》中的实践 (Using the grammar of the documentary to reframe history. Talking at the same time over the realisation of visual history in *The Rise of the Great Powers* and *The Road to Revival*), *Zhongguo guangbo dianshi xuekan* 中国广播电视学刊 ('China Radio & TV Academic Journal'), no. 08: 22–9.

— (2009) 'Lishi tiankongxia de shidai zhi sheng. Dui *Fuxing zhi lu* re de wenhua fanxi' 历史天空下的时代之声。对《复兴之路》热的文化反思 (The voice of the times in historical space. A cultural reflection on the *Road to Revival* fever), *Zhongguo dianshi* 中国电视 ('China Television'), no. 10: 43–4.

Renmin chubanshe xiang Hanguo shuchu 7zhong banquan 人民出版社向韩国输出 7 种版权 (*People's Press* sells seven licences to South Korea) (5 September 2007). Online. Available HTTP: <http://www.gmw.cn/01ds/2007-09/05/content_665733.htm> (last accessed 22 February 2013).

Renov, Michael (1993) 'Introduction. The truth about non-fiction', in Renov, Michael (ed.) *Theorizing Documentary*, New York: Routledge, pp. 1–36.

Richter, Steffi (ed.) (2008) *Contested Views of a Common Past. Revisions of History in Contemporary East Asia*, Frankfurt am Main, New York: Campus.

Riederer, Günter (2006) 'Film und Geschichtswissenschaft. Zum aktuellen Verhältnis einer schwierigen Beziehung', in Paul, Gerhard (ed.) *Visual History. Ein Studienbuch*, Göttingen: Vandenhoeck & Ruprecht, pp. 96–113.

Rioux, Yu Luo (2007) 'Marketing the revolution. Tourism, landscape and ideology in China', unpublished thesis, University of Colorado.

Road to Revival *continues on stage of the National Center* (22 January 2010). Online. Available HTTP: <http://english.cctv.com/program/cultureexpress/20100122/101304.shtml> (last accessed 27 February 2013).

Road to Revival *opens in Beijing* (22 September 2009). Online. Available HTTP: <http://www.china.org.cn/culture/2009-09/22/content_18571688.htm> (last accessed 27 February 2013).

Road to Revival *premiered in Beijing* (22 September 2009). (Originally on CCTV.) Online. Available HTTP: <http://www.china.org.cn/video/2009-09/22/content_18585545.htm> (last accessed 27 February 2013).

Road to Revival *starts China tour* (3 March 2011). Online. Available HTTP: <http://www.chinadaily.com.cn/life/2011-03/03/content_12109112.htm> (last accessed 27 February 2013).

Rosen, Philip (1993) 'Document and documentary. On the persistence of historical concepts', in Renov, Michael (ed.) *Theorizing Documentary*, New York: Routledge, pp. 58–89.

Rosenstone, Robert A. (2001) 'The historical film. Looking at the past in a postliterate age', in Landy, Marcia (ed.) (2001) *The Historical Film. History and Memory in Media*, New Brunswick, NJ: Rutgers University Press, pp. 50–66, originally printed in Kramer, Lloyds S. Reid, D., Barney, William L. (eds) (1994) *Learning History in America: Schools, Cultures, and Politics*, Minneapolis, MN: University of Minnesota, pp. 141–60.

— (2006) *History on Film/Film on History*, Harlow: Pearson.

— (ed.) (1995) *Revisioning History. Film and the Construction of a New Past*, Princeton, NJ: Princeton University Press.

Rosenthal, Alan (ed.) (1988) *New Challenges for Documentary*, Berkeley, CA: University of California Press.

Rozman, Gilbert (1987) *The Chinese Debate about Soviet Socialism, 1978–1985*, Princeton, NJ: Princeton University Press.

— (2010a) 'China's concurrent debate about the Gorbachev era', in Bernstein, Thomas P. and Li, Huayu (eds) *China Learns from the Soviet Union, 1949–Present*, Lanham, MD: Lexington Books, pp. 449–76.

— (2010b) 'Concluding assessment: The Soviet impact on Chinese society', in Bernstein, Thomas P. and Li, Huayu (eds) *China Learns from the Soviet Union, 1949–Present*, Lanham, MD: Lexington Books, pp. 517–25.

Rubinstein, Joshua (1988) 'World War II – Soviet style', in Rosenthal, Alan (ed.) *New Challenges for Documentary*, Berkeley, CA: University of California Press, pp. 465–70.

Rüsen, Jörn (1994) *Historisches Lernen. Grundlagen und Paradigmen*, Köln: Böhlau.

— (1997) 'Geschichtskultur', in Bergmann, Klaus, Fröhlich, Klaus and Kuhn, Annette (eds) *Handbuch der Geschichtsdidaktik*, 5th edn, 2 vols, Düsseldorf: Seelze-Velber, pp. 38–42.

Sachsenmaier, Dominic (2007a) 'Debates on world history and global history: The neglected parameters of Chinese approaches', *Traverse. Zeitschrift für Geschichte*, vol. 3: 67–84.

— (2007b) 'World history as ecumenical history?', *Journal of World History*, vol. 18, no. 4: 465–89.

Schörken, Rolf (1995) *Begegnungen mit Geschichte. Vom außerwissenschaftlichen Umgang mit der Historie in Literatur und Medien*, Stuttgart: Klett-Cotta.

Schwartz, Vanessa R. (2008) 'Film and History', in Donald, James and Renov, Michael (eds) *The Sage Handbook of Film Studies*, Los Angeles, CA: Sage, pp. 199–215.

Scott, David (2012) 'Soft language, soft imagery and soft power in China's diplomatic lexicon', in Lai, Hongyi and Lu, Yiyi (eds) *China's Soft Power and International Relations*, London and New York: Routledge, pp. 39–63.

Scotton, James F. and Hachten, William A. (eds) (2010) *New Media, New China*, Chichester: Wiley-Blackwell.

Shambaugh, David (2008) *China's Communist Party. Atrophy and Adaptation*, Berkeley, CA: University of California Press.

Shambaugh, David and Xiao, Ren (2012) 'China, the conflicted rising power', in Nau, Henry R. and Ollapally, Deepa M. (eds) *Worldviews of Aspiring Powers. Domestic Foreign Policy Debates in China, India, Iran, Japan, and Russia*, New York: Oxford University Press, pp. 36–72.

Shen Zhihua 沈志华 (ed.) (2009) *Yige daguo de jueqi yu bengkui. Sulian lishi zhuanti yanjiu (1917–1991)* 一个大国的崛起于崩溃。苏联历史专题研究 (1917–1991) ('The rise and collapse of a superpower. A research study of Soviet history, 1917–1991'), 3 vols, Beijing: Shehui kexue wenxian chubanshe.

Shi, Tianjian, Lu, Ji and Aldrich, John (2011) 'Bifurcated images of the U.S. in urban China and the impact of media environment', *Political Communication*, vol. 28, no. 3: 357–76.

Shipin: Jilupian Ju an si wei – Sugong wangdang de lishi jiaoxun diyi ji 视频: 纪录片 《居安思危——苏共亡党的历史教训》第一集 (Video: The documentary *Alert to Danger while Dwelling in Safety – the Historical Lesson of the Perishing of the Soviet Communist Party*, part 1) (n.d.). Online. Available HTTP: <http://v.youku.com/v_show/id_XMjIwNTAwNzk2.html> (last accessed 10 March 2013).

Shirk, Susan L. (2011a) 'Changing media, changing China', in Shirk, Susan L. (ed.) *Changing Media, Changing China*, Oxford and New York: Oxford University Press, pp. 1–37.

— (2011b) 'Changing media, changing foreign policy', in Shirk, Susan L. (ed.) *Changing Media, Changing China*, Oxford and New York: Oxford University Press, pp. 225–52.

— (ed.) (2011c) *Changing Media, Changing China*, Oxford and New York: Oxford University Press.

Siemons, Mark (2012) 'Fünftausend Jahre Wurstigkeit', *Frankfurter Allgemeine Zeitung*, no. 216: Z4.

Smith, Greg M. (2003) *Film Structure and the Emotional System*, Cambridge: Cambridge University Press.

Sorlin, Pierre (2001) 'How to look at an "historical" film', in Landy, Marcia (ed.) *The Historical Film. History and Memory in Media*, New Brunswick, NJ: Rutgers University Press, pp. 25–49. (Originally printed in Sorlin, Pierre (1980) *The Film in History: Restaging the Past*, Totowa: Barnes & Noble, Chapter 1).

Spakowski, Nicola (2009) 'National aspirations on a global stage: Concepts of world/global history in contemporary China'. *Journal of Global History*, vol. 4, no. 3: 475–95.

Steinle, Matthias (2009) 'Geschichte im Film: zum Umgang mit den Zeichen der Vergangenheit im Dokudrama der Gegenwart', in Korte, Barbara and Paletschek, Sylvia (eds) *History goes Pop. Zur Repräsentation von Geschichte in populären Medien und Genres*, Bielefeld: transcript Verlag, pp. 147–65.

Stockmann, Daniela (2010) 'Who believes propaganda? Media effects during the anti-Japanese protests in Beijing', *The China Quarterly*, vol. 202: 269–89.

— (2011a) 'Greasing the reels: Advertising as a means of campaigning on Chinese television', *The China Quarterly*, vol. 208: 851–69.

— (2011b) 'Race to the bottom: Media marketization and increasing negativity toward the United States in China', *Political Communication*, vol. 28, no. 3: 268–90.

— (2013) *Media Commercialization and Authoritarian Rule in China*, New York: Cambridge University Press.

Stockmann, Daniela and Gallagher, Mary E. (2011) 'Remote control: How the media sustain authoritarian rule in China', *Comparative Political Studies*, vol. 44, no. 4: 436–67.

Su, Xiaokang *et al.* (1991) *Deathsong of the River. A Reader's Guide to the Chinese TV Series* Heshang, Ithaca, NY: East Asia Program, Cornell University.

Su, Zhiliang (2011) 'The "Others" in Chinese history textbooks: with a focus on the relationship between China and Japan', in Müller, Gotelind (ed.) *Designing History in East Asian Textbooks. Shifting Images of 'Self' and 'Other' between Identity Politics and Transnational Aspirations*, London: Routledge, pp. 147–62.

Sui Xiaofei 隋笑飞 (18 October 2007) 'Zai lishi bianqian zhong chumo xingfu. Daxing dianshi zhenglunpian *Fuxing zhi lu* yinqi guanzhong fanxiang' 在历史变迁中触摸幸福。 大型电视政论片 《复兴之路》 引起观众反响 (Touching upon happiness in historical evolution. The large-scale TV political piece *The Road to Revival* draws the audience's reaction), *Renmin ribao* 人民日报 ('People's Daily'): 9.

Sun, Bin (28 November 2006) *The rise of the great nations – A Chinese documentary*. Online. Available HTTP: <http://sun-bin.blogspot.com/2006/11/rise-of-great-nations-chinese.html> (last accessed 28 February 2013).

— (29 November 2006) *'The great nations', and 'What does China want?'*. Online. Available HTTP: <http://sun-bin.blogspot.com/2006/11/great-nations-and-what-does-china-want.html> (last accessed 28 February 2013).

Sun Ran 孙冉 (2007) 'Dang dianshi jilupian chengwei wenhua naimu' 当电视纪录片成为
文化乳母 (Let TV documentaries become the culture nurse), *Zhongguo xinwen zhoukan*
中国新闻周刊 ('China Newsweek'), no. 41: 78–9.

Tai, Zixue (2006) *The Internet in China. Cyberspace and Civil Society*, New York:
Routledge.

Tang Jin 唐晋 (ed.) (2006) *Daguo jueqi: Yi lishi de yanguang he quanqiu de shiye jiedu yi
15 shiji yilai 9 ge daguo jueqi de lishi* 大国崛起。 以历史的眼光和全球的视野解读
15 世纪以来 9 个世界性大国崛起的历史 (The rise of the Great Powers: Reading the
history of the rise of nine Great Powers since the fifteenth century in a historical view
and a global perspective), Beijing: Renmin chubanshe.

— (ed.) (2007) *Daguo jueqi. Qiye lingdaoren bixu de jiutang guoji caijing xueke*
大国崛起。 企业领导人必须的九堂国际财经学课 (The rise of the Great Powers.
The nine essential lessons in international finance for managers), Taibei: Yifu wenhua.

Tang, Wenfang and Iyengar, Shanto (2011) 'The emerging media system in China: Implications for regime change', *Political Communication*, vol. 28, no. 3: 263–7.

Taylor, Charles (1991) *The Ethics of Authenticity*, Cambridge, MA: Harvard University
Press.

Think of Danger (15 December 2006). Online. Available HTTP: <http://bloodandtreasure.
typepad.com/blood_treasure/2006/12/think_of_danger.html> (last accessed 10 March
2013).

Thornton, Patricia (2011) 'Retrofitting the steel frame: From mobilizing the masses to
surveying the public' in Heilman, Sebastian and Perry, Elizabeth J. (eds) *Mao's Invisible
Hand*, Cambridge, MA, and London: Harvard University Asia Center, pp. 237–68.

Tucker, Nancy B. (1995/6) 'China as a factor in the collapse of the Soviet Union', *Political
Science Quarterly*, vol. 110, no. 4: 501–18.

TV docu stimulates more open attitude to history, China, the world (26 November 2006).
Online. Available HTTP: <http://english.peopledaily.com.cn/200611/26/eng20061126_
325264.html> (last accessed 28 February 2013).

Unger, Jonathan (ed.) (1993) *Using the Past to Serve the Present. Historiography and
Politics in Contemporary China*, Armonk, NY: Sharpe.

Urmersbach, Viktoria (2009) 'Dokudrama zwischen Fakten und Fiktionen', in Hardtwig,
Wolfgang and Schug, Alexander (eds) *History Sells!* Stuttgart: Steiner, pp. 107–17.

Veyrat-Masson, Isabelle (2000) *Quand la Télévision Explore le Temps. L'histoire au Petit
Écran*, Paris: Fayard.

Vickers, Edward (2007) 'Museums and nationalism in contemporary China', *Compare: A
Journal of Comparative Education*, vol. 37, no. 3: 365–82.

Vickers, Edward and Jones, Alisa (eds) (2005) *History Education and National Identity in
East Asia*, London: Routledge.

Wade, Rex A. (ed.) (1993) *Documents of Soviet History*, vol. 2, Gulf Breeze: International
Academic Press.

Wang, Ban (2000) 'Historical trauma in multi-national cinemas: Rethinking history and
trauma', *Tamkang Review*, vol. 31, no. 1: 23–48.

Wang, Jing (1996) *High Culture Fever. Politics, Aesthetics, and Ideology in Deng's China*,
Berkeley, CA: University of California Press.

— (2008) *Brand New China. Advertising, Media, and Commercial Culture*, Cambridge,
MA, and London: Harvard University Press.

Wang Jisi 王缉思 (29 December 2006) Daguo jueqi *zhebu pianzi feichang ling ren
zhenfen* 《大国崛起》 这部片子非常令人振奋 (The piece *The Rise of the Great Powers*
makes people very excited). (Originally in *Xinlang Yule* 新浪娱乐 (sina entertainment).)

Online. Available HTTP: <http://ent.sina.com.cn/v/2006-12-29/17291391617.html> (last accessed 28 February 2013).

Wang, Lixin 王立新 (2007) *Sugong xingwang lun* 苏共兴亡论 (On the rise and fall of the CPSU), Beijing: Zhonggong zhongyang dangxiao chubanshe.

Wang, Q. Edward (2003) 'Encountering the world: China and its other(s) in historical narratives, 1949–89', *Journal of World History*, vol. 14, no. 3: 327–58.

— (2010) ' "Rise of the Great Powers" = rise of China? Challenges of the advancement of global history in the People's Republic of China', *Journal of Contemporary China*, vol. 19, no. 64: 273–89.

Wang, Xi (2007) 'Rise of the Great Nations of Great Powers? Reflections on "daguo jueqi" ', *Chinese Historical Review*, vol. 14, no. 2: 291–301.

Wang Xiaoling 王晓岭 (2007) 'Wangquan zhuanzhi shi daguo jueqi de yuanyin ma. Dui xilie dianshi zhuantipian *Daguo jueqi* de zhiyi' 王权专制是大国崛起的原因吗。对系列电视专题片 《大国崛起》 的质疑 (Is autocratic rule the reason for the rise of the Great Powers? Questioning the topical TV series *The Rise of the Great Powers*), *Xueshujie* 学术界 ('Academics in China'), no. 6: 95–101.

Wang, Zheng (2008) 'National humiliation, history education, and the politics of historical memory: Patriotic Education Campaign in China', *International Studies Quarterly*, vol. 52, no. 4: 783–806.

Wasko, Janet (ed.) (2005) *A Companion to Television*, Malden, MA: Wiley-Blackwell.

Watt, Donald (1988) 'History on the public screen, I', in Rosenthal, Alan (ed.) *New Challenges for Documentary*, Berkeley, CA: University of California Press, pp. 435–43. (Originally printed in Smith, Paul (ed.) (1976) *The Historian and Film*, Cambridge: Cambridge University Press, pp. 169–76.)

White, Geoffrey M. (1997) 'Moving history: The Pearl Harbor film(s)', *Positions*, vol. 5, no. 3: 709–44.

White, James D. (2005) *Global Media. The Television Revolution in Asia*, London: Routledge.

Williams, Kevin (2008) 'Flattened visions from timeless machines. History in the mass media', in Nicholas, Siân, O'Malley, Tom and Williams, Kevin (eds) *Reconstructing the Past. History in the Mass Media 1890–2005*, London: Routledge, pp. 7–28.

Winkler, Heinrich August (2004) 'Einleitung', in Winkler, Heinrich August (ed.) *Griff nach der Deutungsmacht. Zur Geschichte der Geschichtspolitik in Deutschland*, Göttingen: Wallstein, pp. 7–13.

— (2006) 'Dieser Bismarck widerspräche meinen Ausführungen diametral', *Frankfurter Allgemeine Zeitung*, no. 291: 35.

Wirtz, Rainer (2008a) 'Alles authentisch: so war's', in Fischer, Thomas and Wirtz, Rainer (eds) *Alles authentisch? Popularisierung der Geschichte im Fernsehen*, Konstanz: UVK Verlagsgesellschaft, pp. 6–32.

— (2008b) 'Das Authentische und das Historische', in Fischer, Thomas and Wirtz, Rainer (eds) *Alles authentisch? Popularisierung der Geschichte im Fernsehen*, Konstanz: UVK Verlagsgesellschaft, pp. 187–203.

Wolfrum, Edgar (2003) 'Neue Erinnerungskultur? Die Massenmedialisierung des 17. Juni 1953', *Aus Politik und Zeitgeschichte*, vol. B 40–41, pp. 33–9.

— (2010) 'Erinnerungskultur und Geschichtspolitik als Forschungsfelder. Konzepte – Methoden – Themen', in Scheunemann, Jan (ed.) *Reformation und Bauernkrieg. Erinnerungskultur und Geschichtspolitik im geteilten Deutschland*, Leipzig: Evangelische Verlagsanstalt, pp. 13–47.

Wortmann, Volker (2006) 'Was wissen Bilder schon über die Welt, die sie bedeuten sollen? Sieben Anmerkungen zur Ikonographie des Authentischen', in Knaller, Susanne and Müller, Harro (eds) *Authentizität. Diskussion eines ästhetischen Begriffs*, München: Wilhelm Fink, pp. 163–84.

Wu, Jia (23 September 2009). (Road to Revival). *A Musical Tribute to China*. Online. Available HTTP: <http://english.cri.cn/7146/2009/09/23/1261s517804.htm> (last accessed 10 March 2013).

Wu, Nan (15 May 2008) *Chinese bloggers on the history and influence of the 'fifty-cent party'*. Online. Available HTTP: <http://chinadigitaltimes.net/2008/05/chinese-bloggers-on-the-history-and-influence-of-the-fifty-cent-party/> (last accessed 20 December 2012).

Xiao Sanlang 萧三郎 (9 December 2006) Daguo jueqi *yin qianglie fanxiang. Kancheng quanmin lishi xuesi* 《大国崛起》 引强烈反响. 堪称全民历史学习 (*The Rise of the Great Powers* draws strong reactions. It may be called a historical study for the populace). (Originally in *Xinjingbao* 新京报 ('Beijing News').) Online. Available HTTP: <http://ent.sina.com.cn/v/m/2006-12-09/13411363156.html> (last accessed 1 March 2013).

Xu, Luo (2007) 'Reconstructing world history in the People's Republic of China since the 1980s', *Journal of World History*, vol. 18, no. 3: 325–50.

Xu Sheng 徐馨 (29 December 2006) '2006, dianshi pingmu you xi you you' 2006, 电视屏幕有喜有忧 (2006: the TV screen provides positive and deplorable aspects), *Renmin ribao* 人民日报 ('People's Daily'): 14.

Xu Xin 许新 *et al.* (2001) *Chaoji daguo de bengkui. Sulian jieti yuanyin tanxi* 超级大国的崩溃. 苏联解体原因探析 (The collapse of a superpower: An analysis of the reasons for the dissolution of the Soviet Union), Beijing: Shehui kexue wenxian chubanshe.

Xu Xin 徐馨 (1 December 2006) 'Rang lishi zhaoliang weilei – lai zi dianshi jilupian *Daguo jueqi* de qishi' 让历史照亮未来 来自电视纪录片 《大国崛起》 的启示 (Let history illuminate the future: new insights provided by the TV documentary *The Rise of the Great Powers*), *Renmin ribao* 人民日报 ('People's Daily'): 14.

Xue Xiantian 薛衔天 and Kim Donggil 金东吉 (2009) *Minguo shiqi Zhong-Su guanxi shi (1917–1949)* 民国时期中苏关系史 (A history of Sino–Soviet relations during the Republican era, 1917–1949), 3 vols, Beijing: Zhonggong dangshi chubanshe.

Yan, Xuetong (2001) 'The rise of China in Chinese eyes', *Journal of Contemporary China*, no. 26: 33–9.

Yang, Guobin (2009) *The Power of the Internet in China. Citizen Activism Online*, New York: Columbia University Press.

Yang Yumou 杨育谋 (April 2007) 'Daguo ruhe jueqi' 大国如何崛起 (How does a Great Power rise?), *Zhongguancun* 中关村 ('Zhong guan cun Magazine') no. 4: 46–9.

Yangshi bochu Daguo jueqi *jiemeipian. Shehui gejie fanxiang relie* 央视播出 《大国崛起》 姐妹篇. 社会各界反响热烈 (CCTV aired the sister piece to *The Rise of the Great Powers*. The reaction from all walks of society is enthusiastic) (12 October 2007). Online. Available HTTP: <http://ent.sina.com.cn/v/m/2007-10-12/11131746484.shtml> (last accessed 1 March 2013).

Yangshi guoji Fuxing luntan *zhengshi shangxian. Fangwenliang tupo 100wan* 央视国际 《复兴论坛》 正式上线 访问量突破 100 万 (CCTV's international *Forum on Revival* has officially been opened. Visitors' numbers surpass the million mark) (8 October 2007). Online. Available HTTP: <http://media.people.com.cn/GB/40606/6346632.html> (last accessed 1 March 2013).

Yangshi tui Fuxing zhi lu. *Zhuanjia chenggei Zhonggong zhuangdan* 央视推 《复兴之路 》 。 专家称给中共壮胆 (CCTV promotes *The Road to Revival*. Experts prop up the CCP) (6 October 2007). Online. Available HTTP: <http://www.epochtimes.com/gb/7/10/6/n1857844.htm> (last accessed 1 March 2013).

Yin Hong 尹鸿 (2002) *Xin Zhongguo dianying shi* (A television history of New China), Changsha: Hunan meishu chubanshe.

— (2003) *Meaning, Production, Consumption: The History and Reality of Television Drama in China*. Online. Available HTTP: <http://www.sino.uni-heidelberg.de/archive/documents/film/yinhong030718.htm> (last accessed 1 March 2013).

— (1 December 2006) 'Meijie yi sikao, shangdi jiu hui faxiao?' 媒介一思考, 上帝就会发笑？ (Thinking about the media, will God start laughing?), *Renmin ribao* 人民日报 ('People's Daily'): 14.

Yu Du 于都 (December 2007) 'Qishi hongda, zhizuo jingliang. Ping Zhongyang dianshitai bochu de zhenglunpian *Fuxing zhi lu*' 气势宏大制作精良——评中央电视台播出的政论片《复兴之路》 (Impressive and well done. Evaluating CCTV's broadcast political piece *The Road to Revival*), *Junshi jizhe* 军事记者 (Military Reporter) no. 12: 44.

Yu, Haiqing (2009) *Media and Cultural Transformation in China*, London and New York: Routledge.

Yu Qunying 禹群英 (7 September 2008) *'Shijie lishi' xiabi juli* 《世界历史》 瑕疵举例 (Several defects in 'world history'). (Originally in *Bolan qunshu* 博览群书 ('Chinese Book Review Monthly').) Online. Available HTTP: <http://www.gmw.cn/02blqs/2008-09/07/contents_859343.htm> (last accessed 1 March 2013).

Yuan Weishi 袁伟时 (2004) 'Daguo xingshuai zhi wuda shuji' 大国兴衰之五大枢机 (The five nodal points of the rise and fall of Great Powers), *Nanfengchuang* 南风窗 (Window of Southern Breeze), vol. 1, no. 1: 32–5.

Zajda, Joseph and Zajda, Rea (2003) 'The politics of rewriting history. New history textbooks and curriculum materials in Russia', *International Review of Education*, vol. 49, nos. 3 and 4: 363–84.

Zajec, Olivier (September 2008) 'China's naval ambitions', *Le Monde Diplomatique*, English edn: 1.

Zha, Jianying (1995) *China Pop: How Soap Operas, Tabloids and Bestsellers are Transforming a Culture*, New York: New Press.

Zhang Jingwei 张敬伟 (8 December 2006) Daguo jueqi *de dazhong qimeng quexian* 《大国崛起》 的大众启蒙缺陷 (*The Rise of the Great Powers*' neglect of enlightening the masses). (Originally in *Shenzhen shangbao* 深圳商报 ('Shenzhen Economic Daily').) Online. Available HTTP: <http://ent.sina.com.cn/r/m/2006.12.08/17101362360.html> (last accessed 1 March 2013).

Zhang Lei 张雷 (2011) 'Sugong wangdang ershinian hou de xin faxian' 苏共亡党二十年后的新发现 (New discovery after 20 years of the CPSU's perishing), *Baokan huicui* 报刊荟萃 (Journals' Digest), no. 7: 4–8.

Zhang Lifan 章立凡 (2 November 2007) *Fuxing zhi lu de qianshi jinsheng* 复兴之路的前世今生 (*The Road to Revival*'s precursor and present embodiment). (Originally in *Nanfang dushibao* 南方都市报 (Southern Metropolis Daily).) Online. Available HTTP: <http://www.360doc.com/content/07/1111/14/142_816722.shtml> (last accessed 1 March 2013).

Zhang, Tongdao (2008) 'Chinese television audience research', in Zhu, Ying and Berry, Chris (eds) *TV China: a Reader on New Media*, Bloomington: Indiana University Press, pp. 168–79.

Zhang Wei 张炜 (2011) *Daguo zhi dao. Chuanjian yu haiquan* 大国之道。 船舰与海权 (Way of a Great Power. Navy vessels and maritime power), Beijing: Beijing daxue chubanshe.

Zhang, Wei (2012) *'Funktion' und 'Wesen'. Fernsehen und Medienöffentlichkeit in der Volksrepublik China am Beispiel von China Central Television*, Berlin: Lit Verlag.

Zhang Xiaojing 张小劲 (ed.) (2007) *Daguo fuxing zhi lu* 大国复兴之路 (*The Road to Revival of Great Powers*), Beijing: Renmin chubanshe.

Zhang Xiaoling (2011) *The Transformation of Political Communication in China. From Propaganda to Hegemony*, Singapore: World Scientific Publishing.

Zhang Yi 张漪 (1 December 2006) Daguo jueqi *yin guanzhong reyi. Rang lishi zhaoliang xingcheng* 《大国崛起》 引观众热议. 让历史照亮行程 (*The Rise of the Great Powers* draws lively discussions from the audience. Let history shine upon the road ahead). (Originally in *Yangzi wanbao* 扬子晚报 ('Yangtse Evening Post').) Online. Available HTTP: <http://ent.sina.com.cn/v/2006-12-01/07391351169.html> (last accessed 1 March 2013).

Zhang Yi 张毅 and Liang Min 梁敏 (2 November 2007) Fuxing zhi lu *daxing zhuti zhanlan* 《复兴之路》 大型主题展览 (The large-scale thematic exhibition *The Road to Revival*). Online. Available HTTP: <http://www.chinamil.com.cn/site1/2007-11/02/content_1004041.htm> (last accessed 28 February 2012). (As of March 2013, this website seems defunct.)

Zhang Zongtang 张宗堂 (26 September 2009) Guojia bowuguan juban *Fuxing zhi lu* daxing zhanlan 国家博物馆举办 《复兴之路》 大型展览 (The National Museum opens the large-scale exhibition *The Road to Revival*), *Renmin ribao* 人民日报 ('People's Daily'): 4.

Zhao Buhui 赵卜慧 (2008) 'De qi shu er du zhi, bu yi le hu! *Fuxing zhi lu* xilie tushu bianji shouji' 得其书而渎之, 不亦乐乎。 《复兴之路》 系列图书编辑手记 (Isn't it great to read it also from the book! Personal notes from the editor of the book series *The Road to Revival*), *Chuban cankao* 出版参考 ('Information on Publication'), no. 3: 24.

Zhao Huayong 赵华勇 (2007) 'Rang lishi zhaoliang weilai de xingcheng' 让历史照亮未来的行程 (Let history illuminate the future trajectory), in Daguo jueqi: *12 ji daxing dianzi jilupian* 《大国崛起 》 。十二集大型电视纪录片 (*The Rise of the Great Powers*: a 12-part big-format TV-documentary), 3 vols, Beijing: Zhongguo minzhu fazhi chubanshe (no pagination).

Zhao, Suisheng (1998) 'A state-led nationalism: the patriotic education campaign in post-Tiananmen China', *Communist and Post-Communist Studies*, vol. 31, no. 3: 287–302.

— (2004) *A Nation-State by Construction. Dynamics of Modern Chinese Nationalism*, Stanford: Stanford University Press.

Zhao, Yuezhi (1998) *Media, Market, and Democracy in China. Between the Party Line and the Bottom Line*, Urbana *et al.*: University of Illinois Press.

— (2008) *Communication in China. Political Economy, Power, and Conflict*, Lanham *et al.*: Rowman & Littlefield.

— (2011) 'Sustaining and contesting revolutionary legacies in media and ideology', in Heilman, Sebastian and Perry, Elizabeth J. (eds) *Mao's Invisible Hand*, Cambridge, MA, and London: Harvard University Asia Center, pp. 201–36.

Zhao, Yuezhi and Guo, Zhenzhi (2005) 'Television in China: history, political economy, and ideology', in Wasko, Janet (ed.) *A Companion to Television*, Malden: Blackwell, pp. 521–39.

Zheng, Bijian (2005) *China's Peaceful Rise. Speeches of Zheng Bijian, 1997–2005*, Washington, D.C.: Brookings Institution Press.

— (2011) *China's Road to Peaceful Rise. Observations on its Cause, Basis, Connotations and Prospects*, London and New York: Routledge.

Zheng Pengnian 郑彭年 (2008) *Riben jueqi de lishi kaocha* 日本崛起的历史考察 (A historical inquiry into the rise of Japan), Beijing: Renmin chubanshe.

Zheng, Yongnian (2008) *Technological Empowerment. The Internet, State, and Society in China*, Stanford: Stanford University Press.

Zheng, Yongnian and Zhang, Chi (2012) ' "Soft power" and Chinese soft power', in Lai, Hongyi and Lu, Yiyi (eds) *China's Soft Power and International Relations*, London and New York: Routledge, pp. 21–38.

Zhong, Xueping (2010) *Mainstream Culture Refocused. Television Drama, Society, and the Production of Meaning in Reform-Era China*, Honolulu: University of Hawai'i Press.

Zhonggong zhongyang zhengzhiju jiti xuexi (di shiliu jie) 中共中央政治局集体学习 (第十六届) (Collective study session of the Politburo of the CCP (the sixteenth)) (29 November 2005). Online. Available HTTP: <http://news.xinhuanet.com/ziliao/2005-11/29/content_3849521.htm> (last accessed 28 March 2012).

Zhongguo gonchandang dishiqici quanguo daibiao dahui 中国共产党第十七次全国代表大会 (The CCP's seventeenth party congress) (2007). Online. Available HTTP: <http://cpc.people.com.cn/GB/104019/index.html> (last accessed 1 March 2013).

Zhongguo guojia bowuguan 中国国家博物馆 (Chinese National Museum) (1 March 2011) *Zhongguo guojia bowuguan* Fuxing zhi lu *jiben chenlie fuzhan* 中国国家博物馆《复兴之路》 基本陈列复展 (The Chinese National Museum reopens the basic permanent exhibition *The Road to Revival*). Online. Available HTTP: <http://www.chnmuseum.cn/tabid/138/InfoID/33312/frtid/64/Default.aspx> (last accessed 1 March 2013).

Zhonghua renmin gongheguo jiaoyubu 中华人民共和国教育部 (Ministry of Education of the People's Republic of China) (comp.) (2001a) *Quanri-zhi yiwu jiaoyu lishi kecheng biaozhun (shiyangao)* 全日制义务教育历史课程标准 (实验稿) (History curriculum standards for full-time compulsory education (provisional draft).) Beijing: Beijing Normal University Press.

— (2001b) *Quanri-zhi yiwu jiaoyu lishi yu shehui kecheng biaozhun (I) (shiyangao)* 全日制义务教育历史与社会课程标准 (I) (实验稿) (History and society I curriculum standards for full-time compulsory education (provisional draft).) Beijing: Beijing Normal University Press.

— (2003) *Putong gaozhong lishi kecheng biaozhun (shiyan)* 普通高中历史课程标准 (试验) (History curriculum standards for normal senior secondary school (provisional).) Beijing: Renmin jiaoyu.

Zhong-wai meiti canguan Fuxing zhi lu *zhanlan. Jianzheng 60 nian jubian* 中外媒体参观《复兴之路》 展览。见证 60 年巨变 (Chinese and foreign media visit the exhibition *The Road to Revival*. Verifying 60 years of great change) (27 September 2009). Online. Available HTTP: <http://www.cnr.cn/09zt/60zn/zxbd/200909/t20090927_505489505.html> (last accessed 1 March 2013).

Zhou Xincheng 周新城 (2011) 'Yibu kexue di fenxi Sugong wangdang de yuanyin he jiaoxun de lizuo: Du Li Shenming zhubian de *Ju an si wei: Sugong wangdang ershinian de sikao*' 一部科学地分析苏共亡党的原因和教训的力作。 读李慎明主编的 《居安思危。 苏共亡党二十年的思考》 (A rigorous scientific analysis of the reasons and lessons of the CPSU's perishing. Reading *Alert to Danger while Dwelling in Safety: a Reflection at the Twentieth Anniversary of the CPSU's Perishing*, edited by Li Shenming), *Zhonghuahun* 中华魂 (China's Spirit), no. 6: 62–4.

Zhou Yingfeng 周英峰 (1 January 2008) '*Fuxing zhi lu* shizhan jieshu zeqi zhengshi kaizhan. Jiezhi qunian 12 yue 31 ri canguan renshu jin 260 wan 《复兴之路》 试展结束择期正

式开展。截至去年 12 月 31 日参观人数近 260 万 (The provisional exhibition *The Road to Revival* ended and decided upon its official opening. Until 31 December of last year at closure, numbers of visitors had approached 2.6 million), *Renmin ribao* 人民日报 ('People's Daily'): 4.

Zhou, Yongming (2006) *Historicizing Online Politics. Telegraphy, the Internet, and Political Participation in China*, Stanford: Stanford University Press.

Zhu, Ying (2008) *Television in Post-Reform China: Serial Dramas, Confucian Leadership, and the Global Television Market*, London: Routledge.

— (2012) *Two Billion Eyes. The Story of China Central Television*, New York: The New Press.

Zhu, Ying and Berry, Chris (eds) (2008) *TV China: a Reader on New Media*, Bloomington: Indiana University Press.

Zhu, Ying and Keane, Michael. (2008) *TV Drama in China*, Hong Kong: Hong Kong University Press.

Zhuang Liwei 庄礼伟 (8 December 2006) Daguo jueqi *hai keyi paide geng hao yixie* 《大国崛起》还可以拍得更好一些 (*The Rise of the Great Powers* could have been made a bit better). (Originally on *Nanfang baoyewang* 南方报业网 ('nfmedia.com').) Online. Available HTTP: <http://ent.sina.com.cn/r/m/2006-12-08/17091362359.html> (last accessed 1 March 2013).

Zhuanjia yanzhong de Daguo jueqi. *Xin shidai xuyao xin shixue* 专家眼中的《大国崛起》。新时代需要新史学 (*The Rise of the Great Powers* in the eyes of experts. A new time needs a new historiography) (5 December 2006). Online. Available HTTP: <http://ent.sina.com.cn/v/2006-12-05/07171356487.html> (last accessed 1 March 2013).

Zi Zhongjun 资中筠 (2007) 'Shuobujin de daguo xingshuai' 说不尽的大国兴衰 (The inexhaustible [topic of] rise and fall of the Great Powers), *Nanfengchuang* 南风窗 (Window of Southern Breeze), no. 1: 42–7.

Zimmermann, Martin (2008) 'Der Historiker am Set', in Fischer, Thomas and Wirtz, Rainer (eds) *Alles authentisch? Popularisierung der Geschichte im Fernsehen*, Konstanz: UVK Verlagsgesellschaft, pp. 137–60.

Zuo Fengrong 左凤荣 and Jiang Changwu 姜长斌 (2007) 'Dianshi zhenglunpian *Ju an si wei – Sugong wangdang de lishi jiaoxun* shishi zeyi' 电视政论片 《居安思危 —— 苏共亡党的历史教训》 史实质疑 (Factual criticism of the political TV piece *Alert to Danger while Dwelling in Safety – the Historical Lesson of the Perishing of the Soviet Communist Party*), *Dangdai shijie shehuizhuyi wenti* 当代世界社会主义问题 ('Issues of Contemporary World Socialism'), vol. 92, no. 2: 61–71.

Index